Lecture Notes in Computer Science 1885

Edited by G. Goos, J. Hartmanis and J. van Leeuwen

Springer
Berlin
Heidelberg
New York
Barcelona
Hong Kong
London
Milan
Paris
Singapore
Tokyo

Klaus Havelund   John Penix
Willem Visser (Eds.)

SPIN Model Checking and Software Verification

7th International SPIN Workshop
Stanford, CA, USA, August 30 – September 1, 2000
Proceedings

Springer

Series Editors

Gerhard Goos, Karlsruhe University, Germany
Juris Hartmanis, Cornell University, NY, USA
Jan van Leeuwen, Utrecht University, The Netherlands

Volume Editors

Klaus Havelund
John Penix
Willem Visser
NASA Ames Research Center
Moffett Field, California 94035-1000, USA
E-mail: {havelund/jpenix/wvisser}@ptolemy.arc.nasa.gov

Cataloging-in-Publication Data applied for

Die Deutsche Bibliothek - CIP-Einheitsaufnahme

SPIN model checking and software verification : proceedings /
7th International SPIN Workshop, Stanford, CA, USA,
August 30 - September 1, 2000. Klaus Havelund ... (ed.). - Berlin ;
Heidelberg ; New York ; Barcelona ; Hong Kong ; London ; Milan ;
Paris ; Singapore ; Tokyo : Springer, 2000
  (Lecture notes in computer science ; Vol. 1885)
  ISBN 3-540-41030-9

CR Subject Classification (1998): F.3, D.2.4, D.3.1

ISSN 0302-9743
ISBN 3-540-41030-9 Springer-Verlag Berlin Heidelberg New York

This work is subject to copyright. All rights are reserved, whether the whole or part of the material is
concerned, specifically the rights of translation, reprinting, re-use of illustrations, recitation, broadcasting,
reproduction on microfilms or in any other way, and storage in data banks. Duplication of this publication
or parts thereof is permitted only under the provisions of the German Copyright Law of September 9, 1965,
in its current version, and permission for use must always be obtained from Springer-Verlag. Violations are
liable for prosecution under the German Copyright Law.

Springer-Verlag Berlin Heidelberg New York
a member of BertelsmannSpringer Science+Business Media GmbH
© Springer-Verlag Berlin Heidelberg 2000
Printed in Germany

Typesetting: Camera-ready by author, data conversion by PTP-Berlin, Stefan Sossna
Printed on acid-free paper   SPIN: 10722468   06/3142   5 4 3 2 1 0

Preface

The SPIN workshop is a forum for researchers interested in the subject of automata-based, explicit-state model checking technologies for the analysis and verification of asynchronous concurrent and distributed systems. The SPIN model checker (http://netlib.bell-labs.com/netlib/spin/whatispin.html), developed by Gerard Holzmann, is one of the best known systems of this kind, and has attracted a large user community. This can likely be attributed to its efficient state exploration algorithms. The fact that SPIN's modeling language, Promela, resembles a programming language has probably also contributed to its success.

Traditionally, the SPIN workshops present papers on extensions and uses of SPIN. As an experiment, this year's workshop was broadened to have a slightly wider focus than previous workshops in that papers on software verification were encouraged. Consequently, a small collection of papers describe attempts to analyze and verify programs written in conventional programming languages. Solutions include translations from source code to Promela, as well as specially designed model checkers that accept source code. We believe that this is an interesting research direction for the formal methods community, and that it will result in a new set of challenges and solutions. Of course, abstraction becomes the key solution to deal with very large state spaces. However, we also see potential for integrating model checking with techniques such as static program analysis and testing. Papers on these issues have therefore been included in the proceedings.

The workshop featured 17 refereed papers selected from 31 submissions, three invited talks, and three invited tutorials about commercial testing and formal methods tools, represented by three additional papers. Each refereed paper was reviewed by three reviewers. The three invited talks were as follows. Leslie Lamport (Compaq Systems Research Center) talked about model checking specifications; Bill Roscoe (Oxford University Computing Laboratory) talked about the FDR model checker and the verification of scalable real-life systems; and Peter Gluck (NASA's Jet Propulsion Laboratory) talked about testing of the Deep-Space 1 spacecraft software architecture. The three invited tutorials about commercial tools were as follows. Doron Drusinsky (Time Rover) presented the Temporal Rover tool, which performs temporal logic testing; Philippa Broadfoot and Bill Roscoe (Oxford University Computing Laboratory) presented the FDR model checker (developed by Formal Systems, of which Bill Roscoe was one of the founders); and Jerry Harrow (Compaq) presented the Visual Threads tool, which performs runtime analysis of multi-threaded programs.

The first SPIN workshop was held in October 1995 in Montréal. Subsequent workshops were held in New Brunswick (August 1996), Enschede (April 1997), Paris (November 1998), Trento (July 1999), and Toulouse (September 1999). This year's workshop ran for three days and was therefore the longest workshop to date.

Acknowledgments The editors of this volume wish to thank the program committee for its invaluable refereeing effort, resulting in a fine selection of papers. We also want to thank the additional referees supporting the program committee. Since each submitted paper received three reviews, the review effort was substantial. A special thanks goes to the Research Institute for Advanced Computer Science (RIACS) for sponsoring the event. We would also like to thank the Computational Sciences Division at the NASA Ames Research Center for generously providing resources.

August 2000

Klaus Havelund
John Penix
Willem Visser

Organization

SPIN 2000 was organized by the Automated Software Engineering Group within the Computational Sciences Division at the NASA Ames Research Center, California, USA.

Program Committee

Dennis Dams (Eindhoven University, The Netherlands)
David Dill (Stanford University, USA)
Orna Grumberg (The Technion, Israel)
John Hatcliff (Kansas State University, USA)
Bengt Jonsson (Uppsala University, Sweden)
Kim Larsen (Aalborg University, Denmark)
Stefan Leue (Albert-Ludwigs University, Germany)
Doron Peled (Bell Laboratories/Carnegie Mellon University, USA)
Natarajan Shankar (SRI International, USA)
Joseph Sifakis (Verimag, France)
Moshe Y. Vardi (Rice University, USA)
Pierre Wolper (Liege University, Belgium)

Organization

Klaus Havelund (QSS/Recom at NASA Ames Research Center, USA)
Gerard Holzmann (Bell Laboratories, USA)
John Penix (NASA Ames Research Center, USA)
Willem Visser (RIACS at NASA Ames Research Center, USA)

Referees

K. Altisen	M. Geilen	C. Păsăreanu
S. Bensalem	J. Geldenhuys	C. Pecheur
N. Bjørner	P. Godefroid	H. Saïdi
D. Bošnački	G. Goessler	N. Sidorova
M. Bozga	S. Graf	F. van Wijk
D. Bruening	F. Klaedtke	
P. Cuijpers	C. Muñoz	

Sponsoring Institution

Research Institute for Advanced Computer Science (RIACS), California, USA.

Table of Contents

Papers

Tool Tutorials

Symmetric Spin[*]

Dragan Bošnački[1], Dennis Dams[2], and Leszek Holenderski[1]

[1] Dept. of Computing Sci., Eindhoven University of Technology
PO Box 513, 5600 MB Eindhoven, The Netherlands
[2] Dept. of Electrical Eng., Eindhoven University of Technology
PO Box 513, 5600 MB Eindhoven, The Netherlands

{D.Bosnacki,D.Dams,L.Holenderski}@tue.nl

Abstract. We give a detailed description of SymmSpin, a symmetry-reduction package for Spin. It offers four strategies for state-space reduction, based on the heuristic that we presented in [3], and a fifth mode for reference. A series of new experiments is described, underlining the effectiveness of the heuristic and demonstrating the generalisation of the implementation to multiple scalar sets, multiple process families, as well as almost the full Promela language.

1 Introduction

One way to combat the state explosion problem in model checking [5,7] is to exploit symmetries in a system description. In order to grasp the idea of symmetry reduction, consider a mutual exclusion protocol based on semaphores. The (im)possibility for processes to enter their critical sections will be similar regardless of their identities, since process identities (pids) play no role in the semaphore mechanism. More formally, the system state remains behaviorally equivalent under permutations of pids. During state-space exploration, when a state is visited that is the same, up to a permutation of pids, as some state that has already been visited, the search can be pruned. The notion of behavioral equivalence used (bisimilarity, trace equivalence, sensitivity to deadlock, fairness, etc.) and the class of permutations allowed (full, rotational, mirror, etc.) may vary, leading to a spectrum of symmetry techniques.

The two main questions in practical applications of symmetry techniques are how to find symmetries in a system description, and how to detect, during state-space exploration, that two states are equivalent. To start with the first issue: as in any other state-space reduction method based on behavioral equivalences, the problem of deciding equivalence of states requires, in general, the construction of the full state space. Doing this would obviously invalidate the approach, as it is precisely what we are trying to avoid. Therefore, most approaches proceed by listing sufficient conditions that can be statically checked on the system description. The second problem, of detecting equivalence of states,

---

[*] This research has been supported by the VIRES project (Verifying Industrial Reactive Systems, Esprit Long Term Research Project #23498).

© Springer-Verlag Berlin Heidelberg 2000

involves the search for a *canonical* state by permuting the values of certain, symmetric, data structures. In [4] it was shown that this *orbit problem* is at least as hard as testing for graph isomorphism, for which currently no polynomial algorithms are known. Furthermore, this operation must be performed for every state encountered during the exploration. For these reasons, it is of great practical importance to work around the orbit problem. In practice, heuristics for the graph isomorphism problem can be reused to obtain significant speedups. In case these do not work, one can revert to a suboptimal approach in which (not necessarily unique) *normalized* states are stored and compared.

The use of symmetry has been studied in the context of various automated verification techniques. We mention here only a few papers that are most closely related to our work, which is in the context of asynchronous systems. For a more complete overview we refer to the bibliography of [19]. Emerson and Sistla have applied the idea to CTL model checking in [9], with extensions to fairness in [12] and [15]. In [10], Emerson and Trefler extended the concepts to real-time logics, while in [11] they considered systems that are *almost* symmetric. Clarke, Enders, Filkorn, and Jha used symmetries in the context of symbolic model checking in [4]. Emerson, Jha, and Peled, and more recently Godefroid, have studied the combination of partial order and symmetry reductions, see [8,14].

Our work draws upon the ideas of Ip and Dill [17,18,19]. They introduce, in the protocol description language Murφ, a new data type called *scalarset* by which the user can point out (full) symmetries to the verification tool. The values of scalarsets are finite in number, unordered, and allow only a restricted number of operations, that do not break symmetry; any violations can be detected at compile time.

Following up on the approach of Ip and Dill, we have presented in [3] a new heuristic for finding representatives of symmetry equivalence classes. In Section 3, this heuristic and the four strategies based on it are summarised. This is done by redeveloping them on the basis of a generalisation of the notion of lexicographical ordering. By introducing *partial weight functions*, lexicographical orderings are generalised to partial orderings that are not necessarily total, which allows to uniformly capture both the canonical and the non-canonical strategies.

[3] also reports on a number of experiments obtained with a prototype implementation on top of the Spin tool. Based on the results of those experiments, it was deemed worthwhile to extend the implementation so as to provide a more complete integration into Spin. Presently, this extension has been carried out. Compared to the prototype implementation, the current symmetry package has been generalised in a number of essential directions. The main improvements are its capabilities to handle *queues*, *multiple scalar sets*, as well as *multiple process families*. One of the current paper's contributions is to describe the overall implementation in the context of Spin (Section 4). Having implemented this symmetry package, we were also able to run more and larger experiments. The results of these, and their evaluation, form the second main contribution of this paper (Section 5). In the sequel we assume that we are dealing with safety properties (see also Section 6).

2   Preliminaries

A *transition system* is a tuple $T = (\mathcal{S}, s_0, \rightarrow)$ where $\mathcal{S}$ is a set of states, $s_0 \in \mathcal{S}$ is an initial state, and $\rightarrow \subseteq \mathcal{S} \times \mathcal{S}$ is a transition relation. We assume that $\mathcal{S}$ contains an error state $e \neq s_0$ which is a sink state (whenever $e \rightarrow s$ then $s = e$).

An equivalence relation on $\mathcal{S}$, say $\sim$, is called a *congruence* on T iff for all $s_1, s_2, s_1' \in \mathcal{S}$ such that $s_1 \sim s_2$ and $s_1 \rightarrow s_1'$, there exists $s_2' \in \mathcal{S}$ such that $s_1' \sim s_2'$ and $s_2 \rightarrow s_2'$. Any congruence on T induces a quotient transition system $T/\sim = (\mathcal{S}/\sim, [s_0], \Rightarrow)$ such that $[s] \Rightarrow [s']$ iff $s \rightarrow s'$.

A bijection $h : \mathcal{S} \rightarrow \mathcal{S}$ is said to be a *symmetry* of T iff $h(s_0) = s_0$, $h(e) = e$, and for any $s, s' \in \mathcal{S}$, $s \rightarrow s'$ iff $h(s) \rightarrow h(s')$. The set of all symmetries of T forms a group (with function composition).

Any set A of symmetries generates a subgroup $G(A)$ called a *symmetry group* (induced by A). $G(A)$ induces an equivalence relation $\sim_A$ on states, defined as

$$s \sim_A s' \text{ iff } h(s) = s', \text{ for some } h \in G(A)$$

Such an equivalence relation is called a *symmetry relation* of T (induced by A). The equivalence class of s is called the *orbit* of s, and is denoted by $[s]_A$.

Any symmetry relation of T is a congruence on T (Theorem 1 in [18]), and thus induces the quotient transition system $T/\sim_A$. Moreover, s is reachable from s_0 if and only if $[s]_A$ is reachable from $[s_0]_A$ (Theorem 2 in [18]). This allows to reduce the verification of safety properties of T to the reachability of the error state $[e]$ in $T/\sim_A$ (via observers, for example).

In order to extend an enumerative model checker to handle symmetries, i.e., to explore $T/\sim_A$ instead of T, a practical representation for equivalence classes is needed. A common approach is to use a *representative function*, which is a function $rep : \mathcal{S} \rightarrow \mathcal{S}$ that, given a state s, returns an equivalent state from $[s]_A$. For an equivalence class C, the states in $\{rep(s) \mid s \in C\}$ are called the *representatives* of C. Clearly, if $rep(s) = rep(t)$ then states s and t are equivalent. The reverse does not hold in general, but the smaller the set of all representatives of a class, the more often it will hold. The two extremes are $rep = id$ (the identity function), which can obviously be implemented very efficiently but will never succeed to detect the equivalence of two different states ("high speed, low precision"); and $\lambda s \in \mathcal{S}. c_{[s]}$ which returns for any input s a canonical state $c_{[s]}$ that is the *unique* representative for the class $[s]$. Such a *canonical* representative function will detect all equivalences but is harder to compute ("low speed, high precision"). Now, one can explore $T/\sim_A$ by simply exploring a part of T, using $rep(s)$ instead of s. A generic algorithm of this type is given in Section 4. In the sequel, by a *reduction strategy* we mean any concrete rep.

The definition of the representatives is usually based on some partial ordering on states, e.g. by taking as representatives those states that are minimal in a class, relative to the ordering. If the ordering is total, then the representatives are unique for their class.

In practice, a transition system is given implicitly as a *program*, whose possible behaviours it models. In order to simplify the detection of symmetries on the level of the program, we assume that a simple type can be marked as *scalarset*, which essentially means that it is considered to be an unordered, finite enumerated type, with elements called *scalars*. As a representation for scalars, we use integers from 0 to $n-1$, for some fixed n. Syntactical criteria can be identified under which scalarsets induce symmetries on the program's transition system, see [18]. In this presentation, we usually restrict ourselves to one scalarset which is then denoted I. Our implementation is able to deal with multiple scalarsets however.

3   Reduction Strategies

We start with a summary of the strategies from [3].

In the approach of [17], the definition of representatives is based on a lexicographic ordering on state vectors. Normally this is a total ordering, but by defining it relative to a splitting of the state vector in two parts, a hierarchy of non-total orderings is obtained, parameterized by the point at which the vector is split. More precisely, the representatives of a class are those state vectors whose leftmost part (relative to the splitting) is the lexicographical minimum among the leftmost parts of all the vectors in that class. The trade-off between speed and precision may now be tuned by varying the split point. This is a degree of freedom that allows to explore a variety of representative functions, including the two extremes id (split point at the beginning of the state vector) and $\lambda s \in \mathcal{S}. c_{[s]}$ (split point at the end) mentioned in the previous section.

We generalise this approach. Recall that a lexicographic ordering is an ordering on sequences of elements, and it is based on an underlying ordering on the type of the elements. Normally, in lifting this underlying ordering to sequences, "weights" are attached to all positions in the sequence, where the weight increases as the position is further to the left[1] (therefore ab would precede ba in a dictionary). Splitting the state vector and letting only the leftmost part determine the lexicographic value, as done in [17], may be seen as assigning weights only to the leftmost k positions, for some k. In other words, the weight function from positions to weights becomes partial. We generalise this further by dropping the requirement that weights increase as positions are further to the left. Hence, we consider lexicographic orderings that are parameterized by arbitrary partial weight functions. Viewed differently, such a weight function not only truncates the state vector (as in [17]), but also reshuffles it, before computing the lexicographic value in the standard way. Thus, we have extended the freedom in selecting a representative function. In order to explain how this freedom is exploited, we first look into the way the equivalence on states is defined in our particular case.

Symmetry relations between states are generated by permuting scalars. A given *scalar permutation* $p : I \to I$ can be lifted to states. The precise definition of this lifting can be found in [3]. Intuitively, the application of a scalar permutation p to a state vector s replaces every scalar i that occurs in s by $p(i)$.

---

[1] Note that it is only the relative weight of an element w.r.t. other elements in the sequence that counts, not its absolute value.

Because scalars may also occur as indices of arrays, array values may have to be reshuffled in order to get a proper state vector again. An equivalence class is a minimal non-empty set of states that is closed under applying scalar permutations. The representatives of such a class are those states that are minimal under some given (generalised) lexicographic ordering. These representatives are the states that are actually stored as the exploration of the transition system proceeds.

First, we explain how to choose a lexicographic ordering so as to further optimise on the *speed*, i.e. the computational effort in mapping a state s to its representative $rep(s)$. Assume that the program uses an array indexed by scalars and whose elements do not involve scalars; we call this a *main array*. Then take such an array, say M, and choose the partial weight function that assigns weights only to the elements of M (and to nothing else in the state vector), with weights decreasing from the first element $M[0]$ to the last $M[n-1]$. Now observe that under the lexicographic ordering based on this partial weight function, in all representatives (in any equivalence class), M is *sorted*. This gives rise to the following idea in order to compute a representative $rep(s)$: Instead of applying different scalar permutations to s until a minimal state vector is found, *sort M in s*. Depending on the particular sorting algorithm used, this gives rise to a certain scalar permutation, that is then applied to the rest of s in order to obtain a representative. As an example, consider the following picture showing a state vector before and after sorting a main array M, where M has been depicted at the beginning of the state vector to stress the fact that its elements have the highest lexicographic weight.

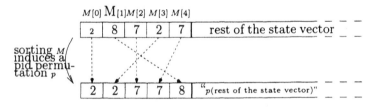

M is indexed by scalars, which in this case range from 0 to 4. M's elements are the numbers 2, 7, and 8, taken from some type that differs from I. Suppose that the particular sorting algorithm being used sorts M as indicated by the dashed arrows. This particular sorting induces the scalar permutation $p = \{0 \mapsto 0, 3 \mapsto 1, 2 \mapsto 2, 4 \mapsto 3, 1 \mapsto 4\}$, which is then applied to the rest of the state vector. This is called the **sorted** strategy. Note that it is not canonical.

Another strategy presented in [3] is based on the **sorted** strategy, and trades some speed for *precision*. It is called the **segmented** strategy. Instead of sorting M in one particular way, it considers all sortings of M. To continue with the example, observe that there are 3 more ways to sort M, depending on how the two 2's and the two 7's are moved around. An example of a corresponding scalar permutation is $p' = \{3 \mapsto 0, 0 \mapsto 1, 4 \mapsto 2, 2 \mapsto 3, 1 \mapsto 4\}$. Furthermore, the **segmented** strategy is based on a lexicographic ordering which, just as **sorted**, gives the highest weights to M's elements, but in addition it assigns weights to all other elements in the state vector as well, i.e., it is a total function. The segmented strategy considers the results of applying the scalar permutations corresponding to all ways to sort M, and selects the lexicographically smallest among these. Clearly, this results in *canonical* representatives[2].

The assumption of an explicit array M can be dropped if the program contains a family $C_0, \ldots, C_{n-1}$ of processes $C = \lambda i : I.C_i$ parameterized by scalars. In every such program there is, in fact, an implicit array indexed by scalars, namely the array of program counters for processes C_i. Thus, we can consider the variants of sorted and segmented in which we use the array of program counters for M. These variants are called pc-sorted and pc-segmented, respectively, the latter one being canonical again.

Finally, full is the (canonical) strategy that generates all scalar permutations and applies each of them to the state s, selecting the (standard) lexicographic minimum as representative. It is used for reference purposes.

4   Extending Spin with Symmetry Reductions

The result of our extension of Spin with a symmetry package is called SymmSpin. When extending an existing enumerative model checker, in the spirit of [18], two essential problems have to be solved. First, the input language must be extended, to allow the usage of scalarsets in a program that specifies a model. Second, a symmetry reduction strategy must be added to the state space exploration algorithm. Both problems are non-trivial. As far as the extension of the input language is concerned, a compiler should be able to check whether the scalarsets really induce a symmetry relation (i.e., whether a program does not rely on the order of the range of integers that represents a scalarset). As far as adding a reduction strategy is concerned, the *rep* function should be implementable in an efficient way.

In order for a model checker to be a successful tool for the verification of symmetric systems, good solutions are needed for both problems. However, there does not seem to be much sense in putting an effort into solving the language extension problem without having an efficient reduction strategy. That is why in SymmSpin we have mainly concentrated on the second problem.

As far as the first problem is concerned, it could be solved just by lifting the syntactical extensions of Murφ [18] to Spin. Although not entirely straightforward, it should not pose fundamental difficulties. Unfortunately, to do it in the right way, one would need to extensively modify the existing Promela parser. In SymmSpin, we have tried to avoid this effort, as explained in Section 4.3.

4.1   A Modified State Space Exploration Algorithm

In principle, extending an existing enumerative model checker to handle symmetries is not difficult, once the *rep* function is implemented. Instead of using a

---

[2] In [3], we prove a more general result stating that for canonicity it is not necessary to extend the partial weight function of the sorted strategy to a full function, but that an arbitrary choice function can be used.

standard algorithm for exploring $T = (\mathcal{S}, s_0, \rightarrow)$, as depicted in Fig. 1, one explores the quotient $T/\sim$ using a simple modification of the algorithm, as depicted in Fig. 2 (this modification is borrowed from [18]).

> $reached := unexpanded := \{s_0\}$;
> while $unexpanded \neq \emptyset$ do
>   remove a state s from $unexpanded$;
>   for each transition $s \rightarrow s'$ do
>   if $s' = $ **error** then
>   stop and report error;
>   if $s' \notin reached$ then
>   add s' to $reached$ and $unexpanded$;

Fig. 1. A standard exploration algorithm

> $reached := unexpanded := \{rep(s_0)\}$;
> while $unexpanded \neq \emptyset$ do
>   remove a state s from $unexpanded$;
>   for each transition $s \rightarrow s'$ do
>   if $s' = $ **error** then
>   stop and report error;
>   if $rep(s') \notin reached$ then
>   add $rep(s')$ to $reached$ and $unexpanded$;

Fig. 2. A standard exploration algorithm with symmetry reductions

In practice, we had to overcome several problems, due to idiosyncrasies of Spin. For example, it turned out that the operation "add $rep(s')$ to $unexpanded$" is difficult to implement reliably, due to the particular way Spin represents the set $unexpanded$ as a set of "differences" between states rather than states themselves. For this reason, we had to change the exploration algorithm given in Fig. 2. In our[3] algorithm, the original states, and not their representatives, are used to generate the state space to be explored, as depicted in Fig. 3.

Obviously, our algorithm is still sound. Beside avoiding the problem with "add $rep(s')$ to $unexpanded$", it has yet another advantage over the algorithm in Fig. 2: it allows to easily regenerate an erroneous trace from the set $unexpanded$, in case an error is encountered. Since Spin explores the state space in a depth first manner, the set $unexpanded$ is in fact structured as a stack. When an error is encountered the stack contains the sequence of states that lead to the error, and its contents can directly be dumped as the erroneous trace. In the algorithm from Fig. 2, the stack would contain the representatives of the original states, and since the representatives are not necessarily related by the transition relation

---

[3] We acknowledge a remark from Gerard Holzmann which led us to this algorithm.

$reached := \{rep(s_0)\}; \; unexpanded := \{s_0\};$
while $unexpanded \neq \emptyset$ do
    remove a state s from $unexpanded$;
    for each transition $s \to s'$ do
      if $s' = $ **error** then
        stop and report error;
      if $rep(s') \notin reached$ then
        add $rep(s')$ to $reached$ and s' to $unexpanded$;

Fig. 3. A modified exploration algorithm with symmetry reductions

in the original model, the stack would not necessarily represent an existing trace in the original model.

Notice that although both algorithms explore the same state space (since they agree on the *reached* set), there could still be a difference in their execution times, if the numbers of successor states s' considered in the loop "for each transition $s \to s'$ do" were different. It can easily be proven that this is not a case. Whenever the algorithm in Fig. 3 computes the successors of s, the algorithm in Fig. 2 computes the successors of $rep(s)$. Since s and $rep(s)$ are related by a symmetry, they must have the same number of successors (recall that any symmetry is a bijection).

4.2   An Overview of SymmSpin

Our goal was first to experiment with various reduction strategies, to check whether they perform well enough to undertake the effort of fully extending Spin with a symmetry package (such as modifying the Promela parser). So the problem was how to extend Spin in a minimal way that would be sufficient to perform various verification experiments with some symmetric protocols. In fact, we have managed to find a way which does not demand any change to the Spin tool itself, but only to the C program generated by Spin.

The C program generated by Spin is kept in several files. Two of them are of particular interest to us: `pan.c` that implements a state exploration algorithm, and `pan.h` that contains the declarations of various data structures used in `pan.c`, including a C structure called `State` that represents a state of the transition system being verified. Our current extension of Spin with symmetry reductions simply adds a particular reduction strategy to `pan.c`. This is done in two steps.

First, we locate in `pan.c` all calls to the procedures that add a newly visited state to the set of already visited states. The calls have the generic form `store(now)` where `now` is a global variable that keeps the current state. All the calls are changed to `store(rep(now))` where `rep` is the name of a C function that implements the reduction strategy. In this way, the representatives, and not the states themselves, are stored in the set of already visited states. The `pan.c` code that computes the successor states of `now` is left unchanged. As a consequence, the original states, and not their representatives, are used to generate the state space to be explored. This agrees with the exploration algorithm in Fig. 3.

Second, the C code for `rep` is generated and added to `pan.c`. This step is not straightforward since we have to scan `pan.h` for various pieces of information needed for the implementation of `rep`.

The two steps are performed by a Tcl script called `AdjustPan` [1]. The current version of the script is about 1800 lines, not counting comments.

4.3 The `AdjustPan` Script

Conceptually, the symmetry relation is deduced from a Promela program, say `foo.pml`, that uses special types called *scalarsets* which are unordered ranges of integers (in SymmSpin, always of the form $0..n-1$, for some constant $n < 256$).

Actually, in order to avoid modifications to the Promela parser, there is no special declaration for scalarsets. Instead, the standard Promela type `byte` is used for this purpose. Also, the symmetry relation is not deduced from `foo.pml` itself. Instead, it is deduced from an additional file, say `foo.sym`, that must accompany the Promela program. The additional file (later called a *system description file*) must be prepared by a user, and must contain all information relevant to the usage of scalarsets in the original Promela program that specifies a symmetric concurrent system.

The precise description of the syntax of the system description file, and its meaning, is beyond the scope of this paper. In short, it resembles the declaration part of Promela, and allows to describe all the data structures and processes, appearing in the original Promela program, that depend on scalarsets. This description is then used by the `rep` function to locate all fragments of the Spin state vector that depend on a particular scalarset, and lift a permutation of the scalarset to the state.

The only important restriction in the current version of SymmSpin is that the concurrent system specified by a symmetric Promela program must be static, in the sense that all the processes must be started simultaneously, by the `init{atomic{...}}` statement.

The `AdjustPan` script is called with two parameters: the name of one of the 5 reduction strategies described in Section 3, and the name of a system description file. The script reads three files: `pan.h`, `pan.c` (both generated by Spin from `foo.pml`), and `foo.sym`. The information in `foo.sym` and `pan.h` is used to modify `pan.c`. The modified version of `pan.c` is stored under the name `pan-sym.c`, and is used to model check the symmetric Promela program.

In summary, SymmSpin is used in the following way:

- Write a symmetric Promela program, say `foo.pml`, and its system description file, say `foo.sym`.
- Run Spin (with the `-a` option) on `foo.pml` (this will generate `pan.h` and `pan.c` files).
- Run `AdjustPan` on `foo.sym` with a particular reduction strategy (this will generate `pan-sym.c` file).
- Compile `pan-sym.c` with the same options you would use for `pan.c`, and run the generated binaries to model check the symmetric Promela program.

4.4   The Implementation of Strategies

In this section we highlight some implementation details of SymmSpin, to give an idea of how the rep function is implemented in an efficient way. To simplify presentation, we assume that only one scalarset is used in a Promela program.

The canonical strategies full, segmented and pc-segmented are implemented by a C function of the following shape:

```
State tmp_now, min_now;

State *rep(State *orig_now) {
  /* initialize */
    memcpy(&tmp_now, orig_now, vsize);
  /* find the representative */
    memcpy(&min_now, &tmp_now, vsize);
    ...
  return &min_now;
}
```

The parameter orig_now is used to pass the current state now. In order to avoid any interference with the original code in pan.c that uses now for its own purposes (for example, to generate the succesor states of the current state), we must assure that rep does not modify now. For this reason, we copy orig_now to the auxiliary state tmp_now.

The representative is found by enumerating permutations of a scalarset, and applying them to (the copy of) the current state. The lexicographically smallest result is kept in min_now. After each permutation, it is updated by the following statement

```
if (memcmp(&tmp_now, &min_now, vsize) < 0)
  memcpy(&min_now, &tmp_now, vsize);
```

In strategies sorted and pc-sorted, only one permutation is considered, so the auxiliary state min_now is not needed. Hence, the strategies are implemented by a function of the following shape:

```
State tmp_now;

State *rep(State *orig_now) {
  /* initialize */
    memcpy(&tmp_now, orig_now, vsize);
  /* find the representative */
    ...
  return &tmp_now;
}
```

In the rest of this section, we present the rep functions for the full, sorted and segmented strategies. The pc-sorted and pc-segmented strategies are similar to the sorted and segmented strategies.

Strategy full

```
State tmp_now, min_now;

State *rep_full(State *orig_now) {
  memcpy(&tmp_now, orig_now, vsize);
  /* find the representative */
    memcpy(&min_now, &tmp_now, vsize);
    permute_scalar(SIZE_OF_SCALAR);
  return &min_now;
}
```

The representative is found by the `permute_scalar` procedure that takes the size of a scalarset, say *size*, and generates all permutations of numbers from 0 to *size* − 1, excluding the identity permutation. Each permutation is then applied to the current state. Applying a permutation may be quite expensive. It can be implemented more efficiently if a permutation is a transposition (i.e, a swap of two numbers). For this reason, the permutations are generated incrementally, by composing successive transpositions (starting from the identity permutation). A tricky algorithm (borrowed from [20], and presented in Fig. 4) is used for this purpose.

It happens that the transpositions generated by the algorithm always swap two succesive elements p and $p + 1$, but we do not rely on this feature. Whe-

```
void permute_scalar(int size) {
  int i, p, offset, pos[MAX_SCALAR_SIZE], dir[MAX_SCALAR_SIZE];

  for (i = 0; i < size; i++) { pos[i] = 1; dir[i] = 1; }
  pos[size-1] = 0;

  i = 0;
  while (i < size-1) {
    for (i = offset = 0; pos[i] == size-i; i++) {
      pos[i] = 1; dir[i] = !dir[i]; if (dir[i]) offset++;
    }
    if (i < size-1) {
      p = offset-1 + (dir[i] ? pos[i] : size-i-pos[i]);
      pos[i]++;

      /* apply transposition p <-> p+1 */
        apply_swap(&tmp_now, p, p+1);
        if (memcmp(&tmp_now, &min_now, vsize) < 0)
          memcpy(&min_now, &tmp_now, vsize);
    }
  }
}
```

Fig. 4. Generating permutations by transpositions

never a new transposition is computed, `permute_scalar` calls `apply_swap`. The `apply_swap` procedure has the following header:

```
void apply_swap(State *state, int v1, int v2)
```

It lifts the transposition of scalar values v_1 and v_2 to a given state. The lifting is performed *in situ*, by modifying the given state. The body of `apply_swap` is generated by `AdjustPan`, using the information given in a system description file. The generated C code is straightforward. It consists of a sequence of guarded assignments that swap v_1 with v_2, for each variable that depends on a scalarset.

For example, if x is a global variable of a scalarset type then the following code fragment is generated:

```
if (state->x == v1) state->x = v2; else
if (state->x == v2) state->x = v1;
```

For arrays, the code is more complex. For example, if x is a global array of a scalarset type, and indexed by the same scalarset, then the following code fragment is generated:

```
/* swap values */
for (i = 0; i < SCALAR_SIZE; i++) {
  if (state->x[i] == v1) state->x[i] = v2; else
  if (state->x[i] == v2) state->x[i] = v1;
}
/* swap indices */
{ uchar tmp; tmp = x[v1]; x[v1] = x[v2]; x[v2] = tmp; }
```

In addition, for every family of processes indexed by a scalarset, say `proctype` `P(scalar i)`, `apply_swap` swaps the two chunks of memory (in a state vector) that correspond to $P(v_1)$ and $P(v_2)$.

Strategy sorted

```
State *rep_sorted(State *orig_now) {
  int perm[MAX_SCALAR_SIZE];
  memcpy(&tmp_now, orig_now, vsize);
  /* sort the main array and compute the sorting permutation */
  ...
  /* find the representative */
    apply_perm(perm, &tmp_now);
  return &tmp_now;
}
```

The main array is sorted using a straightforward algorithm that successively finds minimal elements. Its quadratic complexity is acceptable since the size of a scalarset is usually small. On the other hand, it allows to compute the sorting permutation with minimal cost, since each element is swapped only once.

The `apply_perm` procedure has the following header:

```
void apply_perm(int *perm, State *state)
```

It lifts the given permutation of scalarset values to `state`. As in `apply_swap`, the lifting is performed *in situ*, and it consists of a sequence of guarded assignments, for each variable that depends on a scalarset. For example, if x is a global variable of a scalarset type then the following code fragment is generated:

```
if (state->x < SCALAR_SIZE) state->x = perm[state->x];
```

The guard is needed to solve a subtle problem with the initialization of scalarset variables. Since all variables used in a standard Promela program are automatically initialized with 0, it is common to use 0 to represent an undefined value. Unfortunately, this convention cannot be used for scalarsets. The reason is that in our implementation, a scalarset of size n is a range of integers from 0 to $n - 1$, so 0 must be treated as other well-defined values (otherwise, the symmetry would be broken). Thus, a value outside of the range must be used for an undefined value. By convention, we use n for this purpose, and the guard guarantees that the undefined value is treated in a symmetric way (i.e., it is never permuted, as required in [18]). In fact, any value not less than n can be used to represent the undefined value.

For arrays, the code is more complex. For example, if x is a global array of a scalarset type, and indexed by the same scalarset, then the following code fragment is generated:

```
/* permute values */
for (i = 0; i < SCALAR_SIZE; i++) {
  if (state->x[i] < SCALAR_SIZE) state->x[i] = perm[state->x[i]];
}
/* permute indices */
{ uchar buf[SCALAR_SIZE];
  memcpy(buf, state->x, sizeof(state->x));
  for (i = 0; i < SCALAR_SIZE; i++) state->x[perm[i]] = buf[i];
}
```

Notice that when permuting indices we have to use a buffer.

Strategy segmented

```
State *rep_segmented(State *orig_now) {
  int perm[MAX_SCALAR_SIZE];
  memcpy(&tmp_now, orig_now, vsize);
  /* sort the main array and compute the sorting permutation */
    ...
  /* locate blocks */
    ...
  /* find the representative */
    apply_perm(perm, &tmp_now);
    memcpy(&min_now, &tmp_now, vsize);
    if (num_of_blocks > 0)
      permute_blocks(0, block_start[0], block_size[0]);
  return &min_now;
}
```

First, the main array is sorted as in the sorted strategy. Second, the segments of equal values are located, in the sorted main array, by a straightforward linear algorithm. The information about the segments (called blocks henceforth) is stored in the following global data structures:

```
int num_of_blocks;
int block_start[MAX_SCALAR_SIZE], block_size[MAX_SCALAR_SIZE];
```

Finally, the canonical representative is found by procedure permute_blocks that generates all permutations of indices in successive blocks, excluding the identity permutation. Its code is given in Fig. 5. Each permutation is then applied to the current state, and the lexicographically smallest result is chosen.

The procedure uses double recursion, to assure that the number of calls to apply_swap and comparisons between tmp_now and min_now is minimal. It is a generalization of permute_scalar used in rep_full. Conceptually, the indices of separate blocks, when considered relative to the start of a respective block, can be perceived as separate scalarsets. Inside one block, all transpositions of the block's indices are generated as in permute_scalar. The double recursion is used to properly compose the permutations of separate blocks, by chaining the invocations of permute_blocks.

```
void permute_blocks(int block, int start, int size) {
    int i, p, offset, pos[MAX_SCALAR_SIZE], dir[MAX_SCALAR_SIZE];

    /* go to the last block */
      if (++block < num_of_blocks)
        permute_blocks(block, block_start[block], block_size[block]);
      block--;

    /* the same as permute_scalar, but apply transposition is changed to */
      ...
        swap_in_block(block, p, p+1);
      ...
}

void swap_in_block(int block, int p1, int p2) {
    /* apply transposition p1 <-> p2 */
    apply_swap(&tmp_now, p1, p2);
    if (memcmp(&tmp_now, &min_now, vsize) < 0)
      memcpy(&min_now, &tmp_now, vsize);
    /* permute the next block */
    if (++block < num_of_blocks)
      permute_blocks(block, block_start[block], block_size[block]);
}
```

Fig. 5. Permuting blocks

5 Experimental Results

We tried our implementation on several examples, like Peterson's mutual exclusion algorithm [21], or Data Base Manager from [23] (see also [3] for more details about these and other examples.) The obtained reduction were often very close to the theoretical limits, thus, we were able to obtain reductions of several orders of magnitude in the number of states. Also, due to the significantly smaller number of states that had to be explored, in all the cases the verification with symmetry reduction was faster than the one without it.

The experiments showed that in general there is no favorite among the reduction strategies regarding the space/time ratio. This justifies our decision to have all strategies (maybe except full) as separate options of the extended model-checker.

In the verification experiments we used Spin both with and without the partial order reduction (POR) option. Allowing Spin to use its POR algorithm together with our symmetry reductions is sound due to Theorem 19 in [8] which guarantees that the class of POR algorithms to which the Spin's POR algorithm belongs, is compatible with the generic symmetry reduction algorithm. With a straightforward modification, the theorem's proof is valid for our algorithm as well. In most of the cases there was a synergy between the symmetry and the partial order reductions. The two reduction techniques are orthogonal because they exploit different features of the concurrent systems, therefore, their cumulative effect can be used to obtain more efficient verification.

In the sequel, we present the results for two examples. They were chosen so as to test the capabilities to deal with queues, multiple scalar sets and multiple process families. All experiments were performed on a Sun Ultra-Enterprise machine, with three 248 MHz UltraSPARC-II processors and 2304 MB of main memory, running the SunOS 5.5.1 operating system. Verification times are given in seconds $(s.x)$, minutes $(m{:}s)$, or hours $(h{:}m{:}s)$; the number of states is given directly or in millions (say, 9.1M); $o.m.$ stands for out of memory, and $o.t.$ denotes out of time (more than 10 hours); +POR and −POR mean with and without POR, respectively.

The Initialization Protocol. Assume that we are given a system of n processes each consisting of an initial part and a main part. The data structures can have arbitrary initial values. The role of the Initialization Protocol from [13] is to synchronize the processes such that none of them can enter its main part before all the others have finished their initial parts.[4] Process synchronization is done via shared boolean variables. Each process has so called co-component process whose task is to manage the synchronization of the boolean variables. We refer the reader to [13] for more details.

The protocol is an example of a system with one scalar variable and two process families indexed by this scalar – the family of processes that are synchronized and the family of their co-components. In such a case one can expect

---

[4] Note that this would be trivial if we could assume that the variables' initial values were known.

the same maximal amount of reduction of $n!$ (where n is the family size) as with one family.

Table 1. Results for the Initialization Protocol example.

n		2		3		4		5	
		+PO	-PO	+PO	-PO	+PO	-PO	+PO	-PO
no	states	2578	2578	131484	131484	7.0M	7.0M	o.m.	o.m.
symm.	time	6.4	1.1	19.3	12.2	18:50	16:31	—	—
	states	1520	1521	26389	26399	386457	386536	5.3M	o.m.
full	time	6.2	1.0	11.4	6.0	4:53	4:46	5:38:05	—
seg.	time	6.3	1.0	11.1	5.4	3:19	3:04	2:28:20	—
pc-seg.	time	6.3	0.9	10.1	4.4	1:54	1:39	47:03	—
sorted	states	2344	2344	98602	98602	4.2M	4.2M	o.m.	o.m.
	time	6.3	1.0	17.9	11.0	12:13	12:22	—	—
pc-	states	1607	1607	40395	40395	987830	987830	o.m.	o.m.
sorted	time	6.3	0.1	11.8	5.7	3:55	3:17	—	—

We verified the correctness of the algorithm for several values of n by placing before the main part of each process an assertion which checks that all the other processes have terminated their initial parts.

Because of the intensive use of global variables, partial order reduction had almost no effect in this example. Thus, the state space reduction was mostly due to the symmetry. The canonical heuristic segmented and pc-segmented prevailed over the non-canonical ones regarding both space and time. Compared to full, they were significantly faster for larger values of n. Better performance of pc-segmented and pc-sorted over segmented and sorted respectively, can be explained by the fact that the main array that was used in the latter strategies is of boolean type. This means that the elements of the main array can have only two values, in contrast with the program counter which ranges over at least 15 different values. Intuitively, the greater versatility of values in the pc array means that fewer permutations have to be generated on average in order to canonicalize the state.

Base Station. This example is a simplified version of MASCARA – a telecommunication protocol developed by the WAND (Wireless ATM Network Demonstrator) consortium [6]. The protocol provides an extension of the ATM (Asynchronous Transfer Mode) networking protocol to wireless networks. Our model represents a wireless network connecting $n_s \geq 1$ sending mobile stations and $n_r \geq 1$ receiving mobile stations that may communicate with each other using a limited number ($m \geq 1$) of radio channels provided by one base station BS. More specifically, when sender station A wants to send a message to receiver station B it must request a channel from BS. Provided there are channels available, A is granted one, call it c. If B wants to receive messages, it queries BS. As there is a pending communication for B through c, BS assigns c to B. After the communication has taken place, both A and B return the channel to BS. The results given below are for checking for unreachable code, with $m = 2$ radio channels.

Table 2. Results for the Base Station example.

		$n_s = 2$ $n_r = 2$		$n_s = 3$ $n_r = 2$		$n_s = 2$ $n_r = 3$	
		+PO	-PO	+PO	-PO	+PO	-PO
no	states	4.6M	9.0M	*o.m.*	*o.m.*	*o.m.*	*o.m.*
symm.	time	5:02	13:48	—	—	—	—
full	states	1.2M	2.3M	9.0M	*o.m.*	9.4M	*o.m.*
	time	1:41	5:03	28:57	—	30:32	—
pc-seg.	time	1:32	4:54	19:29	—	20:36	—
pc-	states	1.7M	3.5M	*o.m.*	*o.m.*	*o.m.*	*o.m.*
sorted	time	1:58	6:03	39:02	—	—	—

There are two families of symmetric processes in the model: The family of sending stations and the family of receiving stations. Unlike in the Initialization Protocol, the two families are independent, and, consequently, indexed with two different scalar sets.

On this example we could apply only pc-segmented and pc-sorted because there was no main array that could be used for sorted and segmented. One can see that for the canonical strategies the reduction indeed approaches the theoretical limit $n_s! \cdot n_r!$. (In general, for a system with k independent process families indexed by k scalar sets, the reduction due to symmetry is limited by $n_1! \cdot n_2! \cdot \ldots \cdot n_k!$, where $n_i, 1 \leq i \leq k$, is the number of processes in the i-th family.)

A version of this protocol was analyzed in [3]. There, we had to rewrite the original model such that all the communication was done via global variables. For the experiments in this paper we were able to use the original model in which the communication was modeled with Promela channels. As a result, the contribution of the partial order reduction became visible. One can also notice the already mentioned orthogonality of the two heuristics – namely, the factor of reduction due to symmetry was almost the same with or without POR.

6 Conclusions and Future Work

We have presented SymmSpin, an extension of Spin with a symmetry-reduction package. The package is based on the heuristic presented in [3]. It provides the 4 reduction strategies based on this heuristic (sorted/pc-sorted and segmented/pc-segmented) as well as the full reduction strategy. Compared to the prototype implementation that was used for the feasibility study reported in [3], the current implementation covers a more general class of symmetric systems. Namely, it is able to deal with multiple scalar sets and multiple process families. In addition, almost all Promela features are now handled, including queues. The only remaining restrictions are that the elements of queues are as yet restricted to simple, non-structured types, and that no dynamic process creation is allowed.

The resulting package has been described at a detailed level. For maximal modularity, the implementation is in the form of a Tcl script that operates on the verification engine produced by Spin. We point the interested reader to the web site accompanying this paper, [1], for the full source code.

This enhanced implementation enabled a more extensive series of experiments, exploiting the additional symmetric structure in models and the richer variety of Promela constructs handled. Two of the new experiments are reported here. Naturally, also the experiments reported in [3] have been repeated and successfully reproduced in the process of testing the new implementation.

The most natural next step would be to extend the Promela syntax to allow specifications of scalarsets directly instead of via an accompanying file. This will facilitate the automatic verification of the syntactic conditions along the lines of [18], that are needed to ensure the soundness of the analysis. With the present implementation this is still a task for the user. A more ambitious attempt would be the automatic detection of scalarsets directly from the Promela sources.

On a theoretical level, the symmetry package is compatible with Spin's LTL verification algorithm combined with partial order reduction. What needs to be verified is that our arguments are also valid for the particular implementations in Spin, more precisely, the cycle detection algorithm. Experience has taught us that this kind of issues should be treated cautiously.

References

1. AdjustPan script, http://www.win.tue.nl/~lhol/SymmSpin, April 2000.
2. D. Bošnacki, D. Dams, Integrating real time into Spin: a prototype implementation, in S. Budkowski, A. Cavalli, E. Najm (eds), *Proc. of FORTE/PSTV'98 (Formal Description Techniques and Protocol Specification, Testing and Verification)*, 423–438, Paris, France, Oct. 1998.
3. D. Bošnacki, D. Dams, L. Holenderski, A Heuristic for Symmetry Reductions with Scalarsets, submitted to *FORTE'2000 (The 13th Int. Conf. on Formal Description Techniques for Distributed Systems and Communication Protocols)*.
4. E.M. Clarke, R. Enders, T. Filkorn, S. Jha, Exploiting symmetry in temporal logic model checking, *Formal Methods in System Design*, Vol. 19, 77–104, 1996.
5. E.M. Clarke, O. Grumberg, D.A. Peled, *Model Checking*, The MIT Press, 2000.
6. I. Dravapoulos, N. Pronios, S. Denazis *et al*, *The Magic WAND, Deliverable 3D2, Wireless ATM MAC*, Sep 1997.
7. E.A. Emerson, Temporal and modal logic, in Jan van Leeuwen (ed.), *Formal Models and Semantic*, Vol. B of *Handbook of Theoretical Computer Science*, Chap. 16, 995–1072, Elsevier/The MIT Press, 1990.

8. E.A. Emerson, S. Jha, D. Peled, Combining partial order and symmetry reductions, in Ed Brinksma (ed.), *Proc. of TACAS'97 (Tools and Algorithms for the Construction and Analysis of Systems)*, LNCS 1217, 19–34, Springer, 1997.

9. E.A. Emerson, A.P. Sistla, Symmetry and model checking, in C. Courcoubetis (ed.), *Proc. of CAV'93 (Computer Aided Verification)*, LNCS 697, 463–478, Springer, 1993.

10. E.A. Emerson, R.J. Trefler, Model checking real-time properties of symmetric systems, *Proc. of the 23rd International Symposium on Mathematical Foundations of Computer Science (MFCS)*, 427–436, Aug. 1998.

11. E.A. Emerson, R.J. Trefler, From asymmetry to full symmetry: new techniques for symmetry reduction in model checking, *Proc. of CHARME'99 (The 10th IFIP WG10.5 Advanced Research Working Conference on Correct Hardware Design and Verification Methods)*, Bad Herrenalb, Germany, Sep. 1999.

12. E.A. Emerson, A.P. Sistla, Utilizing symmetry when model-checking under fairness assumptions: an automata-theoretic approach, *ACM Transactions on Programming Languages and Systems*, 19(4):617–638, July 1997.

13. W.H.J.Feijen, A.J.M. van Gasteren, *On a method of multiprogramming*, Springer-Verlag, 1999

14. P. Godefroid, Exploiting symmetry when model-checking software, *Proc. of FORTE/PSTV'99 (Formal Methods for Protocol Engineering and Distributed Systems)*, 257–275, Beijing, Oct. 1999.

15. V. Gyuris, A.P. Sistla, On-the fly model checking under fairness that exploits symmetry, in O. Grumberg (ed.), *Proc. of CAV'97 (Computer Aided Verification)*, LNCS 1254, 232–243, Springer, 1997.

16. G.J. Holzmann, *Design and Validation of Communication Protocols*, Prentice Hall, 1991. Also: http://netlib.bell-labs.com/netlib/spin/whatispin.html

17. C.N. Ip, D.L. Dill, Better verification through symmetry, in D. Agnew, L. Claesen, R. Camposano (eds), *Proc. of the 1993 Conference on Computer Hardware Description Languages and their Applications*, Apr. 1993.

18. C.N. Ip, D.L. Dill, Better verification through symmetry. *Formal Methods in System Design*, Vol. 9, 41–75, 1996.

19. C.N. Ip, *State Reduction Methods for Automatic Formal Verification*, PhD thesis, Department of Computer Science of Stanford University, Dec 1996.

20. V. Lipskiy, Kombinatorika dlya programmistov, Mir, Moscow, 1988. (In Russian)

21. N.A. Lynch, *Distributed Algorithms*, Morgan Kaufmann Publishers, 1996.

22. R. Nalumasu, G. Gopalakrishnan, Explicit-enumeration based Verification made Memory-efficient, *Proc. of CHDL'95 (Computer Hardware Description Languages)*, 617-622, Chiba, Japan, Aug. 1995.

23. A. Valmari, Stubborn sets for reduced state space generation, *Advances in Petri Nets 1990*, LNCS 483, 491–515, Springer, 1991.

Using Garbage Collection in Model Checking

Radu Iosif and Riccardo Sisto

Dipartimento di Automatica e Informatica, Politecnico di Torino
corso Duca degli Abruzzi 24, 10129 Torino, Italy
iosif@athena.polito.it, sisto@polito.it
http://www.dai-arc.polito.it

Abstract. Garbage collection techniques have become common-place in actual programming environments, helping programmers to avoid memory fragmentation and invalid referencing problems. In order to efficiently model check programs that use garbage collection, similar functionalities have to be embedded in model checkers. This paper focuses on the implementation of two classic garbage collection algorithms in dSPIN, an extension of the model checker SPIN which supports dynamic memory management. Experiments carried out show that, besides making a large class of programs tractable, garbage collection can also be a mean to reduce the number of states generated by our model checking tool.

1 Introduction

Applying finite-state verification techniques, such as model checking, to concurrent and distributed software systems looks attractive because they are capable of detecting very subtle defects in the logic design of these systems. Nevertheless, the transition of these techniques from research to actual practice is still slow. One of the reasons is that current finite-state verification tools still adhere to a static representation of systems, while programming environments become more and more dynamic. It is necessary to distinguish here between static and dynamic program information, the former referring to information that can be known at compile-time using static analysis techniques (e.g., data flow analysis), while the later refers to information that occurs only at run-time. In fact, many of the optimizations performed in compilers (and lately in software verification tools [3]) are based on the attempt to over-approximate run-time information using static analysis techniques. Even if static analysis proves to be useful in reducing the size of finite-state program models, there are still cases in which effective reductions can be achieved only at the expense of very complex and time-consuming analysis. Such cases involve pointer analysis [2] which produces a conservative approximation of a pointer alias set that is, the set of objects it may point to at run-time. Besides being very complex, the analysis results can still be too large to be used in finite-state verification.

An alternative approach to software verification involves the representation of dynamic program information directly into the model checking engine. In

K. Havelund, J. Penix, and W. Visser (Eds.): SPIN 2000, LNCS 1885, pp. 20–33, 2000.
© Springer-Verlag Berlin Heidelberg 2000

order to do that, we have extended the model checker SPIN [7] with a number of dynamic features, among which:

- memory references (pointers),
- dynamic object creation and deletion,
- function declaration and call,
- function code references (function pointers).

The extension is called dSPIN (dynamic SPIN) and has been reported in [5]. Even if dSPIN remains a general-purpose model checker, it is intended especially for software verification, allowing for an easy translation of high-level object-oriented programming languages (Java, C++) into its input language, which is a dialect of PROMELA. The size of the transition system is reduced first using a light-weight pointer analysis, and then applying common finite-state reduction techniques such as: partial order reductions, state compression, symbolic representation, etc.

A further step towards improving model checking of software systems is the introduction of garbage collection techniques in dSPIN. This work is motivated by the widespread use of garbage collection in real-life software systems, especially the ones written in Java, where this is the default memory management policy. Indeed, when unused memory is not reclaimed, the program state space may experience an unbounded growth that makes analysis impossible. For example, let us assume that C represents the name of a class declaration in the following fragment of Java code:

```
C x;
while (true) {
    . . .
  x = new C( );
    . . .
}
```

If no garbage collection is performed during model checking, every iteration of the (possibly infinite) loop will add new states to the program state space. When the state space is explored in the depth-first order, this leads to a very fast growth of the state space that exhausts the system resources before any useful results can be given. Instead, when the program model is checked using garbage collection, the first state of the second iteration will (most probably) match the first state of the first one and the loop need not be re-explored.

Without using garbage collection, a solution can be explicit memory deletion. However, using explicit deletion has two drawbacks. On one hand, if the source program does not use explicit deletion statements, inserting such statements into the program model requires expensive pointer analysis. On the other hand, explicit deletes may result in useless changes of the memory configuration, which greatly increases the program state space. Embedding garbage collection into the model checker proves to be quite easy and it has the advantage of eliminating both, the need for complex pointer analysis and dangerous memory fragmentation at the expense of only a small run-time overhead.

It has recently come to our attention that at least one other group is working on implementing garbage collection in a Java byte-code model checker, the Java PathFinder tool [6].

The paper is organized as follows: Section 2 recalls background concepts on dSPIN and garbage collection, Section 3 describes the implementation of two collection algorithms in dSPIN, Section 4 reports a number of experiments that have been carried out and Section 5 concludes.

2   Background

In this section we recall background concepts used throughout the paper. In particular, we present two classic collection algorithms and discuss the data layout in dSPIN. A detailed report on dSPIN can be found in [5].

In what follows, we denote by *garbage* [1] any heap-allocated object that is not reachable by any chain of pointers from program variables. The memory occupied by garbage should be reclaimed for use in allocating new objects. This process is called *garbage collection* and is performed by the program run-time system, in our case the model checking engine.

2.1   Reference Counting Collection

Most of the garbage collection algorithms identify the garbage by first finding out what is reachable. Instead, it can be done directly by keeping track of how many pointers point directly to each object. This is the *reference count* of the object and needs to be recorded with each object. More precisely, we need to keep the reference count for all objects in a separate table, called the *reference table*. Figure 1 shows the general structure of reference counting collection algorithms [1]. Whenever an object reference p is stored into a pointer variable v, the object

```
procedure GCdec(p)
begin
  reference_table [p] --;
  if (reference_table [p] == 0)
  then begin
    for each field f of object p
      GCdec(f);
    delete(p);
  end
end GCdec
procedure GCinc(p)
begin
  reference_table [p] ++;
end GCinc
```

Fig. 1. Reference Counting Collection

reference count is incremented by a call to `GCinc(p)` and the reference count of what v previously pointed to is decremented by a call to `GCdec(v)`. If the decremented count of an object reaches zero then the object is deleted and the reference counts of all other objects pointed to by its fields are decremented by recursive calls to `GCdec`.

Reference counting seems simple and attractive but there is a major drawback: cycles of garbage cannot be reclaimed. Let us consider for example a cyclic list of objects that is not anymore reachable from program variables. Every cons of the list will still have the reference count at least one, which prevents it from being collected.

Considering that a pass of the reference counting collector has collected $N_{collected}$ objects out of a total of $N_{reachable}$ reachable, the time spent can be evaluated as $t_{delete} \times N_{collected}$, where t_{delete} stands for the average object deletion time. The worst-case time of a reference counting collection occurs when all reachable objects are collected i.e., $t_{delete} \times N_{reachable}$. This corresponds to the case in which all reachable objects have the reference count equal to one, which makes the collector reclaim them all.

Despite the previously mentioned problem, regarding the impossibility of reclaiming cyclic-structured data, the cost of a reference counting collection is quite small which makes the algorithm suitable for use in model checking.

2.2   Mark and Sweep Collection

Program pointers and heap-allocated objects form a directed graph. Program variables are the roots of this graph, denoted in what follows by the set ROOTS. A node n in the graph is reachable if there is a path of directed edges leading to n starting at some root r ∈ ROOTS. A graph-search algorithm, such as depth-first search, marks all nodes reachable from all roots. Any node that is not marked is garbage and must be reclaimed. This is done by a sweep of the heap area, looking for nodes that are not marked. As said, these nodes are garbage and they are deleted. The sweep phase should also clear the marking of all nodes, in preparation for the next collection. Figure 2 shows the mark and sweep collection algorithm [1]. The marking of all objects are kept in a global *mark table* used by both the `GCmark` and `GCsweep` procedures.

In order to evaluate the cost of a mark and sweep collection, let us consider that there are $N_{reachable}$ reachable objects. We denote by N_{max} the upper bound of the heap that is, the maximum number of objects that can be allocated. The time taken by the mark phase is proportional to the number of nodes it marks that is, the amount of reachable data. The time taken by the sweep phase is proportional to the size of the heap. Consequently, the overall time of the garbage collection is $t_{mark} \times N_{reachable} + t_{delete} \times (N_{max} - N_{reachable})$, where t_{mark} is the object marking time and t_{delete} is the object deletion time, introduced in the previous section. Once again, this is a worst-case estimation because in practice, only the number of unreachable existent objects needs to be deleted by the collector. As this number depends tightly on the program

```
procedure GCmark(r)
begin
  if (! mark_table [r])
  then begin
    mark_table [r] = true;
    for each field f of object r
      GCmark(f);
  end
end GCmark
procedure GCsweep()
begin
  for each object p
  if (mark_table [p])
  then begin
    mark_table [p] = false;
    delete(p);
  end
end GCsweep
```

Fig. 2. Mark and Sweep Collection

structure, we have chosen to over-approximate it with the maximum number of unreachable objects $N_{max} - N_{reachable}$.

2.3 Overview of dSPIN

In order to make this paper self contained, we need to recall some of the extensions that have been implemented in dSPIN, in particular the ones concerning dynamic memory management. In dSPIN, memory can be dynamically allocated and deleted by means of explicit new and delete statements. Dynamically allocated areas will be denoted in what follows as *objects*. The mechanism to handle objects in dSPIN is called *pointer*, as in most programming languages. Semantically, dSPIN pointers resemble to Java references that is, they can be assigned and the objects they point to can be accessed (dereferenced), but they cannot be used in arithmetic operations, as it is the case in C. A complete description of the syntax and semantics of these language constructs can be found in [8].

In dSPIN, the objects that are dynamically allocated reside on a contiguous memory zone called the *heap area*. Newly created objects are added at the end of the heap area. After deleting an existing object, the heap area is compacted in order to avoid memory losses caused by fragmentation. The object retrieval information is kept into two tables called the *offset table* and the *size table*. The first table holds the offset with respect to the beginning of the heap area, while the second one holds the actual size of the object. In addition, a garbage collector must be able to operate on objects of all types. In particular, it must be able to determine the number of fields in each object, and whether each field is a pointer. Type information is kept for each object in the *type table*. A pointer to an object encodes an integer value which is used to index the three tables. Figure 3 depicts the run-time representation of objects in dSPIN.

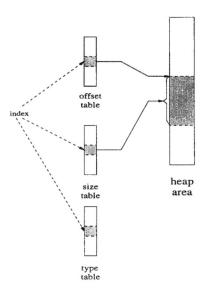

Fig. 3. The Data Layout in dSPIN

Explicit type information is needed at run-time because the input language of dSPIN allows for free pointer conversion. In other words, conversion between any two pointer types is allowed, which makes static type evaluation almost impossible. Let us point out that type information need not be stored into the state vector when performing model checking. The offset, size and type tables are global data structures that are modified only by the allocation and deletion statements. As will be discussed in the following, this information needs to be recorded on the state stack in order to allow the model checker to unwind allocation/deletion forward moves. The memory overhead introduced by garbage collection depends only on the maximum stack depth.

3   Implementation Issues

In this section we present issues related to the implementation of the previously presented collection algorithms, in the dSPIN model checker. In particular, we address aspects related to the compatibility between these algorithms and the model checking run-time environment. As the latter differs from common run-time systems, the way its particularities may interact with garbage collection are considered.

A first point that needs attention is the possibility of duplicating regions of the model checker state space when using garbage collection. For example, let us consider the situation in which the verifier generates a state A in which some objects have become garbage. Let us assume that, like in usual run-time environments, the garbage collector does not necessarily run immediately after this state has been generated. In consequence, all its direct successor states, let us call them $B_1, B_2, \ldots, B_n$ will maintain the garbage. If, at a later point during verification, the model checker generates the state A' that differs from A only by the absence of garbage, the states A and A' will not match. Consequently, none of the direct successors of A', let us call them $B_1', B_2', \ldots, B_n'$ will match the states $B_1, B_2, \ldots, B_n$ respectively. This results in an unwanted duplication of states, because of garbage collection.

The solution is to run the collection as soon as possible in order to avoid states containing any garbage at all. In order to do that, we distinguish three kinds of statements that may produce garbage in dSPIN:

1. pointer *assignment*; the object previously pointed to by the pointer may become garbage.
2. *exit* from function or local scope; the objects pointed to by local pointers may become garbage.
3. explicit *delete*; the objects pointed to by the deleted object fields may become garbage.

Garbage collection is invoked atomically, as part of the transitions fired by the statements above. The model checker will experience an increase of the running time, which is proportional to the overall number of collection attempts.

Another difference between a common run-time system and a model checker regards the possibility of unwinding forward moves. When a model checker, like SPIN[7], encounters an already visited state it performs a backward move that matches its last forward move on the trail stack. As result, the model checker restores the current state to one of its previously visited states. For simple transitions, as for example assignments, only a small amount of unwinding information is kept directly on the trail stack. There are however cases in which a state has to be entirely copied on the stack in order to be used later in performing a backward move. The model checker keeps a separate stack for states that have been thoroughly modified by forward moves, denoted as the *state stack*.

When the garbage collector runs in a transition, it might thoroughly modify the heap area along with the adjacent tables i.e., the offset, size and type table. In order to be able to restore the transition's source state, the model checker needs to save the entire heap area along with the additional tables on the state stack. This is needed because it is actually impossible to predict the behavior of the collector i.e., which objects will be reclaimed. As discussed in Section 2, each garbage collection algorithm keeps some additional information about heap-allocated objects e.g., the reference table. As the latter will be modified by a collector run, it also need to be saved on the state stack. This results in a memory overhead that is proportional with the state stack depth.

The following discussion regards implementation details of each collection algorithm in particular. An estimation of the time and space overhead introduced by each algorithm is reported.

3.1   Reference Counting

The reference counting collector keeps in a global table the number of references to each object. As discussed in Section 2, this is the number of pointers that directly point to the object. The collector runs whenever the reference number has become zero for some objects. These objects are deleted, and then the collector runs recursively for all objects pointed to by the deleted objects fields. The collection stops when no other reachable object can be deleted. The time taken by a collector run is at most $t_{delete} \times N_{reachable}$, where $N_{reachable}$ is the number of objects that are reachable from the set of program pointers, denoted in what follows by ROOTS, at the point where the collection was attempted.

An interesting property of the reference counting collection regards the possibility of performing a partial static evaluation of the set ROOTS, depending on the nature of the statement that might trigger the collection. For pointer assignment statements, the set ROOTS contains only the left-hand side pointer. In this case, garbage collection has to be attempted before the assignment takes place. For statements that exit from functions and local scopes, the set ROOTS contains all the local pointers. The latter situation involves explicit delete statements. In this case, the set ROOTS contains all pointer fields of the deleted object. As said before, the type of an object cannot be statically evaluated, this information being encoded at run-time into the type table. Depending on the given object type, the collector identifies its layout that is, the position of its pointer fields.

In order to estimate the time overhead introduced by the reference counting collection, let us denote by C_{rc} the total number of collector runs. This is the total number of successful collections, which is always less than the total number of the garbage collector invocations, because the reference counting collector stops as soon as no object can be deleted. With the above notations, the worst-case time overhead introduced by the reference counting collection is $t_{delete} \times N_{reachable} \times C_{rc}$. The number $N_{reachable}$ depends on the way program data is structured. Moreover, it may differ from one collection to the next one. In order to be able to evaluate the time of a collection, in what follows we assume that $N_{reachable}$ represents an average value.

The space overhead can be estimated considering that every collection requires the saving of the type and reference table on the state stack. In practice, the size of a type table entry is 4 bytes (integer), while the reference table entry can be represented on 2 bytes (short). Consequently, each collection introduces a space overhead of $6 \times N_{max}$ bytes, where N_{max} is the maximum number of heap objects. If C_{rc} represents the overall number of reference counting collections performed during model checking, each one needing the save of tables on the state stack, the space overhead is $6 \times N_{max} \times \log(C_{rc})$. We have approximated here the maximum depth of the state stack to $\log(C_{rc})$. In practice, the time and space overheads show to be quite small, therefore we have set reference counting to be the default garbage collection mode in dSPIN.

3.2 Mark and Sweep

The mark and sweep collection performs a thorough scan of the reachable data and marks all objects it encounters during the scan. As mentioned in Section 2, the mark phase starts with the set of all live program pointers ROOTS. This cannot be anymore statically evaluated, because the stack layout of every process cannot be statically determined. This problem can be overcome by giving a description of the global pointers and also the local pointers declared in each proctype or function. Such a data structure is called a *pointer map* and is built by the verifier generator.

To find all the roots, the collector starts at the top of each process stack and scans downward, frame by frame. Each frame keys the function or proctype that corresponds to the next frame, giving the entry into the pointer map. In each frame, the collector marks starting from the pointers in that frame and, in the end, it marks starting from the global pointers. The mark phase is recursive, the spanning being done according to the object types, which are kept into the type table.

When the mark phase completes, the sweep phase deletes all unreachable data. In order to do that, the entire heap area must be scanned every time the collector runs. Let us denote by C_{ms} the total number of collector runs. This is the total number of collector invocations, because the mark and sweep collector always performs a complete scan of the reachable data every time it is invoked. With the above notations, the worst-case time overhead introduced by a mark and sweep collection is $(t_{mark} \times N_{reachable} + t_{delete} \times (N_{max} - N_{reachable})) \times C_{ms}$.

The space overhead is introduced also by the need to save the type table on the state stack. As previously explained, the mark table is written by the mark phase and cleared each time by the sweep phase, therefore we don't need to save it on the state stack. The size of the type table entry is 4 bytes. Consequently, the space overhead introduced by a mark and sweep collection is $4 \times N_{max}$ bytes, where N_{max} is the maximum number of objects. The state is saved on the stack each time the collection was successful that is, at least one object has been deleted. We denote this number by C_{ms}^{del}, therefore the overall mark and sweep space overhead is $4 \times N_{max} \times \log(C_{ms}^{del})$.

3.3 Overhead Comparison

Given the evaluations for time and space overheads previously introduced, we attempt to find out under which circumstances reference counting collection is better than mark and sweep or vice-versa. We remind the reader that all evaluations are related to our implementation of these algorithms in dSPIN.

We denote in what follows, for reference counting, the overall time overhead by $t_{rc} = t_{delete} \times N_{reachable} \times C_{rc}$ and space overhead by $s_{rc} = 6 \times N_{max} \times \log(C_{rc})$. For mark and sweep we denote the overall time overhead by $t_{ms} =$

$(t_{mark} \times N_{reachable} + t_{delete} \times (N_{max} - N_{reachable})) \times C_{ms}$ and space overhead by $s_{ms} = 4 \times N_{max} \times \log(C_{ms}^{del})$.

The time overhead comparison is given by:

$$\frac{t_{ms}}{t_{rc}} = \frac{C_{ms}}{C_{rc}} \times \left(\frac{t_{mark}}{t_{delete}} + \frac{N_{max}}{N_{reachable}} - 1 \right) \tag{1}$$

The first term C_{ms}/C_{rc} is always greater than one, because mark and sweep runs every time it is invoked, while reference counting stops when no objects can be deleted. For the second term of the expression we can give a worst-case evaluation. More precisely, it is greater than one if $N_{max} \geq 2 \times N_{reachable}$. This gives us a sufficient condition for reference counting collection to run faster than mark and sweep. We have found that, in practice this condition is usually met by common programs.

The space overhead comparison is given by:

$$\frac{s_{rc}}{s_{ms}} = 1.5 \times \frac{\log(C_{rc})}{\log(C_{ms}^{del})} \tag{2}$$

The second term of the expression depends on the program data layout. If the program does not use cyclic data structures then both collection algorithms reclaim almost the same number of objects that is, $C_{rc} \approx C_{ms}^{del}$ and consequently, $s_{rc}/s_{ms} \approx 1.5$. As will be reported in what follows, in practice the space overhead introduced by mark and sweep is always smaller than the one introduced by reference counting.

4   Experimental Work

We have carried out a number of experiments in order to asses the practical value of garbage collection used in combination with model checking. Obviously, an immediate advantage is tracking down programs that may create an unbounded number of objects. Moreover, using garbage collection reduces the number of states in verification and consequently, the model checker time and space requirements.

The first part of this section reports experiments that are performed on the dSPIN specification of a B-tree structure. The reduction in number of states is compared to the time and space overhead introduced by both collection algorithms. The remainder of this section is concerned with an estimation of the best and worst case complexity in a doubly linked list example. All analysis time reports are obtained from the Unix time command on a 256 Mb RAM Ultra-Sparc 30 at 300MHz workstation. Small times (under 0.5 seconds) tend to be inaccurate because of the operating system overhead.

4.1   The B-Tree Example Revisited

The example considered here is a revision of the test case reported in [5]. The system describes a B-tree structure that is accessed concurrently by two updater processes. A mutual exclusion protocol is used in order to ensure the data consistency while allowing for simultaneous updater accesses to the structure. In order to avoid an unbounded growth of the structure, each updater stops its execution when a predefined maximum depth is reached. The specification was tested for absence of deadlocks. The example is parameterized with respect to the following variables:

- K denotes the B-tree order,
- D denotes the maximum B-tree depth,

In the first case we have explicit delete statements inserted into the model. Table 1 shows the results obtained by performing analysis in presence of explicit delete statements, first without garbage collection, then applying the two collection algorithms, i.e., reference counting (RC) and mark and sweep (MS), that are implemented in dSPIN.

Table 1. Explicit Delete B-tree

K,D	States	Memory (Mb)	GC (runs)	Time (h:m:s)	Options
	4620	3.345	-	0:0:1.0	-
4, 2	4620	3.895	RC (0)	0:0:1.4	-
	4620	3.712	MS (1591)	0:0:1.2	-
	440486	58.062	-	0:1:41.0	COLLAPSE
2, 3	313316	42.858	RC (124)	0:1:39.2	COLLAPSE
	237442	31.837	MS (91247)	0:1:08.7	COLLAPSE
	5.65413e+07	135.772	-	3:33:37.5	BS (9.49519)
2, 4	5.63116e+07	136.468	RC (25745)	4:11:10.4	BS (9.53393)
	5.34694e+07	136.242	MS (33558759)	3:50:04.8	BS (10.0408)

The overall number of collector runs is also presented in the table. For reference counting, this is the total number of successful collections that is, collections in which at least one object has been reclaimed. This comes as a consequence of the fact that reference counting collection stops when it cannot reclaim any more objects. Instead, mark and sweep collection performs exactly one sweep of the heap area every time it is invoked. In this case, the number of collector invocations is the number of collector runs.

It is to be noted that garbage collection acts also as a complexity reduction mechanism. The explicit delete statements that have been inserted into the model tend to increase the overall number of states. Our intuition is that semantically-equivalent states do not match because of different orderings of objects into the heap area. As garbage collection constantly reduces the number of objects it also reduces the number of possible interleavings in the heap representation. Recently, the implementors of the Java PathFinder tool [6] have considered the possibility of representing the heap objects in the same way, disregarding their creation order, which makes a further reduction in the number of states.

In the first case (4, 2) garbage collection is inefficient. Allowing for a maximum tree depth of 2 implies that no object is ever deleted during an update. In this case garbage collection introduces only an overhead in memory and space but does not improve the verification performance. The second case (2, 3) shows clearly how garbage collection reduces the model checker state space and consequently, its time and space requirements. Due to the fact that in our model, the B-tree nodes are doubly linked, mark and sweep collection is more efficient than reference counting. The latter case (2, 4) was analyzed using bitstate hashing (BS). Table 1 shows also the hash factor reported by the verifier (following the BS). It is to be noted that, in this case, using garbage collection reduces the state space complexity and improves the hash factor.

The second suite of experiments has been performed by replacing the explicit deletes with `skip` statements. Table 2 shows the results. In general, the number of states experiences a remarkable decrease, because the lack of explicit deletes makes semantically-equivalent states match in most cases.

Table 2. No Explicit Delete B-tree

K,D	States	Memory (Mb)	GC (runs)	Time (h:m:s)	Options
4, 2	637	1.830	-	0:0:0.1	-
	637	1.920	RC (18)	0:0:0.1	-
	637	1.877	MS (161)	0:0:0.1	-
2, 3	1257	2.497	-	0:0:0.1	-
	1257	2.587	RC (14)	0:0:0.1	-
	1257	2.429	MS (325)	0:0:0.1	-
4, 3	3025	4.935	-	0:0:0.3	-
	3025	4.848	RC (20)	0:0:0.3	-
	3025	4.013	MS (739)	0:0:0.3	-
2, 4	23852	11.987	-	0:0:30.3	COLLAPSE, MA
	23852	11.709	RC (14)	0:0:23.5	COLLAPSE, MA
	30346	9.242	MS (7451)	0:0:30.9	COLLAPSE, MA

In this case, using garbage collection does not reduce the state space, rather tends to slightly increase it, as it is with the case (2, 4) verified using mark and sweep. However, it is to be noticed that the memory requirements tend to decrease, as a consequence of the decrease of the current state size. In the case (4, 2), the memory overhead introduced by the garbage collection balances the gains, resulting in a greater memory requirement. But, as discussed, the space overhead introduced by garbage collection tends to increase logarithmically with the overall number of collections, and therefore with the total number of states.

The following cases (2, 3), (4, 3) and (2, 4) show an actual decrease of memory taken up by the verifier when using garbage collection.

4.2   Worst and Best Case Estimation

We have performed a number of experiments in order to give an upper and lower bound to the efficiency of the collection algorithms. The test case is a specification of a doubly linked list which is updated sequentially by one process. The process does a fixed number of list updates, counted up by an integer variable. The purpose of the counter variable is to ensure that the number of states does not change when garbage collection is used. As the value of the counter is incremented at each iteration, the states from the current iteration will not match the states from previous iterations. The number of states is used as a reference point in our evaluation.

In the worst case, a fixed number of cons cells is inserted into the list. All cells are continuously referenced by the head of the list during program runtime, which makes garbage collection impossible. In the best case, the same number of cons cells is inserted into the list, but after each insertion, every cell is then extracted by resetting the list reference to it. No explicit deletes are performed, the cells being reclaimed only by the garbage collector. Table 3 shows the analysis results.

Table 3. Worst and Best Case Garbage Collection

GC	Runs	States	Memory (Mb)	Time (secs)
i. Worst Case				
-	-	12242	253.009	20.1
RC	0	12242	295.154	20.9
MS	6119	12242	281.105	26.3
ii. Best Case				
-	-	16832	386.079	50.9
RC	1530	16832	231.66	17.3
MS	7650	16832	208.252	8.5

It is to be noticed that the worst-case space overhead introduced by reference counting is greater than the one introduced by mark and sweep. On the other hand, the worst-case time taken up by the reference counting is smaller than the one taken up by mark and sweep. In this case both collection algorithms are inefficient because they cannot reclaim any object. In the best case, mark and sweep yields much better results in both space and time than reference counting, making the analysis more efficient. This comes as a consequence of the fact that, in this case, the rate of successful mark and sweep collections is rather big i.e., at least one occurs in each iteration.

5 Conclusions

Providing model checkers like dSPIN[1] with support for garbage collection allows analysis of a wider class of real-life software systems. This occurs as a consequence of the widespread use of garbage collection in current programming environments. In particular, programs that rely strictly on garbage collection, like the ones written in Java, tend to create untractable models because of the unbounded growth of their working memory. Despite a limited run-time overhead introduced by the collection algorithms, embedding them into model checking seems to improve the analysis results in general, acting also as a state reduction mechanism.

When implementing such algorithms in a model checker, attention has to be paid to the particularities of the model checking environment, such as the possible backward moves. An evaluation of the time and space overhead introduced by garbage collection has been given. Although such an evaluation is tightly related to the layout of the data structures used in the program, worst and best case estimation can be given. Experiments have been carried out in order to assess the practical value of our work.

References

1. Andrew W. Appel: Modern Compiler Implementation in Java. Cambridge University Press, (1998)
2. J. Corbett: Constructing Compact Models of Concurrent Java Programs. Proc. of International Symposium on Software Testing and Analysis (1998)
3. J. Corbett, M. B. Dwyer et al.: Bandera: Extracting Finite-state Models from Java Source Code. Proc. 22nd International Conference on Software Engineering (2000) 439–448
4. C. Demartini, R. Iosif, R. Sisto: A deadlock detection tool for concurrent Java programs. Software: Practice & Experience, Vol 29, No 7 (1999) 577–603
5. C. Demartini, R. Iosif, R. Sisto: dSPIN: A Dynamic Extension of SPIN. Lecture Notes in Computer Science, Vol. 1680, Springer-Verlag, Berlin Heidelberg New York (1999) 261–276
6. G. Brat, K. Havelund, S. Park, W. Visser: Java PathFinder: Second Generation of a Java Model Checker. Workshop on Advances in Verification (2000)
7. G. Holzmann: The Design and Validation of Computer Protocols. Prentice Hall, (1991).
8. R. Iosif: The dSPIN User Manual. http://www.dai-arc.polito.it/dai-arc/auto/tools/tool7.shtml

---

[1] The dSPIN source code is distributed via the URL: http://www.dai-arc.polito.it/dai-arc/auto/tools/tool7.shtml

Model Checking Based on Simultaneous Reachability Analysis*

Bengi Karaçalı** and Kuo-Chung Tai

Department of Computer Science, Box 7534 North Carolina State University
Raleigh, NC 27695-7534, USA
{bkaraca,kct}@eos.ncsu.edu

Abstract. Simultaneous reachability analysis (SRA) is a recently proposed approach to alleviating the state space explosion problem in reachability analysis of concurrent systems. The concept of SRA is to allow a
global transition in a reachability graph to contain a set of transitions of
different processes such that the state reached by the global transition is
independent of the execution order of the associated process transitions.
In this paper, we describe how to apply the SRA approach to concurrent
systems for model checking. We first describe an SRA-based framework
for producing a reduced state graph that provides sufficient information
for model checking. Following this framework, we present an algorithm
that generates a reduced state graph for the extended finite state machine
(EFSM) model with multiple ports. Empirical results indicate that, our
SRA reduction algorithm performs as good as or better than the partial
order reduction algorithm in SPIN.

1 Introduction

For a given finite-state concurrent system and a temporal logic formula specifying some properties, model checking determines whether the concurrent system
satisfies the specified properties [3]. Model checking has been used successfully
to verify computer hardware and software designs. The major challenge in model
checking is dealing with the state space explosion problem. In the last ten years
or so, the partial order reduction approach has been investigated for alleviating
the state space explosion problem. The basic idea of partial-order reduction can
be explained by the following example. Consider a global state $G = (s_1, s_2, ..., s_n)$
of an n-process concurrent system, where s_i, $1 \leq i \leq n$, is a local state of process
P_i. Assume that each s_i, $1 \leq i \leq n$, has exactly one local transition to another
local state s_i' of P_i and that these n local transitions are enabled (i.e., eligible
for execution) and independent from each other (i.e., the result of executing
these transitions is independent of execution order). The traditional reachability analysis generates $n!$ different interleavings of these n transitions from G to
$G' = (s_1', s_2', ..., s_n')$. According to partial-order reduction, only one of these $n!$

---

* This work was supported in part by an IBM fellowship and NSF grant CCR-9901004
** Corresponding author

K. Havelund, J. Penix, and W. Visser (Eds.): SPIN 2000, LNCS 1885, pp. 34–53, 2000.
© Springer-Verlag Berlin Heidelberg 2000

sequences of n transitions is generated from G to G'. Earlier partial order reduction methods were developed for verifying deadlock freedom and other safety properties, while recent partial order reduction methods provide solutions to the model checking problem [3], [4],and [11] .

Simultaneous reachability analysis (SRA) is a recently proposed approach to alleviating the state space explosion problem. SRA differs from partial-order reduction in that the former allows a global transition in a reachability graph to contain a set of independent local transitions. Consider the example mentioned earlier. According to SRA, only one global transition is generated from G to G', with the global transition being the set of these n local transitions. Ozdemir and Ural developed an SRA-based reachability graph generation algorithm for the communicating finite state machine (CFSM) model [10]. Later Schoot and Ural improved the earlier algorithm [15] and showed that combining their new algorithm with partial order reduction techniques improves the performance of partial-order reduction for the verification of CFSM-based concurrent systems [14].

In this paper, we describe how to apply the SRA approach to concurrent systems for model checking. In section 2, we describe a framework for generating a simultaneous reachability graph (SRG) for model checking. In section 3, we define the extended finite state machine (EFSM) model with multiple ports. In section 4, we define the dependency relation for the multi-port EFSM model. In section 5, we present an SRG generation algorithm for the multi-port EFSM model. In section 6, we present preliminary results of our SRA approach to model checking. Finally we present our conclusions in section 7.

2   A Framework for Generating an SRG for Model Checking

In this section, we describe a framework for generating an SRG that provides sufficient information for model checking. Let M be a concurrent system containing processes $P_1, P_2, \ldots, P_n$. Assume that each process P_i, $1 \leq i \leq n$, is represented as a state transition system. Processes may communicate with each other by accessing shared variables and/or message queues. Let $RG(M)$ denote the full reachability graph of M and let $SRG(M)$ denote a reduced reachability graph of M according to SRA. A transition of some process in M is referred to as a transition of M. An edge in $RG(M)$ is a transition of M, while an edge in $SRG(M)$ is a set of transitions of M.

Let t and t' be two transitions. t and t' are process-dependent if they belong to the same process. t and t' are race-dependent if they have a race condition due to access to shared variables or message channels. t and t' are dependent if they are process-dependent or race-dependent, and they are independent otherwise. A transition is visible wrt a temporal logic formula if its execution changes the values of some variables in the formula. A transition is invisible if it is not visible.

Figure 1 shows algorithm Generate_RG, which generates the reachability graph (RG) for a concurrent system in depth-first fashion and performs on-

```
Generate_RG(M: A Concurrent System)
RG: Reachability graph, RG = (V, E), V: nodes, E: edges
open: Set of unexplored nodes of RG
V ← ∅, E ← ∅
Generate the initial global state and put it in open
while open ≠ ∅
    G ← the most recently added global state in open
    remove G from open
    if G is a deadlock state, report deadlock
    else if G is a nonprogress state, report nonprogress
    else G_edges ← Generate_RGEdges(G)
        for each e ∈ G_edges
            determine successor G' of G along edge e
            if G' ∉ V
                V ← V ⋃ {G'} and open ← open ⋃ {G'}
            E ← E ⋃ {e}
return RG
```

Fig. 1. Algorithm Generate_RG

the-fly analysis for detecting deadlock and nonprogress states. Global states that are discovered and not yet expanded are maintained in a set called *open*. The initial global state is placed in *open* at the beginning of the algorithm. At each step, the last global state added to *open* is expanded, unless it is a deadlock or nonprogress state; in which case, the encountered fault is reported. Expanding a state G involves generating the edges and successors of G. Function Generate_RGEdges(G) returns a set of edges where each edge corresponds to an enabled transition of G. The algorithm stops when all reachable states are expanded.

To generate an SRG, we replace Generate_RGEdges(G) in algorithm Generate_RG with Generate_SRGEdges(G), which generates a sets of edges for G, where each edge is a set of transitions. Generate_SRGEdges(G) must satisfy two conflicting goals. On the one hand, it has to generate enough edges for checking the correctness of the specified properties. On the other hand, it has to avoid generating redundant edges. Below we propose a three-step framework for Generate_SRGEdges(G). Let $G_{enabled}$ denote the set of enabled transitions at G.

Step 1: Generate subsets of $G_{enabled}$ that have no process-dependency. Thus, each generated subset contains at most one transition from each process.

Step 2: For each set $E1$ generated by step 1, generate subsets of $E1$ that do not have race-dependency. Thus, each generated subset does not contain two or more enabled transitions belonging to the same process or having race conditions. A solution for step 2 depends on the set of allowed operations that have race conditions.

Step 3: For each set $E2$ generated by step 2, generate subsets of $E2$ that contains at most one visible transition. The reason is to allow the generation of all possible interleavings of visible transitions. Each subset generated in this step is an edge of G.

At the end of step 2, each generated subset contains transitions that are independent with each other. Note that the concept of independent transitions is also used in partial order reduction. The basic idea of partial order reduction is to generate only one of totally ordered transition sequences with the same partial order (based on the dependency relation). SRA, however, generates a sequence of sets of pairwise independent transitions for totally ordered transition sequences with the same partial order. In section 4, we show how to follow the above framework to develop algorithm Generate_SRGEdges for the multi-port EFSM model.

3   The Multi-port EFSM Model

An extended finite state machine (EFSM) is a finite state machine in which each transition is associated with a predicate defined over a set of variables. We consider a set of EFSMs that communicate with each other by sending and receiving messages, where each EFSM contains a set of ports for receiving different types of messages. We refer to this EFSM model as the multi-port EFSM model. Compared to the EFSM models in [8],[2], the multi-port EFSM model has more expressive power. The concept of multiple ports is used in ADA, Estelle, and SDL [1],[13].

Our multi-port EFSM model assumes asynchronous message passing, which involves nonblocking send and blocking receive. A port of an EFSM can receive messages from one or more other EFSMs. Messages that arrive at a port are received in FIFO order. Each port has a bounded queue. The message delivery scheme between EFSMs is assumed to be causal-ordering, meaning that if a message is sent before another message (from the same or different EFSMs) to the same port of an EFSM, then the former arrives at the port before the latter [1].

Formally, a multi-port EFSM P is defined as a 7-tuple $P = < Q, q_0, V, T, I, O, \delta >$, where

1. Q: Set of states of P
2. q_0: Initial state of P
3. V: Set of local variables of P
4. T: Set of port names of P
5. I: Set of input messages for all ports of P
6. O: Set of output messages of P
7. δ: Set of transitions of P

Each transition $t \in \delta$ contains the following information:

- head(t): the start state of t, head(t)$\in Q$.
- tail(t): the end state of t, tail(t)$\in Q$.
- t_{pred}: a predicate involving variables in V, constants, and arithmetic/relational/ boolean operations.
- t_{comp}: a computation block, which is a sequence of computational statements (assignment, loop, etc) involving the received message, variables in V, and constants.
- ?$pn.m$: receive operation, where $pn \in T$ is a port name in P and m an input message in I. in_port(t)=\{pn\} and in_msg(t)=\{m\}. If t has no receive operation, in_port(t)=in_msg(t)=ϵ.

– !$pn.m$: send operation, where $pn \in T$ is a port name of another EFSM and m an output message in O. out_port(t)={pn} and out_msg(t)={m}. If t has no send operation, out_port(t)=out_msg(t)=ϵ.

Determining whether transition t of process P is executable (or enabled) when head(t) is the current state of P involves evaluating t_{pred} and checking the queue for port in_port(t). If t_{pred} is true and the queue is not empty, then t is said to be executable or enabled, meaning that t is eligible for being selected for execution. Otherwise, t is said to be disabled. If t is selected for execution, the first message in the queue for in_port(t) is removed, t_{comp} is executed, the send operation associated with t is performed, and tail(t) becomes the current state of P. Figure 2 illustrates a transition t with in_port(t)={r1} and out_port(t)={r2}. Note that at most three of the following parts may be missing in a transition: the predicate, receive operation, computational block and send operation. If both the predicate and the receive operation are missing, the transition is said to be a spontaneous transition.

Fig. 2. General Format of a Transition

In this paper, we analyze a system of multi-port EFSMs $P_1, P_2, \ldots P_n$, with each P_i, $1 \leq i \leq n$ denoted by $< Q_i, q_{i,0}, V_i, T_i, I_i, O_i, \delta_i >$. Each EFSM P_i is also referred to as a process. $q_{i,0}$ denotes the initial state of P_i and $q_{i,j}$ the jth state of P_i. $T_{i,j}$ refers to the jth port of P_i. For a transition t, proc(t) is the process that contains transition t.

A transition sequence of a system of multi-port EFSMs is composed of zero or more transitions of these EFSMs. Length of a transition sequence ω, denoted by $|\omega|$, is the number of transitions in ω. For example, $\omega = t_1 t_2 \ldots t_n$ has $|\omega| = n$. For any two transition sequences σ and ω, $\sigma\omega$ denotes the concatenation of the two sequences. For a transition sequence $\omega = t_1 t_2 \ldots t_k$ and for any i, $0 \leq i \leq k$, $t_1 \ldots t_i$ is called a prefix of ω. A permutation of a set of transitions is a sequence of these transitions in arbitrary order. For a set T of transitions, perm(T)={ all permutations of transitions in T }. $|T|$ denotes the cardinality of T. If $|T| = n$, then $|\text{perm}(T)|=n!$. For $T_1.T_2 \ldots T_n$, where T_i, $1 \leq i \leq n$, is a set of transitions, perm($T_1.T_2 \ldots T_n$) is defined as perm(T_1).perm(T_1)....perm(T_n).

Definition 1. *A global state G of a system M of multi-port EFSMs contains the local state, the values of local variables and the contents of port queues for each process in M. The initial global state of M, denoted as G_0, contains the initial local states, initial local variable values and empty port queues for all processes in M.*

Definition 2. *Let G be a global state in the reachability graph of a system M of multi-port EFSMs. G' is an immediate sequential successor of G, denoted by $G \xrightarrow{t}_M G'$, if t is an enabled transition of G and G' is the state reached by t from G. $G \xrightarrow{t}_M G'$ is denoted by $G \xrightarrow{t} G'$, if M is implied.*

Definition 3. *A sequential successor G' of G, reached by a transition sequence ω, is denoted by $G \xrightarrow{\omega} *G'$.*

Definition 4. *The reachability graph (RG) of a system of multi-port EFSMs is the set of all global states sequentially reachable from the initial global state of the system.*

Definition 5. *A global state G in the RG of a system of multi-port EFSMs is said to be a nonprogress state if G has no executable transitions. G is said to be a deadlock state if it is a nonprogress state and all port queues for all processes are empty.*

An example system of processes P_1, P_2, P_3, and P_4 is shown in Figure 3. The transitions are labeled with numbers for ease of reference. Final states are designated with double circles. For simplicity, each process $P_i, 1 \leq i \leq 4$, has no local variables and its transitions contain only send and receive operations. The RG of the example system and the details of all global states are also in the figure.

4   Dependency Relation for the Multi-port EFSM Model

Dependency between transitions is a fundamental concept in partial-order reduction. According to [5], a valid dependency relation involves two transitions, while a valid conditional dependency relation involves a global state and two transitions. For the multi-port EFSM model, below we define a valid conditional dependency relation.

Definition 6. *Let G be a global state of a system M of EFSMs. Two transitions t_1 and t_2 of M are said to be independent wrt G if:*

1. *t_1 and t_2 are enabled transitions of G*
2. *$proc(t_1) \neq proc(t_2)$ and*
3. *either $out\_port(t_1) \neq out\_port(t_2)$ or $out\_port(t_1) = out\_port(t_2) = \epsilon$*

t_1 and t_2 are said to be dependent wrt G otherwise. If t_1 and t_2 do not satisfy condition (2), they are said to be process-dependent. If t_1 and t_2 do not satisfy condition (3), they are said to be race-dependent.

Let S be a set of enabled transitions at a global state G of a system of EFSMs. If no two transitions of S are process-dependent (race-dependent), then S is said

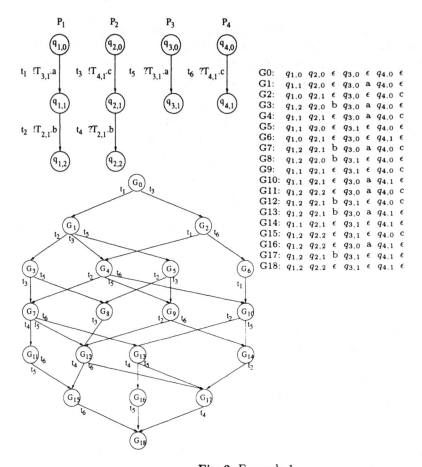

Fig. 3. Example 1

to be process-independent (race-independent) at G. S is said to be an independent transition set at G, if it is process-independent and race-independent at G. S is said to be a maximal independent transition set at G, if G has no enabled transition t, $t \notin S$ such that $S \cup \{t\}$ is an independent transition set at G. In the remainder of this paper, when we mention independent transitions wrt a global state, we often omit *"wrt a global state"* if this global state is implied.

Assume that transitions t_1 and t_2 are independent wrt global state G. If $G \xrightarrow{t_1 t_2} *G'$, then $G \xrightarrow{t_2 t_1} *G'$. Thus, the state reached from G after execution of t_1 and t_2 is independent of the execution order of t_1 and t_2. This property can be generalized to three or more independent transitions wrt a global state, as shown below.

Lemma 1. *Let G be a global state of a system M of EFSMs. Let T be an independent set at G. Let σ and ω be two permutations of T. If $G \xrightarrow{\sigma} *G'$, then $G \xrightarrow{\omega} *G'$.*

Definition 7. *Let G be a global state of a system M of EFSMs. Let t be a transition of M and let $\omega = t_1 t_2 \ldots t_k$ be a transition sequence of M, where $G_1 \overset{t_1}{\to} G_2 \ldots G_k \overset{t_k}{\to} G'$ and $G = G_1$. t and ω are said to be independent wrt G if t and t_i, $1 \le i \le k$ are independent wrt G_i.*

Lemma 2. *Let G be a global state of a system M of EFSMs. Let t be a transition of M and ω be a transition sequence of M. If $G \overset{\omega t}{\to} *G'$ and t and ω are independent wrt G, then $G \overset{t\omega}{\to} *G'$.*

Lemma 3. *Let G be a global state of a system M of EFSMs. Let σ and ω be transition sequences of M. If $G \overset{\omega\sigma}{\to} *G'$ and $\forall t$ in σ, t and ω are independent wrt G, then $G \overset{\sigma\omega}{\to} *G'$.*

The race set of a transition t is defined as the set of transitions that send a message to the same port as t. Formally, $race(t) = \{t' \mid out\_port(t') = out\_port(t), out\_port(t') \ne \epsilon, t \ne t'$, and $proc(t) \ne proc(t')\}$. A transition is referred to as a *racing transition* if its race set is not empty. A port is said to be a race port if two or more EFSMs have transitions with this port as out_port. Thus, for a racing transition t, $out\_port(t)$ is a race port. Let t be a racing transition at a global state G. Since the definition of $race(t)$ is coarse, t does not necessarily have a race with each transition in $race(t)$ at G or at any other state reachable from G. In order to make the set of possible racing transitions more precise, it is necessary to apply some program analysis techniques.

5   Algorithm Generate_SRGEdges

As mentioned in section 2, to generate an SRG for model checking, we replace Generate_RGEdges in algorithm Generate_RG, shown in Figure 1, with Generate_SRGEdges. Following the three-step framework described in section 2, we now present algorithm Generate_SRGEdges(G), where G is a global state, for the multi-port EFSM model.

Definition 8. *An immediate simultaneous successor G' of G reached by an independent transition set T at G, is denoted by $G \overset{T}{\rightsquigarrow} G'$, where $G \overset{\omega}{\to} *G'$ and $\omega \in perm(T)$.*

Definition 9. *A simultaneous successor G' of G reached by a sequence of transition sets $T_1 T_2 \ldots T_l$ is denoted by $G \overset{T_1 T_2 \ldots T_l}{\rightsquigarrow} *G'$.*

In order to illustrate the concept of an SRG, consider example 1, which is shown in Figure 3. Assume that all transitions in this example are invisible. The SRG for example 1 is shown in Figure 4. Note that for each global state in the SRG, its enabled transitions have no process or race-dependency. Thus, each

Fig. 4. SRG for Example 1

global state has exactly one edge, which contains all enabled transitions of this global state.

An edge of an *SRG* state G corresponds to a set of transitions independent wrt G. G_{edges} denotes the set of edges of G. G_{trans} denotes the set of transitions of processes at G. Enabled and disabled transitions of G are referred to as $G_{enabled}$ and $G_{disabled}$, respectively.

5.1   Step 1 of Generate_SRGEdges(G)

This step is to generate subsets of $G_{enabled}$ that have no process-dependency. As mentioned earlier, Ozdemir and Ural [10] developed an SRG generation algorithm for the CFSM model, which has no race conditions. The purpose of that algorithm is to detect deadlock and nonprogress. We use an iterative and more efficient form of their recursive algorithm for step 1. Below we explain our form of the algorithm. (In [15] Schoot and Ural improved that algorithm for the same purpose, but the improved algorithm cannot be used here for model checking.)

An intuitive solution for step 1 is to group transitions in $G_{enabled}$ into sets such that each set is composed of enabled transitions belonging to the same process and then take the Cartesian product of these sets. Figure 5 illustrates this computation for the three processes of example 2, which shows enabled transitions of each process. However, this intuitive solution is not sufficient.

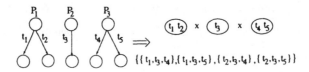

Fig. 5. Example 2

A disabled transition t of process P_i at a global state G is said to be a potentially executable transition if P_i has at least one enabled transition at G and t_{pred}=true. According to the intuitive solution described above, every transition set produced by step 1 contains one enabled transition of P_i. This creates a problem since transition t needs to be executed for fault detection. To solve this problem, we need to delay execution of P_i until t becomes enabled. This can be accomplished as follows. For every transition set S produced by step 1, if S contains an enabled transition t' of P_i, then $S \setminus \{t'\}$ is also produced by step 1.

The term "*potentially executable transitions*" was defined in [10]. In [6] the presence of potentially executable transitions is referred to as confusion. Example 3 in Figure 6 illustrates potentially executable transitions. At G_0, transitions t_1 and t_4 are enabled and t_3 is a potentially executable transition of P_1. So G_0 has 2 global edges $\{t_1, t_4\}$ and $\{t_4\}$. The latter edge ensures that there is a path from G_0 in which P_1 does not make any progress. Note that G_5 is a nonprogress state. If G_0 did not have edge $\{t_4\}$, state G_5 would not be generated.

In order to handle potentially executable transitions, the intuitive solution described above is modified as follows. After grouping the enabled transitions of G into sets of pairwise process-dependent transitions, we add a special transition, t_{null}, to each set formed by enabled transitions of a process with a potentially executable transition. After this modification, the Cartesian product of these sets may produce transition sets containing t_{null}. If a transition set in the Cartesian product contains only t_{null}, then we ignore this transition set. This situation occurs only if each process at G having enabled transitions also has potentially executable transitions. If a transition set in the Cartesian product contains t_{null} as well as other transitions, then we delete t_{null} from this set. This situation occurs when there exists at least one process at G that has both enabled and potentially executable transitions. According to this modified solution, if a generated transition set S has t from a process with a potentially executable transition, then $S \setminus \{t\}$ is also generated by step 1. Note that the use of t_{null} is to simplify the construction of extra edges due to potentially executable transitions. A formal description of the above solution is given in step 1 of algorithm Generate_SRAEdges, which is shown in Figure 9.

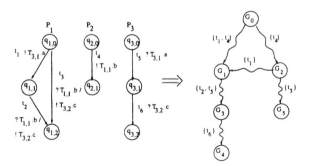

Fig. 6. Example 3

In example 3, shown in Figure 6, G_0 has $\{t_1\}$ and $\{t_4\}$ as process-independent sets. $\{t_1\}$ becomes $\{t_1, t_{null}\}$ due to the existence of a potentially executable transition t_3. Computation of $\{t_1, t_{null}\} \times \{t_4\}$ yields $\{\{t_1, t_4\}, \{t_{null}, t_4\}\}$. After the removal of t_{null}, step 1 produces $\{\{t_1, t_4\}, \{t_4\}\}$.

5.2   Step 2 of Generate_SRGEdges(G)

For each set generated by step 1, this step generates its subsets that do not have race-dependency. According to the definition of dependency for the multi-port EFSM model in section 3, two enabled transitions of G have race-dependency if they have the same out_port that is not ϵ. In [9] we developed an SRG generation algorithm for detecting deadlock and nonprogress in a system of multi-port EFSMs. That algorithm can be used here for model checking. Below we describe an improved version of that algorithm.

Let S be a set generated by step 1. An intuitive solution for step 2 is to group transitions in S into sets such that each set is composed of enabled transitions with the same out_port and then take the Cartesian product of these sets. Figure 7 illustrates this intuitive solution for the sets produced in Figure 5 for example 2. We assume that transitions in example 2 have different out_port except t_1 and t_3. However, this intuitive solution is not sufficient.

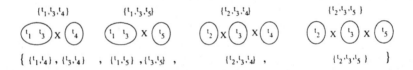

Fig. 7. Step 2 for Example 2

An enabled transition t of process P_i at a global state G may have a race with a transition t' of process P_j, $j \neq i$, at a global state G' such that G' is reachable from G. According to the intuitive solution described above, t' is not taken into consideration in the construction of G_{edges}. As a result, the generated transition sequences from G do not explore the situation where t' occurs before t. Thus, the intuitive solution fails to detect faults that happen in transition sequences from G in which t' occurs before t. t' is referred to as a racing transition of successor states of G.

Consider example 4 shown in Figure 8. Transitions t_1 and t_4 have a race since they send messages to port $T_{3,1}$. We need to generate paths in which t_1 occurs before t_4 and vice versa. However, t_1 is executable at G_0 while t_4 is not even a transition of some process at G_0. In order to construct the path on which t_4 happens before t_1, we need an edge in which t_1 is not executed. In example 4, the enabled transitions of G_0 are t_1 and t_3. Since t_1 is a racing transition, we select sets $\{t_1, t_3\}$ and $\{t_3\}$. G_2 has enabled transitions t_1 and t_4, which have race-dependency. Hence, these transitions are selected on separate edges.

In order to handle racing transitions of successor states, we need to consider the complete system. For a port r, let out_proc(r) be $\{i | P_i$ has at least

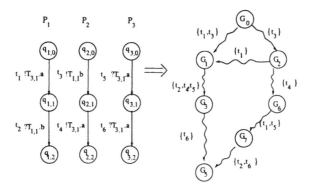

Fig. 8. Example 4

one transition with r as out_port}. For a set A of transitions, let $\text{proc}(A) = \{$ $\text{proc}(t)|t \in A\}$. Let reachable(i, G, k) be true if the local state of process P_i at global state G can reach a transition with port T_k as its out_port.

Let S be a set produced by step 1. We group transitions in S according to their out_port. For a port r, let S_r be the set of transitions in S with r as out_port. Let k be an element in out_port$(r)\backslash\text{proc}(S_r)$. Process P_k contains at least one transition with r as out_port. However, we need to worry about race conditions between transitions in S_r and a future transition of P_k only if the state of P_k in G can reach a transition with r as its out_port. Thus, only under this condition, we add t_{null} to the set of transitions for port r to delay the execution of these transitions. Then we compute the Cartesian product of these sets. If a transition set in the Cartesian product contains only t_{null}, we ignore this transition set. This situation occurs only if t_{null} is added for each out_port involved in S. If a transition set in the Cartesian product contains t_{null} and other transitions, we delete t_{null} from this set. This situation occurs only if t_{null} is added for at least one out_port involved in S. A formal description of the above solution is given in step 2 of algorithm Generate_SRGEdges.

In example 4, shown in Figure 8, G_0 has $\{t_1, t_3\}$ as the maximal process-independent set. Grouping of the transitions in this set according to ports yields $\{t_1\}$ for port $T_{3,1}$ and $\{t_3\}$ for port $T_{1,1}$. Since t_3 is a racing transition, the set for port $T_{3,1}$ is modified to $\{t_1, t_{null}\}$. $\{t_3\} \times \{t_1, t_{null}\}$ yields $\{\{t_1, t_3\}, \{t_{null}, t_3\}\}$. After the removal of t_{null}, G_0 has edges $\{t_1, t_3\}$ and $\{t_3\}$ as shown in Figure 8.

5.3   Step 3 of Generate_SRGEdges(G)

A set of transitions S produced at the end of step 2 for a global state G may contain both visible and invisible transitions. If S has more than one visible transition, then the simultaneous execution of the transitions in S will skip intermediate global states in which values of some variables involved in the specified properties are changed. As a result the generated SRG will not have all the states necessary for model checking. In order to avoid this problem, each

SRG edge can have at most one visible transition. In step 3, we first separate the visible and invisible transitions of S. Let S_{vis} be the set of visible transitions in S. Then, the set of invisible transitions, S_{invis}, is the set $S \setminus S_{vis}$. Each transition $t \in S_{vis}$ can be simultaneously executed with the set S_{invis} to ensure the generation of all global states necessary for model checking. Hence for each $t \in S_{vis}$ we generate $\{t\} \cup S_{invis}$ as an edge. Note that we need to delay the execution of transitions in S_{vis} in order to allow other visible transitions to occur first. In order to do so, we add S_{invis} as an SRG edge of G.

The complete algorithm Generate_SRGEdges is shown in Figure 9. We use set notation throughout the algorithm. Capital letters denote sets and bold face capital letters denote sets of sets. Symbols $\setminus$, $\cup$, and $\cap$ denote set minus, union and intersection, respectively. We refer to elements in a set A as A_i, $1 \leq i \leq |A|$.

5.4   Correctness of Algorithm Generate_SRG

Algorithm Generate_SRG is algorithm Generate_RG modified by replacing Generate_RGEdges(G) with Generate_SRGEdges(G). For a system M of EFSMs, let $RG(M)$ and $SRG(M)$ be the state graphs produced by Generate_RG and Generate_SRG, respectively. To prove that $SRG(M)$ provides sufficient information for model checking, we show that $RG(M)$ and $SRG(M)$ are stuttering equivalent. (See [3] for the definition of stuttering equivalence.) More specifically, we need to show the following:
(a) For each path σ of $RG(M)$ from the initial state, there exists a path η of $SRG(M)$ from the initial state such that σ is stuttering equivalent to any sequence in perm(η).
(b) For each path η of $SRG(M)$ from the initial state, there exists a path σ of $RG(M)$ from the initial state such that any sequence in perm(η) is stuttering equivalent to σ.

The proofs for (a) and (b) are similar to those in section 10.6 of [3], which show the correctness of a partial order reduction algorithm for model checking. The major difference is that an edge of $SRG(M)$ is a set of transitions instead of a single transition. To provide complete proofs for (a) and (b) is a tedious task. Below we show how to prove the portion of (a) that corresponds to the portion immediately before lemma 26 in section 10.6 of [3]. Other proofs for (a) and (b) can be easily derived from the material in section 10.6 of [3].

Let σ be a path of $RG(M)$ from the initial state. We want to show that there exists a path η of $SRG(M)$ from the initial state such that σ is stuttering equivalent to any sequence in perm(η). Let η_i be the prefix of η that has length i. The construction of η_i is as follows. We construct an infinite sequence of strings $\pi_0, \pi_1, \ldots$, where $\pi_0 = \sigma$. Let π_i be $u.\theta_i$, where $u \in perm(\eta_i)$, η_i contains i edges of $SRG(M)$ and θ_i contains transitions of $RG(M)$. For π_0, η_0 is empty and θ_0 is σ. Assume that we have constructed strings $\pi_0, \pi_1, \ldots, \pi_i$, we describe how to construct $\pi_{i+1} = v.\theta_{i+1}$ where $v \in perm(\eta_{i+1})$. Let s_0 be the state in $SRG(M)$ that is reached by η_i and α be the first transition of θ_i.

Let $proc_1 = \{ \ j|P_j$ at s_0 has at least one enabled transition $\}$. Construct the set $T1$ as follows. Initially, $T1$ is empty. For each j in $proc_1$, find the first

---

Generate_SRGEdges(G:GlobalState)

i: Index to processes in the system, $1 \leq i \leq n$, where n is the number of processes

j: Index to ports in the system, $1 \leq j \leq |T|$, where $|T|$ is the number of ports

$\mathbf{G_{edges}} \leftarrow \emptyset$, $\mathbf{Sets1} \leftarrow \emptyset$, $\mathbf{Sets2} \leftarrow \emptyset$, $\mathbf{PD} \leftarrow \emptyset$, $\mathbf{RD} \leftarrow \emptyset$

// *Step 1: Generate transition sets that are process-independent*

For $1 \leq i \leq n$

    $A_i \leftarrow \{$ enabled transitions of P_i at G $\}$ // *Process-dependency*

    if $A_i \neq \emptyset$

        if P_i has a transition t such that $t \in G_{disabled}$ and t_{pred}=true

            $\mathbf{PD} \leftarrow \mathbf{PD} \cup \{A_i \cup \{t_{null}\}\}$ // *Potentially Executable Transition*

        else

            $\mathbf{PD} \leftarrow \mathbf{PD} \cup \{A_i\}$

$\mathbf{CP1} \leftarrow PD_1 \times PD_2 \times PD_3 \times \ldots \times PD_{|PD|}$

for each $D \in \mathbf{CP1}$

    if $D \setminus \{t_{null}\} \neq \emptyset$ then $\mathbf{Sets1} \leftarrow \mathbf{Sets1} \cup \{D \setminus \{t_{null}\}\}$

// *Step 2: For each set in Sets1, generate subsets that are race-independent*

for each $E \in \mathbf{Sets1}$

    $X \leftarrow \{$ transitions in E with empty out_port$\}$

    For $1 \leq j \leq |T|$

        $B_j \leftarrow \{$ transitions in E whose out_port is T_j $\}$ // *Race-dependency*

        if $B_j \neq \emptyset$

            if $\exists \ k \in$ out_proc$(T_j) \setminus$ proc(B_j) st reachable(k, G, j)

                $\mathbf{RD} \leftarrow \mathbf{RD} \cup \{B_j \cup \{t_{null}\}\}$ // *Racing transition of successors*

            else

                $\mathbf{RD} \leftarrow \mathbf{RD} \cup \{B_j\}$

    if $RD = \emptyset$, $\mathbf{Sets2} \leftarrow \{X\}$

    else $\mathbf{CP2} \leftarrow RD_1 \times RD_2 \times RD_3 \times \ldots \times RD_{|RD|}$

        for each $F \in \mathbf{CP2}$

            if $F \setminus \{t_{null}\} \neq \emptyset$, then $\mathbf{Sets2} \leftarrow \mathbf{Sets2} \cup \{F \cup X \setminus \{t_{null}\}\}$

// *Step 3: For each set in Sets2, generate subsets with at most 1 visible transition*

for each $H \in \mathbf{Sets2}$

    $H_{vis} \leftarrow \{$ visible transitions in H $\}$

    $H_{invis} \leftarrow H \setminus H_{vis}$

    if $H_{invis} \neq \emptyset$, $\mathbf{G_{edges}} \leftarrow \mathbf{G_{edges}} \cup \{H_{invis}\}$

    if $H_{vis} \neq \emptyset$

        for each $t \in H_{vis}$

            $\mathbf{G_{edges}} \leftarrow \mathbf{G_{edges}} \bigcup \{H_{invis} \cup \{t\}\}$

return $\mathbf{G_{edges}}$

Fig. 9. Algorithm Generate_SRGEdges

occurrence of a transition of P_j in θ_i such that this transition is independent of all preceding transitions wrt s_0. If such a transition can be found, add it to $T1$. $|T1| > 0$ since $T1$ definitely contains α.

Case A. $|T1| = |proc_1|$. According to algorithm Generate_SRGEdges, T1 is an element in $Sets1$. Since all transitions in $T1$ have distinct out_port, $T1$ is an element in $Sets2$.

A.1. α is a visible transition. According to step 3 for $T1$, s_0 has one edge, say $E3$, that contains α.

A.1.1. $E3 \setminus \{\alpha\}$ is empty. Let η_{i+1} be η_i appended by $\{\alpha\}$ and let θ_{i+1} be θ_i without the first transition.

A.1.2. $E3 \setminus \{\alpha\}$ is not empty. Each transition in $E3 \setminus \{\alpha\}$ is invisible. $RG(M)$ contains a path $u.v$ from state s_0, where u is a sequence in $perm(E3)$ and v is θ_i modified by deleting transitions in $E3$. Let η_{i+1} be $\eta_i.E3$ and let θ_{i+1} be v.

A.2 α is an invisible transition. According to step 3 for $T1$, s_0 contains one edge, say $E3$, that contains α and possibly other invisible transitions, but no visible transitions. Like case A.1.2, let η_{i+1} be $\eta_i.E3$ and let θ_{i+1} be θ_i modified by deleting transitions in $E3$.

Case B. $|T1| < |proc_1|$. Construct the set $T2$ as follows. Initially, $T2$ is empty. For each j in $proc_1 \setminus proc(T1)$, find the first occurrence of a transition of P_j in θ_i such that this transition is an enabled transition of P_j at state s_0. If such a transition can be found, add it to $T2$. Note that each transition in $T2$ is a racing transition. Let $proc_3$ be $\{ k|k \in proc_1$ and P_k has no transitions in $\theta_i\}$. Note that $proc(T1)$, $proc(T2)$ and $proc_3$ are mutually disjoint. For each q that is in $proc_1$, but not in $proc(T1)$, $proc(T2)$. or $proc_3$, the first transition of P_q in θ_i exists and is a potentially executable transition at s_0. According to step 1, the element in PD for P_q contains t_{null}. Thus, $Sets1$ contains an element, say $E1$, that is $(T1 \cup T2 \cup T3)$, where $T3$ contains one enabled transition of each process in $proc_3$ at s_0.

B.1. $proc_3$ is empty. Thus, $E1 = (T1 \cup T_2)$. According to step 2 for $E1$, $Sets2$ contains one element that is exactly $T1$. The proof for this case is similar to that for case A.

B.2. $proc_3$ is not empty. Thus, $E1 = (T1 \cup T2 \cup T3)$, where $T3$ is not empty. According to step 2 for $E1$, the set RD is constructed, where each element of RD contains all transitions in $E1$ with a specific port as out_port and possibly contains t_{null}. Note that if an element of RD does not contain a transition in $T1$ or t_{null}, then it contains only transitions in $T3$. Construct the set $T3'$ as follows. Initially, $T3'$ is empty. For each element in RD, if this element contains only transitions in $T3$, add one of these transitions to $T3'$. $Sets2$ contains one element, say $E2$, such that $E2 = (T1 \cup T3')$. Below we show by contradiction that all transitions in $T3'$ are independent of each transition in θ_i wrt s_0. Assume there is a transition t in $T3'$ such that t is dependent with a transition in θ_i. By construction, all transitions in $T3'$ are in $proc_3$. Hence t cannot have process-dependency with a transition on θ_i. Then t has a race-dependency with a transition in θ_i. Assume that a transition t' in θ_i has the same out_port as t. Since $proc(t')$ is not in $proc_3$, the element in RD that contains t should contain t_{null}. But this is a contradiction to the fact that this element in RD does not contain t_{null}. So t is race-independent with any transition in θ_i. Also, $proc(t)$

has no transitions in θ_i. Therefore, any transition in $T3'$ does not appear in θ_i and is independent of each transition in θ_i wrt s_0.

B.2.1. $T3'$ is empty. Thus, $E2 = T1$. This case is similar to case B.1.

B.2.2. $T3'$ is not empty.

B.2.2.1. α is a visible transition. According to step 3 for $E2$, s_0 has one edge, say $E3$, that contains α.

B.2.2.1.1. $E3 \setminus \{\alpha\}$ is empty. This case is similar to case A.1.1.

B.2.2.1.2. $E3 \setminus \{\alpha\}$ is not empty. Each transition in $E3 \setminus \{\alpha\}$ is invisible. $RG(M)$ contains a path $u.v$ from state s_0, where u is a sequence in perm$(E3)$ and v is θ_i modified by deleting transitions in $E3 \cap T1$. (Note that transitions in $E3 \setminus T1$ do not appear in θ_i.) Let η_{i+1} be $\eta_i.E3$ and let θ_{i+1} be v.

B.2.2.2 α is an invisible transition. According to step 3 for $E2$, s_0 contains one edge, say $E3$, that contains α and possibly other invisible transitions, but no visible transitions. The proof for this case is similar to that for case B.2.2.1.2.

6 Empirical Results

The main goal of our empirical study is to asses the performance of SRA based model checking. We measure the performance in terms of the reduction in the size of the reachability graph constructed by SRA with respect to the full reachability graph. Our system for constructing reachability graphs of EFSMs is implemented in java (JDK12).

Partial order reduction techniques have been shown to provide substantial reduction in the size of the reachability graph for linear-time temporal logic (LTL) model-checking [3]. SPIN [7], which is a widely used model-checker, implements the partial order reduction technique proposed by Peled [4]. In this paper, we compare the performance of our algorithm for SRA based model checking with that of SPIN for the same set of concurrent problems.

SPIN considers each statement in Promela as a transition, while our EFSM model allows a transition to include multiple statements. In order to ensure a fair comparison between SRA and the partial order reduction method implemented in SPIN, we used the same specification style in both EFSM code and Promela code. In accomplishing this we focused on three main issues described below.

First, we adopted the state transition table produced by SPIN for each Promela process to be our EFSM code. As a result, each transition in EFSM code corresponds to a transition in the FSM produced by SPIN and hence a statement in Promela code. [1]

Second, our EFSM code uses ports for message passing, while Promela uses channels. A port is equivalent to a channel with only one receiver. In our empirical studies, we use Promela programs that contain channels with only one receiver. Thus, the difference between ports and channels has no impact on the results of our empirical studies.

---

[1] Since SPIN uses statement merging, a transition in the SPIN FSM may correspond to multiple statements. In such cases, EFSM transition matches the merged statement.

Third, Promela allows global variables, while our EFSM model does not. (We are modifying our EFSM model and its implementation to allow global variables.) In a Promela program, a never claim is used to specify a property to be verified. Global variables used in a never claim cause an increase in the size of the reachability graph produced by partial order reduction, since such variables make some transitions visible. In order to produce the same effect on the reachability graph produced by SRA for an EFSM program, we manually mark transitions that contain variables used in a never claim as visible transitions.

We report two sets of results for each problem. In the first set we show the reachability graphs without never claims. For each problem considered, we first show the sizes of the *RG* and the *SRG* built from the EFSM program and the reduction in the reachability graph achieved by SRA. Second, we report the size of the full reachability graph built by SPIN without using the partial order reduction. Then we report the reduced reachability graph according to partial order reduction of SPIN and the reduction in reachability graph size due to partial order reduction. In the second set, we repeat the above information with the use of never claims.

We considered two concurrent problems, leader election (LD) and readers & writers problem (RW). The algorithm for leader election in a unidirectional ring is adopted from the solution of Dolev, Klawe, and Rodeh found in [12]. In this version, all processes participate in the election. The main idea of the algorithm is as follows: Each node P_i waits until it has received the numbers of its two neighbors to the left , P_k and P_l, where P_k is the nearest. If P_k has the largest number, P_i transmits P_k's number and becomes passive. After a node becomes passive, it merely relays messages. Remaining active nodes repeat the above step until a winner is established.

Table 1. Results for Leader Election Problem

Without Never Claim										
	EFSM				% V Red.	SPIN				%V Red.
LD	RG		SRG			RG		POR		
	V	E	V	E		V	E	V	E	
[3]	379	834	37	36	90.24%	369	808	59	59	84.01%
[4]	2228	6594	45	44	97.98%	2180	6465	77	77	96.47%
[5]	14194	52707	53	52	99.63%	14048	52288	95	95	99.32%
[6]	93194	415807	61	60	99.93%	92895	414808	113	113	99.88%
With Never Claim										
	EFSM				% V Red.	SPIN				%V Red.
LD	RG		SRG			RG		POR		
	V	E	V	E		V	E	V	E	
[3]	381	837	38	37	90.03%	371	812	67	69	81.94%
[4]	2232	6602	46	45	97.94%	2181	6467	78	79	96.42%
[5]	14202	52727	54	53	99.62%	14049	52290	96	97	99.32%
[6]	93210	415855	62	61	99.93%	92897	414812	121	123	99.87%

We considered one never claim for this problem, that is the number of leaders is never more than one. In order to evaluate this never claim, we introduced the global variable *numLeaders* to both EFSM program and Promela program. The transition updating this variable is added to both programs. In the EFSM program, this transition is marked as visible. Table 1 shows the empirical results for the leader election problem. The first column indicates the problem size in terms of the number of nodes participating in the election.

Table 2. Results for Readers and Writers Problem

Without Never Claim									
EFSM				%V Red	SPIN				%V Red
RW	RG		SRG		RG		POR		
	V	E	V	E		V	E	V	E
1,1	111	181	82	132	26.13%	149	240	121	170	18.79%
2,1	712	1330	490	992	31.18%	1023	1901	675	990	34.02%
1,2	1522	2849	1064	2166	30.09%	1733	3218	1201	1800	30.70%
2,2	16867	33130	10581	23796	37.27%	21192	41522	12250	18591	42.20%
With Never Claim									
EFSM				%V Red	SPIN				%V Red
RW	RG		SRG		RG		POR		
	V	E	V	E		V	E	V	E
1,1	178	317	153	297	14.04%	252	452	229	347	9.13%
2,1	1178	2345	1066	2571	9.51%	1759	3534	1603	2563	8.87%
1,2	2410	4811	2185	5328	9.34%	2969	5975	2718	4422	8.45%
2,2	27223	56366	25293	66132	7.09%	36686	76754	33868	55015	7.68%

The second problem we considered is the readers and writers problem. In this problem readers and writers access a shared buffer through a server. The readers and writers have equal access priorities.

For this problem we considered the never claim stating that the total number of readers and writers active in the database is never more than one. This claim involves two global variables *numReaders, numWriters*, which keep track of the active reader and writer instances, respectively. The transitions of the server (total of 4 transitions) that updates these variables are included in both EFSM and Promela programs. In the EFSM program these transitions are marked as visible. Table 2 shows the empirical results for the readers and writers problem. The first column indicates the problem size in terms of readers and writers.

Based on the above results for two concurrent problems, we have the following observations. First, the sizes of the full *RG*s produced by our algorithm and SPIN are not the same. The reason is probably due to some minor differences in the construction of *RG*. Second, for the leader election problem, both SRA reduction and partial order reduction significantly reduced the sizes of the full *RG*s, with SRA reduction producing smaller reduced graphs. Third, for the readers and writers problem, SRA reduction produces about the same number of states as partial order reduction. But the former produces more transitions than the latter.

7   Conclusions

In this paper, we have proposed an SRA-based framework for producing a reduced state graph, called an *SRG*, for a concurrent system in order to allow model checking. We have applied this framework to develop algorithm Generate_SRG, which produces an *SRG* for a system of EFSMs with multiple ports. Based on our preliminary empirical studies, algorithm Generate_SRG performs as good as or better than the partial order reduction algorithm in SPIN.

The three-step SRA-based framework proposed in this paper can be applied to any concurrent system for model checking. Step 2 in the framework deals with race dependency and thus requires different definitions of dependency relations for different models of concurrency. Different solutions can be developed for each step in the framework. How to design solutions to minimize the size of the generated *SRG* for model checking needs further research.

As mentioned in the introduction section, both SRA and partial-order reduction can be used to alleviate the state explosion problem. One major advantage of the SRA approach over the partial-order reduction approach is that the former can be used with compositional techniques while the latter cannot. Compositional techniques build reachability graphs in modular fashion, reducing graphs before using them for composing larger ones. Since it is not known a priori which interleavings of transitions maybe needed in later composition steps, information on all interleavings should be retained. Given n independent transitions at a global state, partial order reduction techniques select only one of the $n!$ interleavings. While this approach is sufficient for analyzing a concurrent program, loss of information on other possible interleavings prohibits using the generated reachability graph for compositional purpose. The SRA approach, on the other hand, maintains information on all interleavings by keeping independent transitions of a global state in one edge. This property permits combining SRA with compositional methods. We are currently investigating how to combine SRA with compositional methods.

References

1. Gregory R. Andrews. *Foundations of Multithreaded Parallel and Distributed Programming*. Addison-Wesley, 2000.
2. P.-Y. M. Chu and Ming T. Liu. Global state graph reduction techniques for protocol validation. In *Proc. IEEE 8th Intl. Phoenix Conf. on Computers and Comm.*, March 1989.
3. Edmund M. Clarke, Orna Grumberg, and Doron Peled. *Model Checking*. MIT Press, 1999.

4. D. Peled. Combining partial order reductions with on-the-fly model-checking. In David L. Dill, editor, *Proceedings of the sixth International Conference on Computer-Aided Verification CAV*, volume 818 of *Lecture Notes in Computer Science*, pages 377–390, Standford, California, USA, June 1994. Springer-Verlag.

5. P. Godefroid and D. Pirottin. Refining dependencies improves partial-order verification methods. In *Proc. (CAV'93)*, volume 697 of *LNCS*, pages 438–449, 1993.

6. P. Godefroid and P. Wolper. Using partial orders for the efficient verification of deadlock freedom and safety properties. In *Proc. (CAV'91)*, volume 575 of *LNCS*, pages 332–342. Springer, 1992.

7. Gerard J. Holzmann. The model checker SPIN. *IEEE Transactions on Software Engineering*, 23(5):279–295, May 1997.

8. Chung-Ming Huang, Yuan-Chuen Lin, and Ming-Juhe Jang. An executable protocol test sequence generation method for EFSM-specified protocols. In *Protocol Test Systems VIII, Proc. 8th Intl. Workshop on Protocol Test Systems*, pages 20–35. Chapman & Hall, 1995.

9. B. Karacali, K.C. Tai, and M.A. Vouk. Deadlock detection of efsms using simultaneous reachability analysis. To appear in The Proceedings from The International Conference on Dependable Systems and Networks (DNS '2000), 2000.

10. Kadir Ozdemir and Hasan Ural. Protocol validation by simultaneous reachability analysis. *Computer Communications*, 20:772–788, 1997.

11. Doron Peled. Ten years of partial order reduction. In *CAV, Computer Aided Verification*, number 1427 in LNCS, pages 17–28, Vancouver, BC, Canada, 1998. Springer.

12. Michel Raynal. *Distributed Algorithms and Protocols*. Wiley & Sons, 1988.

13. K.J. Turner. *Using Formal Description Techniques*. John Wiley Sons Ltd., Amsterdam, 1993.

14. Hans van der Schoot and Hasan Ural. An improvement of partial-order verification. *Software Testing, Verification and Reliability*, 8:83–102, 1998.

15. Hans van der Schoot and Hasan Ural. On improving reachability analysis for verifying progress properties of networks of CFSMs. In *Proc. 18th Intl. Distributed Computing Systems*, pages 130–137, 1998.

Testing SPIN's LTL Formula Conversion into Büchi Automata with Randomly Generated Input

Heikki Tauriainen and Keijo Heljanko*

Helsinki University of Technology,
Laboratory for Theoretical Computer Science
P. O. Box 5400, FIN-02015 HUT, Finland
{Heikki.Tauriainen, Keijo.Heljanko}@hut.fi

Abstract. The use of model checking tools in the verification of reactive systems has become into widespread use. Because the model checkers are often used to verify critical systems, a lot of effort should be put on ensuring the reliability of their implementation. We describe techniques which can be used to test and improve the reliability of linear temporal logic (LTL) model checker implementations based on the automata-theoretic approach. More specifically, we will concentrate on the LTL-to-Büchi automata conversion algorithm implementations, and propose using a random testing approach to improve their robustness. As a case study, we apply the methodology to the testing of this part of the SPIN model checker. We also propose adding a simple counterexample validation algorithm to LTL model checkers to double check the counterexamples generated by the main LTL model checking algorithm.

1 Introduction

Model checking of linear temporal logic (LTL) properties can be done using the automata-theoretic approach [15]. This model checking method employs a translation of properties expressed in LTL into finite-state automata over infinite words (Büchi automata), which are then used to determine whether a given system model satisfies a given LTL property.

An essential requirement for the correctness of model checking results is the correctness of the model checker implementation itself. Therefore, a model checker which has itself been verified or proved correct would certainly be a tremendous advantage in ensuring the correctness of the verification results. However, full verification of complex software of this kind – especially when implemented in an imperative general-purpose programming language such as C – is somewhat out of reach of current software verification techniques. Nevertheless, even methods for only partially improving the robustness of model checkers would still be welcome.

---

* The financial support of Academy of Finland (Project 47754), the Emil Aaltonen Foundation and the Nokia Foundation are gratefully acknowledged.

K. Havelund, J. Penix, and W. Visser (Eds.): SPIN 2000, LNCS 1885, pp. 54–72, 2000.
© Springer-Verlag Berlin Heidelberg 2000

We will propose a method for testing and improving the robustness of a part of a model checker. We focus on the translation of LTL formulas into Büchi automata (LTL-to-Büchi conversion), which seems to be among the most difficult steps in LTL model checking to implement correctly. The method is based on the comparison of several implementations against each other. As a concrete example, we will test the LTL-to-Büchi conversion implementation in the model checker SPIN [6,5] using a random testing methodology. This work can be seen as a continuation of the work published in [13] with the following extensions:

- We describe a systematic method of using the results of the comparison (together with a single behavior in the system model) to find out the particular implementation which failed, an improvement over simply detecting result inconsistencies. The method is based on model checking an LTL formula directly in the witness behavior by applying computation tree logic (CTL) model checking techniques. This special case of model checking LTL in witness behaviors is based on the ideas first presented in an extended version of [8].
- We discuss an additional application of the previous technique in LTL model checking tools for validating counterexamples.
- We extend the test procedure for LTL-to-Büchi conversion algorithm implementations to make use of non-branching state sequences (paths) as reachability graphs, taking advantage of some additional checks provided by the direct LTL model checking method in comparing the behavior of the implementations.
- We present experimental results on using the test procedure on up-to-date versions of SPIN.

The rest of this paper is organized as follows. In Sect. 2, we describe the general testing procedure for comparing the results produced by different LTL-to-Büchi translation algorithm implementations with each other. Section 3 introduces a practical implementation of the test procedure into a randomized testbench for LTL-to-Büchi translation algorithm implementations. In Sect. 4, we propose a method for validating counterexamples provided by LTL model checkers. Section 5 reports the results of using the test procedure on the LTL-to-Büchi translation algorithm implementations of different versions of SPIN. Conclusions with some directions for future work are presented in Sect. 6.

2   Testing Procedure

In order to test the correctness of different LTL-to-Büchi conversion algorithm implementations in practice, the test procedure itself should be efficient in finding errors in the implementations. It should also be as reliable and simple as possible to avoid errors in the test procedure implementation itself.

Testing LTL-to-Büchi conversion algorithm implementations requires input for the implementations, i.e. LTL formulas to be converted into Büchi automata. We could try to test the correctness of a single implementation by using it to construct automata from an LTL formula and its negation and then checking whether the intersection of the languages accepted by these two automata is empty. (This could be checked with the help of a synchronous composition of the two automata, see e.g. [14].) If this result is found to be nonempty, we can conclude that the implementation does not work correctly.

However, this simple method has some disadvantages. First of all, if only a single implementation is used, this check is not sufficient to show that the obtained automata actually represent the formula and its negation correctly. (As a trivial example, this check would not detect the error in an otherwise correct Büchi automaton generator which always negates every input formula before generating the automaton.) We can gain more confidence in the correctness of the implementation by performing the language emptiness check against an automaton constructed for the negation of the formula using another independent conversion algorithm implementation. Therefore, if we have several implementations available, we can use each of them to construct automata from the formula and its negation and then check whether all the pairwise synchronous compositions of some automaton constructed for the formula and another automaton constructed for its negation are empty.

Another problem with this approach is that we cannot use the results of the emptiness checks to infer the correctness of any implementation (even on a single LTL formula) even if no failures are detected. Namely, implementations with errors may generate automata which pass all these checks but which still do not accept the exact languages corresponding to the input formulas. (For example, an implementation which always generates the empty automaton regardless of the LTL formula would always pass the emptiness check with any automaton.)

The test method's reliability in this respect could be increased by extending the procedure with one additional step. In addition to checking the emptiness of the intersection of the languages accepted by a pair of automata constructed from the formula and its negation, we could also check that the *union* of these languages (once again representable as a Büchi automaton, see e.g. [14]) forms the universal language. However, this problem is in general PSPACE-complete in the size of the resulting Büchi automaton, see e.g. [14]. In principle, the universality check can be done with a Büchi automata complementation procedure. However, this is a potentially hard-to-implement task [11], contradicting the goal of trying to keep the test procedure implementation as simple as possible.

In practice, it would also be an advantage if the test procedure were able to give some justification for the incorrectness of an implementation instead of a simple statement that the checks failed without exactly revealing which one of the implementations was in error. For instance, a concrete example of an input incorrectly accepted or rejected by some automaton might be of help in debugging the implementation with errors.

As a compromise between the difficulty of implementation and the reliability and practical applicability of test results, we will not try to compare the obtained automata directly. Instead, we use a testing method based on the automata-theoretic model checking procedure for LTL, see e.g. [4,14,15]. Basically, this involves model checking LTL formulas in models of systems and then checking that the model checking results obtained with the help of each individual LTL-to-Büchi conversion algorithm agree. Although this testing method requires more input (the system models) in addition to the formulas, it can also easily provide counterexamples for confirming the incorrectness of a particular implementation if the verification results are inconsistent. In addition, all steps in this test procedure are relatively straightforward to implement.

In this section, we discuss the general testing procedure and the methods for analyzing the test results. Since the methods for generating input for the testing procedure are independent of the procedure itself, we will leave the description of some possible methods for input generation until Sect. 3.

2.1   Automata-Theoretic Model Checking

We assume the system model to be given as a finite-state reachability graph, an explicit-state representation capturing all the behaviors of the system as infinite paths in the graph. The properties of the system are modeled using a finite set AP of atomic propositions, whose truth values are fixed independently in each state of the graph.

Formally, the reachability graph is a Kripke structure $K = \langle S, \rho, s_0, \pi \rangle$, where

- S is a finite set of states,
- $\rho \subseteq S \times S$ is a total transition relation, i.e. satisfying $\forall s \in S : \exists s' \in S : (s, s') \in \rho$,
- $s_0 \in S$ is the initial state and
- $\pi : S \mapsto 2^{AP}$ is a function which labels each state with a set of atomic propositions. Semantically, $\pi(s)$ represents the set of propositions that hold in a state $s \in S$, and the propositions in $AP \setminus \pi(s)$ are false in s.

The executions of the system are infinite sequences of states $s_0 s_1 \ldots \in S^\omega$ such that s_0 is the initial state of the system and for all $i \geq 0$, $(s_i, s_{i+1}) \in \rho$.

By using the function π for labeling each state with a subset of AP including exactly the propositions which are true in the state, the infinite behaviors of the system can alternatively be represented as infinite strings of state labels.

The task of the conversion algorithms we wish to test is to expand a given LTL property expressed as a formula over AP into a Büchi automaton. This automaton is supposed to accept exactly those infinite strings of state labels (system behaviors) which are models of the formula.

Formally, a Büchi automaton is a 5-tuple $A = \langle \Sigma, Q, \Delta, q_0, F \rangle$, where

- $\Sigma = 2^{AP}$ is an alphabet,
- Q is a finite set of states,
- $\Delta \subseteq Q \times \Sigma \times Q$ is a transition relation,
- $q_0 \in Q$ is the initial state, and
- $F \subseteq Q$ is a set of accepting states.

An execution of A over an infinite word $w = x_0 x_1 x_2 \ldots \in \Sigma^\omega$ is an infinite sequence of states $q_0 q_1 q_2 \ldots \in Q^\omega$ such that q_0 is the initial state and for all $i \geq 0$, $(q_i, x_i, q_{i+1}) \in \Delta$.

Let $r = q_0 q_1 q_2 \ldots \in Q^\omega$ be an execution of A. We denote by $\inf(r) \subseteq Q$ the set of states occurring infinitely many times in r. We say that r is an *accepting* execution of A iff $\inf(r) \cap F \neq \emptyset$.

The automaton accepts an infinite word $w \in \Sigma^\omega$ if and only if there is an accepting execution of A over w.

The goal is now to check whether the reachability graph and the Büchi automaton have any common behaviors, i.e. whether any infinite behavior of the system is accepted by the Büchi automaton. In LTL model checking, the answer to this question is used to confirm or refute whether the system satisfies a given LTL property φ. This actually involves using an automaton $A_{\neg\varphi}$, constructed for the *negation* of the property. Since the model checking of LTL properties requires *all* system behaviors to be considered, any system behavior accepted by $A_{\neg\varphi}$ is sufficient to falsify the given property.

However, in our testing approach, we are not interested in making any such conclusions about the system as a whole. For our needs, it is sufficient to use the LTL-to-Büchi conversion algorithms to construct an automaton A_φ simply for the given property φ. In effect, we will be using the constructed automaton for actually model checking the CTL* formula $\mathbf{E}\,\varphi$ instead of the LTL formula φ in the system [7].

Actually, the reachability graph can be seen as a Büchi automaton whose every state is accepting. This allows checking the existence of common behaviors by computing the synchronous product of the reachability graph with the property automaton (see e.g. [4]). Intuitively, this corresponds to enumerating all the parallel behaviors of the system and the automaton such that the behaviors agree at each step on the truth values of the atomic propositions in the property formula, when both the system and the automaton start their execution in their respective initial states.

Computing the synchronous product (for details, see e.g. [13]) results in another finite-state nondeterministic Büchi automaton having an accepting execution (specifically, a cyclic state sequence with an accepting state) if and only if any infinite system behavior is accepted by the property automaton. The existence of an accepting execution is equivalent to the question whether any nontrivial maximal strongly connected graph component with an accepting state can be reached from the initial state of the product. Determining the answer to this question can be done with the well-known algorithm due to Tarjan [12] for enumerating the maximal strongly connected graph components in linear time in the size of the product automaton.

2.2   Result Cross-Comparison

The existence of system behaviors satisfying the property should not depend on the particular Büchi automaton used for computing the product. However, errors in the LTL-to-Büchi conversion algorithm implementations may result in incorrect Büchi automata.

The basic test objective is to use the different LTL-to-Büchi conversion algorithm implementations to obtain several Büchi automata from a single LTL formula. Each of the automata is then synchronized separately with the reachability graph, and the results are checked for the existence of accepting cycles. Assuming that all the used LTL-to-Büchi implementations are error-free (in which case all the obtained automata will accept the same language), this check should always produce the same set of system states from which an accepting cycle can be reached. Any inconsistencies in the results suggest an error in some conversion algorithm implementation. We will show in Sect. 2.4 how we distinguish the incorrect implementation from those for which the results are correct.

The synchronization of the system with the property automaton is often performed only with respect to the unique initial states of the two automata. However, we proceed by synchronizing the property automaton separately in every state of the reachability graph, i.e. considering each state of the reachability graph in turn as the initial state. In this way, we can obtain more test data for comparison from a single reachability graph. The additional computation corresponds to checking the existence of behaviors satisfying the property in *every* state of the system, instead of only in its initial state. We call this the *global synchronous product*.

It is straightforward to extend the standard method for computing the product to perform all the synchronizations simultaneously. Basically, this requires ensuring that the initial state of the property automaton is paired with each state of the reachability graph while maintaining the product closed under its transition relation. This approach also takes advantage of the possible sharing of substructures between the different product automata, resulting in the same worst-case result size ($|Q| \cdot |S|$) as in the single-state method. (The actual occurrence of the worst case is, however, certainly much more probable with this approach.)

The check for accepting cycles is also easily extended to the global product. The only difference here is that the product automaton now has more than one state in which the reachability of any accepting cycle must be checked.

As a result, we obtain for each Büchi automaton conversion algorithm implementation a set of yes/no answers to the question of the existence of behaviors satisfying the LTL formula beginning at each state of the reachability graph. Assuming the Büchi automata were constructed from an LTL formula φ, these answers correspond to the truth values of the CTL* formula $\mathbf{E}\,\varphi$ in each system state.[1] These answers can then be compared against each other in each individual state as described above.

2.3   Checking the Results for Consistency

Once the previous testing procedure has been completed for a single LTL formula, it is useful to repeat the whole procedure again for the negation of the same formula. In addition to another result cross-comparison check, this allows a simple consistency check to be performed on the two result sets obtained using each individual LTL-to-Büchi conversion algorithm implementation.

The check is based on the fact that no system state can simultaneously satisfy an LTL property *and* its negation, even though both may well remain *unsatisfied* in the state. (For an LTL property, this will occur if there are several behaviors

---

[1]   By exploring the global synchronous product with an on-the-fly version of Tarjan's algorithm, we could thus use the approach also as an efficient LTL model checking subroutine for an on-the-fly CTL* model checker. (See [1].)

beginning at the state, some of which satisfy the property individually, while others satisfy its negation.) However, the *nonexistence* of a behavior satisfying the LTL property implies that the negation of the property holds in that state. Therefore, it follows that the answer to the existence of an accepting execution cannot be negative for both the formula and its negation in any state, as that would imply that both the property and its negation hold in the state at the same time.

This check is very easy to perform on the two result sets obtained using a particular LTL-to-Büchi conversion algorithm implementation. Any violation of the previous fact immediately confirms an error in the implementation.

The basic steps of the test procedure are illustrated in Fig. 1.

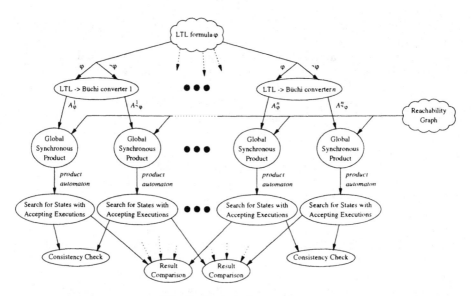

Fig. 1. Basic test procedure

2.4 Cross-Comparison Result Analysis

The result cross-comparison check is not in itself enough to reveal the implementation or implementations in error. Of course, running several independent implementations against each other may help to single out the incorrect one if a pattern can be detected in the occurrence of result inconsistencies, e.g. when the implementations generally agree with each other with the exception of a single implementation which sometimes fails the check with all the other implementations.

However, simply searching for patterns in the detected inconsistencies may not be an adequate strategy if the used implementations are not independent, or if in some cases only few of the many tested implementations are actually correct, while all the others give incorrect results. Therefore, we will need more systematic methods to distinguish the incorrect implementation from the correct ones.

Our approach for detecting the implementation with errors is based on first finding (see below) a concrete example behavior of the system (i.e., a witness) for which the model checking results obtained using two different LTL-to-Büchi conversion algorithm implementations disagree. The LTL formula is then model checked in this example behavior separately. Instead of using for this purpose a general LTL model checking algorithm, whose implementation correctness would be equally difficult to confirm as that of the implementations we wish to test, we use a *direct LTL model checking algorithm for a single state sequence*. This approach is based on the intuition that a restricted algorithm is easier to implement correctly than any of the tested translation algorithms and should therefore be more reliable. Using this algorithm to model check the formula separately in the example behavior, we obtain a strong suggestion about which one of the tested LTL-to-Büchi conversion algorithm implementations had failed.

The first step of the analysis is to find a system state in which the result sets obtained using two LTL-to-Büchi translation algorithms disagree. In this state, another result set claims the existence of an infinite system behavior satisfying the LTL formula. We use the product automaton associated with this result set to extract an actual infinite system behavior which is accepted by the Büchi automaton used for constructing the product. This can be done using the standard model checking techniques for extracting counterexamples (actually witnesses in our case), see e.g. [2].

It is important to note that the obtained infinite system execution always consists of a prefix of system states followed by a state cycle which repeats infinitely often. Another important property of the execution is that each of its states has exactly one successor. The execution is therefore an infinite path in the reachability graph. These characteristics of the execution allow us to apply CTL model checking techniques for evaluating the given LTL formula in the execution.[2] (We use the standard semantics for CTL, see e.g. [7].)

Let τ be a function mapping LTL formulas to CTL formulas, defined recursively as follows:

$$\tau(\text{TRUE}) = \text{TRUE}$$
$$\tau(\text{FALSE}) = \text{FALSE}$$
$$\tau(P) = P \text{ for all atomic propositions } P \in AP$$
$$\tau(\neg\varphi) = \neg\tau(\varphi)$$
$$\tau(\varphi \vee \psi) = \tau(\varphi) \vee \tau(\psi)$$
$$\tau(\mathbf{X}\,\varphi) = \mathbf{AX}\,\tau(\varphi)$$
$$\tau(\varphi\,\mathbf{U}\,\psi) = \mathbf{A}\big(\tau(\varphi)\,\mathbf{U}\,\tau(\psi)\big)$$

---

[2] This idea was first presented as a remark in an extended version of [8], available at URL: http://www.cs.rice.edu/\%7Evardi/papers/.

Intuitively, this transformation simply replaces all temporal operators in the original LTL formula with a corresponding quantified CTL operator.[3] It is clear that the transformation can be done in linear time in the size of the formula.

Let $K = \langle S, \rho, s_0, \pi \rangle$ be a finite-state Kripke structure representing the witness behavior extracted using the product automaton as described above. Each state of this structure has exactly one successor, and every state of the structure is reachable from its initial state. Let $x = s_0 s_1 s_2 \ldots \in S^\omega$ denote the unique infinite state sequence which begins in the initial state $s_0 \in S$.

Let φ be an LTL formula over the atomic propositions in AP. We have the following:

Theorem 1. *The infinite state sequence x satisfies the LTL formula φ if and only if the CTL formula $\tau(\varphi)$ holds in s_0, the initial state of the Kripke structure K.*

Proof. By induction on the syntactic structure of the formula.

This result allows us to use CTL model checking techniques for checking the satisfiability of the LTL formula separately in the system behavior. For example, we can apply a global CTL model checking algorithm (see e.g. [7]) to the path, evaluating each of the subformulas of $\tau(\varphi)$ in turn in each state of the path in order to finally obtain the truth value of $\tau(\varphi)$ in the initial state. The complexity of this algorithm is $\mathcal{O}(|F| \cdot |S|)$, where $|F|$ denotes the number of subformulas of $\tau(\varphi)$. By the previous theorem, the result tells also the truth value of the LTL formula φ in the execution. This result can then be used to detect which one of the tested LTL-to-Büchi converter implementations was probably in error in this test case, i.e. which automaton incorrectly accepted or rejected the execution.

3   Automated Testing of the Implementations

We have implemented the testing procedure of the previous section into a testbench for LTL-to-Büchi translation algorithm implementations. The C++ source code for this program is available through Heikki Tauriainen's homepage at URL: `http://www.tcs.hut.fi/\%7Ehtauriai/`.

3.1   Test Program Operation

The testbench model checks randomly generated LTL formulas in randomly generated reachability graphs, using each of the different LTL-to-Büchi conversion algorithm implementations in turn to expand the LTL formulas and their negations into Büchi automata.

In addition to generating the input, the program performs for each used implementation the global synchronous product computation, together with the

---

[3]   Actually, due to the special characteristics of the executions, even the semantics of the CTL path quantifiers **A** and **E** coincide. Therefore, we could as well use the **E** quantifier without affecting the results presented here.

check for states beginning some execution satisfying the property. Finally, the program compares the results obtained using each LTL-to-Büchi conversion algorithm with each other and reports whether any inconsistencies were detected. After this, the test procedure is repeated using another randomly generated LTL formula and/or a reachability graph.

The testing can be interrupted in case any error is detected, for example, when an implementation fails to generate a Büchi automaton (e.g., due to an internal assertion violation in the implementation). The program provides a command-line interface through which the user can examine the formula, the reachability graph and the Büchi automata generated by the different implementations more closely, optionally invoking a path checking algorithm for LTL to determine which one of the implementations was in error.

The test program collects statistics on the failure rates of the different implementations and records the average sizes of the Büchi automata generated by the individual implementations. Also the average running times of the different implementations are recorded. These capabilities allow the test program to be also used for simple benchmarking of the different implementations.

Interfacing the test program with any LTL-to-Büchi translation algorithm implementation requires writing an additional program module, whose purpose is to translate the input formulas and the outputted Büchi automata between the representations used by the testbench and the LTL-to-Büchi converter implementation. A module is already provided for doing this for SPIN's input syntax and the resulting Büchi automata (called "never claims" in SPIN terminology).

3.2   Generating the Input

The testbench implementation uses randomly generated LTL formulas and reachability graphs as input for the test procedure, allowing the user some control over the behavior of the input generation algorithms through the use of several parameters.

Simple random testing is by no means sufficient for proving the absolute correctness of any LTL-to-Büchi conversion algorithm implementation. In addition, even though seemingly "random" input generation methods are very easy to come up with, these methods may easily create some kind of bias in the output. This makes it hard to analyze the general efficiency of the test procedure in finding errors in the tested implementations. However, since the correctness of the test procedure is independent of any particular input generation method, we do not consider this to be a major weakness. As a matter of fact, it has been our experience that even simple random input generation methods have been quite effective in uncovering flaws in many practical implementations, thus being helpful in improving their robustness.

We shall now describe the input generation methods used in the testbench implementation.

Random LTL Formulas. The test program generates the random LTL input formulas using a recursive algorithm similar to the one in [3] to obtain formulas containing an exact given number of symbols (logical operators, Boolean constants or propositional variables).

The behavior of the algorithm can be customized through the use of several parameters. For example, these parameters allow changing the number of available atomic propositions or setting the relative priorities of choosing any particular logical operator in the algorithm. This can be also used for disabling the use of some operators altogether.

The complete set of available operators for use in the generated formulas is ¬ (logical negation), **X** ("Next"), □ ("Always" or "Globally"), ◇ ("Eventually" or "Finally"), ∧ (logical conjunction), ∨ (logical disjunction), → (logical implication), ↔ (logical equivalence), **U** ("Until"), and **V** ("Release", the dual of **U**).

Pseudocode for the algorithm is shown in Fig. 2. The argument n for the algorithm denotes the desired number of symbols in the generated formula.

```
1     function RandomFormula (n : Integer) : LtlFormula
2     begin
3         if n = 1 then begin
4             p := random symbol in AP ∪ {TRUE, FALSE};
5             return p;
6         end
7         else if n = 2 then begin
8             op := random operator in the set {¬, X, □, ◇};
9             φ := RandomFormula(1);
10            return op φ;
11        end
12        else
13            op := random operator in the set {¬, X, □, ◇, ∧, ∨, →, ↔, U, V};
14            if op ∈ {¬, X, □, ◇} then begin
15                φ := RandomFormula(n − 1);
16                return op φ;
17            end
18            else begin
19                x := random integer in the interval [1, n − 2];
20                φ := RandomFormula(x);
21                ψ := RandomFormula(n − x − 1);
22                return (φ op ψ);
23            end;
24        end;
25    end;
```

Fig. 2. Pseudocode for the formula generation algorithm

Reachability Graphs. The algorithm used in the test program implementation for constructing random reachability graphs is presented in Fig. 3. The goal of the algorithm is to generate graphs with a given number of states n, with the additional requirement of ensuring the reachability of every graph state from the initial state of the graph. Since the test procedure is concerned with infinite system behaviors, the algorithm will also ensure that each graph state has at least one successor.

```
1      function RandomGraph(n : Integer. p : Real ∈ [0.0. 1.0]. t : Real ∈ [0.0. 1.0])
              : KripkeStructure
2      begin
3          S := {s_0, s_1, . . . , s_{n-1}};
4          NodesToProcess := {s_0};
5          UnreachableNodes := {s_1, s_2, . . . , s_{n-1}};
6          ρ := ∅;
7          while NodesToProcess ≠ ∅ do begin
8              s := a random node in NodesToProcess;
9              NodesToProcess := NodesToProcess \ {s};
10             π(s) := ∅;
11             for all P ∈ AP do
12                 if RandomNumber(0.0, 1.0) < t then
13                     π(s) := π(s) ∪ {P};
14             if UnreachableNodes ≠ ∅ then begin
15                 s' := a random node in UnreachableNodes;
16                 UnreachableNodes := UnreachableNodes \ {s'};
17                 NodesToProcess := NodesToProcess ∪ {s'};
18                 ρ := ρ ∪ {(s, s')};
19             end;
20             for all s' ∈ S do
21                 if RandomNumber(0.0, 1.0) < p then begin
22                     ρ := ρ ∪ {(s, s')};
23                     if s' ∈ UnreachableNodes then begin
24                         UnreachableNodes := UnreachableNodes \ {s'};
25                         NodesToProcess := NodesToProcess ∪ {s'};
26                     end;
27                 end;
28             if there is no edge (s. s') in ρ for any s' ∈ S then
29                 ρ := ρ ∪ (s, s);
30         end;
31         return ⟨S, ρ, s_0, π⟩;
32     end;
```

Fig. 3. Pseudocode for the reachability graph generation algorithm

Beginning with the initial state of the graph, the algorithm processes each node of the graph in turn. In order to ensure the reachability and the graph size requirements, the algorithm first chooses a random state already known to be reachable from the initial state (line 8) and connects it to some yet unreachable state, if there are still any available (lines 14–19). Then, random edges are inserted between the chosen node and all other graph nodes (lines 20–27). The probability of inserting these edges can be controlled with the parameter p. Finally, if the chosen state still has no successors, it is simply connected to itself in order to avoid any finite terminating behaviors (lines 28–29).

The truth values of the atomic propositions are chosen randomly in each processed state (lines 10–13). The parameter t denotes the probability with which any of the propositions is given the value "TRUE" in a state.

The algorithm repeats these steps for each state of the graph, until all states have been processed.

Random paths. The test program can also use an alternative method of generating random *paths* as the reachability graphs used as input for the test procedure. These paths simply consist of a given number of states connected to form a sequence whose last state is connected to some randomly chosen previous state in the sequence, thereby forming a cycle. The atomic propositions are then given random truth values in each state as in the previous algorithm.

Generating random paths as reachability graphs has the advantage of allowing us to perform an additional cross-comparison for the model checking results obtained using the different LTL-to-Büchi translation algorithms. The check is based on the use of LTL path checking algorithm based on the methods discussed in Sect. 2.4. This algorithm is first used to evaluate the given LTL formula φ in the executions beginning at each state of the path. In this restricted class of reachability graphs, the previously computed model checking results for the CTL* formula $\mathbf{E}\,\varphi$ using each LTL-to-Büchi translation algorithm should now exactly correspond to the results returned by the path checking algorithm in each state of the path. This follows from the fact that in this class of reachability graphs, the semantics of CTL* path quantifiers $\mathbf{E}$ and $\mathbf{A}$ coincide. For the same reason, the model checking results computed for the CTL* formula $\mathbf{E}\,\neg\varphi$ should be exactly the opposite.

Therefore, using single paths as random reachability graphs gives an additional algorithm to be used in testing the different implementations against each other, providing also for limited testing of a single LTL-to-Büchi conversion algorithm implementation: if the input consisted of more general graphs, at least two implementations would always be required in order to be able to perform any testing based on the cross-comparison of the results given by the different implementations.

4   Application of the LTL Path Checking Algorithm in LTL Model Checking Tools

We suggest an additional application of the methods of Sect. 2.4 for model checking LTL formulas in single state sequences. Namely, an LTL path checking algorithm could also be used in practical LTL model checking tools for validating the counterexamples produced by the tool. Integrating the path checking algorithm as an additional last step of the model checking process into a model checker could give some assurance that the counterexample produced by the tool is really correct. In addition, any errors detected in this phase suggest possible errors in the model checker implementation.

The results of a global CTL model checking algorithm, when applied to the verification of an LTL property in a single system behavior, can also be easily used to automatically produce a proof or a refutation for the property in the behavior. We have used this idea in the testbench implementation for justifying to the user the claim for the failure of one of the tested LTL-to-Büchi conversion implementations when analyzing contradictory results.

5   Testing SPIN's LTL-to-Büchi Conversion

We used our test program implementation for testing the LTL-to-Büchi conversion algorithm implemented in the model checker SPIN [6,5]. The implementation is originally based on the algorithm presented in [4] with several optimizations.

We used the testbench on SPIN versions 3.3.7, 3.3.8, 3.3.9 and 3.3.10, which was the most recent version available at the time of writing.

As a reference implementation, we used another implementation based on an open source C++ class library [10] (extended with some locally developed code), originally a part of the Åbo System Analyser (ÅSA) model checking package [9]. This is an independent, very straightforward implementation of the Büchi automaton construction algorithm in [4]. Even though the tested implementations are based on the same algorithm, we find the independence of the actual implementations far more relevant, since our focus is not on testing the correctness of the abstract algorithm (which is already known to be correct [4]). We have also used the testbench on implementations based on different algorithms for converting LTL formulas into Büchi automata, such as the algorithm of [15] implemented in the tool PROD [16], but due to some limitations in PROD's input syntax (namely, the lack of support for the **X** and **V** operators) we did not include that implementation in the tests made here.

We ran the tests using both the more general random graph algorithm and the random path algorithm for generating reachability graphs with 100 states (in the random graph algorithm, a random edge between two states was added with the probability 0.2). The random LTL formulas used as input for the LTL-to-Büchi translation algorithm implementations consisted of 4 to 7 symbols. Five atomic propositions (with equal probability of being used in a formula) were available for use in the generated formulas. In generating the reachability graphs, each proposition had an equal probability of being true or false in each individual state of the graph. For each reachability graph generation method and for each different number of formula symbols, we ran each LTL-to-Büchi converter implementation on 4,000 randomly generated formulas and their negations. In total, each individual implementation was therefore run on 64,000 input formulas. Additionally, a new reachability graph was generated after every tenth generated formula.

The randomly generated formulas were partitioned into four batches of equal size, using in each batch a different subset of formula symbols in generating the formulas. The symbol sets used in the different batches were

(1) atomic propositions; no Boolean constants; operators $\neg, \Diamond, \Box, \wedge, \vee, \rightarrow, \leftrightarrow,$ **U, V**
(2) atomic propositions; Boolean constants TRUE and FALSE; the same operators as in (1)
(3) atomic propositions; no Boolean constants; all operators in (1) together with the **X** operator
(4) atomic propositions; all Boolean constants and logical operators.

Each available operator had an equal priority of being selected into a generated formula by the algorithm in Sect. 3.2; however, each Boolean constant (when included in the symbol set) had the smaller probability of 0.05 of being selected, compared to the probability of 0.18 used for each of the five propositional variables.

The tests were run using Linux PCs. Table 1 shows the failure rates of each implementation during the conversion of an LTL formula into a Büchi automaton. All the tested implementations except SPIN 3.3.9 sometimes failed to produce acceptable output (interpreted as a failure to generate an automaton). The reported failures of the reference implementation are due to its failure to produce any output after running for 12 hours. On the other hand, all SPIN versions never consumed more than only a few seconds of running time, showing the straightforward reference implementation very inefficient in practice.

Table 1. Büchi automaton generation failure statistics

Number of symbols in formula	Imple- mentation	Number of Büchi automaton generation failures (of 4,000 attempts)			
		(1)	(2)	(3)	(4)
4	ASA	0	0	0	0
	SPIN 3.3.7	38	72	84	92
	SPIN 3.3.8	38	72	84	92
	SPIN 3.3.9	0	0	0	0
	SPIN 3.3.10	0	0	0	0
5	ASA	0	0	0	0
	SPIN 3.3.7	100	158	138	167
	SPIN 3.3.8	100	158	138	167
	SPIN 3.3.9	0	0	0	0
	SPIN 3.3.10	10	13	13	9
6	ASA	0	0	0	0
	SPIN 3.3.7	142	168	215	198
	SPIN 3.3.8	142	168	215	198
	SPIN 3.3.9	0	0	0	0
	SPIN 3.3.10	8	7	8	5
7	ASA	1	2	2	2
	SPIN 3.3.7	138	220	248	293
	SPIN 3.3.8	138	220	248	293
	SPIN 3.3.9	0	0	0	0
	SPIN 3.3.10	12	4	10	5

All but one SPIN version failed in some cases to produce acceptable output. Occasionally, the never claims produced by SPIN versions 3.3.7 and 3.3.8 were syntactically incorrect. Moreover, in some cases both versions failed due to an internal error on some input formulas (all of which contained the logical equivalence operator ↔) without producing any output. Version 3.3.9 never failed to produce correctly formatted output; however, version 3.3.10 again failed on some input formulas, reporting an internal error instead.

Finally, Tables 2 and 3 contain the number of input formulas failing the result cross-comparison check between the implementations. The tables also include the total number of failed consistency checks for each individual implementation. The results of Table 2 were obtained using randomly generated reachability graphs as input for the testing procedure, while the results of Table 3 are based on using randomly generated paths as input. The results are grouped according to the used set of formula symbols.

The results show that there were cases in which SPIN versions 3.3.7, 3.3.8 and 3.3.9 failed the result cross-comparison check with version 3.3.10 and the reference implementation, however SPIN 3.3.9 failed only if the input formulas were

Table 2. Result cross-comparison statistics (random graphs)

Formula symbol set	Implementation	Total number of consistency check failures	Total number of result cross-comparison failures / number of comparisons performed	
(1)			ÁSA	SPIN 3.3.10
	ÁSA	0/4000	—	0/7989
	SPIN 3.3.7	0/3894	907/7788	907/7777
	SPIN 3.3.8	0/3894	907/7788	907/7777
	SPIN 3.3.9	0/4000	0/8000	0/7989
	SPIN 3.3.10	0/3989	0/7989	—
(2)	ÁSA	0/3998	—	0/7985
	SPIN 3.3.7	4/3841	849/7680	849/7669
	SPIN 3.3.8	4/3841	849/7680	849/7669
	SPIN 3.3.9	1/4000	1/7998	1/7987
	SPIN 3.3.10	0/3987	0/7985	—
(3)	ÁSA	0/3998	—	0/7983
	SPIN 3.3.7	0/3811	624/7647	623/7635
	SPIN 3.3.8	0/3811	624/7647	623/7635
	SPIN 3.3.9	0/4000	0/7998	0/7985
	SPIN 3.3.10	0/3985	0/7983	—
(4)	ÁSA	0/3999	—	0/7988
	SPIN 3.3.7	4/3777	747/7582	747/7572
	SPIN 3.3.8	4/3777	747/7582	747/7572
	SPIN 3.3.9	0/4000	64/7999	64/7989
	SPIN 3.3.10	0/3989	0/7988	—

Table 3. Result cross-comparison statistics (random paths)

Formula symbol set	Implementation	Total number of consistency check failures	Total number of result cross-comparison failures / number of comparisons performed	
(1)			ÁSA	SPIN 3.3.10
	ÁSA	0/3999	—	0/7980
	SPIN 3.3.7	0/3897	926/7793	926/7775
	SPIN 3.3.8	0/3897	918/7793	918/7775
	SPIN 3.3.9	0/4000	0/7999	0/7981
	SPIN 3.3.10	0/3981	0/7980	—
(2)	ÁSA	0/4000	—	0/7989
	SPIN 3.3.7	6/3850	923/7700	923/7690
	SPIN 3.3.8	6/3850	921/7700	920/7690
	SPIN 3.3.9	0/4000	0/8000	0/7989
	SPIN 3.3.10	0/3989	0/7989	—
(3)	ÁSA	0/4000	—	0/7984
	SPIN 3.3.7	51/3820	825/7666	825/7650
	SPIN 3.3.8	50/3820	822/7666	819/7650
	SPIN 3.3.9	0/4000	0/8000	0/7984
	SPIN 3.3.10	0/3984	0/7984	—
(4)	ÁSA	0/3999	—	0/7991
	SPIN 3.3.7	60/3820	898/7666	899/7659
	SPIN 3.3.8	60/3820	891/7666	892/7659
	SPIN 3.3.9	0/4000	76/7999	76/7992
	SPIN 3.3.10	0/3992	0/7991	—

allowed to contain Boolean constants or **X** operators. SPIN 3.3.10 never failed the result cross-comparison check with the reference implementation. SPIN versions 3.3.7, 3.3.8 and 3.3.9 also occasionally failed the result consistency check. However, the relatively rare occurrence of these failures seems to suggest that the result cross-comparison check is more powerful of these methods for detecting errors in an implementation. However, unlike the consistency check, this test always requires a separate analysis of the results produced by two implementations to determine which one of them is incorrect.

The test results show a clear improvement in the robustness of SPIN's LTL-to-Büchi conversion algorithm implementation since version 3.3.7. SPIN 3.3.10 was the first to pass all result cross-comparison checks with the reference implementation. However, in these tests this version was slightly more unstable than its immediate predecessor due to the occasional automaton generation failures. This may be a result of some new optimizations made in the newer version to reduce the size of the generated automata, which reminds that extreme care should always be taken when making optimizations into an implementation in order to retain its stability and correctness. This reveals another possible application for the test procedure as a regression testing method to be used in the development of new versions of an LTL-to-Büchi algorithm implementation.

6   Conclusions

We have presented a random testing method for LTL-to-Büchi conversion algorithm implementations. The approach was quite effective in uncovering errors in the SPIN model checker, and this has been our experience also with other model checkers on which we have run a smaller set of tests. (Of the four independent implementations we have tested, the reference implementation ÅSA has been the only one in which no errors have ever been detected using this method.)

This work can be seen as the continuation of the work in [13]. We have improved the methodology presented there by using counterexample validation algorithms (essentially, a global CTL model checker) to decide which one of several disagreeing implementations is incorrect. Also the use of random paths is first introduced here. We present a larger set of experimental results with up-to-date SPIN versions. New to this work is additionally the idea of using a counterexample validation algorithm as the last step of an LTL model checker.

In the future, we would like to extend the approach to also test nondeterministic finite automata generated from (syntactic) safety LTL formulas using the approaches presented in [8]. These (safety) LTL-to-NFA conversion algorithm implementations would need a different (more simple) emptiness checking subroutine, but the results could then be compared against the results obtained from the LTL-to-Büchi conversion tests for the same formula.

We will also continue using the test program on other LTL-to-Büchi converter implementations based on different conversion algorithms than the one used here. For example, it would be interesting to try the test program on the LTL2AUT implementation of [3]. The testbench implementation itself could also be still improved with some of the methods for the direct comparison of Büchi automata as described in the beginning of Sect. 2 (the emptiness check for the synchronous composition of two automata, however without the universality test for the union of the automata).

A very surprising result in the experiments was that using randomly generated paths as input reachability graphs for the testing procedure resulted in a slightly higher failure rate in the tested implementations. However, since there are so many factors affecting the test procedure (details of the input generation algorithms, the particular combination of values chosen for the test parameters, even the tested implementations themselves), it is impossible to say anything conclusive about which one of these graph generation methods might be "better" for uncovering errors in the implementations. The relationship between the test parameters and the failure rates would certainly make an interesting issue to investigate in the future.

We propose that LTL model checkers should be extended with a counterexample validation algorithm as described in Sect. 4. The implementation of this algorithm is quite straightforward, as it can be done based on even a straightforward implementation of a CTL model checker. The running time overhead of such an algorithm should be quite negligible, as it is linear both in the size of the formula and the length of the counterexample. Such an algorithm would increase the confidence in the counterexamples provided by the model checker implementation, and could hopefully help in finding some of the yet unknown implementation errors in the tool. Of course, separate validation of counterexamples only helps in detecting false negatives but not false positives; however, it would still be a step in the right direction.

There are several other places in LTL model checkers which could probably be improved with random testing but which we have not covered here (for example, emptiness checking and partial order reduction algorithms). However, we think that the LTL-to-Büchi conversion algorithm, including all the possibly used optimizations, is one of the most difficult algorithms to implement, and thus should also be regression tested whenever new versions are implemented.

An optimal situation would of course be that the implementation of a model checker were fully verified (and still have adequate performance). Until that is the case, we aim at a more humble goal: to validate a part of the model checker using random testing.

Acknowledgements. The random testing method has been used on SPIN starting from version 3.3.3, on which the first preliminary tests were made in the summer of 1999. More extensive tests have been done on versions 3.3.8, 3.3.9 and 3.3.10 since January 2000. We would like to thank Gerard J. Holzmann for creating new and improved versions of SPIN during the period this work was done.

We would also like to thank Tommi Junttila for critical comments on this work and Mauno Rönkkö for creating a reliable reference implementation. We are also grateful to the anonymous referees whose feedback was very important in improving this work.

References

[1] G. Bhat, R. Cleaveland, and O. Grumberg. Efficient on-the-fly model checking for CTL*. In *Proceedings of 10th Annual IEEE Symposium on Logic in Computer Science (LICS'95)*, pages 388–397. IEEE Computer Society Press, 1995.

[2] C. Courcoubetis, M. Y. Vardi, P. Wolper, and M. Yannakakis. Memory-efficient algorithms for the verification of temporal properties. *Formal Methods in System Design*, 1:275–288, 1992.

[3] M. Daniele, F. Giunchiglia, and M. Y. Vardi. Improved automata generation for linear temporal logic. In *Proceedings of the 11th International Conference on Computer Aided Verification (CAV'99)*, pages 249–260. Springer, 1999. LNCS 1633.

[4] R. Gerth, D. Peled, M. Y. Vardi, and P. Wolper. Simple on-the-fly automatic verification of linear temporal logic. In *Proceedings of 15th Workshop Protocol Specification, Testing, and Verification*, pages 3–18, 1995.

[5] G. Holzmann. On-the-fly, LTL model checking with Spin. URL: http://netlib.bell-labs.com/netlib/spin/whatispin.html.

[6] G. Holzmann. The model checker Spin. *IEEE Transactions on Software Engineering*, 23(5):279–295, May 1997.

[7] E. Clarke Jr., O. Grumberg, and D. Peled. *Model Checking*. MIT Press, 2000.

[8] O. Kupferman and M. Y. Vardi. Model checking of safety properties. In *Proceedings of 11th International Conference on Computer Aided Verification (CAV'99)*, pages 172–183. Springer, 1999. LNCS 1633.

[9] J. Lilius. ÅSA: The Åbo System Analyser, September 1999. URL: http://www.abo.fi/\%7Ejolilius/mc/aasa.html.

[10] M. Rönkkö. A distributed object oriented implementation of an algorithm converting a LTL formula to a generalised Buchi automaton, 1998. URL: http://www.abo.fi/\%7Emauno.ronkko/ASA/ltlalg.html.

[11] S. Safra. *Complexity of automata on infinite objects*. PhD thesis, The Weizmann Institute of Science, 1989.

[12] R. Tarjan. Depth-first search and linear graph algorithms. *SIAM Journal on Computing*, 1(2):146–160, June 1972.

[13] H. Tauriainen. A randomized testbench for algorithms translating linear temporal logic formulae into Büchi automata. In *Proceedings of the Workshop Concurrency, Specification and Programming 1999 (CS&P'99)*, pages 251–262. Warsaw University, September 1999.

[14] M. Y. Vardi. An automata-theoretic approach to linear temporal logic. In *Logics for Concurrency: Structure versus Automata*, pages 238–265, 1996. LNCS 1043.

[15] M. Y. Vardi and P. Wolper. An automata-theoretic approach to automatic program verification. In *Proceedings of the 1st IEEE Symposium on Logic in Computer Science (LICS'86)*, pages 332–344. IEEE Computer Society Press, 1986.

[16] K. Varpaaniemi, K. Heljanko, and J. Lilius. PROD 3.2 - An advanced tool for efficient reachability analysis. In *Proceedings of the 9th International Conference on Computer Aided Verification (CAV'97)*, pages 472–475. Springer, June 1997. LNCS 1254.

Verification and Optimization of a PLC Control Schedule

Ed Brinksma[1] and Angelika Mader[2*]

[1] Faculty of Computer Science, University of Twente
[2] Computer Science Department, University of Nijmegen

Abstract. We report on the use of the SPIN model checker for both the verification of a process control program and the derivation of optimal control schedules. This work was carried out as part of a case study for the EC VHS project (Verification of Hybrid Systems), in which the program for a Programmable Logic Controller (PLC) of an experimental chemical plant had to be designed and verified. The intention of our approach was to see how much could be achieved here using the standard model checking environment of SPIN/Promela. As the symbolic calculations of real-time model checkers can be quite expensive it is interesting to try and exploit the efficiency of established non-real-time model checkers like SPIN in those cases where promising work-arounds seem to exist. In our case we handled the relevant real-time properties of the PLC controller using a time-abstraction technique; for the scheduling we implemented in Promela a so-called *variable time advance procedure*. For this case study these techniques proved sufficient to verify the design of the controller and derive (time-)optimal schedules with reasonable time and space requirements.

1 Introduction

Nowadays, the verification of hybrid systems is a popular topic in the formal methods community. The presence of both discrete and continuous phenomena in such systems poses an inspiring challenge for our specification and modelling techniques, as well as for our analytic capacities. This has led to the development of new, expressive models, such as timed and hybrid automata [3,16], and new verification methods, most notably model checking techniques involving a symbolic treatment of real-time (and hybrid) aspects [10,17,6].

An important example of hybrid (embedded) systems are process control programs, which involve the digital control of processing plants, e.g. chemical plants. A class of process controllers that are of considerable practical importance are those that are implemented using Programmable Logic Computers or PLCs. Unfortunately, both PLCs and their associated programming languages have

---

* supported by an NWO postdoc grant and the EC LTR project VHS (project nr. 26270)

K. Havelund, J. Penix, and W. Visser (Eds.): SPIN 2000, LNCS 1885, pp. 73–92, 2000.
© Springer-Verlag Berlin Heidelberg 2000

no well-defined formal models, c.q. semantics, which complicates the design of reliable controllers and their analysis.

To assess the capacity of state-of-the-art formal methods and tools for the analysis of hybrid systems, the EC research project VHS (Verification of Hybrid Systems) has defined a number of case studies. One of these studies concerns the design and verification of a PLC program for an experimental chemical plant.

In this paper we report on the use of the SPIN model checker for both the verification of a process control program for the given plant and the derivation of optimal control schedules. It is a companion paper to [12], which concentrates on the correct design of the process controller. The intention of our approach was to see how much could be achieved here using the standard model checking environment of SPIN/Promela [7]. As the symbolic calculations of real-time model checkers can be quite expensive it is interesting to try and exploit the efficiency of established non-real-time model checkers like SPIN in those cases where promising work-arounds seem to exist. In our case we handled the relevant real-time properties of the PLC controller using a time-abstraction technique; for the scheduling we implemented in Promela a so-called *variable time advance procedure* [15]. For this case study these techniques proved sufficient to verify the design of the controller and derive (time-)optimal schedules with very reasonable time and space requirements.

The rest of this paper is organised as follows: section 2 gives a description of the batch plant, the nature of PLCs and a description of the control program that was systematically designed in [12]. Section 3 describes the Promela models for the plant and the control process, and their use for the formal verification and optimization. Section 4 contains the conclusions.

2   Description of the System

The system of the case study is basically an embedded system, consisting of a batch plant and a Programmable Logic Controller (PLC), both of which are described in more detail below. The original goal of the case study was to write a control program such that the batch plant and the PLC with its control program together behave as intended. The intended behaviour is that, first, new batches can always be produced, and second, in the second place, that the control schedule is time optimal, i.e. the average time to produce a batch is minimal.

2.1   Description of the Batch Plant

The batch plant (see Figure 1) of the case study is an experimental chemical process plant, originally designed for student exercises. We describe its main features below; a more detailed account can be found in [9]. The plant "produces" batches of diluted salt solution from concentrated salt solution (in container B1) and water (in container B2). These ingredients are mixed in container B3 to

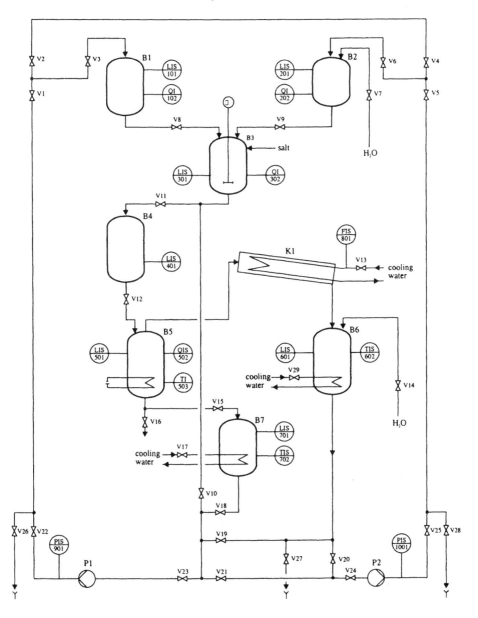

Fig. 1. The P/I-Diagram of the Batch Plant

obtain the diluted solution, which is subsequently transported to container B4 and then further on to B5. In container B5 an evaporation process is started. The evaporated water goes via a condenser to container B6, where it is cooled and pumped back to B2. The remaining hot, concentrated salt solution in B5 is transported to B7, cooled down and then pumped back to B1.

The controlled batch plant is clearly a hybrid system. The discrete element is provided by the control program and the (abstract) states of the valves, mixer, heater and coolers (open/closed, on/off). Continuous aspects are tank filling levels, temperatures, and time. The latter can be dissected into real-time phenomena of the plant on the one hand, such as tank filling, evaporation, mixing, heating and cooling times, and the program execution and reaction times (PLC scan cycle time), on the other. The controller of the batch plant is a nice example of an *embedded system*: the controlling, digital device is part of a larger physical system with a particular functionality.

For the case study we decided to fix the size of a batch: the material is either 4.2l salt solution with a concentration of 5g/l and 2.8l water or, if mixed, 7l salt solution of 3g/l concentration. With these batch sizes containers B1, B2, B4, B6 and B7 are capable of two "units" of material, B3 and B5 only one "unit" of material. The plant description in [9] contains also durations for the transport steps from one tank to another. In our (timed) plant model we used these durations as our basis, although the actual durations might possibly be different.

Table 1. Duration of plant processes in seconds

B1–B3	B2–B3	B3–B4	B4–B5	heat B5	B5–B7	cool B6	cool B7	B6–B2	B7–B1
320	240	70	350	1100	280	300	600	240	220

2.2 Programmable Logic Controllers

PLCs are special purpose computers designed for control tasks. Their area of application is enormous. Here, we briefly emphasize the main characteristics of PLCs in comparison to "usual" computers.

The most significant difference is that a program on a PLC runs in a permanent loop, the so called *scan cycle*. In a scan cycle the program in the PLC is executed once, where the program execution may depend on varible values stored in the memory. The length of a scan cycle is in the range of milliseconds, depending on the length of the program. Furthermore, in each scan cycle there is a data exchange with the environment: a PLC has *input points* connected via an interface with a dedicated *input area* of its memory, and the *output area* of the memory is connected via an interface with the *output points* of the PLC. On the input points the PLC receives data from sensors, on the output points the PLC sends data to actuators. Finally, there are some activities of the operating system (self checks, watchdogs etc.) that take place in a scan cycle. The operating system itself is small and stable, which is prerequisite for reliable real-time control. PLC programs are developed and compiled on PCs in special programming environments and can be loaded to the PLC. There are different programming languages collected in a standard [8]. In our application we used Sequential Function Charts (SFC), a graphical language that is related to Petri-Nets, and the program executed in each scan cycle depends on the places that are active at the moment. In this sense SFC provides a meta-structure and the actual instructions of our application are written in Instruction List, an assembly-like language. In these languages it is possible to make use of *timers* which is also a difference to the programming languages we usually deal with.

The scan cycle mechanism makes PLCs suitable for control of continuous processes (tight loop control). However, it has to be guaranteed that the scan cycle length is always below the minimal reaction time that is required by the plant to control the entire system. In this case study the scan cycle time is a few orders of magnitude smaller than what the reaction time has to be. The execution time of a scan cycle is in the range of a few milliseconds. For some applications the timing behaviour in this range is relevant, e.g. for machine control. For our chemical plant it is not relevant: it does not really matter whether a valve closes 10 ms earlier or later. This property is relevant when modelling the whole system. Here, we can model the PLC as if executing "time-continuously", i.e. a scan cycle takes place in zero time. In comparison to the PLC the plant is so "slow" that it cannot distinguish a real PLC with scan cycles form an ideal time-continuous control. For a more detailed discussion of modelling PLCs see [11].

2.3 The Control Program

The goal of this section is to describe our view on the plant and the control program as we used it in an informal way. Its formal derivation and our other verification activities are presented in [12].

In the plant we identified a number of transport processes, such as transport of 4.2l salt solution from container B1 to B3. All possible transport processes, the evaporation process and two cooling process lead to a number of 12 parallel processes. The activities in each process are simply to open some valves, switch on a mixer, pump or heater, and when the process finishes, close and switch off everything again. Each process starts its activities if its *activation conditions* are fulfilled, and is in a wait state otherwise. An active process (state) remains active until its postconditions are fulfilled. Then it gets back in the waiting state. With this approach we have a so called *closed loop control*: the criterion to change a state is not that time proceeded, but an event occurs. The structure of the program is easy to find back in the SFC (Sequential Function Chart) representation in Figure 2.

Control starts in the state "START" and (because the transition condition is "true") immediately distributes to the 12 parallel wait states. In a wait state a process does nothing. If control comes to state Pi, the program attached to state Pi is executed in every scan cycle as long as control remains in Pi. The programs attached to P1, ..., P12 are contained in figure 3 in the so called Instruction List (IL) format. The instructions of IL are assembly-like. Here, we mainly load the constants true or false to the accumulator and write the accumulator value to the variables, e.g., Vi, representing the valves. The *action qualifier* P1 (at the top of each program) indicates that the instructions right to it are only executed

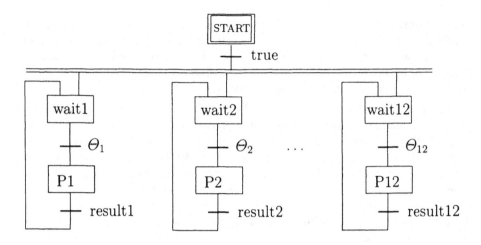

Fig. 2. The control program in Sequential Function Chart

in the first scan cycle when control is here; P0 says that the instructions are only executed in the last scan cycle when control is in this location.

The main complexity of the program is hidden in the activation conditions Θ_i. We assume to have a predicate $Pi.X$ for each step Pi indicating whether control is at the corresponding step or not (these variables are available in PLC programs). The conditions to start a process (i.e. step) are infomally the following:

1. The filling levels of the tanks must allow for, e.g., a transport step: the upper tank must contain enough material, the lower tank must contain enough space, etc. These conditions are encoded in the predicates Φ_i of Figure 4.
2. We do not want a tank to be involved in two processes at a time. E.g., when transferring solution from B4 to B5 there should not be a concurrent transfer from B3 to B4. This requirement can be formulated by conditions on valves: when solution is transferred from B4 to B5 valve V11 must be closed for the duration of the transfer (invariant). These requirements induce a conflict structure on the processes. It is required that control is never at two conflicting processes at the same time. This condition is split into two parts: first, control cannot go to a process if a conflicting process is alraedy active. These conditions are encoded in the predicates Ψ_i of Figure 5. Second, when conflicting processes could get control at the same moment only the one having *priority* gets it. These priorities are fixed, and their priority graph is cycle free. They induce the predicates Θ_i in figure 6.

The execution mechanism of PLCs guarantees a synchronous execution of parallel steps: in each scan cycle each program attached to an active step is executed once. It is this synchronous mechanism that makes the conditions Θ_i to have the intended effect.

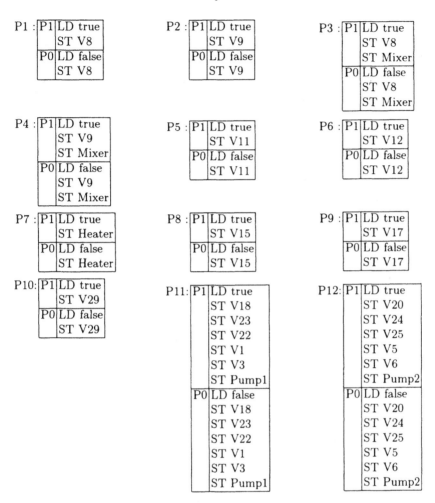

Fig. 3. Instruction List Programs for steps P1. ..., P12

$$\Phi_1 \;\; := \;\; (B1 = \text{sol42C} \lor B1 = \text{sol82C}) \land B3 = \text{empty}$$
$$\Phi_2 \;\; := \;\; (B2 = \text{water28C} \lor B2 = \text{water56C}) \land B3 = \text{empty}$$
$$\Phi_3 \;\; := \;\; (B1 = \text{sol42C} \lor B1 = \text{sol82C}) \land B3 = \text{water28C}$$
$$\Phi_4 \;\; := \;\; (B2 = \text{water28C} \lor B2 = \text{water56C}) \land B3 = \text{sol42C}$$
$$\Phi_5 \;\; := \;\; B3 = \text{sol70C} \land (B4 = \text{empty} \lor B4 = \text{sol70C})$$
$$\Phi_6 \;\; := \;\; (B4 = \text{sol70C} \lor B4 = \text{sol140C}) \land B5 = \text{empty}$$
$$\Phi_7 \;\; := \;\; B5 = \text{sol70C} \land (B6 = \text{empty} \lor B6 = \text{water28C} \lor B6 = \text{water28H})$$
$$\Phi_8 \;\; := \;\; B5 = \text{sol42H} \land (B7 = \text{empty} \lor B7 = \text{sol42C} \lor B7 = \text{sol42H})$$
$$\Phi_9 \;\; := \;\; B7 = \text{sol42H} \lor B7 = \text{sol84H}$$
$$\Phi_{10} \;\; := \;\; B6 = \text{water28H} \lor B6 = \text{water56H}$$
$$\Phi_{11} \;\; := \;\; (B7 = \text{sol42C} \lor B7 = \text{sol84C}) \land (B1 = \text{empty} \lor B1 = \text{sol42C})$$
$$\Phi_{12} \;\; := \;\; (B6 = \text{water28C} \lor B6 = \text{water56C}) \land (B2 = \text{empty} \lor B2 = \text{water28C})$$

Fig. 4. The tank filling conditions

$$
\begin{aligned}
\Psi_1 &:= \Phi_1 \wedge \neg\, P2.X \wedge \neg\, P4.X \wedge \neg\, P5.X \wedge \neg\, P11.X \\
\Psi_2 &:= \Phi_2 \wedge \neg\, P1.X \wedge \neg\, P3.X \wedge \neg\, P5.\,X \wedge \neg\, P12.X \\
\Psi_3 &:= \Phi_3 \wedge \neg\, P2.X \wedge \neg\, P4.X \wedge \neg\, P5.X \wedge \neg\, P11.X \\
\Psi_4 &:= \Phi_4 \wedge \neg\, P1.X \wedge \neg\, P3.X \wedge \neg\, P5.\,X \wedge \neg\, P12.X \\
\Psi_5 &:= \Phi_5 \wedge \neg\, P1.X \wedge \neg\, P2.X \wedge \neg\, P3.X \wedge \neg\, P4.X \wedge \neg\, P6.X \\
\Psi_6 &:= \Phi_6 \wedge \neg\, P5.X \wedge \neg\, P7.X \wedge \neg\, P8.X \\
\Psi_7 &:= \Phi_7 \wedge \neg\, P6.X \wedge \neg\, P8.X \wedge \neg\, P10.X \wedge \neg\, P12.X \\
\Psi_8 &:= \Phi_8 \wedge \neg\, P6.X \wedge \neg\, P7.X \wedge \neg\, P9.X \wedge \neg\, P11.X \\
\Psi_9 &:= \Phi_9 \wedge \neg\, P8.X \wedge \neg\, P11.X \\
\Psi_{10} &:= \Phi_{10} \wedge \neg\, P7.X \wedge \neg\, P12.X \\
\Psi_{11} &:= \Phi_{11} \wedge \neg\, P1.X \wedge \neg\, P3.X \wedge \neg\, P8.X \wedge \neg\, P9.X \\
\Psi_{12} &:= \Phi_{12} \wedge \neg\, P2.X \wedge \neg\, P4.X \wedge \neg\, P7.X \wedge \neg\, P10.X
\end{aligned}
$$

Fig. 5. A process may not start if a conflicting process is active

$$
\begin{aligned}
\Theta_1 &:= \Psi_1 \wedge \neg\, \Psi_5 \\
\Theta_2 &:= \Psi_2 \wedge \neg\, \Psi_1 \wedge \neg\, \Psi_3 \wedge \neg\, \Psi_5 \\
\Theta_3 &:= \Psi_3 \wedge \neg\, \Psi_5 \\
\Theta_4 &:= \Psi_4 \wedge \neg\, \Psi_1 \wedge \neg\, \Psi_3 \wedge \neg\, \Psi_5 \\
\Theta_5 &:= \Psi_5 \wedge \neg\, \Psi_6 \\
\Theta_6 &:= \Psi_6 \wedge \neg\, \Psi_7 \wedge \neg\, \Psi_8 \\
\Theta_7 &:= \Psi_7 \\
\Theta_8 &:= \Psi_8 \wedge \neg\, \Psi_7 \\
\Theta_9 &:= \Psi_9 \wedge \neg\, \Psi_8 \\
\Theta_{10} &:= \Psi_{10} \wedge \neg\, \Psi_7 \\
\Theta_{11} &:= \Psi_{11} \wedge \neg\, \Psi_1 \wedge \neg\, \Psi_3 \wedge \neg\, \Psi_8 \wedge \neg\, \Psi_9 \\
\Theta_{12} &:= \Psi_{12} \wedge \neg\, \Psi_2 \wedge \neg\, \Psi_4 \wedge \neg\, \Psi_7 \wedge \neg\, \Psi_{10}
\end{aligned}
$$

Fig. 6. Of two conflicting processes only the one with priority may get active

3   Verification and Optimization with Spin

This section describes our approach to the verification of the PLC program of Figure 2 and its subsequent optimisation. For the verification we constructed a model of the control program and the plant in Promela, while completely abstracting away from time. We used the model checker Spin to check that all execution sequences of the combined model satisfy the property that "always eventually batches are produced". This implies that under ideal circumstances, in which no material is lost through leakage or evaporation, control is such that new batches will always be produced. The details of the verification procedure are given in section 3.1; the technical conclusions are given in section 4.

To obtain also optimal schedules for the plant, in the sense that the average production time of a batch is minimal, we refined the Promela model by including light-weight real-time features. These sufficed find optimal scheduling sequences as counter-examples to properties stating suboptimal behaviour (cf. [4,14]). This approach is described in more detail in section 3.2, with conclusions in section 4.

3.1   Correctness of the PLC Program

Both the plant as described in section 2.1, and the informal control program description of section 2.3 can be translated into Promela in a straighforward way, the crucial part of the modelling exercise being the real-time properties of the plant in combination with the PLC execution mechanism given in section 2.2. In this case there are two basic principles that allow us to deal with the entire system by essentially abstracting away from time (see also [11] for a more general account in the context of PLCs):

1. The control program works independently of the time that the production steps take. Therefore, in the model each of the production steps P1, ..., P12 may take some unspecified time: if activated (e.g. by opening a valve) it goes to an undefined state that it eventually will leave to reach the final state where the result property holds. By this way of modeling every timing behaviour of the plant is subsumed, including the real one. If we can prove correctness for this general case, then correctness of the special case follows.
2. The excution speed of the control program is much faster than the tolerance of the plant processes, as was already mentioned above. This has two important implications:
   - we can abstract away from the scan cycle time and assume that scan cycles are executed instantaneously.
   - we can assume that the plant is continuously scanned so that state changes are detected without (significant) delay.

In our Promela model of the control program scan cycles are made instantaneous using the **atomic** construct. The model of the combined behaviour of the plant and the control program is obtained by putting the models of the control process and all the plant processes in parallel. Doing this, we must make sure that the continuous execution of the control program does not cause a starvation of the plant processes. This is taken care of by allowing only fair executions in Spin of our Promela model: in each execution no active process may be ignored indefinitely. We must be careful, however, not to lose the other important property, viz. that each state change of the plant is detected "immediately". Our model takes care of this by forcing a control program execution after each potential state change of the plant.

The Promela model of this case study is too big to be part of this paper. The full version can be retrieved from [2]. Here we present two excerpts, one of the plant model and one of the control program model, to illustrate its main features. Figure 7 contains the Promela process that models the transportation of solutions from container B1 to B3. It models the combined behaviour underlying steps S1 and S3.

The model consists of a do-loop that continuously tries to start the transfer of a unit of salt solution from B1 to B3 (corresponding to steps S1 and S3 of the specification). If the right conditions are fulfilled control will enter the body of the loop, and will mark the beginning of the transfer step by instantaneously (using the Promela `atomic` construct) changing the contents of both containers to undefined transitional states. At some later moment it will execute the second part of the body, instantaneously changing the transitional states to the corresponding terminal states, corresponding to the end of the transfer. Here, we have also added an assert statement between these two atomic statements, expressing an invariant that must always hold between the beginning and end of the tranfer step. As this may create a lot of extra states in the verification model this assertion can be removed to improve the performance when checking other properties.

Other observations that may help to understand this Promela model are:

- The `cycle` variable is a global flag that forces the excution of a scan cycle after the execution of each atomic step in the plant (flag is raised at the end of each such atomic step). After the execution of a scan cycle (also modelled as an atomic process, see below) the flag is lowered. Each atomic step in the plant is guarded by the test `cycle==0`.
- The Promela model combines steps in the plant that involve the same set of containers into one process. This reduces the number of processes that must be scheduled fairly.
- The Promela model of the plant models the transportation steps from a "physical" attitude and imposes fewer conditions for a transportation to take place that the formal plant specification in the corresponding steps. E.g. for transportation from B1 to B3 to take place it is only required that B1 is not empty and valve V8 is open.
- To compensate for this all illegal and unwanted states of the plant are explicitly modelled as error states (`error` is defined as `assert(false)`) whose reachability can be checked. This approach gives us more information about the robustness of our controller.

The Promela process that models the control program is listed in Figure 8. This is a straightforward translation of the PLC program of Figure 3.

The do loop of `Control` repeatedly executes an atomic scan cycle, in which the processes P1,...,P12 are scheduled sequentially. To deal with the symmetric subcases of each step (i.e. the disjuncts between brackets in Figure 4) we need a second loop counter j next to the main counter i (because P11 and P12 in fact have 4 subcases P11 is covered by $i \in \{11, 12\}$ and $j \in \{1, 2\}$, and P12 by $i \in \{13, 14\}$ and $j \in \{1, 2\}$). Modulo these small adaptations the `theta(i,j)` correspond to the Θ-predicates of Figure 6, and the `result(i,j)` correspond to analoguous formalisation of result conditions of the PLC program (the uninstantiated result$i$ labels of Figure 2). `PB1(i)` and `PB2(i)` correspond to the code of the P1 part, and the P0 part of the PLC program, respectively. The variables `px[i]` correspond to the Pi.X activity predicates of the program mentioned earlier. Note that at the end of each scan cycle the global flag `cycle` is lowered, as required.

Whereas the assertions in the model served to check on our own understanding the model, the main correctness requirement that "always eventually a new

```
proctype B1toB3()
{   do
    :: atomic{ (cycle==0 && B1!=cempty && v8) ->
                    if
                    :: (B1==sol42C) -> B1=undef1
                    :: (B1==sol84C) -> B1=undef2
                    :: else -> error
                    fi ;
                    if
                    :: (B3==cempty) -> B3=undef1
                    :: (B3==water28C && mix) -> B3=undef2
                    :: else -> error
                    fi ;
                    cycle=1
         } ;
         assert(v8 && (B3!=undef2 || mix)) ;
         atomic{ (cycle==0 && v8) ->
                    if
                    :: (B1==undef1) -> B1=cempty
                    :: (B1==undef2) -> B1=sol42C
                    :: else -> error
                    fi ;
                    if
                    :: (B3==undef1) -> B3=sol42C
                    :: (B3==undef2 && mix) -> B3=sol70C
                    :: else -> error
                    fi ;
                    cycle=1
         }
    od
}
```

Fig. 7. The Promela model of transfer between B1 and B3

```
proctype Control()
{ int i,j ;
    do
    :: atomic{ i=1 ; j=1 ;
            do
            :: (i<15) ->
                if
                :: (theta(i,j) && !px[procnr(i)]) -> PB1(i)
                :: (result(i,j) && px[procnr(i)]) -> PB0(i)
                :: else -> skip
                fi ;
                if
                :: (j==1) -> j=2
                :: (j==2) -> j=1 ; i=i+1
                fi
            :: (i==15) -> goto endcycle
            od ;
            endcycle: cycle=0
         }
    od
}
```

Fig. 8. The Promela model of the control process

batch is produced" was verified using the Spin facilities for model checking LTL formulas. The requirement was formalized as the following LTL property:

$$\Box \Diamond \text{ (B3 == sol70C)} \ \wedge \ \Box \Diamond \text{ (B3 == cempty)} \tag{1}$$

expressing that the contents of container B3 (containing the brine solution that is considered the "production" of the plant) is infinitely often full and infinitely oftem empty (the constant cempty was chosen to be different from the Promela reserved word empty). As these two properties must interleave in each linear execution sequence they are equivalent to the desired requirement.

It turned out to be feasible to run the model checker sequentially on our model initialised with material for 0 up to 8 batches (including the intermediate different possibilities for half batches; 30 runs in total). In order to avoid the explosion of the more than 8100 possible initial configurations that are in principle possible, we considered only configurations filling the plant "from the top", i.e. filling tanks in the order B1,...,B7. The other initializations are reachable from these by normal operation of the plant. As satisfaction of the property that we checked (see below) for our initial configurations implies its satisfaction for all reachable configurations this is sufficient. Using simulations of our model we satisfied ourselves that our model did include the required normal operation steps (here, model checking would run into the same combinatorial explosion).

After initial simulations and model checking runs had been used to remove small (mainly syntactic) mistakes from our model, the model was systematically checked for property (1) for the 30 initializations with different batch volumes described above. No errors were reported, except for initializations with batch volumes 0, 0.5, 7.5 and 8, as should be the case. The model checking was done using Spin version 3.3.7 on a SUN Enterprise E3500-server (6 SPARC cpus with 3.0 GB main memory). The model checking was run in exhaustive state space search mode with fair scheduling. The error states reported unreachable in all runs. The shortest runs were completed in the order of seconds and consumed in the order of 20MB memory; the longest run required in the order of 40 minutes and 100MB.

3.2 Deriving Optimal Schedules

The control schedule of Figure 2 that we have shown to be correct by the procedure sketched in the previous subsection, follows an essentially crude strategy. After each scan cycle it enables *all* non-conflicting processes in the plant whose preconditions it has evaluated to hold true. It is not a priori clear that this strategy would also lead to a plant operation that is optimal in the sense that the average time to produce a batch is minimal.

To determine optimal schedules for the various batch loads of the plant we have refined the models of the previous section as follows:

1. We added a notion of time to the model. To avoid an unnecessary blow-up of the state space due to irrelevant points in time, i.e. times at which nothing interesting can happen, we have borrowed an idea from discrete event simulation, viz. that of *variable time advance procedures* [15].
2. We refined the plant model using the information from Table 1, such that each process in the plant will take precisely the amount of time specified.
3. We refined the model of the control program such that after each scan cycle any non-empty subset of the maximal set of allowed non-conflicting processes determined by the original control program could be enabled.

The search for optimal schedules was then conducted by finding counterexamples for the claim:

$$\Box(\texttt{batches} < \texttt{N}) \tag{2}$$

where `batches` is a global variable that counts the number of times that a brine solution is transferred from B3 to B4. This property is checked for increasing values of N in the context of a given maximal clock value `maxtime`. The assumption is that for `maxtime` large enough such counterexamples will display regular scheduling patterns. Below, we elaborate on each of the above points and the search procedure.

A variable time advance procedure. In real-time discrete event systems events have associated clocks that can be set by the occurrence of other events. An event occurs when its clock expires. Such systems can be simulated by calculating at each event occurrence the point in time at which the *next* event will occur, and then jumping to that point in time. This is known as *variable time advance*.

We wish to apply this idea to our model because it will not litter the global state space with states whose time component is uninteresting, in the sense that there is no process in the plant that begins or ends. As we can only calculate when plant processes will end once they have started, we can only use this time advance procedure if we assume that processes will always be started when others end (or at time 0). It is not difficult to see, however, that we will not lose schedules this way that are strictly faster than what we can obtain using this policy. The informal argument is as follows: assume that a derived scheduling policy can be strictly improved by postponing a given event *e* by some time *t*. Because we are optimising w.r.t. time (and not energy or resource utilisation or the like), the more optimal schedule must exploit this time to start a *conflicting* process (ending a conflicting process would have prevented *e* in the original schedule; any event associated with a non-conflicting process can be executed anyway). Because this process is conflicting it must also finish before *e* occurs. We may therefore assume that in any optimal schedule *e* is excuted when the last preceding conflicting process ends.

The variable time advance procedure is implemented by the Promela process Advance given in Figure 9. The basic idea of Advance is quite simple: when it becomes active it will calculate the next point in time when a plant process will terminate. To do so it uses the global array ptime(i) containing the termination times of the processes i, whose values are calculated as part of the Promela processes modelling the plant, and the global time variable time, which is controlled by Advance. maxstep is a global constant corresponding to the longest possible time step in the model, i.e. the duration of the heating process. All variables related to time are of type short, a unit corresponding to 10 seconds in Table 1 as al its entries are multiples of 10 seconds. Advance will be activated only when the predicate promptcondition holds. This predicate is true if and only if all processses that have been enabled by the control program have indeed become active and none has terminated.

```
proctype Advance()
{ int i ; short minstep ;
    do
    :: atomic{(promptcondition) ->
            minstep=maxstep ; i=1 ;
            do
            :: (i<13) ->
                if
                :: (px[i] && ((ptime(i)-time)<minstep)) ->
                    minstep=(ptime(i)-time)
                :: else -> skip
                fi ;
                i=i+1
            :: (i==13) -> goto step
            od ;
            step: time=time+minstep
    }
    od
}
```

Fig. 9. The Promela model of the time advance process

The refined plant model. The refined model of the plant differs from the original model in the folowing respects:

  − The (atomic) start event of each plant process is used to calculate the termination time of that process.
  − The termination event of each plant process is guarded with the additional condition that the global time time must equal the calculated termination time.
  − The start and termination events include printf statements to record activation and termination times to enable the analysis of simulated executions (of the counterexample trails).

The refined control model. To allow the new model of the control program to enable any nonempty subset of the permissable plant process start events, we have split the loop of the original model of Figure 8, resulting in Figure 10. The first of the two loops scans only for termination conditions of plant processes and executes the corresponding control fragments PB0(i). The second loop subsequently scans the valid preconditions of the plant processes. The corresponding control fragments PB1(i) may or may not be executed. If not, the process number is stored in the local variable last, possibly overwriting a previous value. If the second loop is exited without any processes being active (act is false), then the process with number last is activated.

The idea to retrospectively activate the last plant process that could have been activated to prevent the plant from becoming inactive, cannot be implemented in the original, single control loop. There, plant process terminations occuring after the evaluation of the precondition corresponding to last could invalidate the precondition, rendering subsequent activation impossible.

Both loops of the new version are contained in a new outer loop that monitors the progress of time and will stop control if time exceeds maxtime. This will cause the combined plant and control model to terminate.

Finding optimal schedules. Finding optimal schedules we restricted ourselves to the interesting cases involving initial plant loads of 1 through 7 batches. For our initial experiments we fixed maxtime to be 5000 time units (50,000 s). For each initial load we needed two or three runs to determine the maximal number of batches for which counterexamples could be produced in a very short time (in the order of seconds real time). It turned out that all counterexamples produced contained schedules that rapidly (i.e. within 300 time units) converged to a repeating pattern with a fixed duration.

The initial measurements are collected in Table 2. The interpretation of the columns is as follows:

- load: indicates the number of batches with with the plant is initialised,
- simtime: indicates the the duration (in simulated time units) of the counter-example traces,
- batches: the number of batches produced in that trace,
- states: the number of states visited to produce the trace,
- transitions: the number of transitions visited to produce the trace,
- convergence: the convergence time until periodic behaviour,
- period: period time of periodic behaviour.

A first analysis of Table 2 shows the state space that needs to be searched to produce the counterexamples is very small, and could make one suspicious of the quality of the results that are obtained. Surprisingly enough, five of the measured periods turn out to be optimal schedules! For loads with 1 and 7 batches this can be readily checked by hand by moving a single batch through the plant, or the

```
proctype Control()
{    int i,j,last ; bool precon, postcon ;
     do
     :: (time<maxtime) ->
         atomic{i=1 ; j=1 ;
             do
             :: (i<15) ->
                 postcon=(result(i,j) && px[procnr(i)]) ;
                 if
                 :: postcon -> PB0(i)
                 :: else -> skip
                 fi ;
                 if
                 :: (j==1) -> j=2
                 :: (j==2) -> j=1 ; i=i+1
                 fi
             :: (i==15) -> goto loop2
             od ;
             loop2:
             i=1 ; j=1 ; last=1 ;
             do
             :: (i<15) ->
                 precon=(theta(i,j) && !px[procnr(i)]) ;
                 if
                 :: precon -> PB1(i)
                 :: precon -> last=i
                 :: else -> skip
                 fi ;
                 if
                 :: (j==1) -> j=2
                 :: (j==2) -> j=1 ; i=i+1
                 fi
             :: (i==15) -> goto finish
             od ;
             finish:
             if
             :: (!act) -> PB1(last)
             :: else -> skip
             fi ;
             cycle=0
         }
     :: (time>=maxtime) -> goto endtime
     od ;
     endtime: skip
}
```

Fig. 10. The refined model of the control process

empty space for a batch (the total volume of the plant is 8 batches), respectively, and measuring the total duration of the critical branches of the path.

Initially, we thought that we had made a mistake when we measured the same period of 173 units for loads 2, 3 and 4. Closer analysis of the schedules, however, revealed that this is the result of the fact that the plant has one process that clearly dominates the time consumption during the production of batches, viz. the heating of container B5 (110 time units). Since filling B5, heating it, and emptying B5 must be part of every production cycle, the average production time of a batch must be greater or equal then 35+110+28=173 time units. This makes the schedules underlying the period of 173 for loads 2, 3 and 4 optimal schedules as well.

Table 2. Initial schedule measurements

load	simtime	batches	states	transitions	convergence	period
1	4767	17	1185	1510	56	294
2	4682	28	1916	2450	56	173
3	4972	31	2063	2639	294	173
4	4886	30	2031	2598	208	173
5	3761	20	1449	1866	208	197
6	3885	20	1567	2072	173	195
7	4340	17	1202	1532	173	260

The previous observation made us think that schedules for loads 5 and 6 could be improved upon, as they are in some sense dual to the cases for loads 2 and 3 (moving empty batch space upwards through the plant instead of batches downwards). In fact, inspection of the counterexample for load 6 clearly showed that it could be improved. As increasing the number of batches immediately led to a dramatic increase of the response time for producing counterexamples, we looked for cheaper ways to get feedback more quickly. There are two dimensions that determine the state space to be explored, viz. the depth of the search tree and its branching degree. The first can be made smaller by reducing the value of `maxtime`, the second by exploring fewer scheduling alternatives in the control program.

For the second option we had the original control schedule of Figure 8 at our disposal. This process does not lead to a completely deterministic scheduling, because it may make a difference whether the scan cycle is executed once or more often between plant events. This is because the termination of some processes later in the scan cycle may enable the beginning of other plant processes earlier in the (next) scan cycle. The result therefore stabilises after two scan cycles. Using this much leaner search tree we did in fact find optimal schedules for loads 5 and 6, again with period 173, in a matter of seconds, see Table 3.

Table 3. Measurements for loads 5 and 6 with the original control program

load	simtime	batches	states	transitions	convergence	period
5	3329	20	1380	1761	35	173
6	3467	20	1415	1806	173	173

Also the first option, reducing the search tree by reducing `maxtime`, can be used with success. Reducing the simulated time to 519 time units, we could find an optimal schedule for a system load of 6 producing 3 batches. This option required a more extensive search, however, involving more than 4.5 million states, showing that the optimal schedule here is contained in a part of the tree explored much later than in the previous examples. We did not systematically apply this approach to the other loads.

It must be concluded that the plant can be scheduled in the overall optimal time of 1730 seconds for all loads, except for the extreme loads of 1 and 7. Because of our analysis above, these are not only time optimal but also resource optimal schedules, in the sense that the (expensive) destillation container B5 is in continuous use. From the energy perspective, probably the schedule for load 2 is optimal, as this involves the circulation, heating and cooling of the smallest volume.

4   Conclusions

In this paper we have shown how the Promela/Spin environment can be used to verify and optimize control schedules for a small-size PLC controlled batch plant. The approach in this paper relies quite heavily on the structured design of an initial control program that can be found in [12] and the analysis of formal approaches to PLCs in [11].

It is interesting to see that we succeeded in dealing with this real-time embedded system using standard Promela/Spin. For the verification of the initial control program this was due to a property of the plant, viz. that we could assume instantaneous and immediate scanning of all state changes of the plant. This as a consequence of the tolerance of the plant processes for much slower reaction times than those realised by the PLC control. This makes us conclude that this abstraction can be used for checking non-timed correctness criteria in all process control problems that have this property.

The original task we set ourselves was just to check the correctness of the plant control in the sense that the designed program would in principle always be capable of producing more batches for any reasonable initial load. Having achieved that task we wondered how the model might be used to also look at the optimality of the schedules. As we wanted to treat this in terms of small modifications of the model only, we added time in the form of an explicit time advancing process. This is very close in spirit to the real-time Promela/Spin extension DTSpin [1]. Given the particular properties of the plant, however, viz. that without loss of optimality plant processes can be assumed to start when others terminate, we could do this by only generating those points in time in which plant events could take place. From the schedules that we obtained we can conclude that in this case study this variable time advance procedure reduced the generated state space by approximately a factor of 20.

On the basis of our modified model we could find optimal schedules surprisingly quickly. This is certainly due to the particular characteristics of the given plant, with its very critical heating process. Also, we have been lucky in the sense that the optimal schedules often were found in those parts of the search tree that were explored earlier. Counterexamples were produced so quickly, in fact, that the gain of the factor of 20 by using the time advance procedure seemed immaterial. There is one exception, however, viz. searching the optimal schedule for load 6 using the refined (nondeterministic) Control process. By drastically reducing `maxtime` we obtained an optimal schedule while storing some 4.5 million states. Given the 132 byte state vector, in this case the reduction factor of 20 appears very useful. Although more experiments are certainly needed, we believe that variable time advance procedures can be useful for this kind of application. One way to think of them is as an explicitly programmed analogon of the notion of time regions as in timed automata [3]. Taking advantage of specific properties of systems such as ours an explicit approach can sometimes yield better results.

To apply our technique for finding optimal schedules, viz. by generating counterexamples for claims of suboptimal behaviour, in more general cases, it would be useful to be able to influence the search strategy of the model checker more directly and guide the search first into those parts of the search trees where counterexamples are likely to be found. [5] discusses how branch and bound algorithms could be used for such purposes, especially in the context of model checking for timed automata (UPPAAL [10]). Our results indicate that it can be wortwhile to investigate such guided search methods also for non-real time model checkers like Spin.

Another study of the optimal scheduling for the VHS case study 1 is reported in [13]. Here the problem is analysed using the tools OpenKronos and SMI. It is difficult to compare the results of this approach directly with ours, as they include also the production of the initial loads into their schedules, which we just assume to be present. The more general findings seem to be consistent with ours, however. OpenKronos could be used succesfully to produce optimal schedules for loads of up to 3 batches before falling victim to the state explosion problem. The symbolic model checker SMI produced results 6 batches and more, with a computation time of approximately 17 minutes per batch.

References

1. Dtspin homepage. http://www.win.tue.nl/d̃ragan/DTSpin.html.
2. VHS: Case study 1 sources. http://www.cs.kun.nl/m̃ader/vhs/cs1.html.
3. R. Alur and D.L. Dill. A theory of timed automata. *Th. Computer Science*, (138):183–335, 1994.
4. A. Fehnker. Scheduling a steel plant with timed automata. In *Sixth International Conference on Real-Time Computing Systems and Applications (RTCSA'99)*. IEEE Computer Society Press, 1999.
5. A. Fehnker. Bounding and heuristics in forward reachability algorithms. Technical Report CSI-R0002, University of Nijmegen, Netherlands, February 2000.
6. T.A. Henzinger, P.-H. Ho, and H. Wong-Toi. Hytech: a model checker for hybrid systems. *Software Tools for Technology Transfer*, (1):110–123, 1997.
7. G.J. Holzmann. The model cheker SPIN. *IEEE Trans. on Software Eng.*, 23(5):279–295, May 1997.
8. International Electrotechnical Commission. *IEC International Standard 1131-3, Programmable Controllers, Part 3, Programming Languages*, 1993.
9. S. Kowalewski. Description of case study cs1 "experimental batch plant". http://www-verimag.imag.fr/VHS/main.html, July 1998.
10. K.G. Larsen, P. Petterson, and W. Yi. Uppaal in a nutshell. *Software Tools for Technology Transfer*, (1):134–153, 1997.

11. A. Mader. A classification of PLC models and applications. submitted to WODES, 2000.
12. A. Mader, E. Brinksma, H. Wupper, and N. Bauer.   Design of a plc control program for a batch plant - vhs case study 1. submitted for publication, http://www.cs.kun.nl/~ mader/papers.html, 2000.
13. Peter Niebert and Sergio Yovine.   Computing optimal operation schemes for multi batch operation of chemical plants.   VHS deliverable, May 1999. http://www-verimag.imag.fr/VHS/main.html.
14. Th. Ruys and E. Brinksma. Experience with literate programming in the modelling and validation of systems. In B. Steffen, editor, *Tools and Algorithms for the Construction and Analysis of Systems*, volume 1384 of *Lecture Notes in Computer Science*, pages 393–408. Springer-Verlag, 1998.
15. G.S. Shedler. *Regenerative Stochastic Simulation*. Academic Press, 1993.
16. F.W. Vaandrager and J.H. van Schuppen. *Hybrid Systems: Computation and Control*, volume 1569 of *Lecture Notes in Computer Science*. Springer-Verlag, 1999.
17. S. Yovine. Kronos: a verification tool for real-time systems. *Software Tools for Technology Transfer*, (1):123–134, 1997.

Modeling the ASCB-D Synchronization Algorithm with SPIN: A Case Study

Nicholas Weininger and Darren Cofer

Honeywell Technology Center, Minneapolis MN 55418, USA
{nicholas.weininger,darren.cofer}@honeywell.com

Abstract. In this paper, we describe our application of SPIN [1] to model an algorithm used to synchronize the clocks of modules that provide periodic real-time communication over a network. We used the SPIN model to check certain performance properties of the system; in particular, we were able to verify that the algorithm achieves synchronization within a time bound, even in the presence of certain types of faults. Our results suggest that state space explosion in models of time-dependent systems can be most effectively managed by explicit modeling of time; by imposing determinism on execution orderings, and justifying that determinism in a domain-specific manner; and by splitting up the space of execution sequences according to initial conditions.

1 Introduction

In this paper, we describe our construction of a formal model of the ASCB-D synchronization algorithm using the SPIN model checker. ASCB-D (Avionics Standard Communications Bus, rev. D) is a bus structure designed for real-time, fault-tolerant periodic communications between Honeywell avionics modules. The algorithm we modeled is used to synchronize the clocks of communicating modules to allow periodic transmission. The ASCB-D synchronization algorithm is a particularly good test case for formal methods, for several reasons:

- The algorithm is a good example of a time-dependent, event-driven system. Many safety-critical embedded software systems, particularly real-time systems, are of this type, and so modeling techniques learned in this effort are likely to have wide application.
- The algorithm is sufficiently complex to test the limits of currently available modeling tools. It demands an intelligent and efficient modeling approach: due to the essentially infinite number of timing sequences possible in the system, a naive model would surely be intractable.
- The central performance properties which the algorithm is intended to fulfill are time bounds. For example, the specification states that synchronization must be achieved within 200 milliseconds of initial node startup. It is notoriously difficult to verify that such bounds hold over all possible startup conditions. Furthermore, these bounds must be shown to hold in the presence of numerous hardware faults, some of which are difficult to simulate on actual test hardware.

K. Havelund, J. Penix, and W. Visser (Eds.): SPIN 2000, LNCS 1885, pp. 93–112, 2000.
© Springer-Verlag Berlin Heidelberg 2000

SPIN, in turn, proved to be a particularly good tool for modeling such an algorithm; it allowed us not only to verify timing invariants over the state space of the model, but also to conduct random or guided simulations that shed light on the possible behaviors of the model. The graphical representation of these simulations made debugging the model, and eliciting the causes of invariant violations, much easier. Furthermore, the Promela modeling language allowed us to produce an easy-to-understand model that we later found corresponded remarkably well to the C++ implementation code.

Since the ASCB-D synchronization algorithm contains numerous explicit time constraints, one might reasonably ask why we did not choose a model-checking tool that has time-related primitives as part of its language. We did evaluate one such tool, Kronos [2]. In Kronos, a continuously running clock can be associated with each state in the model, and transition conditions between states can include predicates on clock values. However, Kronos's modeling language, based on an explicit representation of states, made for a much less intuitively obvious representation of the algorithm than we obtained with Promela. The high level of algorithmic complexity, in our judgment, made ease of understanding of the representation an overriding consideration.

Despite that complexity, we were able to integrate almost all of the algorithm's features into the model while keeping the state space small enough to allow exhaustive verification of timing properties. We achieved this, first, by minimizing the number of execution orderings possible in the model, and second, by splitting the space of initial conditions and faults into subspaces.

Although the first versions of our model avoided introducing any explicit representation of time, due to our belief that such representation would add unnecessary state to the system model, we found eventually that an explicit time representation was essential to controlling execution orderings. As we incorporated new features into the model, we learned more about the effects of different kinds of nondeterminism on the state space, and were able to gain steadily deeper insights into the behavior of the real system. Indeed, perhaps the most important general lesson we learned was that an iterative, top-down modeling process is crucial to managing model complexity and maximizing understanding of the system being modeled.

The following sections motivate, describe, and examine the results of the modeling effort. Section 2 describes the algorithm we modeled; terminology from this section is used throughout the rest of the paper. Section 3 gives a history of the model's implementation, from simple original versions to the final version, describing in detail the major structural changes we made along the way. Section 4 discusses the lessons we learned.

Our approach built on our experience with real-time operating system modeling using SPIN [3]. Although SPIN and other model-checking tools have been used to analyze real-time, safety-critical systems [4] [5] [6], we have found few cases in which model checking has been used to verify as complex a real-world system as the synchronization algorithm.

2   Algorithm Overview

The ASCB-D synchronization algorithm is run by each of a number of *NICs*
(Network Interface Cards) which communicate via a series of buses. These NICs
are split into two *sides*, corresponding to the pilot and co-pilot sides of an aircraft.
For each side there are two buses, a primary and a backup bus. Each NIC can
listen to, and transmit messages on, both of the buses on its own side. It can
also listen to, but not transmit on, the primary bus on the other side. From the
viewpoint of a given NIC, other NICs on the same side are called *onside* NICs;
NICs on the other side are *xside* NICs. Likewise, the buses on the NIC's own
side and on the other side are onside and xside buses respectively. The basic
structure of buses and NICs is diagrammed in Figure 1.

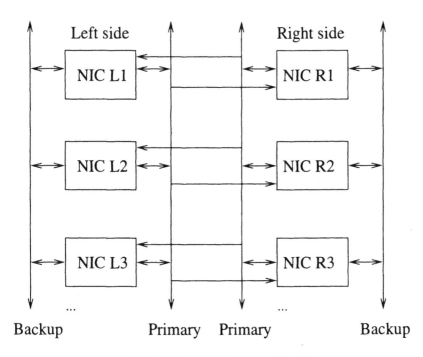

Fig. 1. Structure of the ASCB-D buses.

The operating system running on the NICs produces *frame ticks* every 12.5
msec which trigger threads to run. In order for periodic communication to operate, all NICs' frame ticks must be synchronized within a certain tolerance. The
purpose of the synchronization algorithm is to enable that synchronization to
occur and to be maintained, within certain performance bounds, over a wide
range of faulty and non-faulty system conditions.

The synchronization algorithm works by transmitting special *timing messages* between the NICs. Upon initial startup, these messages are used to designate

the clock of one NIC as a "reference" to which the other NICs synchronize; after synchronization is achieved, the messages are used to maintain synchronization by correcting for the NICs' clock drift relative to each other. The algorithm is required to achieve synchronization within 200 msec of initial startup. It must do this regardless of the order in which the NICs start or the time elapsed between their initial startup.

The synchronization algorithm must also meet the 200 msec deadline in the presence of malfunctions in certain NICs or buses. For example, any one of the NICs might be unable to transmit on, or unable to listen to, one or more of the buses; or it might babble on one of the buses, sending gibberish which prevents other messages from being transmitted; or one of the buses might fail completely at startup, then function again for some period of time, then fail again, then function again, and so on.

3   Implementing the Model

Our implementation of the ASCB-D synchronization algorithm in a SPIN model aimed to begin by modeling the smallest possible nontrivial subset of the specified algorithm, and increase the complexity of the model in stages from there. We therefore began by limiting the scope of the model to the initial "synchronization establishment" phase of the algorithm, omitting the logic dealing with maintaining synchronization after it has been achieved. We initially modeled only two NICs, one on each side. Also, we decided to abstract away from the details of message transmission on the bus, and in general to make the assumption that both transmitting messages and executing code take zero time.

We also initially decided to abstract away from the numerical time calculations used by the algorithm, and to model only the ordering constraints it imposes. This decision was based on a strong initial aversion to the idea of an explicit model of time. Since the state space of a model must be finite, elapsed time has to be measured in discrete units of some fixed granularity; no matter what granularity is chosen, this strategy is prone to errors caused by lumping two different execution orderings together into the same time unit. Furthermore, since time counters can typically take on a very large number of different values, use of time counters can greatly increase the model state space size. The explicit modeling of time eventually turned out to be unavoidable, and we were forced to find ways around its limitations.

3.1   Simplifying Observations

Beyond our initial restrictive assumptions, we can make two observations about the structure of the ASCB-D algorithm which limit the space of execution orderings which we must consider.

First, from a single NIC's standpoint, the algorithm can be viewed as a process driven by the frame tick event. Each time the NIC receives a frame tick, it executes some code and then waits for the next tick. Furthermore, the code executed after a frame tick operates entirely on input data that were collected before the frame tick.

This means that if any two NICs, NIC 1 and NIC 2, are executing at the same time, the execution sequence of NIC 1 cannot depend on anything that NIC 2 does while NIC 1 is executing. Therefore we can construct the model such that iterations of the algorithm on different NICs are atomic with respect to each other. This greatly reduces the size of the state space by eliminating interleavings between different NICs' execution.

Second, the frame ticks of different NICs are related in their periodicity. It is not possible for NIC 1 to go through an arbitrarily large number of frame ticks while NIC 2 gets none, so execution sequences in which this happens should be excluded from the model. In fact, under most circumstances, NIC 1 can only have one frame tick for each tick of NIC 2, and vice versa.

The key phrase here, however, is "under most circumstances." Because frames on different NICs *can* be of different lengths during the initial establishment of synchronization, there are legitimate execution orderings in which NIC 1 gets two ticks to NIC 2's one. The need to include these orderings in the model, without including unrealistic n-to-1 orderings, was the key factor that eventually drove us to implement an explicit numerical representation of time.

3.2 Structure of the Two-NIC Model

In our first and simplest model, the two NIC processes wait for ticks provided by a "time" process; these ticks are communicated through blocking, or rendezvous, channels. When a NIC receives a frame tick event, it queries a buffer process which gives it the contents of the timing messages received in the previous frame. The NIC executes the algorithm logic appropriately, based on the messages received from the buffer process. It then tells the buffer process, again using a rendezvous channel, what (if any) timing message to send in the coming frame. The communications occurring among the processes are diagrammed in Figure 2.

The NIC processes' code is enclosed in atomic statements specifying that they are not to be interleaved with each other. Because the buffer processes are distinct from the NIC processes, however, their message transmissions may be interleaved with NIC executions. We separated buffers from NICs in order to model execution orderings in which messages are sent after a frame tick, and to prevent deadlocks which could occur if each NIC process waited for the other to send a message.

However, in the two-NIC model, the separate buffer processes did not solve the deadlock problem, but only pushed it one step further out. The deadlock sequence instead became one in which NIC 1 was waiting to send to Buffer 1, which was waiting to send to Buffer 2, which was waiting to send to Buffer 1 (and likewise NIC 2 was waiting to send to Buffer 2). Also, introducing separate buffers led to too many spurious execution orderings in which a message was sent to a buffer at the frame tick, but then not sent on to the other NIC until after that NIC had undergone several frame ticks.

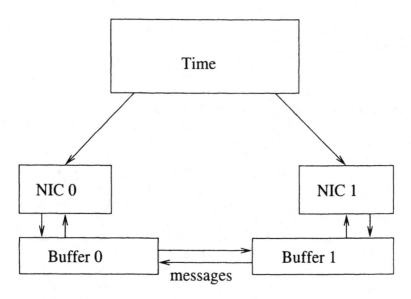

Fig. 2. Processes in the first two-NIC version of our model.

A solution to this problem is to have NICs modify global data structures in order to send messages, rather than making them communicate with separate buffer processes. This approach eliminates deadlocks, since there is no inter-process synchronization mechanism required. However, it tends to expand the state space, since global data structures are less susceptible to SPIN's compression algorithms.

Despite these limitations, the two-NIC model is useful. The logic modeled is very far from the complexity of the real algorithm, but it nevertheless encodes the basic strategy. The model is also sufficient to encode and verify a key system invariant: that no matter what order the two NICs start up in, they always eventually get in sync. In this model, that invariant can easily be encoded as an LTL property and exhaustively verified. By introducing a counter that is incremented each tick after both NICs have started up, we can also bound the time required for both NICs to get in sync.

An LTL verification, with global data structures instead of buffers, that the NICs are both in sync within 12 frames of starting completes in about 15 seconds and visits 150409 states, reaching a search depth of 31741. (All timing figures are for a 300 Mhz UltraSparc II with 1024 MB of RAM). This result led us to predict that modifications would be needed to keep the state space size tractable with a more complex four-NIC model.

3.3   Expanding the Model to Four NICs

Our initial four-NIC model incorporated the following changes:

- We extended the time process straightforwardly to provide ticks to four NICs. Each time that the time process "ticked," it would allow for one frame tick for each NIC; however, it did not restrict the order of the frame ticks corresponding to its tick. This created problems, as we discuss below.
- SPIN verifies LTL properties by generating verifier processes which run concurrently with the model's processes. This increases the state space size considerably. We replaced the LTL property by a simple assertion within the time process:

```
assert(frames_since_started < 9 || (in_sync[0] && in_sync[1]
&& in_sync[2] && in_sync[3]));
```

This assertion is considerably easier for SPIN to verify. It is checked only once per frame tick, but since the variables tested only change once per frame tick, this is sufficient.
- We reintroduced buffer processes, but with a separation of onside and xside buses. Since each NIC sends messages only on its onside bus, but listens to both onside and xside buses, this prevents the buffer processes from deadlocking. We also introduced logic in the algorithm that differentiates between onside and xside timing messages.

Our changes produced a stubbornly intractable model. Even after making further simplifications (e.g. disallowing all those execution sequences where one NIC started up two or more frames before the others), we estimated (by running supertrace verifications) that the state space size was in the tens of millions, and the search depth exceeded 500000. This goes far beyond the capacity of the hardware available to us.

Furthermore, our initial four-NIC model clearly included execution sequences not possible in the real system, because of the fact that the time process did not control the ordering of the NIC ticks corresponding to its tick. For example, if we number the NICs 0 through 3, we can see that the time process would allow ticks and thus message transmissions to occur in a 3-2-1-0-0-1-2-3-3-2-1-0-0-1-2-3 sequence, which is not possible in the real algorithm. However, imposing a fixed order on NIC ticks goes to the opposite extreme, excluding many orderings which the real algorithm does allow. For instance, if a NIC extends its frame length to "sync up" with the others, there could be two frame ticks from another NIC arriving within that NIC's frame.

3.4   The Time/Environment Process

The problems in the four-NIC model clearly necessitated major changes to the basic model structure. The introduction of an explicit numerical time model, and the combination of that time-modeling capability and the message-transmission capability in the same "environment" process, turned out to be the changes we needed to make the model tractable again.

For our first time model, we chose a granularity of 0.5 msec. This allowed us to capture many of delay times in the algorithm, and to represent most time quantities of interest (e.g. the length of frames) within an unsigned byte, minimizing the total number of bytes that must be added to the state space. We later reduced the time granularity to 1 μsec in order to capture more of the delay times precisely; the sufficiency of a 1 μsec granularity is justified in Section 3.8.

The time/environment process keeps track of the time remaining until the next frame tick of each NIC and the messages received by each NIC in the current frame, as well as the total time elapsed since "time zero." It then sits in a loop executing the following algorithm:

```
while(forever)
{
        pick id such that timeToNextTick[id] is minimal;

        send NIC[id] the contents of its message buffers from
        the last frame;

        wait for NIC[id] to send back the length of its next frame,
        plus the contents of the message it wants to send;

        if that message is not empty, send it to the other
        NICs' buffers;

        add timeToNextTick[id] to timeToNextTick[i] for all i != id;

        add timeToNextTick[id] to total_elapsed_time;

        set timeToNextTick[id] to the length of the next frame
        for NIC[id];
}
```

Observe that the above algorithm transfers the responsibility for determining the length of the next frame to the NIC, allowing the introduction of NIC-specific algorithm logic for determining this length. Also, it encapsulates message transmissions in the time process, eliminating the need for separate buffer processes. Since the time process is now dispatching the NICs one by one, there is now no fear of message transmission deadlocks.

The NIC process can then sit in the following loop:

```
while(forever)
{
        wait for the time process to send the contents of the
        message buffers from last frame;

        process the message buffers appropriately depending
        on the NIC's current state;

        compute the length of the next frame and the contents
        of the timing message to send (if any);

        send these data to the time process;
}
```

The communication structure between NIC and environment processes is diagrammed in Figure 3.

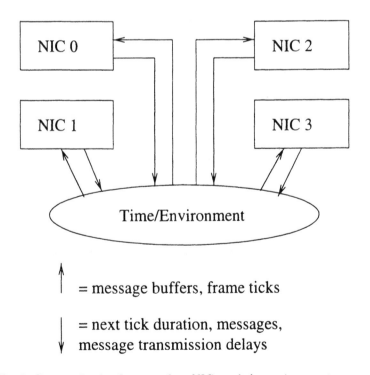

↑ = message buffers, frame ticks

↓ = next tick duration, messages,
message transmission delays

Fig. 3. Communication between four NICs and the environment process.

3.5   Consequences of the Time/Environment Process

A number of fundamental changes in the model follow immediately from this introduction of numerical time. These include:

- The environment process neatly encapsulates all those parts of the system that provide input to the algorithm we wish to model (frame ticks, buffers, and buses), while the NIC process encapsulates that algorithm completely. The interface between the two is simple and localized. As we shall see later, this is perhaps the most powerful advantage of the time/environment model; it allows faults to be injected and complicated hardware interactions to be added with no change required to the NIC code.
- Because the environment process now dispatches ticks one by one, NICs are trivially guaranteed to execute atomically with respect to each other. NICs also execute atomically with respect to the environment process. This simplifies the space of possible execution orderings dramatically; the only order that matters is the order in which ticks and message transmissions occur.
- Complicated tick orderings produced by frames of different lengths are now explicitly and accurately represented in the model.
- We can now easily test for timing-dependent system properties. For instance, we can place an assertion in the environment process, checked before each tick, that states that all NICs should be in sync within 200 msec of the startup time:

```
assert((total_time_elapsed < 400) ||
    (in_sync[0] && in_sync[1] && in_sync[2] && in_sync[3]));
```

- Because the interface between environment and NIC includes all the data that must be shared between them, there is no need for global data structures. This allows SPIN's compression techniques to reduce the memory required to store each state.

The reduction in state space produced by eliminating extraneous buffer processes and impossible interleavings far exceeds the increase produced by having time counter values. However, we still face the problem that letting total time elapsed go off to infinity can expand state space unnecessarily. To solve this problem, we observe that the timing invariants we want to verify in the system provide a natural bound on the maximum "interesting" time value. If we require that all NICs get into sync within 200 msec, then there is no reason to continue searching the state space after $200 + \epsilon$ msec has gone by. Therefore we can put a test in the time process that, when a certain time threshold is passed, places the system in an "acceptance" or valid end state.

Two major issues remain. First, in the above loop description, we stated that the environment process should "choose id such that timeToNextTick[id] is minimal." We did not specify how to choose between two NICs whose ticks are scheduled at the same time: should we make a nondeterministic choice, or put them in some predetermined order? The former will greatly expand the state space; the latter runs the risk of excluding important execution orderings. In our initial model, we opted to choose nondeterministically; further expansion of the model eventually forced us to change to deterministic choice, and to justify that change.

Second, initial startup orderings can now be specified by giving initial times (i.e. times to first tick) for each NIC. This is an important new capability, because we can now ask "what if the NICs started at just these times, and ran from there?" However, it also means that much of the nondeterminism from the original model has now been transferred into the choice of initial starting times. Effectively, we have split the state space of all possible execution sequences into many small slices, one for each possible set of initial conditions. This makes verification runs tractable, but it also forces us to be careful about what we deduce from an exhaustive verification: before we conclude that a timing property always holds in the system, we must verify it for a sufficiently representative set of initial conditions.

We can, of course, introduce nondeterministic choice of initial conditions into the model. Both the initial startup times and the order in which the NICs are assigned to those times can be chosen "randomly." However, choosing randomly over even a small range of possible times quickly expands the state space beyond tractability. One version of our four-NIC model, for example, can verify our 200 msec time-to-sync bound for a fixed set of startup times in about six minutes, storing 3.05 million states and reaching a search depth of 2113. Here we use nondeterministic NIC ordering for that set of startup times, so we are verifying over 24 sets of initial conditions. If we also chose the startup time for each NIC randomly from among a set of five values, we'd have 625 * 24 sets of initial conditions over which to verify; this would likely produce a state space far too large for a single verification run.

3.6   Adding Delayed Message Transmission

Once we model time explicitly, we can introduce into the model the variable delays that occur between frame ticks and timing message transmissions. Since we are modeling the hardware abstractly with the environment process, the approach is simple: let the NIC process send the message delay to the environment process, and have the environment process schedule the message transmission as an event at the appropriate time.

This requires that we add four new events to the list from which the environment must select the "soonest," since each NIC might transmit a timing message each frame. If nondeterministic choices are allowed, this will increase the state space size considerably. We therefore specify that message transmissions always occur after frame ticks. This requires some justification to ensure that real execution orderings are not eliminated from the model; see our more general argument in Section 3.8.

3.7   Adding Multiple Buses and Bus Fault Injection

Once we've made the unified environment process into a single entity distinct
from the NIC processes, it is easy to implement a model of the multiple buses
(primary and backup on each side) that exist in the ASCB-D system. The actual
transmission logic is handled entirely within the environment process. Modeling
multiple buses also provides an opportunity to start injecting bus faults into the
model. Each NIC might be deaf (unable to receive messages) with respect to
the onside primary bus, the onside backup bus, and/or the xside primary bus;
it might also be mute (unable to send messages) on either onside bus.

An example of the relevant logic is shown below. Here what we are seeing
is the code that sends a message from one timing NIC to the other timing NIC
on the same side. The sending NIC transmits the message on both primary and
backup buses; the receiving NIC listens to only one of those buses at a time. In
order for the receiving NIC to get the message successfully, the following must
be true for one of the buses, either primary or backup:

1. The receiving NIC must be listening to that bus.
2. The receiving NIC must not be deaf to that bus.
3. The sending NIC must not be mute to that bus.

If these conditions are satisfied for one of the buses, the message is placed
in the receiving NIC's first onside buffer, and the receiving NIC's second onside
buffer is filled with the former contents of its first onside buffer.

```
if
   ::(listening_primary[(enabled_id + 1) % MAX_NICS] &&
     !onside_primary_deaf[(enabled_id + 1) % MAX_NICS] &&
     !primary_mute[enabled_id]) ||
     (!listening_primary[(enabled_id + 1) % MAX_NICS] &&
     !onside_backup_deaf[(enabled_id + 1) % MAX_NICS] &&
     !backup_mute[enabled_id]) ->
     d_step {
        buffers[(enabled_id + 1) % MAX_NICS].onside_1 =
     buffers[(enabled_id + 1) % MAX_NICS].onside_0;

        buffers[(enabled_id + 1) % MAX_NICS].onside_timestamp[1] =
          buffers[(enabled_id + 1) % MAX_NICS].onside_timestamp[0];

        buffers[(enabled_id + 1) % MAX_NICS].onside_0 =
     last_message[enabled_id];

        buffers[(enabled_id + 1) % MAX_NICS].onside_timestamp[0] =
          timeToNextTick[(enabled_id + 1) % MAX_NICS];
     }
   ::else ->
fi;
```

Now that we have the ability to specify fault conditions, there are several ways to inject faults. The simplest way is to set some combination of fault attributes true at the beginning of the environment process, before any events have occurred; this makes the fault specification part of the initial condition specification. For example, if we wished to model a disabling of the left-side primary bus on powerup, we could set:

```
onside_primary_deaf[0] = true;
onside_primary_deaf[1] = true;
xside_deaf[2] = true;
xside_deaf[3] = true;
```

We might also wish to model a fault that occurs as soon as a certain condition becomes true (e.g. a certain amount of time has elapsed). To do this, we check the condition after every tick or message event processed, and call a fault injection routine when it becomes true.

```
if
::!fault_injected ->
    if
    ::condition ->
        inject_fault();
      fault_injected = true;
    ::else -> skip;
    fi;
::else -> skip;
fi;
```

Furthermore, we might like to model a fault that is injected at a random time; for instance, we might want to model a bus that could malfunction at any time. This can be done as follows:

```
if
::!fault_injected ->
    if
    ::condition ->
        inject_fault();
      fault_injected = true;
    ::true -> skip;
    fi;
::else -> skip;
fi;
```

In these examples, a fault event is something that can occur only once in any execution sequence of the model. However, we might also like to model faults that occur multiple times; a bus, for example, might switch from functional to nonfunctional many times during execution. We can do that by getting rid of the

"fault injected" variable above and modifying the inject_fault() function so that
it "uninjects" a fault already injected. For example, an inject_fault() function
designed to make the onside primary bus malfunction might do this:

```
if
::onside_primary_deaf[0] ->
     onside_primary_deaf[0] = false;
     onside_primary_deaf[1] = false;
     xside_deaf[2] = false;
     xside_deaf[3] = false;
::else ->
     onside_primary_deaf[0] = true;
     onside_primary_deaf[1] = true;
     xside_deaf[2] = true;
     xside_deaf[3] = true;
fi;
```

Note, however, that nondeterministically choosing to execute such a fault
function will greatly increase the state space size, much more than if the fault
can only occur once. We found that introducing a fault condition that could
"flip" arbitrarily many times, as in the above example, made the state space too
large to be tractable for exhaustive verification.

3.8   Adding Sync Phase Behavior to the Model

With the addition of multiple buses and bus faults, our model now incorporated
most of the features of the algorithm relevant to the initial achievement of synchronization. However, most of the complex logic in the ASCB-D synchronization
algorithm, especially logic for detecting and responding to faults, is specific to
NICs in the "already synchronized" state. In principle, adding this logic to the
model should be a relatively simple matter of extending the NIC processes to
do more complex calculations on messages received when in sync; after all, the
environment process cares only about frame ticks and message transmissions,
and not about whether NICs are in sync.

However, our initial experiments quickly showed that the existing environment process, combined with sync phase code, produced intractably large models. The culprit here was clearly the nondeterministic choice between events
that were scheduled to happen at the same time. The defining characteristic of
sync phase is that all NICs in sync should have their frame ticks occur at the
same time. Furthermore, corresponding pairs of NICs (one on each side) transmit timing messages at the same time when in sync; for example, NIC 1 and
NIC 3 transmit at the same time. Thus a four-NIC model in normal operation
with all NICs synced must explore 96 orderings of the NICs' frame ticks and
subsequent sync message transmissions– for *every frame.*

In order to make the model tractable again, we had to impose a deterministic
priority ordering on events scheduled at the same time. Intuitively, we ought to

be able to impose such an ordering and then replicate the execution orderings lost by changing initial conditions. For example, if two timing messages from two different NICs, say A and B, are scheduled at the same time with a certain set of startup times for each NIC, they might come in either order. If we impose an order, say A comes before B, then we can replicate the "lost" execution sequence where B comes before A by making B's startup time slightly earlier, so that the time at which B is scheduled to transmit is strictly earlier than the time A is scheduled to transmit. This works as long as the time increment by which we change B's time is small enough that it will not affect any other event in the system. In effect, we are splitting the old state space into two subspaces, each of which can be covered by a (hopefully) more tractable verification.

We want to formally justify the imposition of an order rule in which:

- when a frame tick and a message transmission are scheduled at the same time, the frame tick comes first.
- when two message transmissions are scheduled at the same time, either could come first.

Our argument can be stated as follows: Suppose there are two events, E_A and E_B, which emanate from NICs A and B respectively, and which in a certain system state S are scheduled at the same time. If such events are nondeterministically ordered, we could have E_A or E_B execute first, leading to consequent states C_1 and C_2. Given an order rule for such events satisfying the above properties, we want to show that there exist states S_A and S_B using that order rule, such that the consequent states of S_A and S_B, C_A and C_B, are equivalent to S_1 and S_2 respectively. Here "equivalent" is defined as "differing only in the values of time counter variables." If this is true, then we've proven that any execution ordering in the nondeterministic model is also in the deterministic model. We proceed by cases.

1. E_A and E_B are both tick events.
   Then $C_1 = C_2$, so we can take $S_A = S_B = S$. This is true because NIC A's processing of its frame tick cannot in itself affect NIC B in any way, and vice versa; furthermore, their resultant timing message transmissions (if any) will be scheduled at just the same times regardless of the order they execute in. Therefore the ordering of E_A and E_B cannot affect future events.
2. E_A is a tick event and E_B is a message transmission, and $A = B$.
   Then we make the assumption that a NIC's message delay time (the time between the occurrence of the frame tick and the transmission of the timing message resulting from that frame tick) is always either:
   - strictly less than the length of its next frame
   - infinity (i.e. the NIC transmits no message from that frame tick)
   This assumption is true for all versions of our model. It implies that if E_A is scheduled at the same time as E_B, then E_B must be the message transmission resulting from E_A. If this is the case, then E_A must execute before E_B, since E_B does not exist until E_A executes. So, whatever order rule we choose, there is only one ordering of these two events.

3. E_A is a tick event and E_B is a message transmission, and $A \neq B$; or E_A and E_B are both message transmissions.

   For the first of these, under our deterministic order rule, we can take $S_A = S$ since E_A is a tick event and so must execute first. For the second, we can again assume that our order rule puts E_A before E_B, so $S_A = S$. In both of these cases, we want to construct S_B by setting an initial state for the system that is the same as the initial state resulting in S, except that the startup time for A is one time unit later.

   If A or B is in sync, then there are only two ways E_A and E_B can occur at the same time:

   a) They are message transmissions from two NICs on different sides. In this case, their order is unimportant, since they go into different buffers for each NIC. We therefore can take $S_B = S$ if this happens.

   b) One of A and B is not in sync with the other. If this is true, we can move the startup time for B back one unit so that E_B occurs before E_A. This works as long as all of the other events before E_B and E_A are not affected by this shift.

   In this case, then, we must ensure that the time granularity is sufficiently small that we can move B's events by one unit without affecting the orderings of those events with respect to others. Once again, the ordering of two ticks is irrelevant, and we can without loss of generality assume that B is out of sync with respect to at least one other NIC. Then it is sufficient to make the time granularity no greater than $D_{min}/(n * F_{max})$, where D_{min} is the shortest nonzero message transmission delay for a non-synced NIC, n is the number of timing NICs, and F_{max} is the maximum number of frames that a NIC can take to get in sync.

   As it happens, for our model, $D_{min} = 500$ μsec, $n = 4$, and $F_{max} \leq 20$. This gives a maximum time granularity of 6.25 μsec, so the 1 μsec time granularity used in the final version of our model is sufficient.

3.9   Including Fault Response Logic

Once we have a tractable model of normal sync operation, we can then model the rules by which NICs detect and respond to bus faults. These situations can be tested in the model by the introduction of appropriate bus faults. For instance, if the left-side primary bus malfunctions after the NICs have achieved sync with a left-side NIC as reference point, the right-side NICs will no longer have a reference point for maintaining synchronization. Eventually one of them will assume the status of a new reference point, and the left-side NICs will have to resynchronize to it.

   In the presence of such resynchronization, verifying the timing invariant becomes more complicated. Now it is clearly not enough to look at the first 200 + ϵ msec of operation. Besides verifying that we initially get into sync within 200 msec, we want to verify that when sync is broken by some fault, resynchronization is achieved within some bounded time. We need two modifications to our time-measurement mechanisms in order to make this work:

1. We introduce, in place of a counter for total elapsed time, a counter variable "total_time_since_resync" that measures the total time since the last resynchronization began. This counter variable is set to 0 at startup, incremented just as the elapsed time variable was before, but reset to 0 upon the occurrence of a resync (i.e. all NICs are in sync, then one NIC drops out of sync).

2. We now cannot cut off the state space when total_time_since_resync passes a certain threshold; there is no obvious bound on how long the system might stay in sync and keep generating new and "interesting" execution orderings. Therefore, when total_time_since_resync exceeds its threshold, instead of jumping to an end state. we set total_time_since_resync back to the threshold value. This prevents it from increasing to infinity, and bounds the state space by causing SPIN to treat two states as the same if they differ only in the amount of time elapsed since resynchronization.

We found that the "in-sync" model remains tractable, given appropriate restrictions. For instance, a verification run for our timing invariant, with a fixed set of startup timings, plus a randomly occurring bus fault, finishes in about five minutes after exploring 2.65 million states, reaching a search depth of 42724. If a totally deterministic startup ordering (all NICs start at the same time) is used, and there is no bus fault, the verification completes in less than a minute, storing 65032 states and reaching a depth of 9472.

Note that this verification run proves less than the same run would have for a version of the model with nondeterministic event ordering. However, this can be remedied by making several verification runs with different sets of startup timings. The important point is that we have kept the model tractable while greatly increasing its complexity, decreasing the time granularity, etc.

3.10   Expanding the Model

As a final test of our model's scalability, we expanded it to include six rather than four NICs. The changes required to the environment process were relatively simple: We added two new events to the event list for the frame ticks of the two new NICs, expanded the appropriate arrays (message buffers, times remaining until the next tick, etc.) to account for the new processes, and expanded the message transmission code to transmit messages to the new NICs.

When we ran an exhaustive verification with six NICs, for a fixed startup ordering and no faults, the run again completed in less than a minute, storing 92951 states and reaching a depth of 13754. This was much less of an increase in state space size than we had feared; it served to confirm the effectiveness of our environment process design, which prohibits interleavings between the user NIC code and the other processes' code. Adding a random bus fault increased the time required to about nine minutes, the state space to 2.65 million states and the search depth to 59050.

However, adding a nondeterministic choice of startup order, with no faults, resulted in the verification using 2 million states, reaching a depth of 14805 and taking 5 minutes to complete. With a randomly occurring bus fault and nondeterministic startup order, the model becomes intractable for exhaustive verification; bitstate verification shows an approximate size of 16 million states. The reason for this is easy to see: whereas with four NICs there were 24 possible startup orderings for any fixed set of startup times, with six NICs there are 720. A six-NIC model, then, is pushing the limits of verifiability with our current computing resources. (The actual system in which the algorithm is used can contain up to 32 NICs, but the NICs are organized into categories such that six are sufficient to represent all possible interactions).

Fortunately, the model's usefulness does not lie only in its capacity for verifying system properties. Our current model, which integrates a large majority of the specified algorithm's features, is a very powerful tool for asking "What if?" questions that are difficult to answer either by manual analysis or by testing on real hardware. If you want to see what happens to the model when, say, the NICs start out at intervals of 0.2 msec, and the right-side primary bus fails 40 msec after the first NIC begins, all you need to do is program in (mostly with #define statements) the appropriate startup timings and fault injection conditions, and run a simulation. The resultant graphical display, although it can be hard to read at first, gives a clear and comprehensive picture of what's happening in the system at any point in time.

4   Lessons Learned

4.1   Efficacy of the Top-Down Modeling Approach

We believe that the success of our modeling effort– our construction of a working, useful, well-understood model of a complex algorithm– demonstrates the efficacy of what we might call a "top-down" modeling process. The crucial characteristic of such a process is that it starts by modeling as small a subset of the system as possible at the highest possible level of abstraction, and builds on that small model in stages, gradually decreasing the level of abstraction and increasing the number of features included. This approach may seem to involve a lot of extra work, but in fact it reduces the model construction time required significantly; most of our model was built by one person with about 1.5 man-months of effort.

There are several reasons why the top-down approach works well. It avoids the conceptual difficulty of trying to comprehend and model a lot of unfamiliar things at the same time; the modelers' understanding of the system is built up in stages as the model itself is built. Because the top-down approach starts with a highly abstracted model and decreases the level of abstraction as time goes on, it facilitates high-level thinking and prevents too much focus on the trees at the expense of the forest. The approach drives the model structure naturally toward modularity and clear separation of functions, leading to an easier-to-understand model. Furthermore, even partial models can provide important insights into a complex specification, and can form the basis for thinking about features of the system that are not yet modeled.

4.2   Modeling Time-Dependent Systems

The ASCB-D modeling effort also taught us quite a bit about modeling systems whose central properties are based on time. Modeling these systems with a purely order-based model introduces large numbers of execution interleavings which do not exist in the real system and which produce spurious violations of safety properties. Furthermore, performance requirements for these algorithms are often expressed in terms of time, so you need a numerical time model to verify them.

Modeling time with an event queue seems to be a feasible, conceptually simple method for event-driven algorithms. However, it requires that careful thought be given to nondeterminism in simultaneously scheduled events. Some restrictions on nondeterminism may have to be justified by algorithm-specific system properties, as we justified the restrictions on event ordering.

4.3   Controlling Model State Space Size

Finally, our experience taught us that controlling nondeterminism and interleavings of concurrent processes is the overriding factor in managing the state space of a model– far more important than limiting the number or size of variables used, reducing the total number of processes in the model, etc. It is useful to assign a single process to be the manager of interleavings, so that other processes can model the desired algorithms in a way that is close to how they would be implemented in the real system. The construction of this process is likely to be less susceptible to automation than the modeling of the algorithm itself, since the structure of this "environment" depends on domain-specific properties of the hardware events that drive the algorithm.

One of the most effective tactics for controlling nondeterminism is using fixed initial condition settings to split the state space of all possible system conditions into numerous subspaces. When attempting to verify an invariant with such a model, it is always necessary to qualify the verification result by noting the set of initial conditions over which the verification was performed. Complex, time-dependent systems are likely to have a space of initial conditions large enough that the system cannot be verified over the whole space in a single run; therefore small subsets of the initial condition space must be chosen intelligently as subjects for verification. The formulation of a small set of initial conditions that are in some sense representative of all the possible ones is a difficult and domain-specific problem, which we have yet to address for the ASCB-D synchronization algorithm.

References

1. G. Holzmann. The SPIN Model Checker. *IEEE Transactions on Software Engineering*, vol. 23, no. 5, May 1997, pp. 279-295.
2. S. Yovine. "Kronos: A verification tool for real-time systems." In *International Journal of Software Tools for Technology Transfer*, vol. 1, no. 1/2, Oct. 1997.

3. J. Penix, W. Visser, E. Engstrom, A. Larson, and N. Weininger. Verification of time partitioning in the deos scheduler kernel. In *Proceedings of the 22nd International Conference on Software Engineering*. ACM Press, June 2000.
4. A. Cimatti, F. Giunchiglia, G. Mongardi, D. Romano, F. Torielli, and P. Traverso. Model Checking Safety Critical Software with SPIN: an Application to a Railway Interlocking System. Presented at SPIN97, the Third SPIN Workshop, April 1997 (online proceedings at http://netlib.bell-labs.com/netlib/spin/ws97/papers.html).
5. K. Havelund, M. Lowry, and J. Penix. Formal Analysis of a Space Craft Controller using SPIN. Presented at SPIN98, the 4th International SPIN Workshop, November 1998 (online proceedings at http://netlib.bell-labs.com/netlib/spin/ws98/program.html).
6. S. Vestal. Modeling and verification of real-time software using extended linear hybrid automata. To appear at Lfm2000, June 2000 (see http://atb-www.larc.nasa.gov/fm/Lfm2000/).

Bebop: A Symbolic Model Checker for Boolean Programs

Thomas Ball and Sriram K. Rajamani

Software Productivity Tools
Microsoft Research
http://www.research.microsoft.com/slam/

Abstract. We present the design, implementation and empirical evaluation of Bebop—a symbolic model checker for boolean programs. Bebop represents control flow explicitly, and sets of states implicitly using BDDs. By harnessing the inherent modularity in procedural abstraction and exploiting the locality of variable scoping, Bebop is able to model check boolean programs with several thousand lines of code, hundreds of procedures, and several thousand variables in a few minutes.

1 Introduction

Boolean programs are programs with the usual control-flow constructs of an imperative language such as C but in which all variables have boolean type. Boolean programs contain procedures with call-by-value parameter passing and recursion, and a restricted form of control nondeterminism.

Boolean programs are an interesting subject of study for a number of reasons. First, because the amount of storage a boolean program can access at any point is finite, questions of reachability and termination (which are undecidable in general) are decidable for boolean programs.[1] Second, as boolean programs contain the control-flow constructs of C, they form a natural target for investigating model checking of software. Boolean programs can be thought of as an abstract representation of C programs that explicitly captures correlations between data and control, in which boolean variables can represent arbitrary predicates over the unbounded state of a C program. As a result, boolean programs are useful for reasoning about temporal properties of software, which depend on such correlations.

We have created a model checker for boolean programs called Bebop. Given a boolean program B and a statement s in B, Bebop determines if s is reachable in B (informally stated, s is reachable in B if there is some initial state such that if B starts execution from this state then s eventually executes). If statement s is reachable, then Bebop produces a shortest trace leading to s (that possibly includes loops and crosses procedure boundaries).

---

[1] Boolean programs are equivalent in power to push-down automaton, which accept context-free languages.

K. Havelund, J. Penix, and W. Visser (Eds.): SPIN 2000, LNCS 1885, pp. 113–130, 2000.
© Springer-Verlag Berlin Heidelberg 2000

```
        decl g;

        main()
        begin
          decl h;
[6]       h := !g;
[7]       A(g,h);
[8]       skip;
[9]       A(g,h);
[10]      skip;
[11]      if (g) then
[12] R:   skip;
          else
[14]        skip;
          fi
        end


        A(a1,a2)
        begin
[20]      if (a1) then
[21]        A(a2,a1);
[22]        skip;
          else
[24]        g := a2;
          fi
        end
```

```
bebop v1.0: (c) Microsoft Corporation.
Done creating bdd variables
Done building transition relations

Label R reachable by following path:

Line 12          State g=1 h=0
Line 11          State g=1 h=0
Line 10          State g=1 h=0
   Line 22       State g=1 a1=1 a2=0
      Line 24 State g=1 a1=0 a2=1
      Line 20 State g=1 a1=0 a2=1
   Line 21       State g=1 a1=1 a2=0
   Line 20       State g=1 a1=1 a2=0
Line 9           State g=1 h=0
Line 8           State g=1 h=0
   Line 22       State g=1 a1=1 a2=0
      Line 24 State g=1 a1=0 a2=1
      Line 20 State g=1 a1=0 a2=1
   Line 21       State g=1 a1=1 a2=0
   Line 20       State g=1 a1=1 a2=0
Line 7           State g=1 h=0
Line 6           State g=1
```

Fig. 1. The **skip** statement labelled R is reachable in this boolean program, as shown by the output of the Bebop model checker.

Example. Figure 1 presents a boolean program with two procedures (main and a recursive procedure A). In this program, there is one global variable g. Procedure main has a local variable h which is assigned the complement of g. Procedure A has two parameters. The question is: is label R reachable? The answer is yes, as shown by the output of Bebop on the right. The tool finds that R is reachable and gives a shortest trace (in reverse execution order) from R to the first line of main (line 6). The indentation of a line indicates the depth of the call stack at that point in the trace. Furthermore, for each line in the trace, Bebop outputs the state of the variables (in scope) just before the line. The trace shows that in order to reach label R, by this trace of lines, the value of g initially must be 1.[2] Furthermore, the trace shows that the two calls that main makes to procedure

---

[2] Note that g is left unconstrained in the initial state of the program. If a variable's value is unconstrained in a particular trace then Bebop does not output it. Thus, it is impossible for g to be initially 0 and to follow the same trace. In fact, for this example, label R is not reachable if g initially is 0.

A do not change the value of g. We re-emphasize that this is a shortest trace witnessing the reachability of label R.

Contributions. We have adapted the interprocedural dataflow analysis algorithm of Reps, Horwitz and Sagiv (RHS) [RHS95,RHS96] to decide the reachability status of a statement in a boolean program. A core idea of the RHS algorithm is to efficiently compute "summaries" that record the input/output behavior of a procedure. Once a summary $\langle I, O \rangle$ has been computed for a procedure **pr**, it is not necessary to reanalyze the body of **pr** if input context I arises at another call to **pr**. Instead, the summary for **pr** is consulted and the corresponding output context O is used. We use Binary Decisions Diagrams (BDDs) to symbolically represent these summaries, which are binary relationships between sets of states.

In the program of Figure 1, our algorithm computes the summary $s = \langle \{g = 1, h = 0\}, \{g' = 1, h' = 0\} \rangle$ when procedure A is first called (at line 7) with the state $\{g = 1, h = 0\}$. This summary will be "installed" at all calls to A (in particular, the call to A at line 9). Thus, when the state $I = \{g = 1, h = 0\}$ propagates to the call at line 9, the algorithm finds that the summary s matches and will use it to "jump over" the call to A rather than descending into A to analyze it again.

A key point about **Bebop** that distinguishes it from other model checkers is that it exploits the locality of variable scopes in a program. The time and space complexity of our algorithm is $O(E \times 2^k)$ where E is the number of edges in the interprocedural control-flow graph of the boolean program[3] and k is the maximal number of variables *in scope* at any program point in the program. In the example program of Figure 1 there are a total of 4 variables (global g, local h, and formals $a1$ and $a2$). However, at any statement, at most three variables are in scope (in **main**, g and h; in A, g, $a1$, and $a2$).

So, for a program with g global variables, and a maximum of l local variables in any procedure, the running time is $O(E \times 2^{g+l})$. If the number of variables in scope is held constant then the running time of **Bebop** grows as function of the number of statements in the program (and not the total number of variables). As a result, we have been able to model check boolean programs with several thousand lines of code, and several thousand variables in a few minutes (the largest example we report in Section 4 has 2401 variables).

A second major idea in **Bebop** is to use an explicit control-flow graph representation rather than encode the control flow of a boolean program using BDDs. This implementation decision is an important one, as it allows us to optimize the model checking algorithm using well-known techniques from compiler optimization. We explain two such techniuqes —live ranges and modication/reference analysis— to reduce the number of variables in support of the BDDs that represent the reachable states at a program point.

Overview. Section 2 presents the syntax and semantics of boolean programs. Section 3 describes our adaption of the RHS algorithm to use BDDs to solve the reachability problem for boolean programs. Section 4 evaluates the performance

---

[3] E is linear in the number of statements in the boolean program.

Syntax	Description
prog ::= *decl* * *proc* *	A program is a list of global variable declarations followed by a list of procedure definitions
decl ::= **decl** *id* + ;	Declaration of variables
id ::= [**a-zA-Z_**] [**a-zA-Z0-9_**] *	An identifier can be a regular C-style identifier
	{ *string* }	or a string of characters between '{' and '}'
proc ::= *id* (*id* *) **begin** *decl* * *sseq* **end**	Procedure definition
sseq ::= *lstmt* +	Sequence of statements
lstmt ::= *stmt*	
	id : *stmt*	Labelled statement
stmt ::= **skip** ;	
	print (*expr* +) ;	
	goto *id* ;	
	return ;	
	id + := *expr* + ;	Parallel assignment
	if (*decider*) **then** *sseq* **else** *sseq* **fi**	Conditional statement
	while (*decider*) **do** *sseq* **od**	Iteration statement
	assert (*decider*) ;	Assert statement
	id (*expr* *) ;	Procedure call
decider ::= ?	Non-deterministic choice
	expr	
expr ::= *expr binop expr*	
	! *expr*	Negation
	(*expr*)	
	id	
	const	
binop ::= '|'	'&'	'∧'	'='	'!='	'⇒'	Logical connectives
const ::= **0**	**1**	False/True

Fig. 2. The syntax of boolean programs.

of Bebop. Section 5 reviews related work and Section 6 looks towards future work.

2   Boolean Programs

2.1   Syntax

Figure 2 presents the syntax of boolean programs. We will comment on noteworthy aspects of it here. Boolean variables are either global (if they are declared outside the scope of a procedure) or local (if they are declared inside the scope of a procedure). Since there is only one type in the boolean programming language, variable declarations need not specify a type. Variables are statically scoped, as in C. A variable identifier is either a C-style identifer or an arbitrary string between the characters "{" and "}". The latter form is useful for creating boolean variables with names denoting predicates in another language (such as {*p==*q}).

There are two constants in the language: 0 (false) and 1 (true). Expressions are built in the usual way from these constants, variables and the standard logical connectives.

The statement sub-language (*stmt*) is very similar to that of C, with a few exceptions. Statements may be labelled, as in C. A parallel assignment statement allows the simultaneous assignment of a set of values to a set of variables. Procedure calls use call-by-value parameter passing.[4] There are three statements that can affect the control flow of a program: **if**, **while** and **assert**. Note that the predicate of these three statements is a *decider*, which can be used to model non-determinism. A *decider* is either a boolean expression which evaluates (deterministically) to 0 or 1, or "?", which evaluates to 0 or 1 non-deterministically.

2.2 Statements, Variables, and Scope

The term *statement* denotes an instance that can be derived from the nonterminal *stmt* (see Figure 2). Let B be a boolean program with n statements and p procedures. We assign a unique *index* to each statement in B in the range $1 \ldots n$ and a unique index to each procedure in B in the range $n + 1 \ldots n + p$. Let s_i denote the statement with index i.

To simplify presentation of the semantics, we assume that variable names and statement labels are globally unique in B. Let $V(B)$ be the set of all variables in B. Let $Globals(B)$ be the set of global variables of B. Let $Formals_B(i)$ be the set of formal parameters of the procedure that contains s_i. Let $Locals_B(i)$ be the set of local variables and formal parameters of the procedure that contains s_i. For all i, $1 \leq i \leq n$, $Formals_B(i) \subseteq Locals_B(i)$. Let $InScope_B(i)$ denote the set of all variables of B whose scope includes s_i. For all i, $1 \leq i \leq n$, $InScope_B(i) = Locals_B(i) \cup Globals(B)$.

2.3 The Control-Flow Graph

This section defines the control-flow graph of a boolean program. Since boolean programs contain arbitrary intra-procedural control flow (via the **goto**), it is useful to present the semantics of boolean programs in terms of their control-flow graph rather than their syntax. To make the presentation of the control-flow graph simpler, we make the minor syntactic restriction that every call c to a procedure **pr** in a boolean program is immediately followed by a skip statement **skip**$_c$.

The control-flow graph of a boolean program B is a directed graph $G_B = (V_B, Succ_B)$ with set of vertices $V_B = \{1, 2, \ldots, n+p+1\}$ and successor function

---

[4] Boolean programs support return values from procedures, but to simplify the technical presentation we have omitted their description here. A return value of a procedure can be modelled with a single global variable, where the global variable is assigned immediately preceding a return and copied immediately after the return into the local state of the calling procedure.

$Succ_B : V_B \to 2^{V_B}$. The set V_B contains one vertex for each statement in B (vertices $1 \ldots n$) and one vertex $Exit_{\mathbf{pr}}$ for every procedure $\mathbf{pr}$ in B (vertices $n + 1 \ldots n + p$). In addition, V_B contains a vertex $Err = n + p + 1$ which is used to model the failure of an **assert** statement. For any procedure $\mathbf{pr}$ in B, let $First_B(\mathbf{pr})$ be the index of the first statement in $\mathbf{pr}$. For any vertex $v \in V_B - \{Err\}$, let $ProcOf_B(v)$ be the index of the procedure containing v.

The successor function $Succ_B$ is defined in terms of the function $Next_B :$ $\{1, 2, \ldots, n\} \to \{1, 2, \ldots, n + p\}$ which maps statement indices to their lexical successor if one exists, or to the exit node of the containing procedure otherwise. $Next_B(i)$ has a recursive definition based on the syntax tree of B (see Figure 2). In this tree, each statement has an $sseq$ node as its parent. The sequence of statements derived from the $sseq$ parent of statement s_i is called the *containing sequence* of s_i. If s_i is not the last statement in its containing sequence then $Next_B(i)$ is the index of the statement immediately following s_i in this sequence. Otherwise, let a be the closest ancestor of s_i in the syntax tree such that (1) a is a *stmt* node, and (2) a is not the last statement in a's containing sequence. If such a node a exists, then $Next_B(i)$ is the index of the statement immediately following a in its containing sequence. Otherwise, $Next_B(s_i) = Exit_{\mathbf{pr}}$, where $\mathbf{pr} = ProcOf_B(i)$.

If s_j is a procedure call, we define $ReturnPt_B(j) = Next_B(j)$ (which is guaranteed to be a **skip** statement because of the syntactic restriction we previously placed on boolean programs).

We now define $Succ_B$ using $Next_B$ and $ReturnPt_B$. For $1 \le i \le n$, the value of $Succ_B(i)$ depends on the statement s_i, as follows:

- If s_i is "**goto** L" then $Succ_B(i) = \{j\}$, where s_j is the statement labelled L.
- If s_i is a parallel assignment, **skip** or **print** statement then $Succ_B(i) = \{Next_B(i)\}$.
- If s_i is a **return** statement then $Succ_B(i) = \{Exit_{\mathbf{pr}}\}$, where $\mathbf{pr} = ProcOf_B(i)$.
- If s_i is an **if** statement then $Succ_B(v) = \{Tsucc_B(i), Fsucc_B(i)\}$, where $Tsucc_B(i)$ is the index of the first statement in the **then** branch of the **if** and $Fsucc_B(i)$ is the index of the first statement in the **else** branch of the **if**.
- If s_i is a **while** statement then $Succ_B(i) = \{Tsucc_B(i), Fsucc_B(i)\}$, where $Tsucc_B(i)$ is the first statement in the body of the **while** loop and $Fsucc_B(i) = Next_B(i)$.
- If s_i is an **assert** statement then $Succ_B(i) = \{Tsucc_B(i), Fsucc_B(i)\}$, where $Tsucc_B(i) = Next_B(i)$ and $Fsucc_B(i) = n + p + 1$ (the Err vertex).
- If s_i is a procedure call to procedure $\mathbf{pr}$ then $Succ_B(i) = First_B(\mathbf{pr})$.

We now define $Succ_B(i)$ for $n + 1 \le i \le n + p$ (that is, for the $Exit$ vertices associated with the p procedures of B). Given exit vertex $Exit_{\mathbf{pr}}$ for some procedure $\mathbf{pr}$, we have

$$Succ_B(Exit_{\mathbf{pr}}) = \{ReturnPt_B(j) \mid \text{statement } s_j \text{ is a call to } \mathbf{pr} \}$$

Finally, $Succ_B(Err) = \{\}$. That is, the vertex Err has no successors.

The control-flow graph of a boolean program can be constructed in time and space linear $n + p$, the number of statements and procedures in the program.

2.4   A Transition System for Boolean Programs

For a set $V \subseteq V(B)$, a *valuation* Ω to V is a function that associates every boolean variable in V with a boolean value. Ω can be extended to expressions over V (see *expr* in Figure 2) in the usual way. For example, if $V = \{x, y\}$, and $\Omega = \{(x, 1), (y, 0)\}$ then $\Omega(x|y) = 1$. For any function $f : D \to R$, $d \in D$, $r \in R$, $f[d/r] : D \to R$ is defined as $f[d/r](d') = r$ if $d = d'$, and $f(d')$ otherwise. For example, if $V = \{x, y\}$, and $\Omega = \{(x, 1), (y, 0)\}$ then $\Omega[x/0] = \{(x, 0), (y, 0)\}$.

A *state* η of B is a pair $\langle i, \Omega \rangle$, where $i \in V_B$ and Ω is a valuation to the variables in $InScope_B(i)$. $States(B)$ is the set of all states of B. Intuitively, a state contains the program counter (i) and values to all the variables visible at that point (Ω). Note that our definition of state is different from the conventional notion of a program state, which includes a call stack. The projection operator Γ maps a state to its vertex: $\Gamma(\langle i, \Omega \rangle) = i$. We can extend Γ to operate on sequences of states in the usual way.

We define a set $\Sigma(B)$ of terminals:

$$\Sigma(B) = \{\sigma\} \cup \{ \langle \mathbf{call}, i, \Delta \rangle, \langle \mathbf{ret}, i, \Delta \rangle \mid \exists j \in V_B, s_j \text{ is a procedure call,}$$
$$i = ReturnPt_B(j), \text{ and}$$
$$\Delta \text{ is a valuation to } Locals_B(j)\}$$

It is clear that $\Sigma(B)$ is finite since all variables in B are boolean variables. Terminals are either σ, which is a place holder, or triples that are introduced whenever there is a procedure call in B. The first component of the triple is either **call** or **ret**, corresponding to the actions of a call to and return from that procedure, the second is the return point of the call, and the third component keeps track of values of local variables of the calling procedure at the time of the call.

We use $\eta_1 \overset{\alpha}{\to}_B \eta_2$, to denote that B can make an α-labeled transition from state η_1 to state η_2. Formally, $\eta_1 \overset{\alpha}{\to}_B \eta_2$ holds if $\eta_1 = \langle i_1, \Omega_1 \rangle \in States(B)$, $\eta_2 = \langle i_2, \Omega_2 \rangle \in States(B)$, and $\alpha \in \Sigma(B)$, where the conditions on η_1, η_2 and α for each statement construct are shown in Table 1. We explain the table below:

- The transitions for **skip**, **print**, **goto** and **return** are the same. All these statements have exactly one control-flow successor. For vertices v such that $Succ_B(v) = \{w\}$, we define $sSucc_B(v) = w$. Each statement passes control to its single successor $sSucc_B(i_1)$ and does not change the state of the program.
- The transition for parallel assignment again passes control to the sole successor of the statement and the state changes in the expected manner.
- The transitions for **if**, **while** and **assert** statements are identical. If the value of the decider d associated with the statement is ? then the successor is chosen non-deterministically from the set $Succ_B(i_1)$. Otherwise, d is a boolean expression and evaluated in the current state to determine the successor.
- The transition for a call statement s_{i_1} contains the α label

$$\langle \mathbf{call}, ReturnPt_B(i_1), \Delta \rangle$$

Table 1. Conditions on the state transitions $\langle i_1, \Omega_1 \rangle \xrightarrow{\alpha}_B \langle i_2, \Omega_2 \rangle$, for each vertex type of i_1. See the text for a full explanation.

i_1	α	i_2	Ω_2
skip print goto return	$\alpha = \sigma$	$i_2 = sSucc_B(i_1)$	$\Omega_2 = \Omega_1$
$x_1, \ldots, x_k :=$ $e_1, \ldots, e_k$	$\alpha = \sigma$	$i_2 = sSucc_B(i_1)$	$\Omega_2 = \Omega_1[x_1/\Omega_1(e_1))]$ $\cdots [x_k/\Omega_1(e_k)]$

if(d)
while(d)
assert(d)
	$\alpha = \sigma$	if $d = ?$
		$i_2 \in Succ_B(i_1)$
		if $\Omega_1(d) = 1$
		$i_2 = Tsucc_B(i_1)$
		if $\Omega_1(d) = 0$
		$i_2 = Fsucc_B(i_1)$
			$\Omega_2 = \Omega_1$

pr($e_1, \ldots, e_k$)	$\alpha = \langle \mathbf{call}, ReturnPt_B(i_1), \Delta \rangle,$ $\Delta(x) = \Omega_1(x), \forall x \in Locals_B(i_1)$	$i_2 = First_B(\mathbf{pr})$	$\Omega_2(x_i) = \Omega_1(e_i),$ $\forall x_i \in Formals_B(i_2)$ $\Omega_2(g) = \Omega_1(g),$ $\forall g \in Globals(B)$
$Exit_{\mathbf{pr}}$	$\alpha = \langle \mathbf{ret}, i_2, \Delta \rangle$	$i_2 \in Succ_B(i_1)$	$\Omega_2(g) = \Omega_1(g),$ $\forall g \in Globals(B)$ $\Omega_2(x) = \Delta(x),$ $\forall x \in Locals_B(i_2)$

where Δ records the values of the local variables at i_1' from the state Ω_1. The next state, Ω_2 gives new values to the formal parameters of the called procedure based on the values of the corresponding actual arguments in state Ω_1. Furthermore, Ω_2 is constrained to be the same as Ω_1 on the global variables.

- Finally, the transition for an exit vertex $i_1 = Exit_{\mathbf{pr}}$ has $\alpha = \langle \mathbf{ret}, i_2, \Delta \rangle$, where i_2 must be a successor of i_1. The output state Ω_2 is constrained as follows: Ω_2 must agree with Ω_1 on all global variables; Ω_2 must agree with Δ on the local variables in scope at i_2.

2.5   Trace Semantics

We now are in a position to give a trace semantics to boolean programs based on a context-free grammar $\mathcal{G}(B)$ over the alphabet $\Sigma(B)$ that specifies the legal sequences of calls and returns that a boolean program B may make.

A context-free grammar $\mathcal{G}$ is a 4-tuple $\langle N, T, R, S \rangle$, where N is a set of nonterminals, T is a set of terminals, R is a set of production rules and $S \in N$ is a start symbol. For each program B, we define a grammar $\mathcal{G}(B) = \langle \{S, M\}, \Sigma(B), Rules(B), S \rangle$, where $Rules(B)$ is defined by the productions of Table 2.

If we view the terminals $\langle \mathbf{call}, i, \Delta \rangle$ and $\langle \mathbf{ret}, i, \Delta \rangle$ from $\Sigma(B)$ as matching left and right parentheses, the language $\mathcal{L}(\mathcal{G}(B))$ is the set of all strings over $\Sigma(B)$ that are sequences of partially-balanced parentheses. That is, every right parenthesis $\langle \mathbf{ret}, i, \Delta \rangle$ is balanced by a preceding $\langle \mathbf{call}, i, \Delta \rangle$ but the converse

Table 2. The production rules $Rules(B)$ for grammar $\mathcal{G}(B)$.

1. $S \to MS$	4. $\forall \langle \mathbf{call}, i, \Delta \rangle, \langle \mathbf{ret}, i, \Delta \rangle \in \Sigma(B)$:
2. $\forall \langle \mathbf{call}, i, \Delta \rangle \in \Sigma(B)$:	$M \to \langle \mathbf{call}, i, \Delta \rangle \ M \ \langle \mathbf{ret}, i, \Delta \rangle$
$\quad S \to \langle \mathbf{call}, i, \Delta \rangle \ S$	5. $M \to MM$
3. $S \to \epsilon$	6. $M \to \epsilon$
	7. $M \to \sigma$

need not hold. The Δ component insures that the values of local variables at the time of a return are the same as they were at the time of the corresponding call (this must be the case because boolean programs have a call-by-value semantics). The nonterminal M generates all sequences of balanced calls and returns, and S generates all sequences of partially balanced calls and returns. This allows us to reason about non-terminating or abortive executions. Note again that the number of productions is finite because B contains only boolean variables.

We assume that B contains a distinguished procedure named **main**, which is the initial procedure that executes. A state $\eta = \langle i, \Omega \rangle$ is *initial* if $i = First_B(\mathbf{main})$ (all variables can take on arbitrary initial values). A finite sequence $\bar{\eta} = \eta_0 \overset{\alpha_1}{\to}_B \eta_1 \overset{\alpha_2}{\to}_B \cdots \eta_{m-1} \overset{\alpha_m}{\to}_B \eta_m$ is a *trajectory* of B if (1) for all $0 \leq i < m$, $\eta_i \overset{\alpha_i}{\to}_B \eta_{i+1}$, and (2) $\alpha_1 \ldots \alpha_m \in \mathcal{L}(\mathcal{G}(B))$. A trajectory $\bar{\eta}$ is called an *initialized trajectory* if η_0 is an initial state of B. If $\bar{\eta}$ is an initialized trajectory, then its projection to vertices $\Gamma(\eta_0), \Gamma(\eta_1), \ldots, \Gamma(\eta_n)$ is called a *trace* of B. The semantics of a boolean program is its set of traces. A state η of B is *reachable* if there exists an initialized trajectory of B that ends in η. An vertex $v \in V_B$ is *reachable* if there exists a trace of B that ends in vertex v.

3   Boolean Programs Reachability via Interprocedural Dataflow Analysis and BDDs

In this section, we present an interprocedural dataflow analysis that, given a boolean program B and its control-flow graph $G_B = (V_B, Succ_B)$, determines the reachability status of every vertex in V_B. We describe and present the algorithm, show how it can be extended to report short trajectories (when a vertex is found to be reachable), and describe several optimizations that we plan to make to the algorithm.

3.1   The RHS Algorithm, Generalized

As discussed in the Introduction, we have generalized the interprocedural dataflow algorithm of Reps-Horwitz-Sagiv (RHS) [RHS95,RHS96]. The main idea of this algorithm is to compute "path edges" that represent the reachability status of a vertex in a control-flow graph and to compute "summary edges" that record the input/output behavior of a procedure. We (re)define path and summary edges as follows:

Path edges. Let v be a vertex in V_B and let $e = First_B(ProcOf_B(v))$. A *path edge* incident into a vertex v, is a pair of valuations $\langle \Omega_e, \Omega_v \rangle$,[5] such that(1) there is a initialized trajectory $\overline{\eta}_1 = \langle First_B(\mathbf{main}), \Omega \rangle \ldots \langle e, \Omega_e \rangle$, and (2) there is a trajectory $\overline{\eta}_2 = \langle e, \Omega_e \rangle \ldots \langle v, \Omega_v \rangle$ that does not contain the exit vertex $Exit_{ProcOf_B(v)}$ (exclusive of v itself). For each vertex v, $PathEdges(v)$ is the set of all path edges incident into v.

A summary edge is a special kind of path edges that records the behavior of a procedure.

Summary edges. Let c be a vertex in V_B representing a procedure call with corresponding statement $s_c = \mathbf{pr}(e_1, e_2, \ldots e_k)$. A *summary edge* associated with c is a pair of valuations $\langle \Omega_1, \Omega_2 \rangle$, such that all the local variables in $Locals_B(c)$ are equal in Ω_1 and Ω_2, and the global variables change according to some path edge from the entry to the exit of the callee. Suppose P is the set of path edges at $Exit_{\mathbf{pr}}$. We define $Lift_c(P, \mathbf{pr})$ as the set of summary edges obtained by "lifting" the set of path edges P to the call c, while respecting the semantics of the call and return transitions from Table 1. Formally

$$
\begin{aligned}
Lift_c(P, \mathbf{pr}) = \{ & \langle \Omega_1, \Omega_2 \rangle \mid \exists \langle \Omega_i, \Omega_o \rangle \in P, \text{ and} \\
& \forall x \in Locals_B(c) : \Omega_1(x) = \Omega_2(x), \text{ and} \\
& \forall x \in Globals(B) : (\Omega_1(x) = \Omega_i(x)) \wedge (\Omega_2(x) = \Omega_o(x)), \text{ and} \\
& \forall \text{ formals } y_j \text{ of } \mathbf{pr} \text{ and actuals } e_j : \Omega_1(e_j) = \Omega_i(y_j) \}
\end{aligned}
$$

For each vertex v in $Call_B$, $SummaryEdges(v)$ is the set of summary edges associated with v. As the algorithm proceeds, $SummaryEdges(v)$ is incrementally computed for each call site. Summary edges are used to avoid revisiting portions of the state space that have already been explored, and enable analysis of programs with procedures and recursion.

Let $Call_B$ be the set of vertices in V_B that represent call statements. Let $Exit_B$ be the set of exit vertices in V_B. Let $Cond_B$ be the set of vertices in V_B that represent the conditional statements **if**, **while** and **assert**.

Transfer Functions. With each vertex v such that $s_v \notin Cond_B \cup Exit_B$, we associate a transfer function $Transfer_v$. With each vertex $v \in Cond_B$, we associate two transfer functions $Transfer_{v,true}$ and $Transfer_{v,false}$. The definition of these functions is given in Table 3. Given two sets of pairs of valuations, S and T, $Join(S, T)$ is the image of set S with respect to the transfer function T. Formally $Join(S, T) = \{ \langle \Omega_1, \Omega_2 \rangle \mid \exists \Omega_j. \langle \Omega_1, \Omega_j \rangle \in S \wedge \langle \Omega_j, \Omega_2 \rangle \in T \}$. During the processing of calls, in addition to applying the transfer function, the algorithm uses the function $SelfLoop$ which takes a set of path edges, and makes self-loops with the targets of the edges. Formally, $SelfLoop(S) = \{ \langle \Omega_2, \Omega_2 \rangle \mid \exists \langle \Omega_1, \Omega_2 \rangle \in S \}$.

Our generalization of the RHS algorithm is shown in Figure 3. The algorithm uses a worklist, and computes path edges and summary edges in a directed, demand-driven manner, starting with the entry vertex of **main** (the only vertex initially known to be reachable). In the algorithm, path edges are used to compute summary edges, and vice versa. In our implementation, we use BDDs to

---

[5] The valuations Ω_e and Ω_v are defined with respect to the set of variables $V = InScope_B(e) = InScope_B(v)$.

Table 3. Transfer functions associated with vertices. These are derived directly from the transition rules given in Table 1

v	$Transfer_v$
skip **print** **goto** **return**	$\lambda\langle \Omega_1, \Omega_2\rangle.(\Omega_2 = \Omega_1)$
$x_1, \ldots, x_k :=$ $e_1, \ldots, e_k$	$\lambda\langle \Omega_1, \Omega_2\rangle.(\Omega_2 = \Omega_1[x_1/\Omega_1(e_1)])\cdots[x_k/\Omega_1(e_k)])$
if(d) **while**(d) **assert**(d)	$Transfer_{v,true} = \lambda\langle \Omega_1, \Omega_2\rangle.((\Omega_1(d) = 1) \wedge (\Omega_2 = \Omega_1))$ $Transfer_{v,false} = \lambda\langle \Omega_1, \Omega_2\rangle.((\Omega_1(d) = 0) \wedge (\Omega_2 = \Omega_1))$
pr$(e_1, \ldots, e_k)$	$\lambda\langle \Omega_1, \Omega_2\rangle.(\Omega_2 = \Omega_1[x_1/\Omega_1(e_1)]\ldots[x_k/\Omega_1(e_k)])$, where $x_1, \ldots, x_k$ are the formal parameters of **pr**.

represent transfer functions, path edges, and summary edges. As is usual with BDDs, a boolean expression e denotes the set of states $\Omega_e = \{\Omega|\Omega(e) = 1\}$. A set of pairs of states can easily be represented with a single BDD using primed versions of the variables in $V(B)$ to represent the variables in the second state. Since transfer functions, path edges, and summary edges are sets of pairs of states, we can represent and manipulate them using BDDs.

Upon termination of the algorithm, the set of path edges for a vertex v is empty iff v is not reachable. If v is reachable, we can generate a shortest trajectory to v, as described in the next section.

3.2   Generating a Shortest Trajectory to a Reachable Vertex

We now describe a simple extension to the algorithm of Figure 3 to keep track of the length of the shortest *hierarchical trajectory* needed to reach each state, so that if vertex v is reachable, we can produce a shortest initialized hierarchical trajectory that ends in v.

A hierarchical trajectory can "jump over" procedure calls using summary edges. Formally, a finite sequence $\bar{\eta} = \eta_0 \overset{\alpha_1}{\to}_B \eta_1 \overset{\alpha_2}{\to}_B \cdots \eta_{m-1} \overset{\alpha_m}{\to}_B \eta_m$ is a *hierarchical trajectory* of B if for all $0 \le i < m$, (1) either $\eta_i \overset{\alpha_i}{\to}_B \eta_{i+1}$, or $\eta_i = \langle v_i, \Omega_i\rangle$, $\eta_{i+1} = \langle v_{i+1}, \Omega_{i+1}\rangle$, $\alpha_i = \sigma$, $v_i \in Call_B$ and $\langle \Omega_i, \Omega_{i+1}\rangle \in SummaryEdges(v_i)$, and (2) $\alpha_1 \ldots \alpha_m \in \mathcal{L}(\mathcal{G}(B))$.

Let v be a vertex and let $e = First_B(ProcOf_B(v))$. For a path edge $\langle \Omega_e, \Omega_v\rangle \in PathEdges(v)$ let $W(\langle \Omega_e, \Omega_v\rangle)$ be the set of all hierarchical trajectories that start from **main**, enter into the procedure $ProcOf_B(v)$ with valuation Ω_e and then reach v with valuation Ω_v without exiting $ProcOf_B(v)$. Note that a hierarchical trajectory in $W(\langle \Omega_e, \Omega_v\rangle)$ is comprised of intraprocedural edges, summary edges, and edges that represent calling a procedure (but not the edges representing a return from a procedure). Instead of keeping all the path edges incident on v as a single set $PathEdges(v)$, we partition it into a set of sets

$$\{PathEdges_{r_1}(v), PathEdges_{r_2}(v), \ldots, PathEdges_{r_k}(v)\}$$

global
PathEdges,SummaryEdges,WorkList

procedure Propagate(v,p)
begin
  if $p \not\subseteq PathEdges(v)$ **then**
    $PathEdges(v) := PathEdges(v) \cup p$
    Insert v into *WorkList* **fi**
  fi
end

procedure Reachable(G_B)
begin
  for all $v \in V_B$ **do** $PathEdges(v) := \{\}$
  for all $v \in Call_B$ **do** $SummaryEdges(v) := \{\}$
  $PathEdges(First_B(\textbf{main})) :=$
    $\{\langle \Omega, \Omega \rangle \mid \Omega$ is any valuation to globals and local variables of **main**$\}$

  $WorkList := \{First_B(\textbf{main})\}$
  while $WorkList \neq \emptyset$ **do**
    remove vertex v from *WorkList*
    switch (v)
      case $v \in Call_B$:
        Propagate($sSucc_B(v)$,$SelfLoop(Join(PathEdges(v), Transfer_v))$)
        Propagate($ReturnPt_B(v)$,$Join(PathEdges(v), SummaryEdges(v))$)
      case $v \in Exit_B$:
        for each $w \in Succ_B(v)$ **do**
          let
            $c \in Call_B$ such that $w = ReturnPt_B(c)$ **and**
            $s = Lift_c(PathEdges(v), ProcOf_B(v))$
          in
            if $s \not\subseteq SummaryEdges(c)$ **then**
              $SummaryEdges(c) := SummaryEdges(c) \cup s$
              Propagate(w,$Join(PathEdges(c), SummaryEdges(c))$);
          ni
      case $v \in Cond_B$:
        Propagate($Tsucc_B(v)$, $Join(PathEdges(v), Transfer_{v,true})$)
        Propagate($Fsucc_B(v)$, $Join(PathEdges(v), Transfer_{v,false})$)
      case $v \in V_B - Call_B - Exit_B - Cond_B$:
        let $p = Join(PathEdges(v), Transfer_v)$ **in**
          for each $w \in Succ_B(v)$ **do**
            Propagate(w,p)
        ni
end

Fig. 3. The model checking algorithm.

where a path edge $\langle \Omega_e, \Omega_v \rangle$ is in $PathEdges_{r_j}(v)$ iff the shortest hierarchical trajectory in $W((\langle \Omega_e, \Omega_v \rangle))$ has length r_j. The set $\{r_1, r_2, \ldots, r_k\}$ is called the set of *rings* associated with v.

We use rings to generate shortest hierarchical trajectories. If vertex v is reachable, we find the smallest ring r such that $PathEdges_r(v)$ exists. Then we pick an arbitrary path edge $\langle \Omega_e, \Omega_v \rangle$ from $PathEdges_r(v)$, and do the following depending on the type of vertex v:

- If $v \neq First_B(ProcOf_B(v))$ then we have two subcases:
  - If s_v is not a **skip** immediately following a call, then we look for a predecessor u of v such that there exists path edge $\langle \Omega_e, \Omega_u \rangle$ in $PathEdges_{r-1}(u)$, and $Join(\{\langle \Omega_e, \Omega_u \rangle\}, Transfer_u)$ contains $\langle \Omega_e, \Omega_v \rangle$.
  - If s_v is a **skip** immediately following a call (say at vertex u), then we look for a path edge $\langle \Omega_e, \Omega_u \rangle$ in $PathEdges_{r-1}(u)$ such that $Join(\{\langle \Omega_e, \Omega_u \rangle\}, SummaryEdges(u))$ contains $\langle \Omega_e, \Omega_v \rangle$.
- If $v = First_B(ProcOf_B(v))$, then it should be the case that $e = v$, and $\Omega_v = \Omega_e$. We find a caller u of $ProcOf_B(v)$, and suitably "lift" Ω_v to a suitable path edge in $PathEdges(u)$. Formally, we find a vertex $u \in Call_B$ such that s_u is a call to procedure $ProcOf_B(v)$, and there exists path edge $\langle \Omega_e', \Omega_u \rangle$ in $PathEdges_{r-1}(u)$ satisfying $Transfer_u(\langle \Omega_u, \Omega_v \rangle)$.

Repeating this process with the vertex u and the path edge found in $PathEdges_{r-1}(u)$, we are guaranteed to reach the entry of **main** in r steps. We may traverse over summary edges in the process. However, we can expand the summary edges on demand, to produce a hierarchical error trajectory, as shown in the Bebop output in Figure 1.

3.3   Optimizations

The basic algorithm described above has been implemented in the Bebop model checker. In this section, we describe a few optimizations based on ideas from compiler optimization [ASU86] that should substantially reduce the size of the BDDs needed to perform the analysis.

Live Ranges. If for some path starting at a vertex v in the control-flow graph G_B, the variable x is used before being defined, then variable x is said to be *live* at v. Otherwise, x is said to be *dead* at v, for its value at v will not flow to any other variable. If variable x is not live at vertex v then we need not record the value of x in the BDD for $PathEdges(v)$. Consider the following boolean program

```
void main()
begin
     decl a,b,c,d,e,f;
L1: a := b|c;      // {b,c,e} live at L1
L2: d := a|e;      // {a,e} live at L2
L3: e := d|e;      // {d,e} live at L3
L4: f := d;        // {d} live at L4
end
```

This program declares and refers to six variables, but at most three variables are live at any time. For example, at the statement labelled L1 only the values of the variables b, c, and e can flow to the statements after L1. As a result, the BDD for the first statement need not track the values of the variables a or d.

MOD/REF sets. A traditional "MOD/REF" (modification/reference) analysis of a program determines the variables that are modified and/or referenced by each procedure **pr** (and the procedures it calls transitively). Let **pr** be a procedure in B such that **pr** nor any of the procedures it calls (transitively) modifies or references global variable g. Although g may be in scope in **pr**, and may in fact be live within **pr**, the procedure **pr** cannot change the value of g. As a result, all that is needed is to record that g remains unchanged, for any summary of **pr**.

4   Evaluation

In this section, we present an evaluation of Bebop on a series of synthetic programs derived from the template T shown in Figure 4. The template allows us to generate boolean programs $T(N)$ for $N > 0$. The boolean program $T(N)$ has one global variable g and $N + 1$ procedures —a procedure main, and N procedures of the form level<i> for $0 < i \leq N$. For $0 < j < N$, the two instances of <stmt> in the body of procedure level<j> are replaced by a call to procedure level<j+1>. The two instances of <stmt> in the body of procedure level<N> are replaced by skip.

As a result, a boolean program $T(N)$ has $N + 1$ procedures, where main calls level1 twice, level1 calls level2 twice, etc. At the beginning of each level procedure, a choice is made depending on the value of g. If g is 1 then a loop is executed that implements a three bit counter over the local variables a, b, and c. If g is 0 then two calls in succession are made to the next level procedure. In the last level procedure, if g is 0 then two skip statements are executed. At the end of each level procedure, the global variable g is negated. Every program $T(N)$ generated from this template has four variables visible at any program point, regardless of N. Note that g is not initialized, so Bebop will explore all possible values for g.

We ran Bebop to compute the reachable states for boolean programs $T(N)$ in $0 < N \leq 800$, and measured the running time, and peak memory used. Figure 4(a) shows how the running time of Bebop (in seconds) varies with N. Figure 4(b) shows how the peak memory usage of Bebop varies with N.

The two curves in Figure 4(a) represent two different BDD packages: CU is the CUDD package from Colorado University [Som98] and CMU is the BDD package from Carnegie Mellon University [Lon93]. We note that the program $T(800)$ has 2401 variables. Model checking of this program takes a minute and a half with the CMU package and four and a half minutes with the CUDD package. Both times are quite reasonable considering the large number of variables (relative to traditional uses of BDDs). The space measurements in Figure 4(b) are taken from the CUDD package, which provides more detailed statistics of BDD space usage.

```
decl g;
void main()
begin
  level1();
  level1();
  if(!g) then
    reach: skip;
  else
    skip;
  fi
end

void level<i>()
begin
  decl a,b,c;
  if(g) then
    a,b,c := 0,0,0;
    while(!a|!b|!c) do
      if (!a) then
        a := 1;
      elsif (!b) then
        a,b := 0,1;
      elsif (!c) then
        a,b,c := 0,0,1;
      fi
    od
  else
    <stmt>; <stmt>;
  fi
  g := !g;
end
```

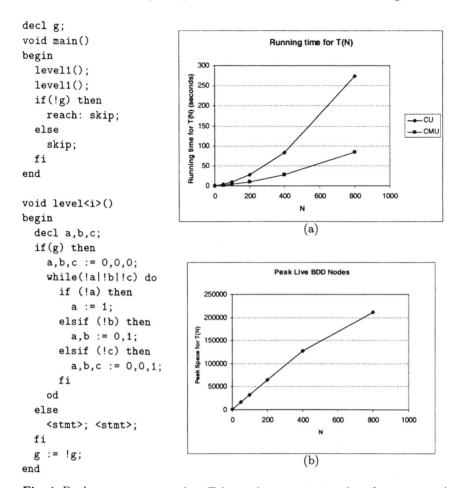

(a)

(b)

Fig. 4. Boolean program template T for performance test and performance results.

We expected the peak memory usage to increase linearly with N. The sublinear behavior observed in Figure 4(b) is due to more frequent garbage collection at larger N. We expected the running time also to increase linearly with N. However, Figure 4(a) shows that the running time increases quadratically with N. The quadratic increase in running time was unexpected, since the time complexity of model checking program $T(N)$ is $O(N)$ (there are 4 variables in the scope of any program point). By profiling the runs and reading the code in the BDD packages, we found that the quadratic behavior arises due to an inefficiency in the implementation of bdd_substitute in the BDD package. Bebop calls bdd_substitute in its "inner loop", since variable renaming is an essential component of its forward image computation. While model checking $T(N)$, the BDD manager has $O(N)$ variables, but we are interested in substituting $O(n)$ variables, for a small n, using bdd_substitute. Regardless of n, we found that bdd_substitute still consumes $O(N)$ time. Both the CUDD and CMU packages had this inefficiency. If this inefficiency is fixed in bdd_substitute, we believe that the running time of Bebop for $T(N)$ will vary linearly with N.

5   Related Work

Model checking for finite state machines is a well studied problem, and several model checkers —SMV [McM93], Murϕ [Dil96], SPIN [HP96], COSPAN [HHK96], VIS [BHSV$^+$96] and MOCHA [AHM$^+$98]— have been developed. Boolean programs implicitly have an unbounded stack, which makes them identical in expressive power to pushdown automata. The model checking problem for pushdown automata has been studied before [SB92] [BEM97] [FWW97]. Model checkers for push down automata have also been written before [EHRS00]. However, unlike boolean programs, these approaches abstract away data, and concentrate only on control. As a result spurious paths can arise in these models due to information loss about data correlations.

The connections between model checking, dataflow analysis and abstract interpretation have been explored before [Sch98] [CC00]. The RHS algorithm [RHS95,RHS96] builds on earlier work in interprocedural dataflow analysis from [KS92] and [SP81]. We have shown how this algorithm can be generalized to work as a model checking procedure for boolean programs. Also, our choice of hybrid representation of the state space in Bebop—an explicit representation of control flow and an implicit BDD-based representation of path edges and summary edges— is novel.

Exploiting design modularity in model checking has been recognized as a key to scalability of model checking [AH96] [AG00] [McM97] [HQR98]. The idea of harnessing the inherent modularity in procedural abstraction, and exploiting locality of variable scoping for efficiency in model checking software is new, though known in the area of dataflow analysis [RHS96]. Existing model checkers neither support nor exploit procedural abstraction. As a result, existing approaches to extract models from software are forced to inline procedure definitions at their points of invocation [CDH$^+$00], which could lead to explosion in both the size of the model and the number of variables.

6   Future Work

Bebop is part of a larger effort called SLAM[6], in progress at Microsoft Research, to extract abstract models from code and check temporal properties of software. We are currently implementing a methodology that uses boolean programs, and an iterative refinement process using path simulation to model check critical portions of operating system code [BR00].

References

[AG00]   A. Alur and R. Grosu. Modular refinement of hierarchic reactive modules. In *POPL 00: Principles of Programming Languages*. ACM Press, 2000.

---

[6] http://www.research.microsoft.com/slam/

[AH96]   R. Alur and T.A. Henzinger. Reactive modules. In *LICS 96: Logic in Computer Science*, pages 207–218. IEEE Computer Society Press, 1996.

[AHM⁺98]   R. Alur, T.A. Henzinger, F.Y.C. Mang, S. Qadeer, S.K. Rajamani, and S. Tasiran. MOCHA : Modularity in model checking. In *CAV 98: Computer Aided Verification*, LNCS 1427, pages 521–525. Springer-Verlag, 1998.

[ASU86]   A. Aho, R. Sethi, and J. Ullman. *Compilers: Principles, Techniques and Tools*. Addison-Wesley, Reading, MA, 1986.

[BEM97]   A. Bouajjani, J. Esparza, and O. Maler. Reachability analysis of pushdown automata: Application to model-checking. In *CONCUR 97: Concurrency Theory*, LNCS 1243, pages 135–150. Springer-Verlag, 1997.

[BHSV⁺96]   R.K. Brayton, G.D. Hachtel, A. Sangiovanni-Vincentelli, F. Somenzi, A. Aziz, S.-T. Cheng, S. Edwards, S. Khatri, Y. Kukimoto, A. Pardo, S. Qadeer, R.K. Ranjan, S. Sarwary, T.R. Shiple, G. Swamy, and T. Villa. VIS: A System for Verification and Synthesis. In *CAV 96: Computer Aided Verification*, LNCS 1102, pages 428–432. Springer-Verlag, 1996.

[BR00]   T. Ball and S. K. Rajamani. Boolean programs: A model and process for software analysis. Technical Report MSR-TR-2000-14, Microsoft Research, February 2000.

[Bry86]   R.E. Bryant. Graph-based algorithms for boolean function manipulation. *IEEE Transactions on Computers*, C-35(8):677–691, 1986.

[CC00]   P. Cousot and R. Cousot. Temporal abstract interpretation. In *POPL 00: Principles of Programming Languages*. ACM Press, 2000.

[CDH⁺00]   James Corbett, Matthew Dwyer, John Hatcliff, Corina Pasareanu, Robby, Shawn Laubach, and Hongjun Zheng. Bandera : Extracting finite-state models from java source code. In *ICSE 2000: International Conference on Software Engineering*, 2000.

[Dil96]   D. L. Dill. The Murφ Verification System. In *CAV 96: Computer Aided Verification*, LNCS 1102, pages 390–393. Springer-Verlag, 1996.

[EHRS00]   J. Esparza, D. Hansel, P. Rossmanith, and S. Schwoon. Efficient algorithms for model checking pushdown systems. Technical Report TUM-I0002, SFB-Bericht 342/1/00 A, Technische Universitat Munchen, Institut fur Informatik, February 2000.

[FWW97]   A. Finkel, B. Willems, and P. Wolper. A direct symbolic approach to model checking pushdown systems. In *INFINITY' 97: Verification of Infinite-state Systems*, July 1997.

[HHK96]   R.H. Hardin, Z. Har'El, and R.P. Kurshan. COSPAN. In *CAV 96: Computer Aided Verification*, LNCS 1102, pages 423–427. Springer-Verlag, 1996.

[HP96]   G.J. Holzmann and D.A. Peled. The State of SPIN. In *CAV 96: Computer Aided Verification*, LNCS 1102, pages 385–389. Springer-Verlag, 1996.

[HQR98]   T.A. Henzinger, S. Qadeer, and S.K. Rajamani. You assume, we guarantee: methodology and case studies. In *CAV 98: Computer Aided Verification*, LNCS 1427, pages 440–451. Springer-Verlag, 1998.

[KS92]   J. Knoop and B. Steffen. The interprocedural coincidence theorem. In *CC 92: Compiler Construction*, LNCS 641, pages 125–140, Springer-Verlag, 1992.

[Lon93]   D. Long. Cmu bdd package. http://emc.cmu.edu/pub, Carnegie Melon University, 1993.

[McM93]   K.L. McMillan. *Symbolic Model Checking: An Approach to the State-Explosion Problem*. Kluwer Academic Publishers, 1993.

[McM97]   K.L. McMillan. A compositional rule for hardware design refinement.
            In *CAV 97: Computer-Aided Verification*, LNCS 1254, pages 24–35.
            Springer-Verlag, 1997.
[RHS95]   T. Reps, S. Horwitz, and M. Sagiv. Precise interprocedural dataflow
            analysis via graph reachability. In *POPL 95: Principles of Programming
            Languages*, pages 49–61. ACM Press, 1995.
[RHS96]   T. Reps, S. Horwitz, and M. Sagiv. Precise interprocedural dataflow
            analysis with applications to constant propagation. *Theoretical Computer
            Science*, 167:131–170, 1996.
[SB92]   B. Steffen and O. Burkart. Model checking for context-free processes. In
            CONCUR 92: Concurrency Theory, LNCS 630, pages 123–137. Springer-
            Verlag, 1992.
[Sch98]   D.A. Schmidt. Data flow analysis is model checking of abstract interpre-
            tation. In *POPL 98: Principles of Programming Languages*, pages 38–48.
            ACM Press, 1998.
[Som98]   F. Somenzi.   Colorado university decision diagram package.
            ftp://vlsi.colorado.edu/pub, University of Colorado, Boulder, 1998.
[SP81]   M. Sharir and A. Pnueli. Two approaches to interprocedural data dalow
            analysis. In *Program Flow Analysis: Theory and Applications*, pages 189–
            233. Prentice-Hall, 1981.

Logic Verification of ANSI-C Code with SPIN

Gerard J. Holzmann

Bell Laboratories, Lucent Technologies,
Murray Hill, New Jersey 07974, USA.
CWgerard@research.bell-labs.com

Abstract. We describe a tool, called AX, that can be used in combination with the model checker SPIN to efficiently verify logical properties of distributed software systems implemented in ANSI-standard C [18]. AX, short for Automaton eXtractor, can extract verification models from C code at a user defined level of abstraction. Target applications include telephone switching software, distributed operating systems code, protocol implementations, concurrency control methods, and client-server applications.
This paper discusses how AX is currently implemented, and how we plan to extend it. The tool was used in the formal verification of two substantial software applications: a commercial checkpoint management system and the call processing code for a new telephone switch.

1 Introduction

The construction of a reliable logic verification system for software systems has long been an elusive goal. It is well-known that in general even simple properties, such as program termination or system deadlock, are formally undecidable [23]. Efforts that target the development of mechanical verification systems therefore usually concentrate on carefully defined subsets of programs. Such subsets can, for instance, be obtained by imposing syntactic restrictions on general programming languages. These restrictions, however, are usually shunned by practicing programmers. An alternative method that we will explore here, is to define a system of abstractions for mechanically extracting verifiable *models* from programs written in a general purpose programming language. The abstractions are defined in such a way that the feasible executions of the modeled programs can be analyzed, if necessary exhaustively, by a model checker.

The staples of the industrial software quality control process from today, i.e., code inspection, peer review, and lab testing, work well for stand-alone, sequential applications that display primarily deterministic behavior. These methods, however, fail when they are applied to distributed software systems. A distributed system is not stand-alone or sequential, and its behavior is typically non-deterministic. It is not too surprising that the behavior of even non-buggy distributed applications can easily defy our human reasoning skills. In many cases, though, it is possible to analyze such systems thoroughly with the help of model checking techniques.

K. Havelund, J. Penix, and W. Visser (Eds.): SPIN 2000, LNCS 1885, pp. 131–147, 2000.
© Springer-Verlag Berlin Heidelberg 2000

Our aim is to develop a system where default abstractions are sufficient to make the verification problem tractable, with a capability to perform fast approximate checks mechanically. By adjusting the abstractions, the user of such a system should be able to increase the level of precision of a check, but it is important that this is not a prerequisite for the applicability of the method. The default checks should return helpful results also without user guidance.

Verification Engine. The verification engine that is central to the work described here is the Bell Labs model checker SPIN [12].[1] Until now, to user of a model checking system will typically manually define an abstract model that captures the essential aspects of an application [2],[13]. Properties can then be formulated as assertions, or more generally as formulae in propositional temporal logic [20]. SPIN can perform either an exhaustive check that proves whether or not the model satisfies the property, or it can deliver a best-effort estimate of this fact within given time or memory constraints. For reasonable constraints (e.g., given a memory arena of around 64 Megabytes, and a runtime constraint of up to ten minutes) the probability of missing a property violation in even a best-effort check is usually small [14].

The use of a mechanical model extraction directly from source code, *without* imposing restrictions to or requiring prior modifications of that source code, can for the first time make it practical to use software model checkers in routine software development. The manual effort is now moved from the construction of the model itself to the definition of a set of abstraction rules, as will be explained. The rules can be checked for soundness and completeness by the model extractor, and may in some cases be generated by default to limit user interaction.

Earlier Work. We earlier attempted to perform direct verification of program sources written in a subset of the CCITT specification language SDL [11]. This lead to the development of the verifier SDLvalid, which was used at our company between 1988 and 1993. Though successful as a verification effort, the restrictions that we had to impose upon the language were too strict for routine programming. Special purposes languages such as SDL also appear to have fallen from favor among programmers, and today most new applications are written in general purpose languages such as C, C++, or Java. Although the tool SDLvalid is itself no longer used, it inspired a number of other verification tools, several being sold commercially today.

An early prototype of a model extractor for C code was constructed in August 1998, to support the direct verification of a commercial call processing application, as documented in [15]. The call processing software is written in ANSI-C, annotated with special markers to identify the main control states. We wrote a parser for this application, and used it to mechanically extract SPIN models from the code. These models were then checked against a library of generic call

---

[1] Online references for SPIN can be found at
http://cm.bell-labs.com/cm/cs/what/spin/Man/.

processing requirements. Over a period of 18 months, the model extraction and verification process was repeated every few days, to track changes in the code and to assure its continued compliance with the requirements. The verification method proved to be thorough and efficient — capable of rapidly intercepting a class of software defects with minimal user involvement. This application of model checking techniques to source level C code is the largest such effort known to us.

In February 2000 we generalized the model extraction method by removing the reliance on the special annotation for control states. The new model extractor was embedded it into a publicly available parser for programs written in full ANSI-standard C, [5]. By doing so we could replace two programs (named Pry and Catch [15]) with a single one (AX). The revision took approximately one month, and produced a fully general model checking environment for programs written in C, without making any assumptions about the specifics of the code and, importantly, without adding any restrictions to the source language.

Related Work. Several attempts have been made to build translators that convert program text literally, without abstraction, into the input language of a model checker. Since no abstraction is used in these cases, one has to resort to imposing restrictions on the input language. Such subsets were defined, for instance, for Ada [4], Java [8],[9], and, as noted, for SDL [11].

For Java, two recent projects are also based on the systematic use of abstraction techniques: the Bandera toolset, in development at Kansas State University [3], and the Pathfinder-2 project at NASA Ames Research Center [24]. The work in [3] bases the model extraction process on the use of program slicing techniques [8],[19],[22]. Both [3] and [24] also target the inclusion of mechanically verified predicate abstraction techniques, by linking the model extraction process to either a theorem prover or a decision procedure for Pressburger arithmetic.

The work we discuss in this paper does not require, but also does not exclude, the use of external tools such as slicers or theorem provers. It is based on the definition of an abstraction filter that encapsulates the abstraction rules for a given body of program code. The method is independent of the manner in which the abstraction rules are generated. Importantly: they allow for the user to define or revise the rules either manually or mechanically. The abstraction rules can be checked for soundness and completeness independently, or they could be machine generated in a predefined way. The problem of syntax conversion from the source language to the model checking language is avoided in [24] by making use of the fact that Java programs can be compiled into a generic byte-code format for a Java virtual machine. The context in which a model extractor for C code has to operate is significantly more complex. There is, for instance, no virtual machine definition for ANSI-C, the use of pointers is unrestricted and can easily defy the pointer-alias analysis algorithms used in program slicers or data dependency algorithms. The use of an abstraction table provides an effective general mechanism for dealing with these practical issues, as we will illustrate here.

A number of other techniques attempt to find a more informal compromise between conventional system testing and simulation on the one side and program verification and logic model checking techniques on the other side. Interesting examples of these are Verisoft [7], which can be used on standard C code, and Eraser [21], which can be used for analyzing Java code. These tools analyze programs by monitoring the direct execution of the code. There is no attempt to compute a representation of the reachable state space, or to check anything other than safety properties. The method that we propose in this paper can be distinguished from these approaches by not only being more thorough (providing full LTL model checking capabilities), but also by allowing us to perform model checking on also partially specified systems.

In the sections that follow we will describe how the AX model extractor works, and we discuss some examples of its use on unrestricted industrial size code.

2   Model Extraction

We can distinguish three separate phases in the model extraction process. Optionally, the three phases described here can be preceded by the use of program slicing and by an independent verification step to prove the soundness of the abstraction rules used. We will not discuss program slicing or soundness checks here, but instead concentrate on the model extraction process itself. The three phases are then as follows. In the *first phase* the model extractor creates a parse tree of the program source text, taking care to preserve all pertinent information about the original source. The *second phase* adds a semantic interpretation based on either a predefined or a user-defined set of abstraction rules, and the *third phase* optimizes the structure thus obtained and generates the verification model. We discuss each of these phases in more detail below.

2.1   First Phase: Parsing

A typical parser for a programming languages attempts to discard as much information as possible about the original program source, since this usually has no further significance to code-generation. In our case this type of information is important, and must be preserved, for instance, to allow for accurate cross-referencing between the executions of the source program and those of the extracted model.

The full parse tree that is built by the model extractor defines the control flow structure for each procedure in the original program, and it contains information about the type and scope of each data object used. The output of the parsing phase could be represented as an uninterpreted model, interpreting only control flow structure of the program, but treating everything else as an annotation. All basic actions (i.e., declarations, assignments, function calls) and branch conditions are collected, and can be tabulated, but they are as yet uninterpreted.

2.2   Second Phase: Interpretation

The *second phase* of the model extraction process applies an interpretation to
each basic action and condition. All basic actions and conditions that appear in
the source of the application can be inserted into a table, where it can be paired
with an interpretation. If no abstraction table is provided the model extractor
can generate one and fill it with a safe default interpretation that we will describe
below. In many cases the default interpretations suffice, but the user can also
revise the table. When model extraction is repeated (it takes just a fraction of a
second) the model extractor will then use the revised abstraction table instead
of the defaults and generate a model that conforms to the new choices. We refer
to the basic actions and conditions as the "entries" in the abstraction table.

The rule table allows us to implement a remarkably broad range of systematic
abstraction techniques. We mention some of the more important types below.

1. Local slicing rules. These rules are used to identify data objects, and their
   associated operations, that are irrelevant to the properties to be proven.
   Each declaration, function call, or statement within the set to be hidden
   from the verification model is interpreted as a skip (a null operation). Each
   condition that refers to a hidden object is made non-deterministic. A data
   dependency analysis can be used to identify the associated operations for
   each data object that is to be sliced away in this manner.
2. Abstraction relations. More general types of abstraction relations can also be
   captured as conversion rules in the table. This includes support for stating
   predicate abstractions [24]. A predicate abstraction is used when the implementation value domain of specific data objects carries more information
   than necessary to carry out a verification. The minimally required information can be captured in boolean predicates. For each such predicate we then
   introduce a boolean variable (replacing the original declaration of the data
   objects in the table), and only the boolean value of the predicate is tracked
   in the model, where possible. In some cases, the loss of access to the full
   value of the original data object can make it impossible to evaluate the predicate. In those cases non-determinism is introduced to indicate that either
   boolean value would be possible. The predicate abstraction relations can be
   derived or checked with separate external tools, such as a theorem prover or
   a decision procedure, as in [24].
3. Syntax conversion. An important class of rules in the table will deal with
   mere syntax conversions, e.g., to accurately represent the transmission or
   reception of messages exchanged between processes, or the creation of new
   asynchronous process threads. We will give some examples of this below.
4. Restriction of verification scope. Finally, the same formalism of the abstraction table can be used to define restrictions to the scope of the verification
   attempt itself, e.g., by limiting buffer sizes, message vocabulary, the number
   of channels or processes, etc.

The use of semantic interpretation of a program through the tabled abstraction methods is at the core of the method introduced here. We discuss more
details in a separate section below.

2.3 Third Phase: Optimization

A notable portion of the source text of an application is often of no direct relevance to the verification of general functional properties of the code. With the corresponding actions *hidden*, the control structure can of course be simplified. For instance, if we find a fragment like (in SPIN's specification language):

```
if
:: true -> /* comment1 */
:: true -> /* comment2 */
fi
```

specifying a nondeterministic choice between two commented out portions of code, clear we can simplify the model without changing its semantics by removing it completely. Similarly, a structure such as

```
if
:: true -> stmnt1
fi;
stmnt2
```

can be reduced to:

```
stmnt1; stmnt2
```

and in a structure like

```
false -> stmnt1; stmnt2; ...
```

everything after the unsatisfiable condition can be omitted. The model extractor uses a small set of rewrite rules to optimize the verification models for these cases.

3 Tabled Abstraction

The larger part of the abstraction table consists of a left-hand side entry, which is a canonicalized representation of a basic statement, a condition or its negation, from the source text of the application, and a right-hand side that specifies its semantic interpretation in the verification model. In many cases, a safe pre-defined interpretation can be applied, assigned automatically by the model extractor. Four predefined types of interpretations for actions are listed in Table 1.

The predefined types from Table 1 can be used to either suppress (slice away) or preserve specific *types* of program statements in the model. The use of data types that are not representable in the input language of the model checker, for instance, is by default suppressed, but can be replaced with a more targeted, and independently verified, type of abstraction by the user. The capability to apply 'local' slicing, at the statement level, is valuable in dealing with the sometimes low-level details of routine applications written in C. It is, for instance, possible to slice away all function calls that can be shown to be redundant to the verification effort with a single entry in the abstraction table.

An example of an abstraction table with three mapping rules and two global Substitute rules, is as follows.

Table 1. Predefined Interpretations.

Type	Meaning
print	Embed source statement into a print action in the model
comment	Include in the model as a comment only
hide	Do not represent in the model
keep	Preserve in the model, subject to global Substitute rules

Substitute FALSE	false
Substitute BOOL	bit
D: int pData=GetDataPointer();	hide
D: BOOL m_bConnected	keep
A: *((int *)pData)=(int)nStatus	print
A: m_bConnected=FALSE	keep

Declarations are prefixed (by the model extractor) with a designation "D:" and assignments are prefixed with "A:". Assume that it can be determined that the use of variable pData is irrelevant to the property to be proven. The variable declaration is suppressed from the model with the mapping hide, but can nonetheless preserve visibility of access to the variable by mapping assignments to print. The print designation means that whenever this statement is encountered the verification model will not execute but print the source text of the statement. The latter capability is important to allow for the proper interpretation of error-trails produced by the model checker.

Data Dependency. To verify that abstraction rules are applied consistently, the model extractor performs a data dependency analysis and checks it against the rules. If, for instance, an assignment to a data object, or its declaration, is hidden (mapped), it is checked that all other read and write accesses to the same data object, and all access to other data objects that are dependent on it, are also hidden (mapped).

If a particular statement does not appear in the abstraction table a default rule is applied. For assignments, the default rule could be print, so in that case the above entry need not be included explicitly in the abstraction table at all. The user can override builtin defaults by entering a new definition for the default rule in an (optional) Preferences file. There can be an entry in this preferences file for each basic type of statement (e.g., declarations, assignments, function calls, conditions), with a corresponding default that will then replace the predefined default.

Point Abstractions. All branch conditions, e.g. those used in iteration and selection statements to effect control flow, are entered twice into the abstraction table by the model extractor: once in positive form as found in the source text, and once in negated form. The reason for this apparent redundancy is that in the verification model we have the option of mapping *both* versions to true, and thus introduce non-determinism into the model. This type of mapping is sometimes called a 'point-abstraction,' and readily shown to preserve soundness. Consider, for instance, the following case:

C:	(device_busy(x->line))	true
C:	!(device_busy(x->line))	true

The precise determination if a given device is idle or busy is considered to be beyond the scope of the verification here. For verification purposes it suffices to state that both cases can occur, and the results of the verification should hold no matter what the outcome of the call is.

Restriction. In a similar vain, though, we can use a mapping to false as a constraint, to restrict the verification attempt to just one case:

F:	(device_busy(x->line))	true
F:	!(device_busy(x->line))	false

Here the verification would check correct operation of the system when the device polled is always busy.

Syntax Conversion. In some cases, the predefined interpretations from Table 1 are not adequate to cover the specifics of a verification. For the applications that we have considered so far, this applied to fewer than 20% of the entries in the machine generated abstraction tables. The following example illustrates typical use.

F:	m_pMon->SendEvent(dest_Id,etype)	destq!etype
F:	_beginthread(assign,0,0)	run assign(0,0)

The first entry defines a syntax conversion for the transmission of a message. The second entry defines the startup of an asynchronous process, executing a given function. Note that within the source text of the application these types of statements can take any form, since there is no generally accepted standard library for such operations. The abstraction table here serves to standardize the format that is used, without impeding the freedom of the programmer to chose an arbitrary representation. Automatic abstraction or checking techniques can generally not verify the correctness of these semantic interpretations. For a given application environment, though, we can manually provide a library of standard interpretations and include them into the abstraction tables.

Domain Restriction. The next table illustrates the definition of a domain reduction, or predicate abstraction, in the use of an integer variable.

D: int timer	bool timer
A: (timer > 0)	keep
A: !(timer > 0)	keep
A: timer = 60	timer = true
A: timer = 10	timer = true
A: timer = 0	timer = false
E: timer–	if :: timer = true :: timer = false fi

We assume here that the precise value of the timer is not relevant to the verification being undertaken, but the fact that the timer is running or not is relevant. We introduce a new boolean variable for the predicate "(timer > 0)", which is true when we know the timer has a non-zero value, and false when the timer-value is zero. We can use a decision procedure, as in [24] to derive the corresponding abstractions, and prove them sound. In this case we can trivially also do this by hand. When the timer variable is decremented, as illustrated in the last entry from the sample table above, the semantic interpretation reflects that the resulting value could be either positive or zero, using non-deterministic choice.

Short-Hands. The abstraction table is generally much smaller than the program text from which it is derived. The user can shorten it still further by exploiting some features of the model extractor. First, any entry that maintains its default mapping can be omitted from a user-maintained table: the model extractor can fill in these missing entries as needed. Second, the user can use patterns to assign the same mapping to larger groups of entries that match the pattern. For instance, suppose that all calls of the C library-functions memcpy and strcpy are to be hidden. We can avoid having to list all different calls by using ellipses, as follows:

F: memcpy(...	hide
F: strcpy(...	hide

This method could be expanded into a more general pattern matching method based on regular expressions. The above prefix match, however, seems to suffice in practice.

The second method for introducing abbreviations uses the Substitute rule that was shown earlier. Substitute rules take effect only on mappings of type keep, and they are applied in the order in which they are defined in the abstraction table.

We will give some statistics on the size and contents of typical abstraction tables in the section on **Application**.

Priorities of Abstraction Rules. Abstraction table, preferences file, and the builtin defaults of the model extractor may all give different instructions for the conversion of a specific fragment of program code. The various rules therefore have different priorities, as follows:

1. If a source fragment is matched in the abstraction table, the mapping from the table always takes precedence.
2. In the absence of an explicit mapping, the model extractor first builds a list of all data objects that are accessed in the given fragment of source code. For each such object, a check is made in the preferences file (if defined) to see if a restriction on that data object was defined. The restriction, if it appears, will be one of the entries of Table 1. If multiple data objects are accessed in a given source fragment, each could define a different restriction. In this case the restriction that appears first in Table 1 is applied. (E.g., print takes the highest priority, and keep the lowest.) If, however, the source fragment is classified as a condition, a mapping to hide or comment is replaced with a mapping to true.
3. If no explicit mapping applies and no data restrictions apply, then the default type rules will be applied. First note that each source fragment at this level can be classified as one of four distinct types: assignment (A), condition (C), declaration (D), or function call (F). For each of these types the model extractor has a builtin mapping to one of the entries from Table 1. The builtin mapping can be overruled by the user with an entry in the preferences file. The redefined rule, however, also in this case remains restricted to the mappings specified in Table 1.

The model extractor can generate the templates for the abstraction table and the preference file automatically, so that any later adjustment to the focus of the verification consists only of making small revisions in one or two pre-populated files.

Synopsis. Note that the use of an abstraction table provides support for a fairly broad range of standard abstraction techniques, including local slicing (data hiding) and point-abstractions (introducing non-determinism), but also model restrictions and, e.g., reductions to the cardinality of a data domain. In addition, the table format allows us to define systematic rules for syntax conversion and model annotation, critical model extraction capabilities that no other method previously described appears to provide.

4   Verification

The output of phases one, two, and three are all executable and can be expressed in a format that is acceptable to the verification engine (which in our case is SPIN). For a meaningful verification, however, two additional items have to be formulated, in as little or as much detail as preferred. First, the user can formulate the functional properties that the application is expected to satisfy. By default the verifier can check for absence of deadlocks, completeness, absence of race conditions, and the like. But, generally, for more precise checks can be made through the use of properties expressed in temporal logic. The same is true in conventional testing: a targeted test of required functionality of the code is far more effective than some default random executions of the system.

The second item that needs to be added to properly direct the verification is an environment model: a stylized set of assumptions about the behavior of the environment in which the application is to be used. Testers often refer to this activity as *test scaffolding* or the construction of a *test harness*. The test harness serves to separate the application from its environment, so that it can be studied in detail under reproducible conditions.

In a verification environment the capability to build environment models and test drivers that can be connected in any way desired to the verification target is particularly rich. It remains to be seen how this power can be made available to those not familiar with the model checking paradigm. One method may be to allow the user to specify the test drivers in C, just like regular test scaffolding that would be constructed to support conventional testing, and to extract the test driver automata from that code, just like the main verification model. In the applications we have pursued we found it simpler to specify the test harness directly in the specification language of the model checker, but this is likely to be a personal preference, not a prescript for general use of the method.

5   Application

A predecessor of AX [15] was used in the verification of the call processing software for the PathStar access server [6]. This version of the tool, like AX, used a abstraction table, but in this case the table was entirely used-defined, and initially had no facility for abbreviations and default designations such as keep, hide, and print. In the PathStar application, all call processing code is grouped into a single module of the system, written in ANSI-C with some small annotations, as discussed earlier in this paper. The details of the verification effort have been described elsewhere. Here we concentrate on the model extraction framework itself.

Approximately 25% of the verification model for this application was handwritten, the remaining 75% mechanically extracted from the program source. The 25% handwritten code consists primarily of a detailed test harness, capturing our assumptions of the possible behaviors of local and remote subscribers and of neighboring switches in the network. The test harness contained six different types of test drivers for this purpose.

In the abstraction table for the call processing code about 60% of the code is mapped to keep, 30% is mapped to either hide or print, and the remaining 10% has an explicit alternate mapping. In most cases, the explicit alternate mapping support a notion of abstraction. Timers, for instance, are mapped from an integer domain into a Boolean domain, to exploit the fact that only the on/off status of the timers was required to verify system properties for this application.

A more recent application of AX was to the code of a checkpoint management system. The code for this application is written in C++, which first had to be converted into ANSI-standard C code to support model extraction. For this application the test harness formed was 31% of the verification model, the remaining 69% mechanically extracted from the source code. A total of ten procedures of interest were identified and mechanically extracted from the code as part of the verification model.

In the abstraction table for the checkpoint manager about 39% of the code is mapped to keep, 40% to either hide, print, or comment, and the remaining 21% was given an explicit mapping, mostly to express simple syntactical translations for message send and receive events.

Table 2. Statistics on Tabled Abstraction.

	PathStar Code	Checkpoint Manager	FeaVer System	Alternating Bit Test	Quicksort Test
Nr. Entries in Map	478	198	104	24	16
Nr. Elipse Rules	34	19	20	1	0
Nr. Substitute Rules	0	5	0	0	0
Default Rules	90%	79%	34%	50%	25%
Explicit Rules	10%	21%	66%	50%	75%
% Model Handwritten	25%	31%	50%	4%	73%
% Model Extracted	75%	69%	50%	96%	27%

Table 2 summarizes these statistics, together with the same metrics for the application of the model extractor to implementations in C of a client-server application that is used to implement the distributed software for the FeaVer verification system from [16].

For comparison the same statistics for two small test cases applications are also included. The first test case is a 54 line implementation in C of the alternating bit protocol [1]. The second test is a deliberately chosen non-concurrent and data-intensive application. For this test we extracted a SPIN model from a 59 line implementation in C of the quicksort algorithm, based on [17]. The model extraction method does not target these types of applications, but it can still be useful to consider how badly the system might perform if it is applied outside its normal domain. For this application the larger part of the model was a handwritten routine for supplying input and for verifying that the output returned was properly sorted.

For the larger applications, the amount of code that can be treated with a default mapping is also the largest, limiting required user actions considerably compared with the effort that would be required to construct the verification models manually. The client-server code for the FeaVer system has more data dependencies, which show up as a larger fraction of the abstraction tables being mapped explicitly. In many cases, these explicit mappings consist of relatively simple syntactical conversions from C code to SPIN code. Once the abstraction table is defined for a given application, it can track changes in the source code with relative ease, and the user need only review occasional additions or revisions of entries in the table to see if the default choices from the model extractor need adjustment.

6   Extensions

The abstraction table used in the prototype version of our model extractor serves two purposes: (1) to define default and user-defined abstractions and (2) to apply syntactic conversions from C to SPIN's input language PROMELA. The current model extractor uses a default rule to print or hide constructs that, because of language differences, would otherwise require user-intervention to be converted into PROMELA code. This applies, for instance, to statements that access data objects via pointers and to statements that contain function calls. These defaults are the 'last resort' of the model extractor, when it encounters a statement that has no obvious representation in PROMELA. The defaults allows the model extractor to generate syntactically correct verification models, that can be used immediately to perform simulations and initial verifications, but clearly the quality of the verification can be improved substantially if the user adjusts the default mappings in these cases by defining abstractions in PROMELA that match the semantics from the statements in C.

The need for syntactic conversions and manual intervention can be reduced if we allow for included C code fragments in a SPIN verification model. Such an extension was, for instance, described in [10] for an early predecessor of SPIN, serving a different purpose. The C code fragments are not parsed by SPIN but included *as is* into the model checking code that is generated from a verification model (which is C source text). Since the data objects that are accessed through the included C code fragments can contribute to the system *state*, they must now be included in the model checker's *state vector* [12]. The model extractor can be adjusted to automatically generate the right information for the most commonly occurring cases. As a syntax for the included code fragments we can consider, for instance,

```
c_decl   ...
c_code   ...
```

respectively for included declarations and included code, both in ANSI C syntax.

The included C code is likely to use memory more liberally than PROMELA would. It may use dynamically allocated memory and might access data in arbitrary ways via pointers. Both issues can in principle be resolved within the model checker. Dynamically allocated memory, for instance, can be tracked in the model checker by monitoring calls to memory allocation routines like sbrk() and malloc(). This gives the model checker an accurate view of all memory that can contain state information. The memory can be compressed and added to the state-vectors. The option would increase the runtime and memory requirements of a search, but would preserve its feasibility.

With bit-state hashing, the memory overhead for the state-space is avoided, though not necessarily the memory overhead for the depth-first search stack. In a bit-state search some state vectors are maintained in uncompressed form on the depth-first search stack (i.e., for actions that have no simple inverse that SPIN can precompute). For exceptionally large state-vectors, this could become prohibitively expensive when elaborate use is made of included C. In this case we can consider using SPIN's disk-cycling option, which maintains only a small portion of the stack in memory with only negligible runtime overhead.

When C code is included into a PROMELA verification model, we can no longer rely on SPIN's builtin interpreter to perform random or guided simulations. To solve this, we plan to add an option to SPIN for generating the simulation code as compilable C code, which can be linked with the related code for model checking that is already generated. Through the extended version of pan.c an identical set of simulation options can then be offered for models with included C code as SPIN does currently for pure PROMELA models.

Despite the hurdles, the option to allow included C code inside SPIN verification models appears to be feasible, and with that the possibility to perform at least approximate verifications of applications written in C. Because of the nature of the problem, it is not possible to provide any guarantees of verifiability. The thoroughness of a check can optionally be improved by a user by replacing included C code with abstracted PROMELA code, or by improving already existing abstractions, using the model extraction method we have described. If the code is entirely abstracted in PROMELA, we obtain a model with properties that are in principle fully decidable. But, also in this case effective verifiability will remain subject to the physical constraints of available memory and time.

The tabled abstraction method allows us to either set the desired level of abstraction, to obtain an increase in thoroughness and precision, or to ignore the issue if the default choices are adequate. The application of model checking techniques to program implementations can add an exceptionally thorough debugging capability to a programmer's toolset, for a class of software faults that is not adequately covered by existing techniques.

On Soundness. The emphasis in this paper has been on the work that is needed to construct a framework for model extraction for a implementation language that is widely used by practicing programmers, yet curiously often shunned by many of us who seek broader use of verification techniques in practice. The abstraction table method proposed here gives the verifier complete control over the abstraction and conversion process, perhaps more control than would at first sight appear to be desirable. Other techniques, beyond the scope of this paper, can be used to check or generate some of the abstractions, e.g., with the help of theorem proving techniques. Our plan is to add such techniques into our framework in a second phase of this work. It should be clear at this point, though, that these techniques by themselves are not sufficient to handle the full generality of applications that can be written in a language such as C. In many cases it will be impossible to formally prove the soundness of an abstraction for a given fragment of C code, or to mechanically generate an adequate abstraction. It is nevertheless desirable that we are able to perform exploratory verifications that are based on such abstractions.

7   Conclusion

Our long-term goal is to develop a reliable testing framework for distributed software applications that can be used without knowledge of model checking techniques. The work on AX is a step in that direction.

The main benefits of the model extraction method we have described can be summarized as follows.

– It allows the application of verification techniques to both high-level design models and low-level implementation code. This makes it possible to track an application throughout a design trajectory, providing an early bug detection capability that currently is not provided by other methodologies.
– After the initial project startup, the application of the fault tracking method based on model extraction requires only modest user intervention.
– The method targets a class of concurrency related software faults that is not addressed by traditional testing techniques. The faults of this type can cause dramatic system failure.
– The use of model checking allows us to introduce reproducibility, controllability, and observability into a test environment for distributed systems: three required elements of a reliable testing strategy.

The applications most suitable for verification with AX and SPIN are control-oriented, rather than data-oriented. Our model extraction method exploits the fact that control information can always be extracted automatically from program sources, and data use can be abstracted where relevant. Applications such as the call processing code used in telephone switches, or more generally data communications protocols, client-server applications, and distributed operating systems code, contain large fragments of control-oriented code, and are therefore good targets for this methodology.

Once the capability for mechanically extracting verification models from program source code exists, the motivation to construct verification models by hand is seriously undermined. The mechanically extracted models are almost always more accurate, easier to manipulate, and can track changes in the source code more easily.

Having a reliable model extractor has allowed us to undertake verification efforts that we would not have attempted before, specifically of larger and more complex applications. An advantage of the method we have described is that the source of an application need not be complete before verification is attempted. Only the part that needs checking has to be provided, the rest can be abstracted in test drivers that become part of the verification model. For large software applications (e.g., a telephone switch) not all the software is generally available, and even if it were, it could not be compiled and executed on just any machine, for the purposes of formal verification. The method based on model extraction can be applied to any fragment of the code that is available, to confirm its properties.

To combine the benefits of program slicing with the tabled abstraction method that is described in this paper, we are currently developing support for property-based slicing of PROMELA models, i.e., as a generic *model* slicing capability. The difficult pointer aliasing problem from programming languages such as C reappears in this context, but in a much simplified form, as a *channel* aliasing problem. The manner in which channels can be aliased in PROMELA, however, are very limited, which greatly simplifies data dependency analysis and slicing.

References

1. K.A. Bartlett, R.A. Scantlebury, and P.T. Wilkinson, A note on reliable full-duplex transmission over half-duplex lines, *Comm. of the ACM*, Vol. 12, No. 5, pp. 260–261, May 1969.
2. Chan, W., Anderson, R.J., Beame, P., et al., Model checking large software specifications. *IEEE Trans. on Software Engineering*, Vol. 24, No. 7, pp. 498–519, July 1998.
3. J. Corbett, M. Dwyer, et. al. Bandera: Extracting Finite-state Models from Java Source Code. *Proc. ICSE 2000*, Limerick, Ireland, to appear.
4. M.B. Dwyer, and C.S. Pasareanu. Filter-based Model Checking of Partial Systems *Proc. ACM SIGSOFT Sixth Int. Symp. on the Foundation of Software Engineering*, November 1998.
5. S. Flisakowski, C-Tree distribution, available from
   http://www.cs.wisc.edu/~flisakow/.
6. J.M. Fossaceca, J.D. Sandoz, and P. Winterbottom, The PathStar^{TM} access server: facilitating carrier-scale packet telephony. *Bell Labs Technical Journal*, Vol. 3, No. 4, pp. 86–102, Oct-Dec. 1998.
7. P. Godefroid, R.S. Hammer, L. Jagadeesan, Systematic Software Testing using Verisoft, *Bell Labs Technical Journal*, Volume 3, Number 2, April-June 1998.
8. J. Hatcliff, M.B. Dwyer, and H. Zheng, Slicing software for model construction, *Journal of Higher-Order and Symbolic Computation*, to appear 2000.
9. K. Havelund, T. Pressburger Model Checking Java Programs Using Java Path-Finder *Int. Journal on Software Tools for Technology Transfer*, to appear 2000.
10. G.J. Holzmann, and R.A. Beukers, The Pandora protocol development system, *Proc. 3rd IFIP Symposium on Protocol Specification, Testing, and Verification*, PSTV83, Zurich, Sw., June 1983, North-Holland Publ., Amsterdam, pp. 357–369.
11. G.J. Holzmann, and J. Patti, Validating SDL Specifications: An Experiment, *Proc. Conf on Protocol Specification, Testing, and Verification*, Twente University, Enschede, The Netherlands, June, 1989, pp. 317-326.
12. G.J. Holzmann, The model checker SPIN. *IEEE Trans. on Software Engineering*, Vol 23, No. 5, pp. 279–295, May 1997.
13. G.J. Holzmann, Designing executable abstractions, *Proc. Formal Methods in Software Practice*, March 1998, Clearwater Beach, Florida, USA, ACM Press.
14. G.J. Holzmann, An analysis of bitstate hashing, *Formal Methods in System Design*, Kluwer, Vol. 13,, No. 3, Nov. 1998, pp. 287–305.
15. G.J. Holzmann, and M.H. Smith, A practical method for the verification of event driven systems. *Proc. Int. Conf. on Software Engineering*, ICSE99, Los Angeles, pp. 597–608, May 1999.
16. G.J. Holzmann, and M.H. Smith, Automating software feature verification, *Bell Labs Technical Journal*, April-June 2000, Special Issue on Software Complexity, to appear.

17. B.W. Kernighan, and R. Pike, *The Practice of Programming*, Addison-Wesley, Cambridge, Mass., 1999, p.33.

18. B.W. Kernighan, and D.M. Ritchie, *The C Programming Language, 2nd Edition*, Prentice Hall, Englewood Cliffs, N.J., 1988.

19. L. Millett, and T. Teitelbaum, Slicing PROMELA and its applications to protocol understanding and analysis, Proc. 4th Spin Workshop, November 1998, Paris, France.

20. A. Pnueli, The temporal logic of programs. *Proc. 18th IEEE Symposium on Foundations of Computer Science*, 1977, Providence, R.I., pp. 46–57.

21. S. Savage, M. Burrows, G. Nelson, P. Sobalvarro, and T.E. Anderson. Eraser: A dynamic data race detector for multi-threaded programs. *ACM Transactions on Computer Systems (TOCS)*, 15(4):391–411, November 1997.

22. F. Tip, A survey of program slicing techniques. *Journal of Programming Languages*, Vol. 3, No. 3, Sept. 1995, pp. 121–189.

23. A.M. Turing, On computable numbers, with an application to the Entscheidungs problem. *Proc. London Mathematical Soc.*, Ser. 2–42, pp. 230-265 (see p. 247), 1936.

24. W. Visser, S. Park, and J. Penix, Applying predicate abstraction to model checking object-oriented programs. *Proc. 3rd ACM SOGSOFT Workshop on Formal Methods in Software Practice*, August 2000.

Interaction Abstraction for Compositional Finite State Systems

Wayne Liu

Department of Electrical and Computer Engineering
University of Waterloo
wbliu@uwaterloo.ca

Abstract. A new algorithm for reducing the state space of compositional finite state systems is introduced. Its goal is similar to compositional minimization algorithms as it tries to preserve only the relevant information for checking properties. It works better than compositional minimization because it reduces components individually and does not need to compose components. Hence it does not suffer from state explosion. Instead, it uses information about interactions with other components, and merges interactions that do not lead to different relevant behaviour. Experiments show that it reduces state spaces dramatically in the cases when only a part of the system's behaviour is of interest

1 Introduction

Model-checking encounters the state-explosion problem. To keep the state space manageable for model-checkers, models of systems should only include features relevant to the property being checked. Holzmann[12] showed it is possible check useful properties using very small models—less than 100 states. Unfortunately, it is often too expensive to manually create a separate model for each property to check. Thus, a single model of a system must be used to verify many different properties of the system.

In these situations, it is desirable to have an algorithm that can abstract away irrelevant features of the model, to create a reduced state space that preserves the property being checked.

A conceptual basis for this kind of abstraction is provided by equivalences of models, such as observation equivalence. Efficient minimization algorithms exist for observation equivalence. Unfortunately, minimization algorithms require the global state space to be generated, which means the reduction requires more effort than checking the model directly.

An approach to alleviate this problem is by compositional minimization, that is composing and minimizing subsets of the system components. Nevertheless, subsystems of components must be composed before they can be reduced, and which may cause state explosion in intermediate state spaces. Another problem is 'spurious behaviour', where a subsystem may exhibit behaviour that is not possible when it is a part of the system as a whole. Interface processes[17,5] have been proposed to reduce spurious behaviour. However, small and effective interface processes are very difficult to find.

K. Havelund, J. Penix, and W. Visser (Eds.): SPIN 2000, LNCS 1885, pp. 148–162, 2000.
© Springer-Verlag Berlin Heidelberg

Furthermore, removing spurious behaviour still leaves much 'redundant' behaviour in the reduced subsystems. Redundant interactions are interactions with the rest of the system that do not affect the property being checked.

The interaction abstraction algorithm is a new algorithm that has similar goals to compositional minimization. However, it automatically uses information about interactions with the rest of the system to remove redundant information from the model, while keeping information necessary to preserve the property being checked.

2 Abstraction Interaction Algorithm

2.1 Basic Notation

The algorithm is based on labelled transition systems (LTS)[16].

DEFINITION: An **LTS** is defined as a tuple (Q, A, Δ, q_0) where

- Q is a set of states
- A is a set of labels (or events)
- Δ is a set of transitions, $p_1 \longrightarrow a \rightarrow q_2$, where $p_1, q_2 \in Q$ and $a \in A$
- $q_0 \in Q$ is the initial state

DEFINITION: The **composition** of two LTSs, $S = (P_1, A_1, \Delta_1, p_{10})$ and $T = (P_2, A_2, \Delta_2, p_{20})$, is the LTS $S \parallel T$, defined as (Q, A, Δ, q_0) where

- $A = A_1 \cup A_2$,
- $Q = P_1 \times P_2$,
- Δ is the set of transitions of the form $(p_{11}, p_{21}) \longrightarrow a \rightarrow (p_{12}, p_{22})$ where
  - if $a \notin A_1 \cap A_2$ and $p_{11} \longrightarrow a \rightarrow p_{12}$, then $(p_{11}, p_{21}) \longrightarrow a \rightarrow (p_{12}, p_{21}) \in \Delta$
  - if $a \notin A_1 \cap A_2$ and $p_{21} \longrightarrow a \rightarrow p_{22}$, then $(p_{11}, p_{21}) \longrightarrow a \rightarrow (p_{11}, p_{22}) \in \Delta$
  - and if $a \in A_1 \cap A_2$ and $p_{11} \longrightarrow a \rightarrow p_{12}$ and $p_{21} \longrightarrow a \rightarrow p_{22}$, then $(p_{11}, p_{21}) \longrightarrow a \rightarrow (p_{12}, p_{22}) \in \Delta$
- the initial state is $q_0 = (p_{10}, p_{20})$

The LTS formalism models abstraction through hiding of labels. Labels that are not of interest in the system (e.g. not mentioned in property to be checked, and not used to interact with other components) can be hidden by renaming them to the special label, τ. A sequence of 0 or more transitions with hidden labels is written as $p_1 = \tau \Rightarrow p_2$ if exist $p_1 \longrightarrow \tau \rightarrow \ldots \longrightarrow \tau \rightarrow p_i$, $i \geq 0$. The weak transition relation is defined as $p_1 = a \Rightarrow p_2$, if exists $p_1 = \tau \Rightarrow p_3, \longrightarrow a \rightarrow p_4 = \tau \Rightarrow p_2$. The weak transition relation enables any number of hidden actions to take place without affecting the observable properties of the system. A system S in which only labels in a set L are visible, and the rest are hidden, is denoted $S<L>$.

Various notions of equivalence exist for LTS, including the well-known observation equivalence[16]. Observation equivalence is defined using a family of bisimulation relations:

- $R_0 \equiv Q \times Q$,
- $R_{k+1} \equiv \{(p_1,p_2) \mid \forall a \in A \ \forall p_1'(p_1 = a \Rightarrow p_1' \Rightarrow \exists p_2'(p_2 = a \Rightarrow p_2' \wedge (p_1',p_2') \in R_k) \wedge$
  $\forall p_2'(p_2 = a \Rightarrow p_2' \Rightarrow \exists p_1'(p_1 = a \Rightarrow p_1' \wedge (p_1',p_2') \in R_k)\}$

The (observation) equivalence relation is defined as $\sim \equiv \bigcup_0^\infty R_k$. Thus, $p_1 \sim p_2$ if $(p_1,p_2) \in R_k$ for all k. Two systems are observation equivalent if their initial states are equivalent.

Given a classification of the states of S, where $[p]$ denotes the class of p, the **quotient** of S, is the LTS $[S] = ([Q], A, [\Delta], [q_0])$ where

- $[Q] = \{[q]\}$ for all $q \in Q$
- $[\Delta] = \{[p_1] \longrightarrow a \rightarrow [q_2]\}$ for all $p_1 \longrightarrow a \rightarrow q_2 \in \Delta$

2.2 Effect of Interactions

To get an intuition for how the algorithm works, consider the composition of two systems, $S \parallel T$, in Figure 1. The goal is to find reduced versions, $[S]$ and $[T]$, so that $(S \parallel T)<a_1, a_2, a_3> \sim ([S] \parallel [T])< a_1, a_2, a_3>$.

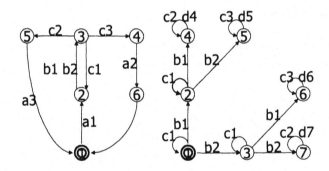

Fig. 1. Example system with two components.

The component on the left can be thought of as a simple model of a telephone, and the component on the right can be thought of as a simple model of a phone directory. Thus, the telephone can go offhook (a1), then a '1' is dialed (b1), then the number is found to be incomplete (c1), in which case, a '2' is dialed (b2), and it is found to be a complete, and valid number (c3). The telephone then connects to the other phone (a2), and so on. On the other hand, dialing a second '1' would result in an invalid number (c2), and the telephone would give a busy tone (a3).

Suppose we are interested only in the actions offhook, connect, or busy tone (a1, a2, a3). In particular, we are not interested in which numbers are dialed (b1, b2), nor the internal interactions between the components (c1, c2). Intuitively, the directory model can be reduced to just three states: from the initial state, it can move to a state with a valid phone number, or an invalid one. The telephone model can be reduced to move from state 2 directly to 5 or 4.

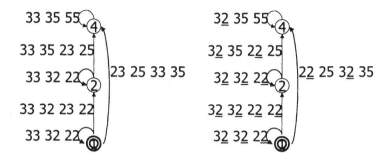

Fig. 3. Part of component relabelled with transitive effect of interactions.

The idea is to achieve the reduction is to record the effect of the interactions of the components, rather than the actual labels. As a first attempt, we can use this idea directly, and relabel the directory model as in Figure 2. For example, the transition $1—b1→2$ is relabelled by the effect of the interaction on the phone model. The phone model makes the transition $2—b1→3$, so the directory model gets the transition $1—23→2$.

This relabelling allows the merging of states $\{4,7\}$, $\{2,3\}$ and $\{5,6\}$. However, the reduce graph is still unsatisfactory in that the merged state $\{2,3\}$ is distinguished from state $\{1\}$. That means the model tracks how many numbers must be dialed to get a complete number. However, from the point of view of observational equivalence, it does not matter how many internal steps occur between externally visible steps.

The approach to obtain full reduction is to label the model with the transitive closure of the effects of individual interactions. Part of the model labelled with the transitive closure is shown in the left part of Figure 3. The labelling shows the source and destination of the other component, after a sequence of internal interactions. An extra transition between states 1 and 4 has been added.

Unfortunately, the model still cannot be further reduced, as state 1 has a transition $—23→$ that leads to state 2, while state 2 does not have a transition $—23→$ that leads to an equivalent state. The problem is the phone model's states 2 and 3 are distinct.

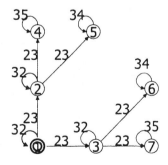

Fig. 2. Component relabelled with effect of interactions.

to an equivalent state. The problem is the phone model's states 2 and 3 are distinct. But they do not need to be, as they do not result in different external behaviour (as internal interactions are not observable). If states 2 and 3 of the phone model can be merged (labelled as '2'), then the portion of the directory model becomes the right side of Figure 3, where it can be seen that states 2 and 1 can be merged.

The idea is to track whether interactions cause the other model to move to equivalent states, rather than just the same states. Unfortunately, which states can be considered equivalent in the other model also depends on which states can be considered equivalent in this model, and vice versa. Thus, the equivalence reduction needs to be computed iteratively.

At the end, the interaction labels in the two reduced models must be matched in order to allow the models to compose.

2.3 Algorithm

The steps of the interaction abstraction algorithm for one component are as follows:
1. Calculate transitive effect of interactions:

    - Store tuple (p, q, p', q') iff whenever the state (p,q) is reachable, there is a transition $(p,q) = \tau \Rightarrow (p',q')$ in $(S \parallel T) < L >$
2. For a given classification $[T]_0$ of T, relabel S with assumed equivalent effects, to obtain S_1:

    - Remove all transitions with labels not in $L \cup \{\tau\}$
    - Add a transition $p - q[q']_0 \rightarrow p'$ for each tuple (p, q, p', q')
3. Classify S_1 to obtain $[S]_1$:

    - Set $[p_1]_1 = [p_2]_1$ iff $p_1 \sim p_2$ in S_1

The iteration for two components is as follows:
4. Repeat Steps 2 and 3 until $[S]_k$ and $[T]_k$ are the same as $[S]_{k-1}$ and $[T]_{k-1}$:

    - Update $[T]_k$ using $[S]_{k-1}$ if changed, and vice versa
5. Finally, label interactions in $[S]=[S]_k$ and $[T]=[T]_k$:

    - Remove transitions with labels not in L
    - For each tuple (p, q, p', q') add transitions $[p] - [p][q][p'][q'] \rightarrow [p']$ in $[S]$, and $[q] - [p][q][p'][q'] \rightarrow [q']$ in $[T]$

After Step 5, $[S]$ and $[T]$ can be composed using the "interaction labels".

2.4 Proof of Correctness

We want to prove that, at the end of the algorithm, $(S \parallel T) < L > \sim ([S] \parallel [T]) < L >$ by proving that for all (p,q) reachable, $(p,q) \sim ([p],[q])$. And since the initial state (p_0,q_0) is reachable, then the two compositions are equivalent. First, we prove some properties of the algorithm.

LEMMA 1:

If $[p_1]_k=[p_2]_k$ then all of the following are true:

a) for all transitions $p_1 =\tau\Rightarrow p_1'$ there exists a transition such that $p_2 =\tau\Rightarrow p_2'$ where $[p_2']_k=[p_1']_k$

b) for all transitions $p_2 =\tau\Rightarrow p_2'$ there exists a transition such that $p_1 =\tau\Rightarrow p_1'$ where $[p_2']_k=[p_1']_k$

c) for all tuples (p_1, q, p_1', q_1'), there exists a tuple (p_2, q, p_2', q_2') where $[p_2']_k=[p_1']_k$ and $[q_2']_k=[q_1']_k$

d) for all tuples (p_2, q, p_2', q_2'), there exists a tuple (p_1, q, p_1', q_1') where $[p_1']_k=[p_2']_k$ and $[q_1']_k=[q_2']_k$

PROOF:

$[p_1]_k=[p_2]_k$

$\Rightarrow p_1 \sim p_2$ in S_k, by definition of $[S]_k$

$\Rightarrow$ for all transitions $p_1 =a\Rightarrow p_1'$ there exists a transition $p_2 =a\Rightarrow p_2'$ where $p_2' \sim p_1'$ in S_k, by corollary to the definition of $\sim$

$\Rightarrow$ for all transitions $p_1 =\tau\Rightarrow p_1'$ there exists a transition $p_2 =\tau\Rightarrow p_2'$ where $[q_2']_{k-1}= [q_1']_{k-1}$, by definition of $[T]_{k-1}$, by which follows cases (a) and (b).

For cases (c) and (d), if there exists a tuple (p_1, q, p_1', q_1')

$\Rightarrow$ there exists a transition $p_1 —q[q_1']_{k-1} \rightarrow p_1'$

$\Rightarrow$ there exists a transition $p_2 =q[q_1']_{k-1} \Rightarrow p_2'$ where $[p_2']_{k-1}=[p_1']_{k-1}$ since $p_1 \sim p_2$

And since tuples contain transitive effects (Step 1), there exists a tuple (p_2, q, p_2', q_2') where $[q_2']_{k-1}=[q_1']_{k-1}$.

■

LEMMA 2:

a) If there exists a transition $(p,q)=\tau\Rightarrow(p',q')$ in $(S \parallel T)<L>$ then there exists a transition $([p],[q])=\tau\Rightarrow([p'],[q'])$ in $([S] \parallel [T])<L>$

b) If there exists a transition $p=a\Rightarrow p'$ in S, where $a\notin L$, then there exists a transition $[p]=a\Rightarrow[p']$ in $[S]$

PROOF:

Proof of (a):

$(p,q)=\tau\Rightarrow(p',q')$ in $(S \parallel T)<L>$

$\Rightarrow$ exist tuples (p, q, p', q') by Step 1

$\Rightarrow$ exist transitions $[p]—[p][q][p'][q']\rightarrow[p']$ in $[S]$, and $[q]—[p][q][p'][q']\rightarrow[q']$ in $[T]$ by Step 5

$\Rightarrow$ $([p],[q])=\tau\Rightarrow([p'],[q'])$ in $([S] \parallel [T])<L>$ by composition.

Proof of (b): True since the quotient keeps transitions of elements of a class, and the algorithm does not relabel transitions with label a in L.

■

LEMMA 3 (inverse of Lemma 2):

a) If there exists a transition $([p],[q]) = \tau \Rightarrow ([p'],[q'])$ in $([S] \parallel [T]) <L>$ and (p,q) is reachable, then there exists a transition $(p,q) = \tau \Rightarrow (p_1',q_1')$ in $(S \parallel T) <L>$ where $[p_1'] = [p']$, $[q_1'] = [q']$.

b) If there exists a transition $[p] = a \Rightarrow [p']$ in $[S]$, where $a \notin L$, then there exists a transition $p = a \Rightarrow p_1'$ in S where $[p_1'] = [p']$.

PROOF:

Proof of (a):

$([p],[q]) = \tau \Rightarrow ([p'],[q'])$

Since the only interactions are through the interaction labels, then by composition and hiding,

$\Rightarrow$ exist transitions $[p] = [p][q][p'][q'] \Rightarrow [p']$ in $[S]$ and $[q] = [p][q][p'][q'] \Rightarrow [q']$ in $[T]$

$\Rightarrow$ exist transitions $[p] = \tau \Rightarrow [p_2] - [p][q][p'][q'] \rightarrow [p_2] = \tau \Rightarrow [p']$ in $[S]$, and $[p_2] = [p]$, $[p_2] = [p']$ (by Step 5)

Since $[S]_k = [S]_{k-1}$ and $[T]_k = [T]_{k-1}$,

$\Rightarrow$ exist transitions $p_1 - q_1 [q']_k \rightarrow p_1'$ in S_k where $[p_2]_k = [p_1]_k = [p]_k$, $[p_2]_k = [p']_k$

$\Rightarrow$ exist tuples (p_1, q_1, p_1', q_1'), where $[q_1]_k = [q]_k$, $[p_1]_k = [p']_k$

$\Rightarrow$ exist tuples (p, q_1, p_1', q_1'), where $[q_1]_k = [q]_k$ (By Lemma 1(c) and (d), since $[p_1]_k = [p]_k$)

$\Rightarrow$ exist tuples (p, q, p_1', q_1') (By Lemma 1 applied to $[T]_k$)

$\Rightarrow$ if (p,q) is reachable, then there exists a transition $(p,q) = \tau \Rightarrow (p_1',q_1')$ in $(S \parallel T) <L>$ where $[q_1'] = [q']$ and $[p_1'] = [p']$

Proof of (b): True by definition of quotient and by Lemma 1(a) and (b).   ∎

THEOREM: If (p,q) reachable in $(S \parallel T) <L>$, then $(p,q) \sim ([p],[q])$ in $([S] \parallel [T]) <L>$.

PROOF:

The proof is a simple application of the definitions. It only uses the properties of the algorithm given in Lemmas 2 and 3.

Obviously for all (p,q) reachable, $((p,q), ([p],[q]))$ in R_0.

Assume for all (p,q) reachable, $((p,q), ([p],[q]))$ in R_{k-1}.

$(p,q) = a \Rightarrow (p',q')$ where a in L

$\Rightarrow (p,q) = \tau \Rightarrow (p_1,p_1) - a \rightarrow (p_2,q_2) = \tau \Rightarrow (p',q')$ by definition of $= a \Rightarrow$

$\Rightarrow ([p],[q]) = \tau \Rightarrow ([p_1],[p_1]) = a \Rightarrow ([p_2],[q_2]) = \tau \Rightarrow ([p'],[q'])$ by lemma 1 (a) and (b)

$\Rightarrow ([p],[q]) = a \Rightarrow ([p'],[q'])$ by definition of $= a \Rightarrow$

And by induction hypothesis, $((p',q'), ([p'],[q']))$ in R_{k-1}

For the other direction:

$([p],[q]) = a \Rightarrow ([p'],[q'])$

$\Rightarrow ([p],[q]) = \tau \Rightarrow ([p_1],[p_1]) - a \rightarrow ([p_2],[q_2]) = \tau \Rightarrow ([p'],[q'])$ by definition of $= a \Rightarrow$

$\Rightarrow (p,q) = \tau \Rightarrow (p_3,q_3) = a \Rightarrow (p_4,q_4) = \tau \Rightarrow (p_5,q_5)$ where $[p_3] = [p_1]$, $[q_3] = [p_1]$, $[p_4] = [p_2]$, $[q_4] = [q_2]$, $[p_5] = [p']$, and $[q_5] = [q']$ by lemma 2 (a) and (b)

$\Rightarrow (p,q) = a \Rightarrow (p_5,q_5)$ where $[p_5] = [p']$, and $[q_5] = [q']$

$\Rightarrow (p,q) = a \Rightarrow (p_s', q_s')$ where $[p_s'] = [p']$, and $[q_s'] = [q']$

And by induction hypothesis, $(\ (p_s', q_s'), ([p'],[q'])\ )$ in R_{k-1}.

Thus, $(\ (p,q), ([p],[q])\ )$ in R_k for all k

∎

Next, it is necessary to show the algorithm always terminates, which can be done using the following lemma.

LEMMA: Let the classification $[T]_k$ be a refinement of the classification $[T]_{k-1}$. Then $[S]_{k+1}$ computed using $[T]_k$ is a refinement of $[S]_k$ computed using the labelling $[T]_{k-1}$.

PROOF:

Suppose $[p_1]_k = [p_2]_k$. We want to show that $[p_1]_{k+1} = [p_2]_{k+1}$, that is, if $p_1 \sim p_2$ in S_k, then $p_1 \sim p_2$ in S_{k+1}.

Since $[T]_k$ is a refinement of $[T]_{k-1}$, if labels $q_1[q_1']_{k-1} = q_1[q_2']_{k-1}$, then labels $q_1[q_1']_k = q_1[q_2']_k$. Thus, if two transitions in S_k have the same labels using the labelling $= q_1[q_1']_{k-1} \Rightarrow$, the transitions in S_{k+1} will still have the same labels using the labelling $= q_1[q_2']_k \Rightarrow$.

Supose $p_1 \sim p_2$ in S_k

$\Leftrightarrow$ for any transition $p_1 = a_1 \Rightarrow p_1'$, there is a corresponding transition $p_2 = a_1 \Rightarrow p_2'$, and $p_1' \sim p_2'$ in S_k

Since the labels a_1 of the two transitions $p_1 = a_1 \Rightarrow p_1'$ and $p_2 = a_1 \Rightarrow p_2'$ are guaranteed to be the same in S_{k+1} as in S_k,

$\Rightarrow$ for any transition $p_1 = a_1 \Rightarrow p_1'$, there is a corresponding transition $p_2 = a_1 \Rightarrow p_2'$, and $p_1' \sim p_2'$ in S_{k+1}

$\Leftrightarrow p_1' \sim p_2'$ in S_{k+1}

∎

The lemma shows that the algorithm is monotonic, that is, each iteration computes a refinement of the classification of the previous iteration. Since the number of refinements is finite, the number of iterations is finite and the algorithm must terminate.

2.5 Multiple Components and Multi-way Interactions

It has been shown how to compute the reduction for two components. For multiple components with 2-way interactions, the interactions between each pair of components are collected and labelled separately.

For Step 1, we can simply store $S_iS_j:(p_i, p_j, p_i', p_j')$ if there is a transition $(p_i, p_j) = \tau \Rightarrow (p_i', p_j')$ in $(S_i \| S_j)<L>$. This satisfies the condition that $S_iS_j:(p_i, p_j, p_i', p_j')$ is stored iff whenever the state $(\ldots p_i, \ldots, p_j, \ldots)$ is reachable, there is a transition $(\ldots p_i, \ldots, p_j, \ldots) = \tau \Rightarrow (\ldots p_i', \ldots, p_j', \ldots)$ in $(S_1 \| \ldots \| S_n)<L>$ (only the i and j components change). For Step 2, the labels are added as $p_i - p_j[p_j']_0 \rightarrow p_i$ for all tuples $S_iS_j:(p_i, p_j, p_i', p_j')$. For the iteration Step 4, update all $[S_i]_k$ if any $[S_j]_{k-1}$ with which it interacts has changed. For Step 5, for all tuples $S_iS_j:(p_i, p_j, p_i', p_j')$, add transitions $[p_i] - S_iS_j:[p_i][p_j][p_i'][p_j'] \rightarrow [p_i']$ in $[S_i]$ and $[p_j] - S_iS_j:[p_i][p_j][p_i'][p_j'] \rightarrow [p_j']$ in $[S_j]$.

Lemma 1 is changed to

a)   for all tuples $(p_{i1}, p_j, p_{i1}', p_{j1})$, there exists a tuple $(p_{i2}, p_j, p_{i2}', p_{j2})$ where $[p_{i2}']_k=[p_{i1}']_k$ and $[p_{j2}]_k=[p_{j1}]_k$

b)   for all tuples $(p_{i2}, p_j, p_{i2}', p_{j2})$, there exists a tuple $(p_{i1}, p_j, p_{i1}', p_{j1})$ where $[p_{i1}']_k=[p_{i2}']_k$ and $[p_{j1}]_k=[p_{j2}]_k$

Lemma 2 is changed to

a)   If there exists a transition $(...p_i,..., p_j,...) \Longrightarrow^\tau (...p_i',..., p_j',...)$ in $(S_1 || ... || S_n)<L>$ then there exists a transition $(...[p_i],..., [p_j],...) \Longrightarrow^\tau (...[p_i'],..., [p_j'],...)$ in $([S_1] || ... || [S_n])<L>$

b)   If there exists a transition $p_i \Longrightarrow^a p_i'$ in S_i, where $a \notin L$, then there exists a transition $[p_i] \Longrightarrow^a [p_i']$ in $[S_i]$

Similarly, change Lemma 3 and all the proofs. That is, p, q is replaced with $...p_i,..., p_j,...$ and $S || T$ is replaced with $S_1 || ... || S_n$. The proof of the theorem is changed so that a τ-transition $(p_1,..., p_n) \Longrightarrow^\tau (p_1',..., p_n')$ in $(S_1 || ... || S_n)<L>$ must be broken down into a sequence of constituent τ-transitions with pair-wise interactions, such as $(...p_i,..., p_j,...) \Longrightarrow^\tau (...p_i',..., p_j',...)$. Then, the lemmas are applied to each constituent τ-transition.

For multi-way interactions, interactions for each subset of interacting components is collected and labelled separately. For example, for a 3-way interaction, the stored vectors are $S_iS_jS_k(p_1, p_2, p_3, p_1', p_2', p_3')$ if there is a transition $(p_1, p_2, p_3) \Longrightarrow^\tau (p_1', p_2', p_3')$ in $(S_1 || S_2 || S_3 || ... || S_n)<L>$. The conditions, the other steps, and the proof proceed similarly.

2.6 Algorithm Complexity

A bound for the algorithm complexity can be obtained by adding up the cost of basic operations.

Since interactions with each pair of components are collected separately, the stored interactions (for 2-way interactions) is $S_iS_j(p_i, p_j, p_i', p_j')$. Thus, the maximum number of interactions of S_i is at worst nm^4 for a system of n components, all with m states. For multi-way interactions, the number of interactions is at worst nm^{2k} if there are at most k-way interactions.

Minimization of each component by observational equivalence can be performed in $O(ne)$ time, where e is the number of transitions of the relabelled components. The number of transitions is the number of interactions plus the number of visible transitions. At worst, this is lm^2+nm^4, where l is the number of externally visible labels. Assuming l is unrelated to m and n, then the number of transitions is $O(nm^4)$. (Typically, l should be small.) Thus, the minimization has complexity $O(n^2m^4)$. (For k-way interactions, the minimization has complexity $O(n^2m^{2k})$).

During one iteration, at most n minimizations is required. The number of iterations is at most the sum of the states of the components, nm, since the size of one reduced component must increase or else the algorithm terminates. Thus, the number of minimizations is at most $O(n^2m)$, and the overall complexity is $O(n^4m^5)$. (For k-way interactions, complexity is $O(n^4m^{2k+1})$).

2.7 Algorithm Notes

Collecting interactions with each pair of components separately means reductions can be computed without composing the rest of the system. However, the disadvantage is that interactions with different components are being distinguished from each other, thus lessening the amount of reduction possible. For example, interactions of S_i with two different components would still be distinguished even if the interactions do not change the states of either of the other components. In particular, a system with all labels hidden would not reduce to a set of 1-state abstractions!

An optimization can be made in the number of edges added to components. In many cases, the same edges in S (labelled $p_1[p_2]$) may cause many different edges in T (labelled $q_1[q_2]$). But, for the purpose of reducing the components, many of the labels $q_1[q_2]$ are redundant. Two labels $q_1[q_2]$ are redundant if they always appear together in all transitions labelled $p_1[p_2]$, since they can never be used to distinguish any states in S.

Formally, it is safe to merge the labels a and b if, whenever there is a transition labelled with $p_1 = a \Rightarrow p_2$, then there is also a transition labelled with $p_1 = b \Rightarrow p_2$, and vice versa. Experiments show this optimization greatly reduces the number of transitions, and significantly speeds up the minimization of components.

2.8 Scalability of Algorithm

In theory, the abstraction algorithm avoids state explosion by avoiding composition of components and abstracting each component individually. Nevertheless, the theoretical complexity of $O(n^4 m^5)$ looks quite daunting for practical use. However, the actual situation is much better in experiments.

The major factor in the cost is the set of interactions between two components. This set has a theoretical size complexity of $O(m^4)$. This level of complexity can occur in practice with components that are basically data structures. It is important to realize, however, that this complexity simply results from interactions between two components. Any type of model-checking that takes into account interactions between components must face at least this level of complexity.

Let us assume that individual components are small, so that the tools built are able to handle compositions of two components in a reasonable (i.e. constant) time. This assumption eliminates the powers of m. Also at the most four iterations of reductions were required for each component in experiments. That is much better than the worst case of $O(n^2)$ minimizations of each component. Further, assume that components only interact with a limited (i.e. bounded) number of other components. This eliminates one power of n.

Thus, the actual observed complexity under these assumptions is proportional to $O(n)$ and the effort depends linearly on the number of components.

3 Implementation and Results

The algorithm has been implemented in a prototype tool as part of the Component Interaction Testing project. One of the goals of the project is to generate test cases from formal design models of software. The other parts of the project include

- the ObjectState formal object-oriented modelling language with features similar to UML for Real-Time[15]
- formal interaction coverage criteria for generating test requirements from models of component (Event-flow[14])
- tools to translate design models and test requirements to the LTS formalism (or Promela[10]), and generate test cases, exploiting the abstraction algorithm.

The tool uses the Caesar-Aldebaran Development Package (CADP)[6]. The CADP toolbox provides facilities to generate LTS files, compute compositions and minimizations. It does not have facilities to compute hook compositions.

The performance of the algorithm was tested using a model of a private branch exchange (PBX) software. The design model is 1000 lines of ObjectState code, while the implementation of the PBX is 16 000 lines of C code.

The following model-checking tools and algorithms were compared:

- SPIN[10], using depth-first, partial-order reduction, supertrace
- Exhibitor, part of CADP, using simple on-the-fly breadth-first search
- Araprod[19] using on-the-fly breadth-first search with partial-order reduction
- Aldebaran, part of CADP, using minimal model generation[3], BDDs
- new analyzer using incremental test generation (observational minimization)
- new analyzer with incremental test generation, and interaction abstraction.

The tools were chosen because they implement advanced and successful model-checking algorithms. All the tools are freely obtainable for research purposes.

3.1 Test Results

Beginning with only one component and the test requirement, the tools were given more components to analyze until they exceeded available memory or failed to give an answer in a reasonable amount of time (i.e. 24 hours).

The test results are shown in Table 1. The components of the PBX model as listed as CH (call handler), DB (database), CM (call manager), LS (line scan), and REQ (the test requirement).

The interaction abstraction algorithm allows much larger models to be analyzed than possible with the other tools. Even for the simplest case of finding a path for a single component, the Aldebaran and Araprod tools failed. SPIN failed for the interaction of two components. The simple breadth-first search in Exhibitor performed better than the more complex algorithms, but it eventually failed to compute a path for three components. With incremental test generation (observational minimization), an additional component can be analyzed. Adding interaction abstraction, five components can be analyzed. However, it also fails when the sixth component was included.

Component subset	PROD	Alde-baran	SPIN	Exhibi-tor	Increment test gen	Interact abstract
REQ +CH	Memory out	Time out	554	790	365	4113
REQ +CH +DB	-	-	Not found	7644	534	6158
REQ +CH +DB +CM	-	-	-	Memory out	677	6311
REQ +2×CH +DB +CM	-	-	-	-	Time out	8436
REQ +3×CH +DB +CM	-	-	-	-	-	10431
REQ +2×CH +DB +CM +LS	-	-	-	-	-	Memory out

Table 1. Times (seconds) for generating paths by each tool

The reason the interaction abstraction failed was the large number of interactions with the sixth component (LS). Recall that there are worst $O(m^4)$ interactions, and this seems to occur in this case. This number of interactions overwhelms the available memory.

The sizes of the models and the impressive reductions achieved by interaction abstraction are shown in Table 2. Each table shows a subset of components that was analyzed. Note that the number of states of a component can be different in different subsets because the component may have to interact with different numbers of other components, and hence require more states. Also the test generation procedure is incremental, and makes several passes. Thus, the actual number of states for each pass is usually much smaller than the maximum shown.

Note that the implementation currently has an error in it that causes it to over-reduce components in some cases, and hence generate incorrect test cases. However, all the test cases generated in the examples shown are correct. Thus, it is likely that the reductions are correct for these examples.

4 Related Work

There are many state space reduction algorithms, and they target different kinds of redundancy in the state space representation. Many redundancies exist as some type of shared state space structure, such as symmetry[13], partial-order equivalence[9], hierarchical state machines[1], shared state representation (using BDDs[4], state compression[8]), and so on. Interaction abstraction, on the other hand, exploits redundancy in model interactions that do not lead to different relevant behaviour. For example, models of systems may deal with many aspects, but only one aspect is of interest at a time.

	REQ	CH1
RAW	7	85956
MIN	5	12790
ABS	5	315

	REQ	DB	CH1
RAW	7	291	85956
MIN	5	4	12390
ABS	5	2	383

	REQ	DB	CM	CH1
RAW	7	291	146	85956
MIN	5	4	125	12790
ABS	5	2	37	392

	REQ	DB	CM	CH1	CH2
RAW	7	579	390	85956	85956
MIN	5	7	223	12790	12790
ABS	5	2	18	63	156

	REQ	DB	CM	CH1	CH2	CH3
RAW	7	579	390	85956	85956	85956
MIN	5	7	223	12790	12790	12790
ABS	5	2	172	102	174	81

	REQ	DB	CM	LS	CH1	CH2
RAW	7	579	390	41371	85956	85956
MIN	5	7	223	1665	12790	12790
ABS	5	2	166	861	326	408

Table 2. Number of states of components, after observation minimization. after interaction abstraction (maximum over all test generation passes)

Interaction abstraction can be used as a preprocessing step for other reduction techniques. After abstraction, other techniques can be applied, including compositional minimization, on-the-fly search, or partial-order reduction. This approach exploits the greatest amount of redundancy in models.

The most closely related algorithms are compositional minimization algorithms. Interaction abstraction differs compositional minimization in that it does not need to compose components of a subsystem, but reduces each component by itself using information about interactions with other components. Thus it avoids the state-explosion problem. Also, it takes into account context of components (its interactions with the rest of the system). Unlike methods using interface processes[5][17], it is completely automatic, and multiple contexts are taken into account without needing to compose the contexts. In addition, interaction abstraction merges redundant interactions, and only preserves behaviour that is relevant to the property being checked, allowing for greater reduction.

While compositional minimization typically tries to construct a single minimal global model on which many different properties can be evaluated, interaction abstraction is much more effective when few behaviours are observable. Therefore, it is more effective to create a specific abstraction for each property to be checked.

5 Conclusions

A new algorithm has been presented to reduce the state space of a model for model checking by abstracting component interactions that are not relevant to the property being checked. It is proved that the algorithm preserves behaviour of interest. Abstraction is performed without composing components, thus avoiding the state space explosion problem.

The algorithm is most useful when models of systems may deal with many aspects, but only one aspect is of interest at a time. It is not useful for properties that depend on all behaviours of a system, such as absence of deadlock.

The complexity of the algorithm is $O(n^4 m^5)$ for a system with n components that have m states maximum. (For systems where k components interact simultaenously, complexity is $O(n^4 m^{2k+1})$). However, for systems that are made up of many small, loosely-coupled components, and each component communicates with a limited number of other components, the algorithm performs well.

Interaction abstraction can be used in conjunction with other reduction techniques, such as compositional minimization, on-the-fly search, or partial-order reduction. By combining different methods, the greatest amount of redundancy in models is exploited.

Experiments show the algorithm is very effective in reducing state spaces, and allowing much larger models to be analyzed than previously possible.

Research is needed to achieve greater reduction. Especially, the algorithm should handle multiple components better. Rather than distinguishing interactions with different components, it is desirable to only consider the final result of interactions with all other components. The problem is how to achieve this without an explosion in the number of interactions that must be stored. In addition, the algorithm should be extended to preserve coarser equivalence relations, such as safety equivalence[2] or trace equivalence. Finally, the algorithm should be incorporated into industrial-strength tools in order to be used for practical applications.

References

1. R. Alur and M. Yannakakis. "Model checking of hierarchical state machines". Sixth ACM Symposium on the Foundations of Software Engineering, pp. 175-188, 1998
2. A. Bouajjani, J.-C. Fernandez, S. Graf, C. Rodriguez and J. Sifakis. Safety for Branching Time Semantics. 18th ICALP, Springer-Verlag, July 1991.
3 A. Bouajjani, J.C. Fernandez, N. Halbwachs, C. Ratel, and P. Raymond. "Minimal state graph generation". Science of Computer Programming, 18(3), June 1992.
4. J.R. Burch, E.M. Clarke, K.L. McMillan, D.L. Dill, and J. Hwang. "Symbolic Model Checking: 10^{20} states and beyond". Technical Report, Carnegie Mellon University, 1989.
5. S. C. Cheung and J. Kramer. Context Constraints for Compositional Reachability Analysis. ACM Transactions on Software Engineering and Methodology. October 1996.
6. Jean-Claude Fernandez, Hubert Garavel, Alain Kerbrat, Radu Mateescu, Laurent Mounier, and Mihaela Sighireanu. CADP: A Protocol Validation and Verification Toolbox. Proceedings of the 8th Conference on Computer-Aided Verification (New Brunswick, New Jersey, USA), pages 437-440, August 1996

7. Jean-Claude Fernandez. An Implementation of an Efficient Algorithm for Bisimulation Equivalence. Science of Computer Programming, volume 13, number 2-3, pages 219-236, May 1990.

8. J-Ch. Grégoire, "State space compression in SPIN with GETSs", Second SPIN Workshop, August 1996.

9. P. Godefroid and P. Wolper. "A partial approach to model checking". In Proc. 6th Annual Symposium on Logic in Computer Science, pages 406-415, July 1991.

10. G. J. Holzmann. Design and Validation of Computer Protocols. Prentice Hall 1991.

11. G.J. Holzmann. The engineering of a model checker: the Gnu i-protocol case study revisited. Proc. of the 6th Spin Workshop LNCS, Vol. LNCS 1680, Springer Verlag, Toulouse France, Sept. 1999.

12. G.J. Holzmann. Designing executable abstractions. Proc. Formal Methods in Software Practice, ACM Press, Clearwater Beach Florida USA, March 1998.

13. K. Jensen. Coloured Petri Nets. Volume 2, Analysis Methods. Monographs in Theoretical Computer Science 575, Springer-Verlag 1992, pp.192-202.

14. Wayne Liu and Paul Dasiewicz. Selecting System Test Cases for Object-oriented Programs Using Event-Flow. Proceedings of the Canadian Conference on Electrical and Computer Engineering (CCECE '97)

15. Andrew Lyons. UML for Real-Time Overview. RATIONAL Software Corporation Whitepaper, April 1998, Available at http://www.rational.com/.

16. R.Milner (1980), A calculus of communication systems, LNCS 92, Springer-Verlag

17. B. Steffen, S. Graf, G. Lüttgen "Compositional Minimization of Finite State Systems". International Journal on Formal Aspects of Computing, Vol. 8, pp. 607-616, 1996.

18. A. Valmari. The State Explosion Problem. Lectures on Petri Nets I: Basic Models, Lecture Notes in Computer Science 1491, Springer-Verlag 1998, pp. 429-528

19. Kimmo Varpaaniemi, Jaakko Halme, Kari Hiekkanen, and Tino Pyssysalo. PROD reference manual. Technical Report B13, Helsinki University of Technology, Digital Systems Laboratory, Espoo, Finland, August 1995.

Correctness by Construction: Towards Verification in Hierarchical System Development

Mila Majster-Cederbaum and Frank Salger

Universität Mannheim
Fakultät für Mathematik und Informatik,
D7, 27, 68131 Mannheim, Germany
{mcb, fsalger}@pi2.informatik.uni-mannheim.de

Abstract. In many approaches to the verification of reactive systems, operational semantics are used to model systems whereas specifications are expressed in temporal logics. Most approaches however assume, that the initial specification is indeed the intended one. Changing the specification thus necessitates to find an accordingly adapted system and to carry out the verification from scratch. During a systems life cycle however, changes of the requirements and resources necessitate repeated adaptations of specifications. We here propose a method that supports *syntactic action refinement* (SAR) and allows to automatically obtain (a priori) correct systems by hierarchically adding details to the according specifications. More precisely, we give a definition of SAR for formulas φ of the *Modal Mu-Calculus* (denoted by $\varphi[\alpha \rightsquigarrow Q]$) that conforms to SAR for *TCSP*-like process terms P (denoted $P[\alpha \rightsquigarrow Q]$) in the following sense: The system induced by a process term P satisfies a specification φ if and only if the system induced by the refined term $P[\alpha \rightsquigarrow Q]$ satisfies the refined specification $\varphi[\alpha \rightsquigarrow Q]$. *Model checking* is used to decide, whether the initial system satisfies the initial specification. If we are not satisfied with the obtained refinement $P[\alpha \rightsquigarrow Q]$ or $\varphi[\alpha \rightsquigarrow Q]$ we reuse already gained verification information (P satisfies φ that is) as the basis for other refinement steps. This can be conceived as a method to reengineer systems. Syntactic action refinement allows to handle infinite state systems. Further, the system induced by P might be exponentially smaller that the system induced by $P[\alpha \rightsquigarrow Q]$. We explain how our results can thus also be exploited to enhance model checking techniques. Finally, we apply our results to an example.

1   Introduction

Faults of *reactive systems* (like, for example of air traffic control systems) can imply severe consequences, whence proving the correctness of such systems with respect to the expected behaviour is inevitable. We are concerned with a dual language approach to verification in which systems are modelled operationally whereas specifications are given in an appropriate temporal logic. The obvious method to obtain verified systems is to come up with a specification of the intended system and subsequently invest experience and guess work to design an

K. Havelund, J. Penix, and W. Visser (Eds.): SPIN 2000, LNCS 1885, pp. 163–180, 2000.
© Springer-Verlag Berlin Heidelberg 2000

according system. *Model checking* can then be used for the verification to follow. However, adaptation of the system and subsequent verification has to be undergone repeatedly until the system meets the specification, a time consuming task. Another method uses transformational methods to construct a (a priori correct) system directly from the specification [CE81,MW84,PR89,AE89], thereby avoiding the need for an explicit verification.

However, the above methods implicitly assume, that the actual specification is indeed the desired one, and that subsequent changes of it will not become necessary. During a systems life cycle however, specifications (and hence the according systems) are most often subject to repeated adaptations actuated by changed requirements or resources. Such changes also emerge in realistic scenarios for system development where the specification is arrived at by successivly enriching the initial specification with details.

It would thus be desirable to extend the above mentioned approaches in the following way: Once it has been proved that a system P satisfies a specification φ (denoted $P \models \varphi$), transforming φ into a modified specification φ' should entail a transformation of P into P' such that $P' \models \varphi'$. This paradigm supports (a priori) correct system maintenance and stepwise *development of correct reactive systems*. Reversely, *reengineering* amounts to the ability to infer $P \models \varphi$ from $P' \models \varphi'$. This allows to reuse verification knowledge that has already been gained through preceding steps in a development sequence.

We here present an action based development/reengineering-technique that exploits the method of *syntactic action refinement* (see [GR99] for a survey), SAR for short. Intuitively, SAR means to refine an (atomic) action α occurring in a process term P by a more complex process term Q thereby yielding a more detailed process description $P[\alpha \rightsquigarrow Q]$. SAR however complicates the task of verification. For example, many behavioural equivalences used for verification [BBR90] are not preserved under SAR [CMP87]. Considering a verification setting based on process algebras and (action based) logics, the following problem arises: Knowing that the system induced by a process term P satisfies a particular formula does not tell us which formulas are satisfied by the system induced by the refined term $P[\alpha \rightsquigarrow Q]$.

To overcome this problem, we define SAR for formulas φ of the Modal Mu-Calculus [Koz83] that conforms to SAR for $TCSP$-like process terms P and show the validity of the assertion

$$T(P) \models \varphi \text{ iff } T(P[\alpha \rightsquigarrow Q]) \models \varphi[\alpha \rightsquigarrow Q] \quad (*)$$

where $T(P)$ is the transition system induced by P and the operator $\cdot[\alpha \rightsquigarrow Q]$ denotes syntactic action refinement, both on process terms and formulas. The distinguishing features of our approach are

- The use of SAR. This supports hierarchical development of infinite state systems: As opposed to semantic action refinement, SAR is applied to process terms whence state spaces do not have to be handled algorithmically to implement SAR.
- The refinement operator implicitly supplies an *abstraction technique* that, by the syntactic nature of the refinement operator, relates system descriptions. Again, this allows infinite state systems to be considered.

- Using assertion (*), correctly developing (or adapting) a system with respect to adding details to the actual specification (or by changing it) boils down to 'gluing' refinement operators to formulas and process terms. On the other hand, reengineering amounts to replacing refinement operators, that is, to first 'cutting away' inappropriate refinement operators (stepping backwards through a development sequence) and subsequently resuming the development procedure. This development/reengineering-technique is illustrated by Figure 1.
- As the Modal Mu-Calculus subsumes many other process logics [EL86,Dam94], we believe that our results provide a basis for similar investigations employing these logics and other semantics for concurrency.

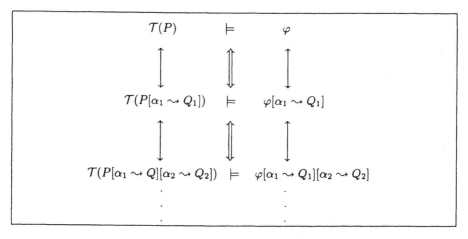

Fig. 1. Developing/Reengineering Correct Systems

If not applied in the context of developing/reengineering reactive systems, assertion (*) can still be usefull to support model checking techniques for systems that could not be handled otherwise due to the (huge or infinite) size of their state spaces: If we can find a process term P_s and a formula φ_s (an abstraction of the formula φ under consideration) and establish an appropriate abstraction (induced by applications of the refinement operator), for example $P = P_s[\alpha_1 \rightsquigarrow Q_1] \ldots [\alpha_n \rightsquigarrow Q_n]$ and $\varphi = \varphi_s[\alpha_1 \rightsquigarrow Q_1] \ldots [\alpha_n \rightsquigarrow Q_n]$ then P_s might well be manageable by a model checker since the state space of P_s might be exponentially smaller then the state space of P due to the well known state explosion problem[1]. We can then apply the model checker to decide $P_s \models \varphi_s$ and conclude via assertion (*) whether $P \models \varphi$ holds or not. Thus, our approach is also conceptually related to a large body of research which invertigates techniques to enhance model checking techniques (see Section 5 for an application of our abstraction technique and Section 6 for related methods).

---

[1] A linear reduction of the number of actions in a process term might entail an exponential reduction of the underlying state space.

We show how 'metalevel reasoning' (involving bisimulations and logical reasoning) can also be exploited in the development/reengineering procedure. We apply our results to a simple case study.

In Section 2 we introduce a $TCSP$-like process calculus which contains an operator for syntactic action refinement. SAR for the Modal Mu-Calculus is defined in Section 3. Section 4 provides the link between those two refinement concepts. The case study is presented in Section 5. Related work is discussed in Section 6. A summary of the results is given in Section 7. Some elementary definitions are collected in Section 8.

2   Syntactic Action Refinement in the System Model

In this section we fix the framework used to model reactive systems. Let $\alpha, \beta, \dots$ range over a fixed set Act of *(atomic) actions*. Two languages are used to build up process terms of the form $P[\alpha \rightsquigarrow Q]$. The language $R\Delta$ supplies the terms Q whereas the language $R\Sigma$ provides the terms P. Let $R\Delta$ be the language of process terms generated by the grammar

$$Q ::= \alpha \mid (Q + Q) \mid (Q; Q) \mid Q[\alpha \rightsquigarrow Q]$$

and $R\Sigma$ be the language of process terms generated by the grammar

$$P ::= 0 \mid \alpha \mid x \mid (P + P) \mid (P; P) \mid (P\|_A P) \mid fix(x = P) \mid P[\alpha \rightsquigarrow Q]$$

where x ranges over a fixed set of *identifiers*, $A \subseteq Act$ is a *synchronisation set* and $Q \in R\Delta$.

Let $sync(P)$ denote the union of all synchronisation sets that occur in P. As usual, the term 0 denotes a process that cannot perform any action. Let Σ, Δ be the languages of process expressions generated by the grammars for $R\Sigma$, $R\Delta$ respectively, without the rule $P ::= P[\alpha \rightsquigarrow Q]$. These two languages will subsequently be used to define logical substitution (see Definition 1).

An identifier x is *guarded* in a term $P \in R\Sigma$ iff each free occurrence of x only occurs in subexpressions F where F lies in a subexpression $(E; F)$ such that $E \notin \sqrt{}$, that is E can execute an action (see Appendix A1). A term $P \in R\Sigma$ is called *guarded* iff we have that in each subexpression $fix(x = Q)$ occurring in P the identifier x is guarded in the term Q.

A term $P_1 \in R\Sigma$ is called *alphabet-disjoint* from a term $P_2 \in R\Sigma$ iff P_1 and P_2 share no common actions.

A term $P \in R\Sigma$ is called *uniquely synchronized* iff for all terms $(P_1\|_A P_2)$ that occur in P, $sync(P_i) = A$ for $i = 1, 2$.

To give a meaning to refined terms $P[\alpha \rightsquigarrow Q]$, we make use of a *reduction function red* : $R\Sigma \rightarrow \Sigma$ which removes all occurrences of refinement operators in a process expression by syntactic substitution. To this end we adapt the definitions of [GGR94] for our purposes and extend it, such that the recursion operator fix can be handled (see Appendices A2 and A3). We illustrate the reduction function by the following example.

Example 1. Consider the process expression $P = ((\alpha; \beta)\|_{\{\alpha\}}\alpha)[\alpha \rightsquigarrow (\alpha_1 + \alpha_2)]$. Then we have that $red(P) = (((\alpha_1 + \alpha_2); \beta)\|_{\{\alpha_1, \alpha_2\}}(\alpha_1 + \alpha_2))$.   □

The operational semantics of the language Σ is given as usual (see Appendix A4). The semantics of a process expression P is a *labelled transition system with termination*, that is, a tuple $\mathcal{T}(P) = (P, \Sigma, Act, \rightarrow, \sqrt{})$ where $\sqrt{}$ is the termination predicate (see Appendix A1). Since the terms $P[\alpha \rightsquigarrow Q]$ and $red(P[\alpha \rightsquigarrow Q])$ are supposed to behave identically, we define $\mathcal{T}(P) := \mathcal{T}(red(P))$ to supply semantics for terms $P \in R\Sigma$ (see also [AH91]). In what follows we sometimes identify the term P with the transition system $\mathcal{T}(P)$ if the context avoids ambiguity.

Remark 1. The absence of the parallel composition operator in terms $Q \in R\Delta$ is no severe restriction. For any finite state system it is possible to replace $\|_A$ by appropriate combinations of sequential composition and binary choice operators without changing the semantics (up to strong bisimulation equivalence [Mil80]). The exclusion of the empty process term 0 from the language $R\Delta$ means that we disallow 'forgetful refinement'[2]. As the refinement of a (terminating) action by some infinite behaviour violates the intuition [GR99], no expression of the form $fix(x = P)$ is allowed to occur in a term $Q \in R\Delta$.   □

3 Syntactic Action Refinement in the Modal Mu-Calculus

We use the *Modal Mu-Calculus* [Koz83] $\mu\mathcal{L}$ to specify properties of reactive systems. It is generated by the grammar

$$\Phi ::= \top \mid \bot \mid Z \mid (\Phi_1 \vee \Phi_2) \mid (\Phi_1 \wedge \Phi_2) \mid [\alpha]\Phi \mid \langle\alpha\rangle\Phi \mid \nu Z.\Phi \mid \mu Z.\Phi$$

where α ranges over the set *Act* of actions and Z ranges over a fixed set *Var* of *variables*. Let $R\mu\mathcal{L}$ be the language generated by the grammar for $\mu\mathcal{L}$ augmented with the rule $\Phi ::= \Phi[\alpha \rightsquigarrow Q]$ where $Q \in R\Delta$. Let $R\mu\mathcal{L}_{(\cdot)}$ ($R\mu\mathcal{L}_{[\cdot]}$) be the language generated by the grammar for $R\mu\mathcal{L}$ without the rule $\Phi ::= [\alpha]\Phi$ ($\Phi ::= \langle\alpha\rangle\Phi$ resp.). We let σ range over the set $\{\mu, \nu\}$.

A *fixed point formula* has the form $\sigma Z.\varphi$ in which σZ *binds* free occurrences of Z in φ. A variable Z is called *free* iff it is not bound. A $R\mu\mathcal{L}$-formula φ is called *closed* iff every variable Z that occurs in φ is bound.

A $R\mu\mathcal{L}$-formula φ is called *guarded* iff every occurrence of a variable Z in φ lies in the scope of a modality $[\alpha]$ or $\langle\alpha\rangle$.

A formula $\varphi \in R\mu\mathcal{L}$ is called *alphabet-disjoint* from a term $P \in R\Sigma$ iff φ and Q share no common actions. Next we introduce a concept of logical substitution which will be used to define the reduction of formulas.

Definition 1. *Let* $Q, Q_1, Q_2 \in \Delta$ *and* $\phi, \varphi, \psi \in \mu\mathcal{L}$. *The operation of* logical substitution, $(\phi)\{\alpha \rightsquigarrow Q\}$ *is defined as follows:*

$$(*)\{\alpha \rightsquigarrow Q\} := *\quad \text{if } * \in \{\top, \bot\} \cup Var$$

---

[2] Such refinements cannot be explained by a change in the level of abstraction [vGG89] and are usually avoided.

$((\varphi \odot \psi))\{\alpha \rightsquigarrow Q\} := ((\varphi)\{\alpha \rightsquigarrow Q\} \odot (\psi)\{\alpha \rightsquigarrow Q\})$ $if \odot \in \{\wedge, \vee\}$

$(\Delta_\beta \varphi)\{\alpha \rightsquigarrow Q\} := \Delta_\beta(\varphi)\{\alpha \rightsquigarrow Q\}$ $if \ \alpha \neq \beta$

$(\Delta_\alpha \varphi)\{\alpha \rightsquigarrow Q\} :=$

$$\begin{cases} \Delta_\beta(\varphi)\{\alpha \rightsquigarrow Q\} & if \ Q = \beta \\[2mm] ((\Delta_\gamma(\varphi)\{\alpha \rightsquigarrow Q\})\{\gamma \rightsquigarrow Q_1\} \wedge (\Delta_\delta(\varphi)\{\alpha \rightsquigarrow Q\})\{\delta \rightsquigarrow Q_2\}) & if \ Q = (Q_1 + Q_2) \\[2mm] (\Delta_\gamma(\Delta_\delta(\varphi)\{\alpha \rightsquigarrow Q\})\{\delta \rightsquigarrow Q_2\})\{\gamma \rightsquigarrow Q_1\} & if \ Q = (Q_1; Q_2) \end{cases}$$

$(\sigma Z.\varphi)\{\alpha \rightsquigarrow Q\} := \sigma Z.(\varphi)\{\alpha \rightsquigarrow Q\}$

where in each clause Δ_ϵ means throughout either $\langle \epsilon \rangle$ or $[\epsilon]$ for all $\epsilon \in Act$. We require that γ, δ are fresh actions, that is, γ and δ do neither occur in ϕ nor in Q in the term $(\phi)\{\alpha \rightsquigarrow Q\}$.   □

Example 2. Let $\varphi = \mu Z.[\alpha](\langle \beta \rangle Z \vee [\alpha]\perp)$ and $Q = (\delta + \xi)$ where $\alpha, \beta, \delta, \xi \in Act$. Then

$$(\varphi)\{\alpha \rightsquigarrow Q\} = \mu Z.([\delta](\langle \beta \rangle Z \vee ([\delta]\perp \wedge [\xi]\perp)) \wedge [\xi](\langle \beta \rangle Z \vee ([\delta]\perp \wedge [\xi]\perp)))$$

□

We can now define the reduction for formulas.

Definition 2. *Let $Q \in R\Delta$ be a process expression and $\varphi, \psi \in R\mu\mathcal{L}$ be formulas. We define the logical reduction function $\mathcal{R}ed : R\mu\mathcal{L} \to \mu\mathcal{L}$ as follows:*

$\mathcal{R}ed(*) := *$ *if $* \in \{\top, \perp\} \cup Var$* $\mathcal{R}ed(\varphi[\alpha \rightsquigarrow Q]) := (\mathcal{R}ed(\varphi))\{\alpha \rightsquigarrow red(Q)\}$

$\mathcal{R}ed((\varphi \odot \psi)) := (\mathcal{R}ed(\varphi) \odot \mathcal{R}ed(\psi))$ *if $\odot \in \{\wedge, \vee\}$*

$\mathcal{R}ed([\beta]\varphi) := [\beta]\mathcal{R}ed(\varphi)$, $\mathcal{R}ed(\langle \beta \rangle \varphi) := \langle \beta \rangle \mathcal{R}ed(\varphi)$

$\mathcal{R}ed(\sigma Z.\varphi) := \sigma Z.\mathcal{R}ed(\varphi)$ □

To cater for refinement, we extend the usual satisfaction relation (see Appendix A5) with the clause $P \models_\vartheta \varphi[\alpha \rightsquigarrow Q]$ iff $P \models_\vartheta \mathcal{R}ed(\varphi[\alpha \rightsquigarrow Q])$. We say P *satisfies* φ (with respect to ϑ) iff $P \models_\vartheta \varphi$. For a closed $R\mu\mathcal{L}$-formula φ we simply write $P \models \varphi$.

Example 3. Let $\phi = \nu Z.([\alpha]\perp \wedge [\beta]Z)$ and $\psi = \mu Z.(\langle \alpha \rangle \top \vee \langle \beta \rangle Z)$. Then ϕ intuitively expresses the (strong) safety property 'there is no α-action executable on any β-path' and ψ expresses the (weak) liveness property 'there exists a β-path along which a state will eventually be reached at which the action α can be executed'. Let $P = fix(x = ((\beta; x); \alpha))$. Then we have $P \models \phi$ and $P \not\models \psi$. □

Example 4. Consider the process terms

$$P_1 = fix(x = ((\alpha\|_\emptyset \beta); x)) \text{ and } P_2 = fix(y = (((\alpha; \beta) + (\beta; \alpha)); y))$$

and the formula
$$\varphi = \nu Z.(\langle\alpha\rangle\langle\beta\rangle Z \wedge \langle\beta\rangle\langle\alpha\rangle Z).$$
Let $Q := \gamma[\gamma \rightsquigarrow (\alpha_1; \alpha_2)]$. Then we have $P_i \models \varphi$ and $P_i[\alpha \rightsquigarrow Q] \models \varphi[\alpha \rightsquigarrow Q]$ for $i = 1, 2$. In addition we have $P_1[\alpha \rightsquigarrow Q] \models \langle\alpha_1\rangle\langle\beta\rangle\langle\alpha_2\rangle\top$ whereas $P_2[\alpha \rightsquigarrow Q] \not\models$ $\langle\alpha_1\rangle\langle\beta\rangle\langle\alpha_2\rangle\top$. □

4   Simultaneous Syntactic Action Refinement

In this section we provide the link between the concept of SAR for the process calculus used and SAR for the logical calculus. Let us first give the general result.

Theorem 1. *Let $P \in R\Sigma$ be a guarded process term and $\varphi \in R\mu\mathcal{L}$ be a closed and guarded formula. Further let $Q \in R\Delta$, such that P and φ are alphabet-disjoint from Q. Then $P \models \varphi \Leftrightarrow P[\alpha \rightsquigarrow Q] \models \varphi[\alpha \rightsquigarrow Q]$.*

Proof (Idea). The proof can be achieved by structural induction as follows: Fixed point formulas are treated by 'syntactically unrolling' them. This leads us to the *infinitary Modal Mu-Calculus*[3] since the considered systems might be infinite state. By the condition of closedness and guardedness we obtain a well ordering, along which an argument by transfinite induction carries through. This argument uses a subsidiary induction on the structure of $Q \in R\Delta$, which in turn exploits a series of lemmata that relate the behaviour induced by a process term P with the behaviour induced by the refined term $P[\alpha \rightsquigarrow Q]$. Alphabet-disjointness of P from Q is needed to avoid the introduction and the resolvement of deadlocks through SAR. On the other hand, alphabet-disjointness of φ from Q ensures that φ remains satisfiable under SAR. ∎

Remark 2. Note that the equivalence in Theorem 1 guarantees that the reduction functions *red* and *Red* are defined appropriately as it excludes the use of nonsensical reduction functions: Using the definition $\mathcal{R}ed(\varphi) = \top$ would trivially validate the implication from left to right. □

Remark 3. It is clear, that (logical) SAR as used in Theorem 1 is not complete in the sense, that we cannot derive every (interesting) formula ψ from a formula φ. We believe however, that Theorem 1 can always be useful to provide 'basic knowledge' in the overall development procedure. □

It is well known, that the Modal Mu-Calculus induces bisimulation equivalence (in the sense of [Mil80]) on the set of (finitely branching) transition systems. To exploit this fact for our approach, we lift bisimulation equivalence to the set $R\Sigma$ by defining $P \sim_b P'$ iff $\mathcal{T}(P) \sim_b \mathcal{T}(P')$. As a direct consequence of Theorem 1 we then obtain the following 'vertical modularity' result.

---

[3] Please consult [Sti96] for the relevant definitions.

Corollary 1. *Let* $P, P' \in R\Sigma$ *be guarded process terms and* $\varphi \in R\mu\mathcal{L}$ *be a closed and guarded formula. Let* $Q \in R\Delta$, *such that* P *and* φ *are alphabet-disjoint from* Q. *Let* $[\alpha \leadsto Q]_n$ *abbreviate* $[\alpha_1 \leadsto Q_1], \ldots, [\alpha_n \leadsto Q_n]$. *If* $P \sim_b P'$ *then* $P[\alpha \leadsto Q]_n \models \varphi[\alpha \leadsto Q]_n \Leftrightarrow P'[\alpha \leadsto Q]_n \models \varphi[\alpha \leadsto Q]_n$.

Corollary 1 can thus be used after any development sequence to syntactically interchange the original 'target'-process term P with a term P', provided P and P' are strongly bisimular.

Remark 4. Clearly, we can replace the premise $P \sim_b P'$ by the premise $P' \models \varphi$. Using model checking however, the best algorithm known hitherto needs time $O(alt(\varphi)^2(N_P + 1)^{\lfloor alt(\varphi)/2 \rfloor + 1})$ to decide $P' \models \varphi$ and space about $N_P^{alt(\varphi)/2}$ where $alt(\varphi)$ is the alternation depth of fixed point operators in φ, and N_P is the number of states of $\mathcal{T}(P)$ (see [LBC+94]). In contrary, deciding bisimilarity for two processes P, P' needs time $O(M_P + M_{P'} \log N_P + N_{P'})$ and space $O(M_P + M_{P'} + N_P + N_{P'})$ (see [PT87]) where M_P is the number of transitions of $\mathcal{T}(P)$. □

In Theorem 1, we can meet the conditions that P and φ are alphabet-disjoint from Q by renaming the actions of Q in the obvious way. This renaming is consistent with the usual approach to action refinement since an action α which is to be refined in the term $P[\alpha \leadsto Q]$ is the abstraction of the term Q whence it should not be considered equal to any action that occurs in Q itself. This supports the separation of different levels of abstraction [GGR94]. Disjoint sets of actions are necessary as can be seen in the following.

Example 5. Consider the process expression $P := (\alpha \|_{\{\beta\}} \alpha)$ and the formula $\varphi := \langle \alpha \rangle \langle \alpha \rangle \top$. We have $P \models \varphi$ but $P[\alpha \leadsto \beta] \not\models \varphi[\alpha \leadsto \beta]$. Note that P is not alphabet-disjoint from Q. □

Though renaming of action can often be applied successfully, alphabet disjointness rules out the possibility to conduct particular refinement steps which can become important in the development of reactive systems: Suppose the system P can execute the atomic actions a, b. At the current level of abstraction, the action a (b) is considered to be the name of a procedure Q_a (Q_b resp.) which is not yet implemented. In an intermediate development step, Q_a and Q_b are implemented making use of a common subsystem S which we might assume has been provided by a system library. Hence, alphabet disjointness of Q_a and Q_b does not hold. However, while dropping the conditions on alphabet-disjointness, we can still derive two special cases of Theorem 1. For the following let $alph(\varphi)$ be the set of actions that occur in a formula $\varphi \in R\mu\mathcal{L}$.

Theorem 2. *Let* $P \in R\Sigma$ *be a guarded and uniquely synchronized process term and* $\varphi \in R\mu\mathcal{L}_{(\cdot)}$ *be a closed and guarded formula. Further let* $Q \in R\Delta$, *such that no action in* $sync(P)$ *occurs in* Q. *If* $\alpha \notin sync(P)$ *or* $alph(\varphi) \subseteq sync(P)$ *then* $P \models \varphi \Rightarrow P[\alpha \leadsto Q] \models \varphi[\alpha \leadsto Q]$.

Theorem 3. *Let* $P \in R\Sigma$ *be a guarded and uniquely synchronized process term and* $\varphi \in R\mu\mathcal{L}_{[\cdot]}$ *be a closed and guarded formula. Further let* $Q \in R\Delta$, *such that no action in* $sync(P)$ *occurs in* Q. *If* $\alpha \notin sync(P)$ *or* $alph(\varphi) \subseteq sync(P)$ *then* $P \models \varphi \Leftarrow P[\alpha \leadsto Q] \models \varphi[\alpha \leadsto Q]$.

It is clear, that we cannot hope for a result like Theorem 1 for any fragment $L \subseteq R\mu\mathcal{L}$ in which it is allowed to compose formulas $\varphi \in L$ containing both types of modalities, i.e. $\langle \alpha \rangle$ and $[\alpha]$ without accepting any restrictions on alphabet disjointness. This is the reason why we considered the logics $R\mu\mathcal{L}_{\langle . \rangle}$ and $R\mu\mathcal{L}_{[.]}$ where only one modality type might occur in the formulas.

The logic $R\mu\mathcal{L}_{[.]}$ can be used to express interesting properties of reactive systems, like unless-properties, for example 'φ remains true in every computation unless ψ holds' or safety properties such as 'φ never holds again whenever ψ has become true'. Moreover, $R\mu\mathcal{L}_{[.]}$ can be used to express liveness-properties under fairness and cyclic-properties (see [Sti96]). $R\mu\mathcal{L}_{\langle . \rangle}$-formulas can be used to formalize properties like for example 'there exists a computation sequence of P in which φ holds infinitely often' or 'there exists a computation sequence of P along which φ is always attainable.'

Whereas Theorem 2 can still be used to develop (correct) systems, the contrapositive form of Theorem 3 can be used to debug a complex (concrete) system $P[\alpha \rightsquigarrow Q]$ (with respect to $\varphi[\alpha \rightsquigarrow Q]$) by debugging the (abstract) system P with respect to φ.

5   The Case Study

While the application of Theorem 1 to develop/reengineer reactive systems can readily be seen, applying Theorem 1 as an abstraction technique to enhance model checking might require some further illustration. To this end, we consider a 'data processing-environment' (DPE) which consists of a central data base and several users of the data base. Conceptually, our example is similar to Milner's *scheduler* [Mil80] or to the *IEEE Futurebus+* (considered for example in [CFJ93]) as several structurally equal subsystems are executed in parallel. To ensure the consistency of the data base, it must be accessed in mutual exclusion by the users. Thus, the data base represents a critical section and accessing it is controlled by parameterized read-and write semaphores.

We assume a situation where a DPE has already been implemented and we want to prove, that the given implementation has a desirable property. In order to demonstrate how our approch allows to fix bug's at high levels of abstraction (instead of fixing the bug at the complex concrete level) we deliberately start with a faulty implementation.

Instead of model checking that the concrete system is faulty, we first construct an abstract system and model check that the abstract system contains an according (abstract) bug. Using Theorem 1, we then infer that the concrete system is faulty as well. We then fix the bug on the abstract level and model check that the 'abstract' bug has been removed. Finally, Theorem 1 is applied again to automatically derive a corrected concrete system from the corrected abstract system.

Let us start with giving some implementation details. The i-th user of the DPE is modelled by the process term[4]

$$User_i := fix((x_i = PD_i; x_i) + (v_i^r; read_i; p_i^r; x_i) + (v_i^w; write_i; p_i^w; x_i)).$$

---

[4] In the example, we sometimes omit pharenthesis in order to support readability.

We define $USER^n := (User_1\|_\emptyset User_2\|_\emptyset, \ldots \|_\emptyset User_n)$. $User_i$ can either process (local) data by executing the subsystem PD_i or access the data base (to read or write data) by coordinating with a particular control process $Cont_i$. For user $User_i$ we thus use a control process $Cont_i$, implemented by the process term

$$Cont_i := fix(y_i = (v_i^r; read_i; p_i^r; y_i) + (v_i^w; write_i; p_i^w; y_i)).$$

Let us first consider a faulty control component defined by

$$CONT^n := (Cont_1\|_\emptyset, Cont_2\|_\emptyset, \ldots, \|_\emptyset Cont_n).$$

A correct control component is

$$CorrCONT^n := (Cont_1 + Cont_2 + \ldots + Cont_n).$$

We next define a faulty and a correct DPE parameterized with respect to the number of users, that is,

$$DPE(n) = (USER^n\|_{\{v_i^r, v_i^w, read_i, write_i, p_i^r, p_i^w \mid 1 \le i \le n\}} CONT^n)$$

and

$$CorrDPE(n) = (USER^n\|_{\{v_i^r, v_i^w, read_i, write_i, p_i^r, p_i^w \mid 1 \le i \le n\}} CorrCONT^n).$$

$User_i$ can read data from the data base if $User_i$ and $Cont_i$ can jointly execute v_i^r ($User_i$ occupies the read-semaphore), $read_i$ ($User_i$ reads data) and p_i^r ($User_i$ releases the read-semaphore). As PD_i is assumed to be a 'local subsystem' of $User_i$, it is reasonable to require that PD_i and PD_j contain no common actions for $i \ne j$. Since the control component $CONT^n$ executes the control processes $Cont_i$ ($1 \le i \le n$) concurrently, mutual exclusive access to the data base is not guaranteed.

   We now consider a (faulty) 'four user DPE' $DPE(4)$. We would like to prove that $User_1$ and $User_2$ cannot write data at the same time as long as only actions from $User_1$ and $User_2$ are executed by $DPE(4)$. In other words, we would like to show that $DPE(4)$ has no computation sequence (that consists of actions from $User_1$ and $User_2$) which leads to a state where the actions $write_1$ and $write_2$ can both be executed. This amounts to show, that $DPE(4)$ has no such computation path which leads to such a 'bad state'. In order to do this, we try to disprove that $DPE(4)$ has a computation path along which a bad state is reachable. This property can be expressed by the Modal Mu-Calculus formula

$$\phi_{error}^{i,j} = \mu Z.((\langle write_i\rangle\top \wedge \langle write_j\rangle\top) \vee \langle alph(User_i) \cup alph(User_j)\rangle Z$$

for $i = 1$ and $j = 2$. In the above formula, $alph(P)$ denotes the set of actions that occur in a process term P and $\langle A\rangle\varphi$ abbreviates the formula $\langle\alpha_1\rangle\varphi \vee \langle\alpha_2\rangle\varphi, \ldots, \langle\alpha_n\rangle\varphi$ for $\alpha_1, \ldots, \alpha_n \in A$.

   It turns out that the considered implementation of the DPE is faulty, that is, $DPE(4) \models \phi_{error}^{1,2}$. This could be proved directly by using a model checker. However, depending on the terms PD_i ($i = 1, 2, 3, 4$), the state space of $DPE(4)$

can become tremendous due to the state explosion problem. In order to model check that $DPE(4) \models \phi_{error}^{1,2}$ we first abstract away those implementation details of $DPE(4)$ that are irrelevant for the verification. To this end, we define

$$SmallUser_i := fix(x_i = (pd_i; x_j + (r_i; x_i + w_i; x_i))$$

and

$$SmallCont_i := fix(x_i = r_i; x_i + w_i; x_i).$$

Using these process terms, we define

$$DPE4_{small} = \Big(USER^2 \|_{\emptyset} SmallUser_3 \|_{\emptyset} SmallUser_3 \|_L$$

$$CONT^2 \|_{\emptyset} SmallCont_3 \|_{\emptyset} SmallCont_4 \Big)$$

where $L = \{v_i^r, v_i^w, read_i, write_i, p_i^r, p_i^w, r_j, w_j \mid i = 1, 2 \text{ and } j = 3, 4\}$. We can then establish the refinement

$$T = DPE4_{small}[pd_3 \rightsquigarrow PD_3][r_3 \rightsquigarrow v_3^r; read_3; p_3^r][w_3 \rightsquigarrow v_3^w; write_3; p_3^w]$$

$$DPE(4) = T[pd_4 \rightsquigarrow PD_4][r_4 \rightsquigarrow v_4^r; read_4; p_4^r][w_4 \rightsquigarrow v_4^w; write_4; p_4^w].$$

Note that the formula $\phi_{error}^{1,2}$ remaines unchanged under the above refinements followed by logical reduction[5]. By Theorem 1 it suffices to model check that $DPE4_{small} \models \phi_{error}^{1,2}$ to conclude that $DPE(4) \models \phi_{error}^{1,2}$. In what follows, we let PD_i be implemented by three sequential actions. Then the state space of $DPE4_{small}$ only contains 10 states whence it is about 8 times smaller than the state space of $DPE(4)$.

We can now fix the bug on the abstract level by using the correct control component:

$$CorrDPE4_{small} = \Big(USER^2 \|_{\emptyset} SmallUser_3 \|_{\emptyset} SmallUser_4 \|_L$$

$$(CorrCONT^2 + SmallCont_3 + SmallCont_4) \Big)$$

Model checking can now be used on the abstract level to show that we have $CorrDPE4_{small} \not\models \phi_{error}^{1,2}$. For

$$T' = CorrDPE4_{small}[pd_3 \rightsquigarrow PD_3][r_3 \rightsquigarrow v_3^r; read_3; p_3^r][w_3 \rightsquigarrow v_3^w; write_3; p_3^w]$$

$$CorrDPE(4) = T'[pd_4 \rightsquigarrow PD_4][r_4 \rightsquigarrow v_4^r; read_4; p_4^r][w_4 \rightsquigarrow v_4^w; write_4; p_4^w].$$

we can immediatly conclude (using Theorem 1 again) that

$$CorrDPE(4) \not\models \phi_{error}^{1,2}.$$

---

[5] Let ψ be the formula that arises by applying the above refinement operators to the formula $\phi_{error}^{1,2}$. Then $\phi_{error}^{1,2} = \mathcal{R}ed(\psi)$ whence $P \models \psi$ iff (by definition) $P \models \mathcal{R}ed(\psi)$ iff $P \models \phi_{error}^{1,2}$.

The example above shows, that those parts of the system description that share no actions with the formula under consideration can be immediatly abstracted. We believe that this makes precise, which parts of the system description are completely irrelevant for the actual verification task and that such situations (where the property of interest 'refers' only to a part of the system) often occur in practice. We conjecture, that the above sketched strategy can be automated efficiently.

It is clear, that the state space of $DPE(i)$ grows exponentially in the number i of DPE-users. The state space of $DPE(8)$ contains about 13000 states whereas a system abstracted with the above strategy contained 19 states, a 680-fold reduction of the state space[6]. Note that we can exploit the above sketched strategy to disprove mutual exclusive write-access (in the above sense) of all users $User_i$. This property can be expressed by the formula

$$\Phi^n_{error} = \bigwedge_{i < j \leq n} \phi^{i,j}_{error} .$$

The application of model checking to verify all conjuncts in the above formula amounts to check a total of about 530 states in order to prove that $DPE(8) \models \Phi^8_{error}$. In contrary, classical model checking would necessitate to create the whole state space of 13000 states in order to verify this property.

Additional logical reasoning (based on the structure of the system) might be neccessary if we want to abstract parts of the process term, that share action with the formula under consideration. For further abstracting the (faulty) $DPE(4)$-example, assume $PD_i = t^i_1; t^i_2; t^i_3$ $(i = 1, 2)$. We can then use the formula

$$\Psi_{error} = \mu Z.((\langle write_1 \rangle \langle p^w_1 \rangle \top \wedge \langle write_2 \rangle \langle p^w_2 \rangle \top) \vee \langle t^1_1 \rangle \langle t^1_2 \rangle \langle t^1_3 \rangle \langle t^2_1 \rangle \langle t^2_2 \rangle \langle t^2_3 \rangle Z$$

to carry out some more abstractions since we have that $DPE4_{small} \models \Psi_{error}$ implies $DPE4_{small} \models \phi^{1,2}_{error}$ (showing the validity of this implication is the above mentioned additional logical reasoning). We proceed as follows:
Let $DPE4_{VerySmall}$ be the process term that arises from $DPE4_{small}$ by substituting the process term PD_i by the action pd_i, the term $read_i; p^r_i$ by the action r_i and the term $write_i; p^w_i$ by the action w_i where $i = 1, 2$. If

$$T = DPE4_{VerySmall}[pd_1 \rightsquigarrow PD_1][pd_2 \rightsquigarrow PD_2][r_1 \rightsquigarrow read_1; p^r_1]$$

then

$$DPE4_{small} = T[r_2 \rightsquigarrow read_2; p^r_2][w_1 \rightsquigarrow write_1; p^w_1][w_2 \rightsquigarrow write_2; p^w_2].$$

Now consider the formula

$$\Theta_{error} = \mu Z.((\langle w_1 \rangle \top \wedge \langle w_2 \rangle \top) \vee \langle pd_1 \rangle \langle pd_2 \rangle Z.$$

We have that

$$\psi = \Theta_{error}[pd_1 \rightsquigarrow PD_1][pd_2 \rightsquigarrow PD_2][r_1 \rightsquigarrow read_1; p^r_1]$$

---

[6] We used the Edinburgh Concurrency Workbench 7.0 (see for example [Cle93]) to calculate the size of the state spaces.

$$\Psi_{error} = \psi[r_2 \rightsquigarrow read_2; p_2^r][w_1 \rightsquigarrow write_1; p_1^w][w_2 \rightsquigarrow write_2; p_2^w].$$

We use model checking to show that $DPE4_{VerySmall} \models \Theta_{error}$. By Theorem 1 follows $DPE4_{small} \models \Psi_{error}$ and hence $DPE4_{small} \models \phi_{error}^{1,2}$.

User-guidance (involving additional logical reasoning) seems to be necessary in situations, where system parts that share actions with the formula under consideration are abstracted. We intend to investigate, to what extend techniques from compiler optimization (for example, exploiting common subexpressions) can support the presented method.

6   Related Work

Adressing a dual language development/reengineering-paradigm, [Huh96] showed that a *synchronisation structure* S satisfies a formula φ if and only if a (semantical) refinement of S satisfies a particular refinement of φ. It is not clear however, to what extend this approach can be used in practice: Reactive behaviour can only be modelled by infinite synchronisations structures. This does not allow to give a straightforward implementation of the involved method of semantic action refinement. Further, a linear time temporal logic is used wheres we use the branching time Modal Mu-Calculus.

If not used to develop and reengineer systems, assertion $(*)$ can still be used to support model checking techniques for systems that could not be handled otherwise due to the (huge or infinite) size of their state spaces as was illustrated by the case study in section 5. Thus, our approach is also conceptually related to a large body of research which invertigates techniques to enhance model checking techniques for huge or infinite state spaces [CAV]. *'On the fly' model checking* [SW91,BS92,Hun94,Sti95] focusses on generating only those parts of the state space that are relevant for the property under consideration. Other techniques exploit *partial order reduction* (surveyed in [Pel98]) or *binary decision diagrams* [Bry86] with the aim to compactify state spaces without loosing information about the systems.

Closest to our approach are the widely investigated *abstraction techniques*, that are mostly based on the framework of *abstract interpretations* (see for example [CC92,Cou96]). Theorem 1 relates process terms and formulas with syntactic refinements of them. The abstractions used in [CGL94,Gra94,BLO98,SS99] are established on the system description as well.

Syntactic action refinement allows to create hierarchical system descriptions. In [AHR98], a model checking technique is presented that directly exploits the hierarchical structure of the considered systems: The BDD-based algorithm traverses 'abstract' transitions by expanding the according 'concrete' transition systems on the fly. Hence, the system is analysed at different levels of abstraction which alleviates the state explosion problem.

Those abstraction techniques differ from our approach in that only the systems are subject to abstractions whereas both, systems and formulas are abstracted in our approach. Furthermore, our abstraction technique is exact whereas most abstraction techniques found in literatur are only conservative: Let S^A be the abstraction of the system S. Then we cannot infere $S \not\models \varphi$ from $S^A \not\models \varphi$

if the involved abstraction is only conservative. On the other hand, some of the above mentioned approaches allow to create abstract finite state systems from concrete infinite state systems which is not possible using our results.

Another method to enhance model checking exploits symmetries which are often exhibited by concurrent systems (see for example [CFJ93,ES93]). Whereas those methods aim to 'merge' the symmetries that occur in the transition graph of a system, our technique exploits the structural equalities that occur in the process descriptions (process terms, that is).

7 Conclusion

We defined syntactic action refinement (SAR) for formulas φ of the Modal Mu-Calculus and showed that the presented definition conforms to SAR for $TCSP$-like process terms P in the sense that

$$P \models \varphi \Leftrightarrow P[\alpha \rightsquigarrow Q] \models \varphi[\alpha \rightsquigarrow Q] \quad (*)$$

The operator $\cdot[\alpha \rightsquigarrow Q]$ denotes syntactic action refinement both on formulas and process expressions. Assertion $(*)$ is valid provided some particular conditions on alphabet-disjointness are obeyed. However, two special cases of assertion $(*)$ which do not rely upon the condition of alphabet-disjointness were presented.

Assertion $(*)$ can be applied in various ways to the verification of reactive systems one of which is the (a priori) correct transformation of systems induced by the syntactic refinement of specifications: Provided we know $P \models \varphi$, refining φ into $\varphi[\alpha \rightsquigarrow Q]$ automatically yields $P[\alpha \rightsquigarrow Q]$ such that $P[\alpha \rightsquigarrow Q] \models \varphi[\alpha \rightsquigarrow Q]$.

Further, we explained how the obtained results can be used as an abstraction technique, allowing to model check systems that would remain unfeasable otherwise.

We explained that assertion $(*)$ can be combined with model checkers. Hence, assertion $(*)$ extends this verification technique which leads to settings, that allow to automatically develop/reengineer formally correct reactive systems by hierarchically enriching/abstracting specifications with details.

We used the expressive Modal Mu-Calculus as specification formalism and the intuitive notion of transition systems as the semantic model for reactive systems. We thus believe that our results can provide a basis for similar investigations that employ other logics and semantic models.

Further case studies are necessary to determine the practical applicability of our approach. Defining an explicit abstraction operator and investigations to what extend our abstraction technique can be fully automated are a future topic of our research. Work is already in progress that extends the above results: We study whether the conditions of alphabet-disjointness can be further relaxed and how the reduction of formulas can be determined efficiently. The consequences of introducing the 'hiding'-operator to the process algebra used will be investigated.

8   Appendix

<u>A1. Terminated States:</u>

To evaluate the semantics of the operator ';' it is common to use a special predicate $\sqrt{}$: Let $\sqrt{} \subseteq R\Sigma$ be the least set which contains the term 0 and is closed under the rules $(P_1 \in \sqrt{} \wedge P_2 \in \sqrt{}) \Rightarrow (P_1 \ op \ P_2) \in \sqrt{}$ where $op \in \{\|_A, +, ;\}$ and $(P \in \sqrt{}) \Rightarrow fix(x = P) \in \sqrt{}$ and $(P \in \sqrt{}) \Rightarrow P[\alpha \rightsquigarrow Q] \in \sqrt{}$.

<u>A2. Syntactic Substitution:</u>

Let $P, P_1, P_2 \in \Sigma$ and $Q \in \Delta$ be process expressions and let $alph(Q)$ denote the set of actions that occur in Q. Syntactic substitution, denoted $(P)\{Q/\alpha\}$ is defined as follows:

$$(*)\{Q/\alpha\} := * \text{ where } * \in \{0\} \cup Idf$$

$$(\alpha)\{Q/\beta\} := \begin{cases} Q \text{ if } \alpha = \beta \\ \alpha \text{ otherwise} \end{cases}$$

$$((P_1 \ op \ P_2))\{Q/\alpha\} := ((P_1)\{Q/\alpha\} \ op \ (P_2)\{Q/\alpha\}) \text{ where } op \in \{+, ;\}$$

$$((P_1 \|_A P_2))\{Q/\alpha\} := \begin{cases} ((P_1)\{Q/\alpha\} \|_{A \setminus \{\alpha\} \cup alph(Q)} (P_2)\{Q/\alpha\}) \text{ if } \alpha \in A \\ ((P_1)\{Q/\alpha\} \|_A (P_2)\{Q/\alpha\}) \qquad\qquad \text{ if } \alpha \notin A \end{cases}$$

$$(fix(x = P))\{Q/\alpha\} := fix(x = P\{Q/\alpha\})$$

<u>A3. Reduction Function:</u>

Let $P, P_1, P_2 \in R\Sigma$ and $Q \in R\Delta$ be process expressions.
The function $red : R\Sigma \rightarrow \Sigma$ is defined as follows:

$$red(*) := * \text{ for } * \in \{0\} \cup Idf \cup Act$$

$$red((P_1 \ op \ P_2)) := (red(P_1) \ op \ red(P_2)) \text{ where } op \in \{+, ;, \|_A\}$$

$$red(P[\alpha \rightsquigarrow Q]) := (red(P))\{red(Q)/\alpha\}$$

$$red(fix(x = P)) := fix(x = red(P))$$

<u>A4. Operational Semantics:</u>

Let $P, Q \in \Sigma$ be process expressions.

$$\frac{}{\alpha \xrightarrow{\alpha} 0} \qquad \frac{P \xrightarrow{\alpha} P'}{(P+Q) \xrightarrow{\alpha} P'} \qquad \frac{Q \xrightarrow{\alpha} Q'}{(P+Q) \xrightarrow{\alpha} Q'}$$

$$\frac{Q \xrightarrow{\alpha} Q'}{(P;Q) \xrightarrow{\alpha} Q'} \text{ if } P \in \sqrt{} \qquad \frac{P \xrightarrow{\alpha} P'}{(P;Q) \xrightarrow{\alpha} (P';Q)}$$

$$\frac{P \xrightarrow{\alpha} P'}{(P\|_A Q) \xrightarrow{\alpha} (P'\|_A Q)} \text{ if } \alpha \notin A \qquad \frac{Q \xrightarrow{\alpha} Q'}{(P\|_A Q) \xrightarrow{\alpha} (P\|_A Q')} \text{ if } \alpha \notin A$$

$$\frac{P[fix(x=P)/x] \xrightarrow{\alpha} Q}{fix(x=P) \xrightarrow{\alpha} Q} \qquad \frac{P \xrightarrow{\alpha} P' \quad Q \xrightarrow{\alpha} Q'}{(P\|_A Q) \xrightarrow{\alpha} (P'\|_A Q')} \text{ if } \alpha \in A$$

A5. Satisfaction:

Let $P \in R\Sigma$, $Q \in R\Delta$ be process expressions, $\varphi, \psi \in R\mu\mathcal{L}$ be formulas, $Z \in Var$ be a variable and $\vartheta : Var \rightarrow 2^{R\Sigma}$ be a valuation function. The customary updating notation is used: $\vartheta[\mathcal{E}/Z]$ is the valuation ϑ' which agrees with ϑ on all variables $Z \in Var$ except Z, and $\vartheta'(Z) = \mathcal{E}$.

$P \models_\vartheta \top$, $\qquad P \not\models_\vartheta \bot$, $\qquad P \models_\vartheta Z$ iff $P \in \vartheta(Z)$

$P \models_\vartheta (\varphi \wedge \psi)$ $\qquad$ iff $P \models_\vartheta \varphi$ and $P \models_\vartheta \psi$

$P \models_\vartheta (\varphi \vee \psi)$ $\qquad$ iff $P \models_\vartheta \varphi$ or $P \models_\vartheta \psi$

$P \models_\vartheta [\alpha]\varphi$ $\qquad$ iff $P \in \{E \in R\Sigma | \forall E' \in R\Sigma(E \xrightarrow{\alpha} E' \Rightarrow E' \models_\vartheta \varphi)\}$

$P \models_\vartheta \langle\alpha\rangle\varphi$ $\qquad$ iff $P \in \{E \in R\Sigma | \exists E' \in R\Sigma(E \xrightarrow{\alpha} E'$ and $E' \models_\vartheta \varphi)\}$

$P \models_\vartheta \mu Z.\varphi$ $\qquad$ iff $P \in \bigcap \{\mathcal{E} \subseteq R\Sigma | \{E \in R\Sigma | E \models_{\vartheta[\mathcal{E}/Z]} \varphi\} \subseteq \mathcal{E}\}$

$P \models_\vartheta \nu Z.\varphi$ $\qquad$ iff $P \in \bigcup \{\mathcal{E} \subseteq R\Sigma | \mathcal{E} \subseteq \{E \in R\Sigma | E \models_{\vartheta[\mathcal{E}/Z]} \varphi\}\}$

References

[AE89]   P. C. Attie and E. A. Emerson. Synthesis of concurrent systems with many similar sequential processes (extended abstract). In ACM, editor, *POPL '89. Proceedings of the sixteenth annual ACM symposium on Principles of programming languages, January 11–13, 1989, Austin, TX*, pages 191–201, New York, NY, USA, 1989. ACM Press.

[AH91]   L. Aceto and M. Hennessy. Adding action refinement to a finite process algebra. *Lecture Notes in Computer Science*, 510:506–519, 1991.

[AHR98]   R. Alur, T. A. Henzinger, and S. K. Rajamani. Symbolic exploration of transition hierarchies. *Lecture Notes in Computer Science*, 1384:330–344, 1998.

[BBR90]   In W. P. De Roever G. Rozenberg J. W. De Bakker, editor, REX Workshop on *Stepwise Refinement of Distributed Systems: Models, Formalism, Correctness*, Mook, The Netherlands, May/June 1989, volume 430 of *Lecture Notes in Computer Science*. Springer-Verlag, 1990.

[BLO98]   S. Bensalem, Y. Lakhnech, and S. Owre. Computing abstractions of infinite state systems compositionally and automatically. In Alan J. Hu and Moshe Y. Vardi, editors, *Computer-Aided Verification, CAV '98*, volume 1427 of *Lecture Notes in Computer Science*, pages 319–331, Vancouver, Canada, June 1998. Springer-Verlag.

[Bry86]   R.E. Bryant. Graph-Based Algorithms for Boolean Function Manipulation. *IEEE Transactions on Computers*, C-35(8):677–691, August 1986.

[BS92]   J. Bradfield and C. Stirling. Local model checking for infinite state spaces. *Theoretical Computer Science*, 96(1):157–174, April 1992.

[CAV]   *International Conf. on Computer-Aided Verification*, volume (LNCS) 407 (1989), 531 (1990), 575 (1991), 663 (1992), 697 (1993), 818 (1994), 939 (1995), 1102 (1996), 1254 (1997), 1427 (1998), 1633 (1999), New York, NY, USA. Springer-Verlag Inc.

[CC92]   P. Cousot and R. Cousot. Abstract interpretation frameworks. *Journal of Logic and Computation*, 2(4):511–547, 1992.

[CE81]   E.M. Clarke and E.A. Emerson. Design and Synthesis of Synchronization Skeletons using Branching Time Temporal Logic. In D. Kozen, editor, *Proceedings of the Workshop on Logics of Programs*, volume 131 of *Lecture Notes in Computer Science*, pages 52–71, Yorktown Heights, New York, May 1981. Springer-Verlag.

[CFJ93]   E. M. Clarke, T. Filkorn, and S. Jha. Exploiting symmetry in temporal logic model checking. In Courcoubetis, editor, *Proceedings of The Fifth Workshop on Computer-Aided Verification*, June/July 1993.

[CGL94]   E. Clarke, D. Grumberg, and D. Long. Model Checking and Abstraction. *ACM Transactions on Programming Languages and Systems*, 16(5):1512–1542, 1994.

[Cle93]   R. Cleaveland. The concurrency workbench: A semantics-based verification tool for the verification of concurrent systems. *ACM Transactions on Programming Languages and Systems*, 15(1):36–72, January 1993.

[CMP87]   L. Castellano, G. De Michelis, and L. Pomello. Concurrency vs interleaving: an instructive example. *Bulletin of the European Association for Theoretical Computer Science*, 31:12–15, February 1987. Technical Contributions.

[Cou96]   P. Cousot. Abstract interpretation. *Symposium on Models of Programming Languages and Computation, ACM Computing Surveys*, 28(2):324–328, June 1996.

[Dam94]   M. Dam. CTL* and ECTL* as fragments of the modal μ-calculus. *Theoretical Computer Science*, 126(1):77–96, April 1994.

[EL86]   E. A. Emerson and C. L. Lei. Efficient model checking in fragments of the propositional μ-calculus. In *Symposium on Logic in Computer Science (LICS '86)*, pages 267–278, Washington, D.C., USA, June 1986. IEEE Computer Society Press.

[ES93]   E. A. Emerson and A. P. Sistla. Symmetry and model checking. In C. Courcoubetis, editor, *Proceedings of The Fifth Workshop on Computer-Aided Verificaton*, June/July 1993.

[GGR94]   U. Goltz, R. Gorrieri, and A. Rensink. On syntactic and semantic action refinement. *Lecture Notes in Computer Science*, 789:385–404, 1994.

[GR99]   R. Gorrieri and A. Rensink. Action refinement. Technical Report UBLCS-99-9, University of Bologna (Italy). Department of Computer Science., April 1999.

[Gra94]   S. Graf. Verification of distributed cache memory by using abstractions. In David L. Dill, editor, *Proceedings of the sixth International Conference on Computer-Aided Verification CAV*, volume 818 of *Lecture Notes in Computer Science*, pages 207–219, Standford, California, USA, June 1994. Springer-Verlag.

[Huh96]   M. Huhn. Action refinement and property inheritance in systems of sequential agents. In Ugo Montanari and Vladimiro Sassone, editors, *CONCUR '96: Concurrency Theory, 7th International Conference*, volume 1119 of *Lecture Notes in Computer Science*, pages 639–654, Pisa, Italy, 26–29 August 1996. Springer-Verlag.

[Hun94]   H. Hungar. Local model checking for parallel compositions of context-free processes. *Lecture Notes in Computer Science*, 836:114–128, 1994.

[Koz83]   D. Kozen. Results on the propositional mu -calculus. *Theoretical Computer Science*, 27(3):333–354, December 1983.

[LBC+94]   D. E. Long, A. Browne, E. M. Clarke, S. Jha, and W. R . Marrero. An improved algorithm for the evaluation of fixpoint expressions. In David L. Dill, editor, *Proceedings of the sixth International Conference on Computer-Aided Verification CAV*, volume 818 of *Lecture Notes in Computer Science*, pages 338–350, Standford, California, USA, June 1994. Springer-Verlag.

[Mil80]   R. Milner. *A Calculus of Communicating Systems*. Springer, Berlin, 1 edition, 1980.

[MW84]   Z. Manna and P. Wolper. Synthesis of communicating processes form temporal logic specifications. *ACM Transactions on Programming Languages and Systems*, 6:68–93, 1984.

[Pel98]   D. Peled. Ten years of partial order reduction. *Lecture Notes in Computer Science*, 1427:17–28, 1998.

[PR89]   A. Pnueli and R. Rosner. On the synthesis of a reactive module. In ACM, editor, *POPL '89. Proceedings of the sixteenth annual ACM symposium on Principles of programming languages, January 11–13, 1989, Austin, TX*, pages 179–190, New York, NY, USA, 1989. ACM Press.

[PT87]   R. Paige and R. E. Tarjan. Three partition refinement algorithms. *SIAM Journal on Computing*, 16(6):973–989, December 1987.

[SS99]   H. Saïdi and N. Shankar. Abstract and model check while you prove. In Nicolas Halbwachs and Doron Peled, editors, *Computer-Aided Verification, CAV '99*, volume 1633 of *Lecture Notes in Computer Science*, pages 443–454, Trento, Italy, July 1999. Springer-Verlag.

[Sti95]   C. Stirling. Local model checking games (extended abstract). In Insup Lee and Scott A. Smolka, editors, *CONCUR '95: Concurrency Theory, 6th International Conference*, volume 962 of *Lecture Notes in Computer Science*, pages 1–11, Philadelphia, Pennsylvania, 21–24 August 1995. Springer-Verlag.

[Sti96]   C. Stirling. Modal and temporal logics for processes. *Lecture Notes in Computer Science*, 1043:149–237, 1996.

[SW91]   C. Stirling and D. Walker. Local model checking in the modal mu-calculus. *Theoretical Computer Science*, 89(1):161–177, October 1991.

[vGG89]   R. van Glabbeek and U. Goltz. Equivalence notions for concurrent systems and refinement of actions. In A. Kreczmar and G. Mirkowska, editors, *Proceedings of the Conference on Mathematical Foundations of Computer Science*, volume 379 of *LNCS*, pages 237–248, Berlin, August28 September–1 1989. Springer.

Linking ST_eP with SPIN

Anca Browne, Henny Sipma, and Ting Zhang*

Computer Science Department
Stanford University
Stanford, CA 94305-9045
sipma@cs.stanford.edu

Abstract. We have connected ST_eP, the Stanford Temporal Prover, with SPIN, an LTL model checker. In this paper we describe the translation of fair transition systems into Promela, in particular how weak and strong fairness constraints are handled. The paper presents some preliminary experimental results using this connection.

1 Introduction

The Stanford Temporal Prover, ST_eP, supports the computer-aided formal verification of concurrent and reactive systems based on temporal specifications [BBC+95]. ST_eP combines *algorithmic* with *deductive methods* to allow for the verification of a broad class of systems, including parameterized (N-process) programs, and programs with infinite data domains. Systems are analyzed modularly [FMS98]: components and subsystems can be analyzed individually and properties proven over these components are then automatically inherited by systems that include them. This allows a selective use of tools appropriate for the module at hand.

In the original version of ST_eP, ST_eP1, we provide a full range of verification tools. Deductive tools include *verification rules*, which reduce simple temporal properties to first-order verification conditions [MP95], and an interactive theorem prover. Algorithmic tools include an explicit-state and a symbolic model checker, an integrated suite of decision procedures [Bjø98] that automatically check the validity of a large class of first-order formulas, and tools for invariant generation to support the deductive tools. *Verification diagrams* [MBSU98], which reduce the proof of arbitrary temporal properties to first-order verification conditions and an algorithmic model check, combine the deductive and algorithmic tools.

In the new version of ST_eP, ST_eP2, we are moving towards a more *open architecture*. Realizing that it is impossible and also undesirable to single-handedly

* This research was supported in part by the National Science Foundation under grant CCR-98-04100 and CCR-99-00984 ARO under grants DAAH04-96-1-0122 and DAAG55-98-1-0471, ARO under MURI grant DAAH04-96-1-0341, by Army contract DABT63-96-C-0096 (DARPA), by Air Force contract F33615-99-C-3014, and by ARPA/Air Force contracts F33615-00-C-1693 and F33615-99-C-3014

support and further develop the full range of tools, we have decided to focus our efforts on methods for high-level proof construction, including abstraction, modularity, diagrams, and hybrid system reduction, and take advantage of specialized, and highly optimized tools such as SPIN [Hol91,Hol97] to provide the algorithmic support.

In this abstract we describe the current interface between $STeP$ and SPIN. As we have only recently started the integration, this work is still very much in progress; we are convinced that as we get more familiar with SPIN, many optimizations can be made. We also hope to benefit from input from more experienced SPIN users and developers.

2   Computational Model and Specification Language

In $STeP$ we represent reactive systems as *fair transition systems* (FTS) [MP95]. A fair transition system $\langle \mathcal{V}, \Theta, \mathcal{T}, \mathcal{J}, \mathcal{C} \rangle$ is given by a finite set of system variables $\mathcal{V}$, defining a state space Σ, an *initial condition* Θ, which is a subset of Σ, a set of *transitions* $\mathcal{T}$, each of which is a binary relation over Σ, describing how the system can move from one state to the next, and the *justice and compassion* requirements $\mathcal{J} \subseteq \mathcal{T}$, and $\mathcal{C} \subseteq \mathcal{T}$, respectively.

In our framework, we assume an *assertion language* based on first-order logic. Θ is expressed as an assertion over the system variables, and each transition τ is described by its *transition relation* $\rho_\tau(\mathcal{V}, \mathcal{V}')$, an assertion over $\mathcal{V}$ and a set of *primed variables* $\mathcal{V}'$ indicating their next-state values. We assume that $\mathcal{T}$ includes an *idling transition*, whose transition relation is $\mathcal{V} = \mathcal{V}'$.

A *run* of S is an infinite sequence of states $s_0, s_1, \ldots$, where s_0 satisfies Θ and for every s_i there is a transition $\tau \in \mathcal{T}$ such that (s_i, s_{i+1}) satisfy ρ_τ.

The fairness requirements state that just (or *weakly fair*) transitions $\tau \in \mathcal{J}$ cannot be continuously enabled without ever being taken. Compassionate (or *strongly fair*) transitions cannot be enabled infinitely often without being taken. Every compassionate transition is also just. A *computation* is a run that satisfies these fairness requirements.

Properties of systems are expressed as formulas in *linear-time temporal logic* (LTL). *Assertions*, or state-formulas, are first-order formulas with no temporal operators, and can include quantifiers. *Temporal formulas* are constructed from assertions, boolean connectives, and the usual *future* ($\Box, \Diamond, \bigcirc, \mathcal{U}, \mathcal{W}$) and *past* ($\boxminus, \diamondsuit, \ominus, \mathcal{B}, \mathcal{S}$) temporal operators [MP95]. A *model* of a temporal property φ is an infinite sequence of states $s_1, s_2, \ldots$ that satisfies φ. For a system S, we say that φ is *S-valid* if all the computations of S are models of φ.

3   Translating FTS into Promela

To enable model checking with SPIN, the FTS must be translated into Promela, the system description language of SPIN. Since the definition of a transition system in $STeP$ is very general, the translation is applicable only to a subset of transition systems, namely those (1) that are syntactically finite-state (that is, all datatypes are finite), and (2) whose transition relations are all of the form

$$\rho_\tau = \bigvee_i \rho_{\tau^i}$$

with τ^i being called a mode of τ, and

$$\rho_{\tau^i} = enabled(\tau^i) \wedge \bigwedge_{v \in V} action(v)$$

where $enabled(\tau^i)$ is an assertion over unprimed variables, characterizing the set of states on which τ^i is enabled, and $action(v) : v' = e$, with e an expression over unprimed variables.

A transition system $\Phi = \langle V, \Theta, \mathcal{T}, \mathcal{J}, \mathcal{C} \rangle$ is translated into Promela by creating an initialization process for Θ, and one process for each transition $\tau \in \mathcal{T}$, as shown in Figure 1. The translation strategy reflects the intuition that a transition represents a single atomic process, and the modes of the transition correspond to the different activities of the process.

proctype P_τ *() {*

    do

      :: *atomic* {*enabled*(τ^1) $\rightarrow$ *action*(τ^1); }

      ⋮

      :: *atomic* {*enabled*(τ^n) $\rightarrow$ *action*(τ^n); }

    od

    }

Fig. 1. Translation from τ to $\mathcal{P}_\tau$

The translation of the *STeP* LTL specification to SPIN format is straightforward. SPIN automatically generates a *stuttering-closed* automaton from any future LTL formula without the $\bigcirc$ (next-state) operator.

3.1   Handling Fairness Constraints

In *STeP* transitions may be unfair, weakly fair or strongly fair. SPIN supports weak fairness at the level of the processes, and thus by translating each transition into a separate proctype, each transition is, by default, modeled as weakly fair.

Unfair transitions simulate possibly non-terminating statements. They are modeled in Promela by adding an empty statement to the transition process, as shown in Figure 2. Note that the *idling transition* τ_I is *unfair* and is included in every Promela program translated from an FTS.

```
proctype Pτ () {
        do
        :: atomic {enabled(τ¹); }
        :: atomic {enabled(τ¹) → action(τ¹); }

              ⋮

        :: atomic {enabled(τⁿ); }
        :: atomic {enabled(τⁿ) → action(τⁿ); }
        od

    }
```

Fig. 2. Translation from τ to P_τ

Strong fairness states that if a transition is enabled infinitely often it must be taken infinitely often. This property can be expressed in LTL as

$$\Box\Diamond enabled(\tau) \rightarrow \Box\Diamond taken(\tau)$$

A convenient way to represent the predicate $taken(\tau)$ is by introducing a new global variable $t : [1 \ldots N]$, with $N = |\mathcal{T}|$, to $\mathcal{V}$ and to augment every transition $\tau_i \in \mathcal{T}$ (assuming an arbitrary order on $\mathcal{T}$) with the assignment $t' = i$. Now the predicate $taken(\tau_i)$ can be expressed by

$$taken(\tau_i) \Longleftrightarrow t = i$$

We now can incorporate the strong fairness requirements in the specification as follows:

$$\Phi = \left(\bigwedge_{\tau \in \mathcal{T}} (\Box\Diamond enabled(\tau) \rightarrow \Box\Diamond taken(\tau)) \right) \rightarrow \varphi$$

Note that the validity of safety properties is independent of the fairness requirements of the system, so for proofs of safety formulas (currently identified by a conservative syntactic check) the strong fairness constraints are omitted from the specification for obvious efficiency reasons.

4   Implementation and Preliminary Results

Implementation The current interface between $STeP$ and SPIN is file-based. Upon clicking the SPIN button on the $STeP$ user interface, the transition system is translated into Promela and stored in a file. Then SPIN is invoked to generate a never claim for the specification in another file, and SPIN is run on these two files, to generate the C-files. The C-files are compiled and the resulting file *pan* is executed, currently with search depth 10,000. The output of all these steps is collected in a log file, which, upon completion of *pan* is examined by $STeP$ to

Table 1. Experiment Results

Peterson's Algorithm (12 proctypes)			
Metric	Mutual Exclusion	Accessibility	One Bounded Overtaking
Formula Template φ	$\Box \neg(p \wedge q)$	$\Box(p \to \Diamond q)$	$\Box(p \to q_1 \ W \ q_2 \ W \ q_3 \ W \ q_4)$
Automaton $\neg\varphi$ Size (lines)	9	11	163
Automaton $\neg\varphi$ Generation Time	0m0.01s	0m0.00s	7m25.04s
Verification Time	0m0.19s	0m0.33s	0m0.22s
Verification Result	True	True	True
Semaphores (10 proctypes)			
Metric	Mutual Exclusion	Accessibility	One Bounded Overtaking
Formula Template φ	$\Box \neg(p \wedge q)$	$\Box(p \to \Diamond q)$	$\Box(p \to q_1 \ W \ q_2 \ W \ q_3 \ W \ q_4)$
Automaton $\neg\varphi$ Size (lines)	9	166	163
Automaton $\neg\varphi$ Generation Time	0m0.01s	1m11.78s	6m55.91s
Verification Time	0m0.08s	0m0.50s	0m0.10s
Verification Result	True	True	False
Dining Philosophers(6 philosophers, 42 proctypes)			
Metric	Mutual Exclusion	Accessibility	One Bounded Overtaking
Formula Template φ	$\Box \neg(p \wedge q)$	$\Box(p \to \Diamond q)$	$\Box(p \to q_1 \ W \ q_2 \ W \ q_3 \ W \ q_4)$
Automaton $\neg\varphi$ Size (lines)	9	-	163
Automaton $\neg\varphi$ Generation Time	0m0.00s	-	7m17.63s
Verification Time	3m58.94s	-	0m0.66s
Verification Result	True	-	False

*Above results obtained using SPIN 3.3.10 on Sun Ultra 2 with Solaris 2.6

determine the result of the model checking. There are three types of outcomes:
(1) SPIN found a counterexample, in which case it generates a file *step.trail*, (2)
the search depth is exceeded, or (3) the property is valid. The current translation
only applies to unparameterized transition systems. We are currently extending
it parameterized transition systems with a fixed number of processes.

Preliminary Experimental Results We tested our current implementation
on some typical properties (*mutual exclusion, accessibility and 1-bounded over-
taking*) for three classic concurrent programs (*Semaphores, Peterson's algorithm
and Dining Philosophers*) [MP95]. The results are shown in Table 1. Note that
accessibility is a liveness property while the other two are safety properties. In
the *Semaphores* case, the increase of automaton size for accessibility is due to the
incorporation of two *strong fairness* conditions. For the *Dining Philosophers* [1]
case, with 12 *strong fairness* conditions, the automaton could not be constructed,
because it was too large.

References

[BBC+95] N.S. Bjørner, A. Browne, E.S. Chang, M. Colón, A. Kapur, Z. Manna,
H.B. Sipma, and T.E. Uribe. STeP: The Stanford Temporal Prover, User's Manual. Technical Report STAN-CS-TR-95-1562, Computer
Science Department, Stanford University, November 1995. available from
http://www-step.stanford.edu/.

---

[1] There are six philosophers in total, each of which is represented by seven transitions.
Of the seven transitions, two are semaphore requests which are compassionate. See
[MP95] page 199 for details.

[Bjø98]   N.S. Bjørner. *Integrating Decision Procedures for Temporal Verification.* PhD thesis, Computer Science Department, Stanford University, November 1998.

[FMS98]   B. Finkbeiner, Z. Manna, and H.B. Sipma. Deductive verification of modular systems. In W.P. de Roever, H. Langmaack, and A. Pnueli, editors, *Compositionality: The Significant Difference, COMPOS'97*, vol. 1536 of *Lecture Notes in Computer Science*, pages 239–275. Springer-Verlag, December 1998.

[Hol91]   G. Holzmann. *The Design and Validation of Computer Protocols.* Prentice Hall Software Series. Prentice Hall, 1991.

[Hol97]   G. Holzmann. The model checker spin. *IEEE Transaction on Software Engineering*, 23(5):279–295, May 1997.

[MBSU98] Z. Manna, A. Browne, H.B. Sipma, and T.E. Uribe. Visual abstractions for temporal verification. In A. Haeberer, editor, *Algebraic Methodology and Software Technology (AMAST'98)*, vol. 1548 of *Lecture Notes in Computer Science*, pages 28–41. Springer-Verlag, December 1998.

[MP95]   Z. Manna and A. Pnueli. *Temporal Verification of Reactive Systems: Safety.* Springer-Verlag, New York, 1995.

Abstraction of Communication Channels in Promela: A Case Study*

Elena Fersman and Bengt Jonsson

Dept. of Computer Systems,
P.O. Box 325, S-751 05 Uppsala, Sweden,
{elenaf,bengt}@docs.uu.se

Abstract. We present a case study of how abstractions can be applied to a protocol model, written in Promela, in order to make in amenable for exhaustive state-space exploration, e.g., by SPIN. The protocol is a simple version of the Five Packet Handshake Protocol, which is used in TCP for transmission of single messages. We present techniques for abstracting from actual values of messages, sequence numbers, and identifiers in the protocol. Instead, an abstract model of the protocol is constructed of variables which record whether variables and parameters of messages are equal or unequal. The abstraction works because the protocol handles identifiers and parameters of messages in a simple way. The abstracted model contains only on the order of a thousand states, and safety properties have been analyzed by SPIN.

1 Introduction

When trying to analyze any reasonable communication protocol using a model-checker, one of the biggest problems is to model it in such a way that the model-checker can analyze it exhaustively. Anyone who has used a model-checker can testify that this is not a trivial problem. In order to overcome the problem, one must deal with those aspects of a protocol that case the state-space to blow up: unbounded channels, large domains of sequence numbers and data, other data structures, etc. An experienced protocol modeler can make judicious modeling of such aspects without compromising the results of analysis. There are also general principles, e.g., based on abstract interpretation, that can guide approximation in modeling. However, we still do not have a generally available "cookbook" of standard recipes to be used in protocol modeling. This lack becomes apparent, e.g., in teaching. Students easily become frustrated when they discover the limitations of a model-checker; being able to provide well-proven and generally applicable cures to overcome such limitations would very likely contribute to the spreading of modeling and model-checking.

This paper does not attempt to present a "cook-book", but rather illustrate abstraction techniques techniques that can be applied to some common causes of

---

* support in part by the ASTEC competence center, and by the Swedish Board for Industrial and Technical Development (NUTEK)

K. Havelund, J. Penix, and W. Visser (Eds.): SPIN 2000, LNCS 1885, pp. 187–204, 2000.
© Springer-Verlag Berlin Heidelberg 2000

state-space explosion in model-checking. More precisely, we present a case-study on the modeling in Promela of the so-called Five Packet Handshake Protocol, which is used in TCP for transmission of single messages. Descriptions of the protocol appear, e.g., in [Bel76] and [Lyn96, pp. 718–729]. We focus on abstraction of some aspects of the protocol that makes it hard to model and analyze it in SPIN:

- The protocol works under rather general assumption about the communication channel, which can reorder, lose, and duplicate messages.
- The protocol uses an unbounded set of identifiers.

These two aspects usually imply that it is not possible to perform exhaustive state-space exploration of a naive Promela model. We will therefore present some abstraction techniques which allow to decrease the state-space significantly, in order to make exhaustive analysis possible. The abstraction is based on the observation that the protocol handles identifiers and parameters of messages in a simple way: the only operation performed is equality test and generation of new identifiers. Inspired by this observation, we construct an abstract model of the protocol, where the values of variables and message parameters are totally removed. Instead, a set of boolean variables is used to record whether variables and message parameters are equal or unequal to each other. Based on a choice of boolean variables, an abstract model of the protocol is constructed, which simulates the original one in the usual sense of being a safety-preserving abstraction (e.g., [CGL94,DGG97]).

Related Work The basic principles underlying the construction of an abstract models are understood from e.g., [CC77,CGL94,DGG97]). Recently, they have become used as a means to make a model of a concurrent system amenable to model checking. One approach is based on *predicate abstraction*, proposed by Graf and Saïdi [GS97], in which the state-space of the abstract model is defined by a set of boolean variables. Each boolean variable corresponds to a set of concrete states, i.e., it can be regarded as a predicate on the states of the concrete model. The transitions of the abstract model are constructed by proving theorems about the pre- and postconditions of the statements of the concrete model. Graf and Saïdi use the interactive theorem prover PVS for this purpose. Das et al. [DDP99] instead use a specialized automated theorem-prover. Other works in this area are, e.g., by Bensalem et al. [BLO98], by Colon and Uribe [CU98], by Lesens and Saïdi [LS97], and by Saïdi and Shankar [SS99]. These works have not explicitly considered unbounded channels in the way considered in this paper.

The idea of abstracting contents of unbounded channels by recording only relevant information is in some sense the basis for some symbolic approaches to model checking of lossy channel systems [AJ96], and Petri Nets [AČJYK96]. In some sense, we have used the idea of "data-independence" [Wol86,JP93]. A contribution is to do this in a setting with unbounded channels.

Outline In the next section, we give a brief outline of the five packet handshake protocol. A Promela model of the protocol can be found in Section 2. In Section 3, we discuss how the state-space of the protocol can be reduced by some abstractions. We also try to provide some general principles underlying these abstractions. Section 4 reporst on the effect of performing a drastic abstraction on the protocol Section 5 contains conclusions and directions for future work.

2   A Five Packet Handshake Protocol

In this section, we describe the Five Packet Handshake Protocol, which is used in TCP for transmission of single messages. Descriptions of the protocol appear, e.g., in [Bel76] and [Lyn96, pp. 718–729].

The protocol is intended to transmit single messages from a sender to a receiver. Before each message transmission, a pair of initialization messages must be exchanged in order to establish an appropriate sequence number, which will be associated with the message in question. After the transmission of a message, its receipt must be appropriately acknowledged, again by a pair of messages. Thus, five messages are required for the transmission of a single message, hence the name of the protocol.

The protocol is intended to work in the presence of losses, duplications, reorderings, and arbitrary delays in the channel. Additionally, the sender and receiver may crash, and be forced to reinitialize. Under these liberal conditions, the protocol may sometimes lose a message, but never transmit duplicates. It is well-known [Lyn96, Thm 22.13] that no protocol can implement a perfect FIFO channel under these assumptions.

Let us give a more detailed description of the protocol. The protocol consists of a Sender, a Receiver, and a communication medium, which can reorder, lose, and duplicate messages. The Sender receives a stream of messages from the environment, and it is the task of the protocol to transmit these in order to the Receiver, which then forwards them to its environment. In order to recover from crashes, both the Sender and the Receiver maintain a set of *unique identifiers* (UIDs), taken from an infinite set, in stable memory (i.e., this set is not affected by crashes). The set represents the set of UIDs that have previously been used, and shall not be used again.

The transmission of a message consists of exchanging five packets.

1. The *Sender* sends a packet of form *needuid*(v), in which v is a fresh UID. This is a request for a UID from the Receiver to be used for the message transmission.
2. The *Receiver* sends a packet of form *accept*(u, v) where v is the UID received in the previous *needuid* message, and u is a fresh UID to be used for the message transmission
3. The *Sender* sends the message m in a packet of form *send*(m, u), where u is the UID just received in the *accept* message
4. The *Receiver* acknowledges the message by an *ack*(u) message
5. The *Sender* closes the packet exchange by a *cleanup*(u) message, which also tells the Receiver to stop using the UID u in any future packet exchange.

In order to recover from packet losses, any packet can be retransmitted if the next expected packet does not arrive within some time. In the description in [Lyn96, pp. 718–729], there is a difference in retransmission policy between different packet types: packets of type *needuid*, *accept*, and *send* can be retransmitted an arbitrary number of times, whereas an *ack* packet is transmitted only on the receipt of a *send* packet; this is done even if the *send* packet is for an "outdated" UID. A *cleanup* packet can be sent in two situations.

– on the receipt of an *ack* packet,
– on the receipt of an "outdated" *accept* packet.

When a Sender or a Receiver crashes, they return to their initial state, but keep the record of used UIDs. In a crash, the Sender may lose some messages that were scheduled for transmission to the Receiver.

In the following, we give a naive simplified Promela model of the protocol, which is taken rather directly from the model of [Lyn96, pp. 718–729]. For readability, we have here not included some aspects of the model:

– We have not included our modeling of the imperfections in the channels (loss, reordering, duplication). These can be modeled in different ways: either by changing the Promela code that sends and/or receives messages, or by adding a demon process which scrambles the contents of Channels.
– In the analyzed model, each message reception and the following sequence of local operations of a process are included within atomic brackets. A standard rule of thumb (e.g., [Lam90,MP92] is to to enclose any sequence triggered by a receive, potentially containing a resulting send, in atomic brackets. In the version shown here, we have omitted the atomic brackets for readability.

Some modeling conventions must be made before the protocol description can be turned into a Promela Model:

– The sequence of messages to be transmitted from Sender to Receiver will be the sequence of numbers $0, 1, 2, \ldots$ upto a maximum number MaxMsg.
– The sequence of UIDs used will similarly be chosen as the sequence $0, 1, 2, \ldots$ upto a maximum number
– We use a separate channel for each packet type, e.g., the channel Sendchan to carry packets of form $send(m, u)$.

Following is the naive Promela model of the protocol.

```
#define NULL        0       /* Undefined value of lastUID */
#define MaxSeq      200     /* How many messages to check*/
#define ChanSize    5       /* channel size */

chan Needuidchan = [ChanSize] of { byte };
chan Acceptchan = [ChanSize] of { byte , byte };
chan Sendchan = [ChanSize] of { byte , byte };
chan Ackchan = [ChanSize] of { byte };
chan Cleanupchan = [ChanSize] of { byte };
```

```
active proctype Sender()
{   byte    SaccUID,        /* UID used to get new sequence number */
            SmsgUID,        /* UID used as sequence number */
            SnextMsg;       /* The message to be transmitted */
    byte    u,v;            /* Used to receive parameters of messages */

Sidle: SnextMsg < MaxSeq ->             /* get next message to send*/
                    SnextMsg++ ;
        SaccUID < MaxSeq ->             /* get fresh UID*/
                    SaccUID++ ;
Sneeduid: do
            :: Needuidchan! SaccUID     /* (re)transmit first packet */
            :: Acceptchan? u, v ->      /* on reception of accept message */
                if
                :: v == SaccUID ->      /* if correct uid start sending */
                        SmsgUID = u ; break
                :: else ->              /* otherwise send cleanup */
                        Cleanupchan ! u
                fi
            :: Ackchan? u ->            /* on a spurious ack */
                Cleanupchan ! u         /* reply with cleanup */
            :: goto Scrash              /* crash */
            od;

Ssend: do
        :: Sendchan!SnextMsg,SmsgUID    /* (re)transmit message */
        :: Ackchan? u ->                /* on reception of ack */
            if
            :: (u == SmsgUID) ->        /* if correct uid */
                    Cleanupchan!u;      /* send cleanup and restart */
                    goto Sidle
            :: else -> Cleanupchan!u    /* otherwise send cleanup */
            fi
        :: Acceptchan? u,v ->           /* if spurious accept */
            if
            :: (u != SmsgUID) ->        /* if old, send cleanup */
                    Cleanupchan!u
            :: else -> skip             /* if current, do nothing */
            fi
        :: goto Scrash                  /* crash */
        od ;

Scrash:   do                           /* lose some input msgs */
            :: SnextMsg < MaxSeq -> SnextMsg++
            :: skip -> break
            od;
            goto Sidle
}
```

```
active proctype Receiver()
{   byte    RaccUID,    /* UID used to ge new sequence number */
            RmsgUID,    /* UID used as sequence number */
            RlastUID,   /* rembembers last sequence number */
            RexpMsg;    /* The message to be received */
    byte    m,u,v;      /* Used to receive parameters of messages */

Ridle: RmsgUID < MaxSeq -> RmsgUID++ ; /* get fresh sequence number */
       do
       :: Needuidchan? RaccUID ->       /* when needuid arrives */
                       break            /* start sending accept */
       :: Sendchan?m,u ->               /* spurious send */
             if                         /* if old uid arrives */
             :: (u != RlastUID) -> Ackchan!u   /* send ack */
             :: else -> skip
             fi
       :: Cleanupchan?u -> skip         /* ignore cleanup */
       :: goto Rcrash                   /* crash */
       od;

Raccept: do
         :: Acceptchan! RmsgUID , RaccUID  /* (re)transmit msg 2 */
         :: Sendchan ? m , u ->           /* on reception of send */
              if
              :: (u == RmsgUID) ->        /* if correct uid */
                   RlastUID = u;          /* remember uid */
                   assert(m >= RexpMsg);  /* check ordering */
                   RexpMsg = m+1; break   /* update expected Msg */
              :: (u != RmsgUID && u != RlastUID) -> /* if old uid */
                                   Ackchan!u   /* send ack */
              :: else -> skip
              fi
         :: Needuidchan? v -> skip        /* ignore needuid */
         :: Cleanupchan? u ->
              if
              :: (u == RmsgUID) ->        /* on cleanup */
                   RlastUID = NULL;       /* clean RlastUID */
                   goto Ridle
              :: else -> skip
              fi
         :: goto Rcrash                   /* crash */
         od;
Rack: do
      :: Ackchan!RmsgUID                  /* (re)transmit ack */
      :: Cleanupchan?u ->                 /* when cleanup arrives */
              if
              :: (u == RlastUID) ->       /* if current uid */
                   RlastUID = NULL;       /* restart */
                   goto Ridle
              :: else -> skip             /* else skip */
              fi
```

```
      :: Sendchan ? m , u ->            /* spurious send msg */
              if
              :: (u != RlastUID) ->     /* if old uid */
                    Ackchan!u           /* send ack */
              :: else -> skip
              fi
      :: Needuidchan? v -> skip         /* ignore needuid */
      :: goto Rcrash                    /* crash */
      od;
Rcrash:   RlastUID=NULL;
          goto Ridle
}
```

3   Abstractions

A protocol model such as the one shown in the preceding section has far too many states for an exhaustive analysis to be feasible. We therefore present, in this subsection, how to obtain a rather drastic abstraction of the protocol. The basic idea is to represent only as much information as needed to infer the possible continued behavior of the protocol. The abstraction will abstract the state variables and channels of the (concrete) protocol model by a set of (abstract) boolean variables. The concrete and the abstract model are related by a concretization function γ, which maps sets of states of the abstract model to sets of states of the concrete model. For each boolean variable b, we can regard the predicates b and $\neg b$ as sets of abstract states (the sets of states where b, resp. $\neg b$, is true). These sets correspond to the sets $\gamma(b)$ and $\gamma(\neg b)$ of concrete states. Note that, unlike some other approaches to predicate abstraction (e.g., [GS97, DDP99], the sets $\gamma(b)$ and $\gamma(\neg b)$ need not be disjoint. We do this for convenience, in the hope of getting a smaller abstract model. Having defined $\gamma(b)$ and $\gamma(\neg b)$ for all boolean variables, the function γ is extended to arbitrary sets in the natural way by

$$\gamma(\phi \wedge \phi') \equiv \gamma(\phi) \wedge \gamma(\phi')$$
$$\gamma(\phi \vee \phi') \equiv \gamma(\phi) \vee \gamma(\phi') \quad .$$

The control states of the abstract model are identical to the control states of the concrete model.

We note that the only operations on the variables of the protocol are check for equality, and assignment of a fresh value to a variable. For the variables SnextMsg and RnexpMsg that model the transmitted messages, this is not quite true, but we can make it true by not modeling them as integers. Instead, we let each new message, which is to be transmitted by the Sender, be a fresh value. When receiving a message, we let the receiver check that the received message is equal to the message that the Sender is trying to send. We use a boolean flag to check for duplicate receptions.

We construct an abstraction for variables that are used in this way by including, for each pair x, x' of state variables of the protocol, an abstract boolean variable, named x_eq_x', which is true if and only if $x = x'$. This means that

$$\gamma(x\_eq\_x') \equiv x = x' \qquad \text{and} \qquad \gamma(\neg\, x\_eq\_x') \equiv x \neq x'$$

The abstraction of channel contents is slightly more complicated. Intuitively, the contents of a channel may influence the future behavior of the protocol by containing messages. The potential influence of receiving a message can be determined by checking whether its parameters are equal or unequal to state variables of the protocol, and also to parameters of other messages, possibly in other channels.

Based on this idea, we construct an abstraction of channel contents using boolean variables as follows. We regard each message as a tuple of parameters. For instance, the messages in channels Needuidchan, Ackchan, and Cleanupchan are tuples with one elements, and the messages in channels Acceptchan and Sendchan are tuples with two elements. An abstract variable b will record whether some channel c contains a message, whose elements satisfy some equality constraint over its elements. An *equality constraint* over a set of parameters is a conjunction of formulas of form $v = v'$ or $v \neq v'$, where v, v' are either program variables or parameters of the message. We use the name c_mc_ψ for the boolean variable, which records whether the channel c *may contain* a message $\langle u_1, \ldots, u_n \rangle$ which satisfies the equality constraint ψ over the parameters $u_1, \ldots, u_n$. Note the formulation *may contain* (abbreviated to mc in the variable name): since any message in a channel can be lost arbitrarily, we can only be sure that a certain message is *not* in the channel (i.e., if it was never sent). Formally, this is reflected by defining the concretization of c_mc_ψ, as follows.

$$\gamma(c\_mc\_\psi) \equiv true$$
$$\gamma(\neg\, c\_mc\_\psi) \equiv \neg \exists \langle u_1, \ldots, u_n \rangle \in c \,.\, \psi \qquad .$$

Note that $\gamma(c\_mc\_\psi)$ and $\gamma(\neg\, c\_mc\_\psi)$ overlap. We do this in the hope of creating a small abstract model. Namely, if we would have defined $\gamma(c\_mc\_\psi)$ as the negation of $\gamma(\neg\, c\_mc\_\psi)$, then for any reachable abstract state where $\gamma(c\_mc\_\psi)$ is true, we would also have to include the corresponding abstract state where $\gamma(c\_mc\_\psi)$ is false, since the channel can always lose messages. As a further slight optimization, we require that at least one conjunct of ψ is an equality: if all conjuncts in ψ are inequalities, then any strange or outdated message will make the variable $\gamma(c\_mc\_\psi)$ true in the abstract model, meaning that the variable is uninteresting.

As an example, the abstract variable Needuidchan_mc_$(u = \text{SaccUID})$ (which in the Promela code will be written Needuidchan_mc_SaccUID) records whether the channel Needuidchan may contain a message $\langle u \rangle$ such that u is equal to SaccUID.

In principle, the abstraction could contain a boolean variable x_eq_x' for each pair x, x' of program variables, and a variable c_mc_ψ for each channel c and corresponding equality constraint ψ. Many of these will turn out to be dead variables in a static analysis of the abstract model, and so are not necessary.

Having chosen a set of abstract variables, with corresponding meanings, we should now construct an abstract Promela model, which simulates the concrete protocol model. This means that if the concrete model can make an atomic step from control point p to p' while changing the state of variables and channels from s to s', then for each state t of the abstract variables such that $\gamma(t) = s$, there should be a state t' of the abstract variables such that $\gamma(t') = s'$ and such that the abstract model can make a step from control point p to p' while changing the state of variables t to t'. All safety properties of the abstract model will then also be satisfied by the concrete model [CGL94,DGG97]). Below, we make one suggestion for how this can be carried out.

We regard the concrete Promela model as consisting of a collection of guarded commands. For instance, an atomic statement of form

```
Somechan?u1, u2 -> if
              :: guard₁ -> stmts₁
                     . . .
              :: guardₙ -> stmtsₙ
              fi
```

is regarded as consisting of a set of atomic guarded commands of form

$$GC_i \quad \equiv \quad \texttt{Somechan?}u1, u2 \rightarrow guard_i \rightarrow stmts_i$$

for $i = 1, \ldots, n$ (We assume that the statement can not deadlock after reception of a message from Somechan).

For each GC_i, we construct a set of abstract statements, which are guarded by an expression g over abstract variables such that the set $\gamma(g)$ includes the set $\exists\langle u1, u2\rangle \in \texttt{Somechan} \wedge guard_i$ corresponding to the guard of GC_i. Furthermore, the abstract statements must update all abstract variables that may be affected by the assignments and send statements in $stmts_i$. The updates to each such abstract variable b is guided by a postcondition $sp(GC_i, true)$ of GC_i with respect to the predicate $true$. More precisely, b is assigned to TRUE under a condition $truecond$, such that $\gamma(truecond)$ is implied by the conjunction of $sp(GC_i, true)$ and $\gamma(b)$. Analogously, b is assigned to FALSE under a condition $falsecond$, such that $\gamma(falsecond)$ is implied by the conjunction of $sp(GC_i, true)$ and $\gamma(\neg b)$. Alternatively, abstract variables of form x_eq_x' can be updated by an expression exp such that such that $x = x' \Leftrightarrow \gamma(exp)$ is implied by $sp(GC_i, true)$. Note that the postcondition may refer to the values of variables before the statement.

Let us consider some examples. The statement

```
Ackchan? u ->
        if
        :: (u == SmsgUID) -> Cleanupchan!u;   goto Sidle
        :: else -> Cleanupchan!u
        fi
```

which occurs within atomic brackets, is regarded as two guarded commands. The first one,

```
Ackchan? u -> (u == SmsgUID) -> Cleanupchan!u;   goto Sidle
```

has the guard

$$\exists \langle u \rangle \in \texttt{Ackchan} \,.\, u = \texttt{SmsgUID}$$

and the postcondition (disregarding the goto)

$$\exists \langle u \rangle \in \texttt{Ackchan}^- \,.\, u = \texttt{SmsgUID} \,\wedge\, \texttt{Cleanupchan} = \texttt{Cleanupchan}^- \cup \langle \texttt{SmsgUID} \rangle$$

where we use v^- to denote the value of v before the statement. The guard can be abstracted by the predicate $\texttt{Ackchan\_mc\_}(u = \texttt{SmsgUID})$, which in the code is given the name $\texttt{Ackchan\_mc\_SmsgUID}$. Since the channel $\texttt{Cleanupchan}$ is updated, the abstract statement must update variables of form $\texttt{Cleanupchan\_mc\_}\psi$. For instance, the variable $\texttt{Cleanupchan\_mc\_}(u = \texttt{RmsgUID})$ will be true after the statement, if either it was true before the statement, or if $\texttt{RmsgUID}$ is equal to $\texttt{SmsgUID}$. The same holds for a variable of form $\texttt{Cleanupchan\_mc\_}(u = \texttt{RlastUID})$. Summarizing, the corresponding abstract statement will have the form

```
Ackchan_mc_SmsgUID ->
    Cleanupchan_mc_RmsgUID = (Cleanupchan_mc_RmsgUID || RmsgUID_eq_SmsgUID);
    Cleanupchan_mc_RlastUID = (Cleanupchan_mc_RlastUID || RlastUID_eq_SmsgU);
    goto Sidle
```

Similarly, the second statement, which can be written

```
Ackchan? u -> (u != SmsgUID) -> Cleanupchan!u
```

can be abstracted to

```
Cleanupchan_mc_RmsgUID =
  (Cleanupchan_mc_RmsgUID || (Ackchan_mc_RmsgUID && ! SmsgUID_eq_RmsgUID));
Cleanupchan_mc_RlastUID =
  (Cleanupchan_mc_RlastUID || (Ackchan_mc_RlastUID && ! SmsgUID_eq_RlastUID))
```

Note here that we have transformed the control structure by omitting the guard, which would be abstracted by $\texttt{Ackchan\_mc\_}(u \neq \texttt{SmsgUID})$. Such a guard will probably be true most of the time, so we omit it.

4   Abstraction of the Protocol

In this section, we report on our manual application of the abstraction technique of the previous section to the Five Packet Handshake Protocol. In the abstract protocol model, boolean variables are chosen as described in the previous section. A (manual) dependency analysis is used to avoid including abstract variables that do not affect (directly or indirectly) the control flow of the protocol. The code of the abstract model is generated according to the principles in the preceding section. Some things to mention are the following.

- The set of messages, which in the concrete model are represented by integers, and assigned to variables SnextMsg and RexpMsg, is treated in the same way as UIDs. In order to do that, we must first change the mechanism for checking that messages are not duplicated by the protocol. In the model of Section 2, this mechanism relies on the fact that messages are generated as increasing integers. We change this mechanism as follows. When a message is received, it is checked that it is equal to the message SnextMsg that the sender is trying to send. In addition, a boolean flag received_SnextMsg records whether this message has been received previously. The flag is reset when a new message is considered for transmission by the sender.

- Since the boolean variables for comparisons are not local to any process, we make all variables global.
- Names of variables are chosen to reflect their meaning: for instance, RaccUID_eq_SaccUID is *true* iff the variables RaccUID and SaccUID have the same value. The variable Accchan_mc_neg_RmsgUID_and_SaccUID is *true* if the channel Acceptchan may contain a message u,v, where the value of u is different from that of RmsgUID and v is equal to SaccUID.
- Most of the abstract statements have been constructed in a rather uniform way. One statement, which maybe was not so straightforward, is the abstraction of

    Acceptchan? u, v -> v == SaccUID -> SmsgUID = u ; break

which is the normal reception of an *accept* message by the Sender, at control point Sneeduid. One problem concerned the update of Ackchan_mc_SmsgUID, which records whether the channel Ackhan may contain the message SmsgUID. The problem is that the above statement assigns a value of SmsgUID, about which it gives no information. A safe abstraction would be to set Ackchan_mc_SmsgUID to true. This abstraction is sufficient to prove absense of duplication, but cannot prove that the protocol delivers all messages in the absense of crashes: the reason is that the abstract statement Ackchan_mc_SmsgUID = TRUE automatically "inserts" an acknowledgment into the channel Ackchan.

A better solution is to guard the statement Ackchan_mc_SmsgUID = TRUE by some checks. For instance, if the channel Acceptchan does not contain any message ⟨u,v⟩ where u is different from RmsgUID and v is equal to SmsgUID, then the statement can be guarded by Ackchan_mc_RmsgUID = TRUE, since u must then be equal to RmsgUID. We can make a similar check for RlastUID. The result is the abstract statement

```
Ackchan_mc_SmsgUID =
    (    (Accchan_mc_neg_RmsgUID_and_SaccUID
         && Accchan_mc_neg_RlastUID_and_SaccUID
         )
    || (Accchan_mc_RmsgUID_and_SaccUID && Ackchan_mc_RmsgUID)
    || (Accchan_mc_RlastUID_and_SaccUID && Ackchan_mc_RlastUID)
    ) ;
```

A version of the abstract protocol model, without comments, is given in the appendix.

Analysis of Abstract Model The abstract Protocol model shown above has a state space defined by control points and 20 boolean variables. The number of reachable states, as reported by SPIN, is 575. SPIN was used to analyze that the protocol delivers messages without duplication. On the other hand, the protocol can lose messages. If the possibility of crashes is excluded, then the number of reachable states becomes only 46, and SPIN could check that no messages are lost. This check was conducted using the boolean flag received_SnextMsg.

5   Discussion and Conclusion

We have reported on the modeling and verification in SPIN of a protocol for single message transmission in TCP. A naive model of the protocol has far too many states for making an exhaustive analysis of the state-space possible. This situation is typical for any protocol which uses asynchronous message passing, where there are more than a couple of different message types.

The main part of the paper presents some techniques for reducing the state space by abstracting away the channels and data variables with unbounded ranges. In the particular case of this protocol, we could replace variables and channels by equality constraints, which were adapted to expressing properties of messages in channels. A contribution is to do this in a setting with unbounded channels. Since we cannot perform symbolic manipulations in SPIN, we have to represent the equality constraints in some way: we have chosen to represent each relevant equality constraint by a boolean variable. Other representations could have been possible, such as choosing a small finite domain where values are reused in an appropriate way (as done, e.g., in [JP93]), but we guess that such a representation would be less efficient in the presence of message channels.

In this work, we have produced the abstraction manually. This introduces a substantial risk for errors, and it would, of course, be desirable to perform the abstractions automatically. The abstractions of most statements were rather straight-forward, but a few required some care in order to generate a sufficiently detailed abstract model.

One motivation for the work is our experience that, as part of teaching formal methods, and protocol validation, it is important to teach good techniques for producing compact and manageable protocol models. In order not to lose the essence of formality, it is important that students understand how to make "correct" simplifications of a protocol, by means of abstractions (preferably safe abstractions), protocol transformations, etc. The principles for making abstractions are known, but a limited number of examples of their practical use have been published in the literature, in a way that can be read by students. With time, a well-documented library of safe abstractions should be developed.

Acknowledgments. We are grateful to the reviewers for insightful comments, which helped improve the paper considerably.

References

[AČJYK96]   Parosh Aziz Abdulla, Karlis Čerāns, Bengt Jonsson, and Tsay Yih-Kuen. General decidability theorems for infinite-state systems. In *Proc. 11th IEEE Int. Symp. on Logic in Computer Science*, pages 313–321, 1996.

[AJ96]   Parosh Aziz Abdulla and Bengt Jonsson. Verifying programs with unreliable channels. *Information and Computation*, 127(2):91–101, 1996.
[Bel76]   D. Belsnes. Single-message communication. *IEEE Trans. on Computers*, COM-24(2):190–194, Feb. 1976.
[BLO98]   S. Bensalem, Y. Lakhnech, and S. Owre. Computing abstractions of infinite state systems automatically and compositionally. In Alan J. Hu and Moshe Y. Vardi, editors, *Computer Aided Verification*, volume 1427 of *Lecture Notes in Computer Science*, pages 319–331. Springer-Verlag, 1998.
[CC77]   P. Cousot and R. Cousot. Abstract interpretation: A unified model for static analysis of programs by construction or approximation of fixpoints. In *Proc. 4th ACM Symp. on Principles of Programming Languages*, pages 238–252, 1977.
[CGL94]   E. M. Clarke, O. Grumberg, and D.E. Long. Model checking and abstraction. *ACM Trans. on Programming Languages and Systems*, 16(5), Sept. 1994.
[CU98]   M.A. Colon and T.E. Uribe. Generating finite-state abstractions of reactive systems using decision procedures. In *Proc. 10th Int. Conf. on Computer Aided Verification*, volume 1427 of *Lecture Notes in Computer Science*, pages 293–304. Springer Verlag, 1998.
[DDP99]   S. Das, D.L. Dill, and S. Park. Experience with predicate abstraction. In *Proc. 11th Int. Conf. on Computer Aided Verification*, volume 1633 of *Lecture Notes in Computer Science*, 1999.
[DGG97]   Dennis Dams, Rob Gerth, and Orna Grumberg. Abstract interpretation of reactive systems. *ACM Transactions on Programming Languages and Systems*, 19(2), 1997.
[GS97]   S. Graf and H. Saidi. Construction of abstract state graphs with PVS. In *Proc. 9th Int. Conf. on Computer Aided Verification*, volume 1254, Haifa, Israel, 1997. Springer Verlag.
[JP93]   B. Jonsson and J. Parrow. Deciding bisimulation equivalences for a class of non-finite-state programs. *Information and Computation*, 107(2):272–302, Dec. 1993.
[Lam90]   L. Lamport. A theorem on atomicity in distributed algorithms. *Distributed Computing*, 4(2):59–68, 1990.
[LS97]   D. Lesens and H. Saidi. Abstraction of parameterized networks. *Electronic Notes in Theoretical Computer Science*, 9, 1997.
[Lyn96]   N. Lynch. *Distributed Algorithms*. Morgan Kaufmann Publishers, 1996.
[MP92]   Z. Manna and A. Pnueli. *The Temporal Logic of Reactive and Concurrent Systems*. Springer Verlag, 1992.
[SS99]   H. Saidi and N. Shankar. Abstract and model check while you prove. In *Proc. 11th Int. Conf. on Computer Aided Verification*, volume 1633 of *Lecture Notes in Computer Science*, 1999.
[Wol86]   Pierre Wolper. Expressing interesting properties of programs in propositional temporal logic (extended abstract). In *Proc. 13th ACM Symp. on Principles of Programming Languages*, pages 184–193, Jan. 1986.

A   Promela Code of the Abstract Model

In this appendix, we give a complete Promela listing of an abstract model of the protocol. The abstraction was performed by hand. In order to fit the code on paper, names of variables have been abbreviated in comparison with their description in the paper.

For instance, the variable Accchan_mc_RmsgUID_and_neg_SaccUID, which records whether the channel Acceptchan may contain a message ⟨RmsgUID, v⟩ such that v is different from the value of SaccUID is written as Acc_mc_RmsgID_a_n_SaccID.

```
#define FALSE      0
#define TRUE       1

bit RaccID_eq_SaccID;
bit RmsgID_eq_SmsgID, RlastID_eq_SmsgID, RmsgID_eq_RlastID;
bit       Nu_mc_SaccID,

          Acc_mc_RmsgID_a_SaccID,
          Acc_mc_RmsgID_a_n_SaccID,
          Acc_mc_n_RmsgID_a_SaccID,
          Acc_mc_RlastID_a_SaccID,
          Acc_mc_RlastID_a_n_SaccID,
          Acc_mc_n_RlastID_a_SaccID,

          Send_mc_SmsgID,
          Send_mc_SnextMsg_a_RmsgID,
          Send_mc_n_SnextMsg_a_RmsgID,

          Ack_mc_SmsgID,
          Ack_mc_RmsgID,
          Ack_mc_RlastID,

          Cu_mc_RmsgID,
          Cu_mc_RlastID;

bit Received_SnextMsg = TRUE;

active proctype Sender()
{

Sidle: atomic{
       Send_mc_SnextMsg_a_RmsgID = FALSE;
       Received_SnextMsg = FALSE;

       RaccID_eq_SaccID = FALSE;
       Nu_mc_SaccID = FALSE;
       Acc_mc_RmsgID_a_SaccID = FALSE;
       Acc_mc_n_RmsgID_a_SaccID = FALSE;
       Acc_mc_RlastID_a_SaccID = FALSE;
       Acc_mc_n_RlastID_a_SaccID = FALSE
       };
```

```
SneedID: do
    :: Nu_mc_SaccID = TRUE      /* (re)transmit the needID message */
    :: atomic{(Acc_mc_RmsgID_a_SaccID || Acc_mc_n_RmsgID_a_SaccID) ->
        Ack_mc_SmsgID =
        (   (Acc_mc_n_RmsgID_a_SaccID && Acc_mc_n_RlastID_a_SaccID)
         || (Acc_mc_RmsgID_a_SaccID && Ack_mc_RmsgID)
         || (Acc_mc_RlastID_a_SaccID && Ack_mc_RlastID)
        ) ;
        if :: Acc_mc_RmsgID_a_SaccID -> RmsgID_eq_SmsgID = TRUE
           :: Acc_mc_n_RmsgID_a_SaccID -> RmsgID_eq_SmsgID = FALSE
        fi;
        if :: Acc_mc_RlastID_a_SaccID -> RlastID_eq_SmsgID = TRUE
           :: Acc_mc_n_RlastID_a_SaccID -> RlastID_eq_SmsgID = FALSE
        fi;
        break
      }
    :: atomic{Cu_mc_RmsgID = (Cu_mc_RmsgID || Acc_mc_RmsgID_a_n_SaccID);
         Cu_mc_RlastID = (Cu_mc_RlastID || Acc_mc_RlastID_a_n_SaccID)
      }
    :: atomic{Cu_mc_RmsgID = (Cu_mc_RmsgID || Ack_mc_RmsgID);
              Cu_mc_RlastID = (Cu_mc_RlastID || Ack_mc_RlastID)
      }
    :: goto Scrash
    od;
Ssend: do
    :: atomic{Send_mc_SnextMsg_a_RmsgID =
                  (Send_mc_SnextMsg_a_RmsgID || RmsgID_eq_SmsgID);
              Send_mc_SmsgID = TRUE
      }
    :: atomic{Ack_mc_SmsgID ->
              Cu_mc_RmsgID = (Cu_mc_RmsgID || RmsgID_eq_SmsgID);
              Cu_mc_RlastID = (Cu_mc_RlastID || RlastID_eq_SmsgID);
              goto Sidle
      }
    :: atomic{Cu_mc_RmsgID =
                  (Cu_mc_RmsgID || (Ack_mc_RmsgID && ! RmsgID_eq_SmsgID));
              Cu_mc_RlastID =
                  (Cu_mc_RlastID || (Ack_mc_RlastID && ! RlastID_eq_SmsgID))
      }
    :: atomic{Cu_mc_RmsgID =
           (   Cu_mc_RmsgID
            || ((Acc_mc_RmsgID_a_SaccID ||Acc_mc_RmsgID_a_n_SaccID)
               && ! RmsgID_eq_SmsgID));
          Cu_mc_RlastID =
            (   Cu_mc_RlastID
             || ((Acc_mc_RlastID_a_SaccID ||Acc_mc_RlastID_a_n_SaccID)
                && ! RlastID_eq_SmsgID));
      }
    :: goto Scrash
    od ;
```

```
Scrash: goto Sidle
}

active proctype Receiver()
{

Ridle: atomic{
        RmsgID_eq_SmsgID = FALSE;
        RmsgID_eq_RlastID = FALSE;
        Acc_mc_RmsgID_a_SaccID = FALSE;
        Acc_mc_RmsgID_a_n_SaccID = FALSE;
        Send_mc_SnextMsg_a_RmsgID = FALSE;
        Send_mc_n_SnextMsg_a_RmsgID = FALSE;
        Ack_mc_RmsgID = FALSE;
        Cu_mc_RmsgID = FALSE};

    do
    :: atomic{Nu_mc_SaccID -> RaccID_eq_SaccID = TRUE; break}
    :: atomic{TRUE -> RaccID_eq_SaccID = FALSE; break}
    :: atomic{Ack_mc_SmsgID =
            (Ack_mc_SmsgID || (Send_mc_SmsgID && ! RlastID_eq_SmsgID));
        Ack_mc_RmsgID =
            (    Ack_mc_RmsgID
             || ((Send_mc_SnextMsg_a_RmsgID ||Send_mc_SnextMsg_a_RmsgID)
                 && ! RmsgID_eq_RlastID))
        }
      :: goto Rcrash
    od;

Raccept:
    do
    :: atomic{Acc_mc_RmsgID_a_SaccID =
                (Acc_mc_RmsgID_a_SaccID || RaccID_eq_SaccID);
            Acc_mc_RmsgID_a_n_SaccID =
                (Acc_mc_RmsgID_a_n_SaccID || ! RaccID_eq_SaccID);
            Acc_mc_RlastID_a_SaccID =
                (Acc_mc_RlastID_a_SaccID
                 || (RmsgID_eq_RlastID && RaccID_eq_SaccID));
            Acc_mc_RlastID_a_n_SaccID =
                (Acc_mc_RlastID_a_n_SaccID
                 || (RmsgID_eq_RlastID && ! RaccID_eq_SaccID));
            Acc_mc_n_RlastID_a_SaccID =
                (Acc_mc_n_RlastID_a_SaccID
                 || (! RmsgID_eq_RlastID && RaccID_eq_SaccID))
        }
    :: assert (    !(Send_mc_n_SnextMsg_a_RmsgID
                  || (Send_mc_SnextMsg_a_RmsgID && Received_SnextMsg)))
    :: atomic{(Send_mc_SnextMsg_a_RmsgID ||Send_mc_n_SnextMsg_a_RmsgID)
                -> RmsgID_eq_RlastID = TRUE;
                    RlastID_eq_SmsgID = RmsgID_eq_SmsgID;
```

```
                    Acc_mc_RlastID_a_SaccID = Acc_mc_RmsgID_a_SaccID;
                    Acc_mc_RlastID_a_n_SaccID = Acc_mc_RmsgID_a_n_SaccID;
                    Acc_mc_n_RlastID_a_SaccID = Acc_mc_n_RmsgID_a_SaccID;
                    Cu_mc_RlastID = Cu_mc_RmsgID;
                    Received_SnextMsg = TRUE;
                    break
          }
   :: atomic{(Send_mc_SmsgID && ! RmsgID_eq_SmsgID && ! RlastID_eq_SmsgID)
                     -> Ack_mc_SmsgID = TRUE
          }
   :: atomic{Cu_mc_RmsgID ->
                 RmsgID_eq_RlastID = FALSE;
                 RlastID_eq_SmsgID = FALSE;
                 Acc_mc_n_RlastID_a_SaccID =
                     (Acc_mc_n_RlastID_a_SaccID || Acc_mc_RlastID_a_SaccID);
                 Acc_mc_RlastID_a_SaccID = FALSE;
                 Acc_mc_RlastID_a_n_SaccID = FALSE;
                 Ack_mc_RlastID = FALSE;
                 Cu_mc_RlastID = FALSE;
                 goto Ridle
          }
     :: goto Rcrash
   od;
Rack:
   do
   :: atomic{Ack_mc_RmsgID = TRUE;
                 Ack_mc_SmsgID = (Ack_mc_SmsgID || RmsgID_eq_SmsgID);
                 Ack_mc_RlastID = (Ack_mc_RlastID || RmsgID_eq_RlastID)
          }
   :: atomic{Cu_mc_RlastID ->
                 RmsgID_eq_RlastID = FALSE;
                 RlastID_eq_SmsgID = FALSE;
                 Acc_mc_n_RlastID_a_SaccID =
                     (Acc_mc_n_RlastID_a_SaccID || Acc_mc_RlastID_a_SaccID);
                 Acc_mc_RlastID_a_SaccID = FALSE;
                 Acc_mc_RlastID_a_n_SaccID = FALSE;
                 Ack_mc_RlastID = FALSE;
                 Cu_mc_RlastID = FALSE;
                 goto Ridle
          }
   :: atomic{
            Ack_mc_SmsgID =
              (Ack_mc_SmsgID || (Send_mc_SmsgID && ! RlastID_eq_SmsgID));
            Ack_mc_RmsgID =
              (    Ack_mc_RmsgID
               || ((Send_mc_SnextMsg_a_RmsgID ||Send_mc_SnextMsg_a_RmsgID)
                       && ! RmsgID_eq_RlastID))
          }
     :: goto Rcrash
   od;
```

```
Rcrash: atomic{RmsgID_eq_RlastID = FALSE;
                RlastID_eq_SmsgID = FALSE;
                Acc_mc_n_RlastID_a_SaccID =
                    (Acc_mc_n_RlastID_a_SaccID || Acc_mc_RlastID_a_SaccID);
                Acc_mc_RlastID_a_SaccID = FALSE;
                Acc_mc_RlastID_a_n_SaccID = FALSE;
                Ack_mc_RlastID = FALSE;
                Cu_mc_RlastID = FALSE;
                goto Ridle
        }
}
```

A Language Framework for Expressing Checkable Properties of Dynamic Software*

James C. Corbett[1], Matthew B. Dwyer[2], John Hatcliff[2], and Robby[2]

[1] University of Hawaii
Honolulu HI, 96822, USA.
corbett@hawaii.edu

[2] SAnToS Laboratory, Kansas State University
234 Nichols Hall, Manhattan KS, 66506, USA.
http://www.cis.ksu.edu/santos, {dwyer,hatcliff,robby}@cis.ksu.edu

Abstract. Research on how to reason about correctness properties of software systems using model checking is advancing rapidly. Work on extracting finite-state models from program source code and on abstracting those models is focused on enabling the tractable checking of program properties such as freedom from deadlock and assertion violations. For the most part, the problem of specifying more general program properties has not been considered.

In this paper, we report on the support for specifying properties of dynamic multi-threaded Java programs that we have built into the Bandera system. Bandera extracts finite-state models, in the input format of several existing model checkers, from Java code based on the property to be checked. The Bandera Specification Language (BSL) provides a language for defining general assertions and pre/post conditions on methods. It also supports the definition of observations that can be made of the state of program objects and the incorporation of those observations as predicates that can be instantiated in the scope of object quantifiers and used in describing common forms of state/event sequencing properties. We describe BSL and illustrate it on an example analyzed with Bandera and the Spin model checker.

1 Introduction

Several current projects [18,4,16,1,7] are aiming to demonstrate the effectiveness of model-checking as a quality assurance mechanism for software source code. Tools developed in these projects typically use one of the following two strategies: (1) they take program source code and compile it to the model description language of an existing model-checker (*e.g.*, Promela – the description language of the Spin model-checker [17]), or (2) they use a dedicated model-checking engine to process a model that is derived on-the-fly from source code. Both of these strategies have relative strengths and weaknesses when it comes to attacking what we

---

* This work supported in part by NSF under grants CCR-9633388, CCR-9703094, CCR-9708184, and CCR-9701418 and DARPA/NASA under grant NAG 21209.

K. Havelund, J. Penix, and W. Visser (Eds.): SPIN 2000, LNCS 1885, pp. 205–223, 2000.
© Springer-Verlag Berlin Heidelberg 2000

call the *model construction problem*: the challenging problem of taking real-world software components built with sophisticated language constructs that give rise to gigantic state-spaces and, from these, forming correct compact representations suitable for tractable model-checking.

Our software model-checking project, called Bandera, adopts a generalization of the first strategy: it provides an environment for compiling finite-state models from Java source code into several existing model-checking engines including Spin, dSpin [8], and NuSMV [3]. The environment includes numerous optimization phases including (a) a program slicing phase to remove program components that are irrelevant for the property being model-checked and (b) an abstraction phase to reduce the cardinality of data sets being manipulated. Just like in a conventional compiler, the translation process is carefully engineered through various intermediate languages so that adding a new back-end model-checker requires relatively little work.

Besides attacking the model-construction problem, we are also devoting significant resources to what we call the *requirement specification problem*: the problem of providing powerful yet easy to use mechanisms for expressing temporal requirements of software source code. Within the context of the Bandera project, one option would be to have developers express requirements in the specification language of one of the underlying model-checkers (e.g., in Spin's Linear Temporal Logic (LTL) specification language, or Computational Tree Logic (CTL) of NuSMV). This has several disadvantages.

1. Although temporal logics such as LTL and CTL are theoretically elegant, practitioners and even researchers sometimes find it difficult to use them to accurately express the complex state and event sequencing properties often required of software. Once written, these specifications are often hard to reason about, debug, and modify.
2. In the Bandera project, following this option forces the analyst to commit to the notation of a particular model-checker back-end. If more than one checker is to be used, the specifications may have to be recoded in a different language (*e.g.*, switching from LTL to CTL), and then perhaps simultaneously modified if the requirement is modified.
3. This option is also problematic because it forces the specification to be stated in terms of the *model's representation of program features* such as control-points, local and instance variables, array access, nested object dereferences as rendered, *e.g.*, in Promela, instead of in terms of the source code itself. Thus, the user must understand these typically highly optimized representations to accurately render the specifications. This is somewhat analogous to asking a programmer to state assertions in terms of the compiler's intermediate representation. Moreover, the representations may change depending on which optimizations were used when generating the model. Even greater challenges arise when modeling the *dynamism* found in typical object-oriented software: components corresponding to dynamically created objects/threads are dynamically added to the state-space during execution. These components are *anonymous* in the sense that they are often not bo-

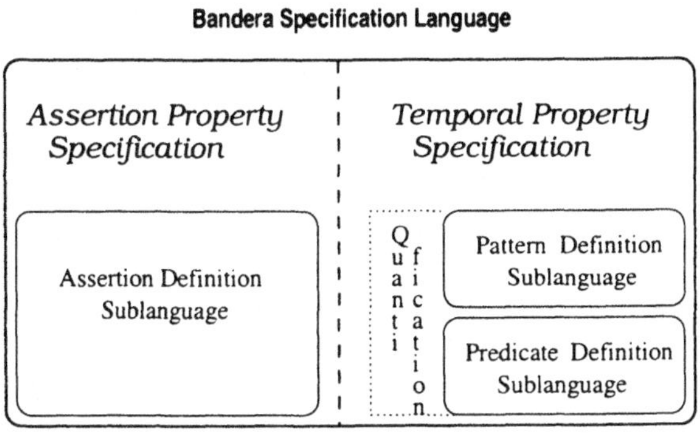

Bandera Specification Language

Fig. 1. BSL organization

und directly to variables appearing in the source program. The lack of fixed source-level component names makes it difficult to write specifications describing dynamic component properties: such properties have to be expressed in terms of the model's representation of the heap.

4. Finally, depending on what form of abstraction is used, the specifications would have to be modified to reference *abstractions of source code features* instead of the source code features themselves.

In this paper, we describe the design and implementation of the Bandera Specification Language (BSL) — a source-level, model-checker independent language for expressing temporal properties of Java program actions and data. BSL addresses the problems outlined above and provides support for overcoming the hurdles one faces when specifying properties of dynamically evolving software. For example, consider a property of a bounded buffer implementation stating that *no buffer stays full forever*. There are several challenges in rendering this specification in a form that can be model-checked including

- defining the meaning of *full* in the implementation,
- quantifying over time to insure that full buffers eventually become non-full, and
- quantifying over all dynamically created bounded buffers instances in the program.

BSL separates these issues and treats them with special purpose sub-languages as indicated in Figure 1.

- An *assertion* sublanguage allows developers to define constraints on program contexts in familiar assertion-style notation. Assertions can be selectively enabled/disabled so that one can easily identify only a subset of assertions for checking. Bandera exploits this capability by optimizing the generated models (using slicing and abstraction) specifically for the selected assertions.

– A temporal property sublanguage provides support for defining *predicates* on common Java control points (*e.g.*, method invocation and return) and Java data (including dynamically created threads and objects). These predicates become the basic *propositions* in temporal specifications. The temporal specification language is based not on a particular temporal logic, but on a collection of field-tested temporal specification patterns developed in our earlier work [13]. This pattern language is extensible and allows for libraries of domain-specific patterns to be created.

Interacting with both the predicate and pattern support in BSL is a powerful quantification facility that allows temporal specifications to be quantified over all objects/threads from particular classes. Quantification provides a mechanism for *naming* potentially anonymous data, and we have found this type of support to be crucial for expressive reasoning about dynamically created objects.

Assertions and predicates are included in the source code as Javadoc comments. This allows for HTML-based documentation to easily be extracted and browsed by developers, and for special purpose doclet-processing to provide a rich tool-based infra-structure for for writing specifications.

Even though BSL is based on Java, and, to some extent is driven by the desire to abstract away from the collection of model-checker back-ends found in Bandera, we believe that the general ideas embodied in this language will be useful in any environment for model-checking software source code.

The rest of the paper is organized as follows. Section 2 discusses some of the salient issues that influenced our design of the language. Section 3 presents a simple Java program that we use to illustrate the features of the language, and gives a brief overview of how Bandera models concurrent Java programs. Section 4 describes the design and implementation of the assertion sublanguage. Section 5 describes the design and implementation of the temporal specification sublanguage. A brief discussion of the implementation of BSL in Bandera and its application to check properties of an example is given in Section 6. Section 7 discusses related work and Section 8 describes a variety of extensions to the current implementation of BSL that are under development and concludes.

2   Design Rationale

BSL is the latest in a series of languages and systems that we have created to support specification of temporal properties of software systems. Experience with an earlier simple property language for Ada software [11] and with a system of temporal specification patterns [13] has yielded the following design criteria that we have tried to follow as we address the challenging issues surrounding specifying properties of Java source code.

1. The specification language must hide the intricacies of temporal logic by emphasizing common specification coding patterns.

2. Even though details of temporal logics are to be hidden, expert users should be allowed "back doors" to write specifications (or fragments of specifications) directly in, e.g., LTL.
3. The language must support specification styles that are already used by developers such as assertions, pre/post-conditions, etc.
4. The specification artifacts themselves should be strongly connected to the code. The specifications will reference features from the code (e.g., variable names, method names, control points), so the principal specification elements should be located with the code so that developers can easily maintain them, read them for documentation, and browse them.
5. Finally, and perhaps must importantly, the language must include support for reasoning about language features used in real software such as dynamic object/thread creation, interface definitions, exceptions, etc. These often give rise to heap-allocated structures that are reachable by following chains of object references, but are effectively anonymous when considering a Java program's static fields and local variables.

Criterion (1) derives from experience with the Specification Patterns Project. BSL provides a macro facility that implements all the patterns from [13]. Conforming to criterion (2), it also allows expert users to write their own patterns or code their temporal logic specifications directly.

Following criterion (3), the design and presentation of BSL has been influenced by various Java assertion languages such as iContract [21]. In each of these languages above, developers write their specifications in Java comments using the Javadoc facility. We have also followed this approach because it is an effective way to address criterion (4): browse-able HTML documentation for BSL specifications can be created, and the close physical proximity of comments and code encourages regular maintenance.

BSL currently does not address all the program features mentioned in criterion (5) (e.g., we don't discuss specifying properties of exceptions in this work), but it does make significant steps in handling heap-allocated data/threads.

3   Example

Figure 2 gives the implementation of a simple bounded buffer implementation in Java that is amenable to simultaneous use by multiple threads. This code illustrates several of the challenges encountered in specifying the behavior of Java programs. Each instance of the BoundedBuffer class maintains an array of objects and two indices into that array representing the head and tail of the active segment of the array. Calls to add (take) objects to (from) the buffer are guarded by a check for a full (empty) buffer using the Java condition-wait loop idiom. Comments in the code contain various BSL declarations, and we will discuss these in the following sections.

Bandera models a concurrent Java program as a finite-state transition system. Each state of the transition system is an abstraction of the state of the

```
/**
 * @observable
 *   EXP Full: (head == tail);
 *   EXP TailRange: (tail >= 0 &&
 *                   tail < bound);
 *   EXP HeadRange: (head >= 0 &&
 *                   head < bound);
 */
class BoundedBuffer {
  Object [] buffer;
  int bound, head, tail;

  /**
   * @assert
   *   PRE PositiveBound: (b > 0);
   */
  public BoundedBuffer(int b) {
    bound = b;
    buffer = new Object[bound];
    head = 0;
    tail = bound - 1;
  }

  /**
   * @observable
   *   RETURN ReturnTrue:
   *           ($ret == true);
   */
  public synchronized
        boolean isEmpty() {
    return head ==
        ((tail + 1) % bound);
  }
}
```

```
/**
 * @assert
 *   POST AddToEnd:
 *         (head == 0) ?
 *           buffer[bound-1] == o :
 *           buffer[head-1] == o;
 * @observable
 *   INVOKE Call;
 */
public synchronized
        void add(Object o) {
  while ( tail == head )
    try { wait(); }
    catch (InterruptedException ex) {}
  buffer[head] = o;
  head = (head+1) % bound;
  notifyAll();
}

/**
 * @observable
 *   RETURN Return;
 */
public synchronized Object take() {
  while ( isEmpty() )
    try { wait(); }
    catch (InterruptedException ex) {}
  tail = (tail+1) % bound;
  notifyAll();
  return buffer[tail];
}
}
```

Fig. 2. Bounded Buffer Implementation with Predicate Definitions

Java program and each transition represents the execution of one or more statements transforming this abstract state. The state of the transition system records the current control location of each thread, the values of program variables relevant to the property being checked, and run-time information necessary to implement the concurrent semantics: the run state of each thread, the lock states, and the lock and wait queues of each object. We bound the number of states in the model by limiting the number of objects each allocator (e.g., new ClassName) can create to k (a parameter of the analysis).

```
import assertion BoundedBuffer.BoundedBuffer.*;
import assertion BoundedBuffer.add.*;
import predicate BoundedBuffer.*;

// Enable PositiveBound pre-cond. assertion of BoundedBuffer
BufferAssertions: enable assertions { PositiveBound, AddToEnd };

// Indices always stay in range
IndexRangeInvariant:forall[b:BoundedBuffer].
                    {HeadRange(b) && TailRange(b)} is universal globally;

// Full-buffers eventually get emptied
FullToNonFull:forall[b:BoundedBuffer].
            {!Full(b)} responds to {Full(b)} globally;

// Empty-buffers must be added to before being taken from
NoTakeWhileEmpty:forall[b:BoundedBuffer].
                {BoundedBuffer.take.Return(b)} is absent
                after {BoundedBuffer.isEmpty.ReturnTrue(b)}
                until {BoundedBuffer.add.Call(b)};
```

Fig. 3. Bounded Buffer Properties rendered in BSL

4   The Assertion Sublanguage

4.1   Rationale

An assertion facility provides a convenient way for a programmer to specify a constraint on a program's data space that should hold when control reaches a particular control location. In C and C++ programming, assertions are typically embedded directly in source code using an **assert** macro, where the location of the assertion is given by the position of the macro invocation in the source program.

Due to Java's support for extracting HTML documentation from Java source code comments via Javadoc technologies, several popular Java assertion facilities, such as iContract [21], support definition of assertions in Java method header comments. BSL also adopts this approach. For example, Figure 2 shows the declaration of the BSL assertion PRE PositiveBound: (b > 0). In this assertion, the data constraint is (b > 0) and the control location is specified by the occurrence of the tag @assert PRE in the method header documentation for BoundedBuffer constructor: the constraint must hold whenever control is at the first executable statement in the constructor.

```
<assertions> ::= @assert <assertion-set-name>? <comment>* <assertion>*

<assertion-set-name> ::= <java-id> | <assertion-set-name> . <java-id>
<label>               ::= <java-id>
<assertion-name>      ::= <java-id>

<assertion>
  ::= PRE <assertion-name> : <exp> ; <comment>*
    | LOCATION '[' <label> ']' <assertion-name> : <exp> ; <comment>*
    | POST <assertion-name> : <exp> ; <comment>*
```

Fig. 4. BSL assertion syntax

4.2   Syntax and Informal Semantics

Figure 4 gives the syntax of BSL assertions. Sets of assertions are defined using the Javadoc tag @assert in the header documentation for methods or constructors. Each assertion set defined by an @assert tag can be given an optional name, and this name along with the name for each assertion in the set, is used to uniquely identify the assertion so that it be can be selectively enabled/disabled. If the set name is omitted, the fully qualified name of the corresponding method is used as the name for the assertion set. The optional name is followed by zero or more Java newline comments.

Besides precondition assertions as illustrated above, BSL supports location assertions and postcondition assertions. LOCATION[<label>] <assertion-name>: <exp> is satisfied if <exp> is true when control is at the Java statement labeled by <label> in the corresponding method).[1] POST <assertion-name>: <exp> is satisfied if <exp> is true immediately *after* the execution of any of the corresponding method's return statements or after the execution of the last statement in the method if it has no return statement. The expression <exp> can refer to the return value of the method using the Bandera reserved identifier $ret.

There are various other well-formedness conditions associated with variable scoping that we will not discuss in detail here. For example, a precondition assertion cannot reference local variables for the method since these have not been initialized when the byte-code for the method body begins executing, and a label assertion can only reference variables are in scope at the point where the given label appears in the source code.

Once assertions have declared, a selection of the assertions can be presented to Bandera as an *assertion specification* to be model-checked. Figure 3 presents a BSL file where the first specification BufferAssertions enables checking of the PositiveBound and AddtoEnd assertions of Figure 2. Violated assertions are reported back to the user by presenting a trace through the source program that terminates at the location in which the data condition is violated.

---

[1] Even though Java does not include goto's, it includes labels to indicate the targets of break and continue statements.

4.3 Implementation Issues

As with other Java assertion tools, the BSL assertion implementation acts as a preprocessor: it transforms the source code and embeds each enabled assertion using a Bandera library method `Bandera.assert(boolean)`. A little bit of extra work is needed to maintain proper label correspondence in `LOCATION` assertions and to calculate the value of the variable `$ret` in `POST` assertions, but the transformation is otherwise straightforward. One can also hardcode assertions directly with `Bandera.assert`, but this is discouraged. When Bandera generates models for Spin, each `Bandera.assert` call is translated to a Promela `ASSERT` statement.

5   The Temporal Specification Sublanguage

While assertions provide a convenient way to write constraints on data at particular program points, they are not powerful enough to directly specify interesting temporal relationships between system actions. Since such temporal properties are often required of concurrent systems, model-checkers usually support a temporal property specification language based on, e.g., LTL or CTL. These temporal specification languages subsume assertions in the sense that any assertion (l, c), where l is a location and c a condition on the data at that location, can be encoded in a temporal property: along all paths, it must be true in every state s that if s's control point is l then c holds. However, model-checkers, such as Spin, provide support for assertions because they can be checked much more efficiently than general temporal properties. To take advantage of the potential for faster checks, BSL separates assertion and general temporal properties.

In this section, we describe BSL's temporal specification sublanguage. First, we introduce a system of predicates on program features including common control points such as method entry and exit, and both class and instance data. These predicates become the primitive propositions that one reasons about when writing temporal property specifications. We describe our extensible pattern-based system for constructing temporal specifications. Woven throughout both the predicates and the temporal patterns is a notion of object quantification that provides a mechanism for generating names of dynamically created objects.

5.1   Predicate Definition Sublanguage

BSL provides two kinds of predicates: location insensitive predicates—predicates that are used for defining observables regardless of program points, and location sensitive predicates—predicates that are used for defining observables at specific program points. For example, Figure 2 shows a declaration of a location insensitive predicate `EXP Full: (head == tail)` in the class `BoundedBuffer` header documentation. This form of predicate, called an *expression predicate*, is often used to define class invariants or to indicate distinguished states (*e.g.*, a full buffer) in class or instance data. Since expression predicates do not refer to

```
<predicates> ::= @observable <predicate-set-name>? <comment>* <predicate>*

<predicate-set-name> ::= <java-id> | <predicate-set-name> . <java-id>
<label>              ::= <java-id>
<predicate-name>     ::= <java-id>

<predicate>
  ::= static? EXP <predicate-name> : <exp> ; <comment>*
    | INVOKE <predicate-name> [: <exp>]? ; <comment>*
    | LOCATION '[' <label> ']' ' <predicate-name> [: <exp>]? ; <comment>*
    | RETURN <predicate-name> [: <exp>]? ; <comment>*
```

Fig. 5. BSL predicate definition syntax

particular control points in methods, they can only be defined in class header documentation.

In addition to categorizing predicates based on location sensitivity, we also categorize predicates based on the kinds of fields or code to which they refer. *Static predicates* are used to reason about static fields (class variables) or program points of static Java methods. *Instance predicates* are used to reason about instance fields (memory cells that appear in each object of a given class) or program points in Java virtual methods. For example, the Full predicate is an instance predicate, because it refers to instance data members of the BoundedBuffer class. The static modifier is used in an expression predicate declaration to indicate that it is a static predicate. When an instance predicate is used in a specification, it must be passed a parameter to indicate the instance to which the predicate applies. For example, the FullToNonFull property of Figure 3 shows the Full predicate being parameterized by the quantified variable b.

Syntax and informal semantics. Figure 5 gives the syntax of BSL predicate definitions. Sets of predicates are defined using the Javadoc tag @observable in the header documentation for classes or methods. Each predicate set defined by an @observable tag can be given an optional name, and this name along with the name for each predicate in the set, is used to uniquely identify the predicate so that it can be referred to in a temporal property specification. If the set name is omitted, the fully qualified name of the corresponding class or method is used as the name for the predicate set. The optional name is followed by zero or more Java newline comments.

Besides expression predicates as illustrated above, BSL supports invocation predicates, location predicates, and return predicates, which are all location sensitive predicates that are defined in method header documentation. These location sensitive predicates are static if they are defined for static methods.

INVOKE <predicate-name> [: <exp>]? is true when control is at the first executable statement in the corresponding method and <exp> is true; absence of <exp> defaults to true. For instance INVOKE predicates, an additional constraint applies: the supplied object parameter must match the *receiver object* (*i.e.*, the object upon which the method was invoked). For example, in the NoTakeWhileEmpty property of Figure 3, the instance INVOKE predicate add.Call holds only when the add method is invoked on the object referenced by the quantified variable b.

The semantics of LOCATION '[' <label> ']' <predicate-name> [:<exp>]? is similar to that of the invoke predicate, except that the relevant control point is the Java statement labeled by <label> in the corresponding method.

RETURN <predicate-name> [:<exp>]? is similar to an invoke predicate, except that the relevant control points are the points immediately *after* any of the corresponding method's return statements or after the last statement in the method if it has no return statement. The expression <exp> can refer to the return value of the method using the Bandera reserved identifier $ret. For example, in the NoTakeWhileEmpty property of Figure 3, the instance RETURN predicate ReturnTrue holds iff the isEmpty method was invoked on the object referenced by the quantified variable b and control is immediately after the return statement of isEmpty and the return value of the method is true.

The Java expressions that are supported in <exp> are Java expressions that are guaranteed to have no *side-effects*. Currently we restrict Java expressions to exclude assignments, array or object creations, and method invocations to assure side-effect freedom.

There are various other well-formedness conditions associated with variable scoping that we will not discuss in detail here. For example, a return predicate cannot refer to local variables of the method since there might be several return statements for the method with each having a different set of visible local variables.

Implicit Constraints. Since the execution of certain Java/BSL operators can throw run-time exceptions (e.g., NullPointerException), expressions containing such operators are conjoined with implicit constraints prohibiting such exceptions (which might otherwise interfere with the model checking). For example, the predicate expression x.f is interpreted as (x != null) && x.f—if x == null, the predicate is false. If static analysis can determine that such exceptions will not be thrown, then the constraints can be omitted.

5.2 Specifying Temporal Patterns

The automata and temporal-logic formalisms that are commonly used to describe state and event sequencing properties of concurrent systems can be subtle and difficult to use correctly. Even people with significant experience with temporal logics find it difficult to specify common software requirements in their formalism of choice. Consequently it is a significant challenge to make these formalisms amenable to effective use by practicing software developers.

To address this issue, in previous work [10] we identified a small number of commonly occurring classes of temporal requirements, e.g., invariance, response, and precedence properties. We refer to these classes as *specification patterns*; there are five basic patterns:

- *universal* properties require the argument to be true throughout the execution
- *absence* properties require that the argument is never true in the execution
- *existence* properties require that the argument is true at some point in the execution
- *response* properties require that the occurrence of a designated state/event is followed by another designated state/event in the execution
- *precedence* properties require that a designated state/event always occurs before the first occurrence of another designated state/event

In addition several *chain* patterns allow for the construction of sequences of dependent response and precedence relationships to be specified. A web-site [12] presents the current set of eight patterns and their variations as well as translations into five different common temporal specification formalisms, including LTL and CTL.

In developing this system of patterns we found that it was useful to distinguish the required pattern of states/events from the region of system execution in which this pattern was required. *Pattern scopes* define variations of the basic patterns in which checking of the pattern is disabled during specified regions of execution. There are five basic scopes; a pattern can hold

- *globally* throughout the system's execution,
- *after* the first occurrence of a state/event,
- *before* the first occurrence of a state/event,
- *between* a pair of designated states/events
- during the interval, or *after* one state/event *until* the next occurrence of another state/event or throughout the rest of the execution if there is no subsequent occurrence of that state/event

In subsequent work [13], we validated that these specification patterns were representative of a large majority of the temporal requirements that researchers and users of finite-state verification tools had written. We studied over 600 property specifications and found that over 94% were instances of the patterns; interestingly over 70% of the properties were either universal or response properties.

We believe that there are several advantages to a pattern based approach. It can shorten the learning curve by presenting a smaller collection of concepts to specification writers. These patterns are expressible in nearly all of the commonly used specification languages for existing finite-state verification tools, thus, patterns provide some degree of tool independence. Finally, techniques for optimizing the construction of finite-state models can exploit information about the structure of the patterns.

BSL builds off of this work by providing a structured-English language front-end for the patterns which is illustrated in the fourth and fifth rule sets of Figure 6. Common synonyms are supported. For example, *invariance* and *universal*

```
<temporal>    ::= <id> : <quantifier>* <pattern>

<quantifier> ::= forall [ <ids> : <java-id> ] .

<ids>         ::= <id>
                | <ids> , <id>

<pattern>     ::= <pred-expr> is universal <scope>
                | <pred-expr> is invariant <scope>
                | <pred-expr> is absent <scope>
                | <pred-expr> exists <scope>
                | <pred-expr> precedes <pred-expr> <scope>
                | <pred-expr> leads to <pred-expr> <scope>
                | <pred-expr> responds to <pred-expr> <scope>

<scope>       ::= globally
                | before <pred-expr>
                | after <pred-expr>
                | between <pred-expr> and <pred-expr>
                | after <pred-expr> until <pred-expr>

<pred-expr>   ::= <predicate-name>
                | <predicate-name> ( <id> )
                | ( <pred-expr> )
                | ! <pred-expr>
                | <pred-expr> && <pred-expr>
                | <pred-expr> || <pred-expr>
                | <pred-expr> -> <pred-expr>
```

Fig. 6. BSL Pattern and Quantifier Syntax

patterns and *leads to* can be used to express the FullToNonFull property from Figure 3 as

```
FullToNonFull: forall[b:BoundedBuffer].
   {Full(b)} leads to {!Full(b)} globally
```

These pattern specifications are then translated into the specification formalism for the chosen checker. For example, if using Spin the *leads to* part of this property would be translated to the following LTL

```
[]( {Full(b)} -> <> {!Full(b)} )
```

Bandera supports user defined extension of BSL patterns. Users can define their own patterns and mappings to low-level specification formalisms. In this way, an expert specifier can customize a collection of patterns for the use of the developers on a project.

5.3   Specifying Properties for Class Instances

One of the chief difficulties in specifying properties of Java programs lies in naming the objects that constitute the state of the system. The majority of program state is heap allocated and is referenced through local thread variables by navigating chains of object references. We believe that, in general, one is interested in stating properties about all instances of a class or by distinguishing instances of a class by observing their state. One way to achieve this is to provide the ability to state properties for all instances of a class created during a program run.

The syntax for universal *class instance quantification* is given in Figure 6. BSL provides this through a mechanism that is independent of the specific checker used to reason about the property defined in the scope of the quantifier. This is achieved by customizing the model based on the quantifiers used and by embedding the property to be checked in a specification pattern that assures it will be checked only over the objects in the quantifier's domain.

For clarity, we describe the customization of the model in terms of a source program transformation rather than as a transformation on Bandera's intermediate program representation. This transformation requires the use of non-determinism in the model, which is not available in Java, so we introduce a static method `Bandera.choose` that is translated by Bandera to non-deterministic choice among its arguments in the model checker input. We also describe the embedding of a quantified LTL property; the approach is similar for other formalisms.

Universal Class Instance Quantification. Universal quantification is achieved as follows, for a quantified formula `forall[var:QuantifiedClass].P(var)`

1. For the bound variable `var` in the quantification, introduce a static field `var` of type `QuantifiedClass` in the public class `BoundVariables`. This will introduce a *global* state variable for each such field in the finite-state model for the program.
2. For each field in `BoundVariables` define a predicate `var_selected` which is true when `var` is not null.
3. At the end of each constructor for `QuantifiedClass` introduce the following code fragment:

```
if (BoundVariables.var == null)
   if (Bandera.choose(true,false)) BoundVariables.var = this;
```

where `Bandera.choose(true,false)` introduces a non-deterministic choice between `true` and `false` values in the finite-state model for the program.
4. The temporal formula, P, to be checked on the generated model is modified in two ways. First, the pattern, P, in the scope of the quantifier, is expanded using the name `var` as parameters to the referenced predicates; call this expanded formula P_var. Second, this expanded formula is embedded in a context which controls the sequences of states on which P_var is evaluated. Specifically, for LTL, the expanded formula has the form:

```
(!var_selected U (var_selected && P_var)) || []!var_selected
```

Checking the modified formula on the modified model exploits the exhaustive nature of model checkers. For each trace of the unmodified model that would be generated by Bandera, the modified model creates a trace in which each instance of the QuantifiedClass will be bound to var. At the state in which the binding is established the modified temporal formula will trigger the checking of P_var.

Note that when nested quantification is used the var_selected condition is defined such that it is true only when all of the bound variables in the quantifiers have been assigned a non-null value.

Implementation Issues. There are several advantages to implementing support for quantification early in the process of extracting finite-state models from Java programs : checker independence and optimization.

The technique described above is applied to the internal representation of Java code prior to the generation of model checker input, e.g., Promela for Spin. Thus, quantified temporal specifications can be checked with any of the supported verifiers. Furthermore, since it is possible to generate Java from our internal representation, it is possible for Java model checkers, such as Java Pathfinder 2 from NASA's Ames Laboratory, to check quantified temporal specifications as long as they map the Bandera.choose method calls to non-deterministic choice in the underlying model.

The scopes in specification patterns define the end-points of regions in which the pattern should be checked. If those end-points do not occur, then the specification is vacuously true. For this reason, by performing object flow analyses [14] we can determine the set of objects that can possibly influence the satisfaction of scope delimiting predicates. This information can be used to restrict the set of objects over which a quantifier must range. Consider the specification

```
forall[s:SuperType].
   {Pred(s)} is absent after {init.Return(s)}
```

in this case we need only calculate the set of instances of SuperType for which the init method is called. An upper approximation of this set can by calculated in terms of the sub-types of SuperType that can appear as the receiver object of an init invocation. The code from step 3, described above, need only be added to those sub-types; this may significantly reduce the cost of checking the quantified property by reducing the number of values that will be assigned to the bound variable, s.

6   Implementation and Preliminary Results

BSL support has been implemented in the latest version of the Bandera toolset [4]. The user interface provides a significant advance over the previous interface for specifying program properties [5] by extracting assertions and predicates

Property	Sliced	Never-claim States	States Stored
Deadlock	No	-	240047
Deadlock	Yes	-	51757
BufferAssertions	No	-	280575
BufferAssertions	Yes	-	17797
IndexRangeInvariant	Yes	14	45215
IndexRangeInvariant, BufferAssertions	Yes	14	115387
FullToNonFull	Yes	25	64687
FullToNonFull, BufferAssertions	Yes	25	154842

Fig. 7. BoundedBuffer Property Check Data

and presenting the latter as building blocks for instantiating temporal pattern specifications.

To illustrate the benefits of selectively analyzing program properties we built a simple environment for the `BoundedBuffer` class. The environment consists of four threads: a main thread that instantiates two `BoundedBuffers` loads one of the buffers until it is full, then passes the pair of buffers to threads that read from one buffer and write to the other such that a *ring* topology is established. An additional thread repeatedly polls the state of the two `BoundedBuffers` to determine if they are empty. With this environment all of the properties in Figure 3 will be true, yet the buffers will be forced through all of their internal states given their **bound**.

Figure 7 shows the size of the state space for checks of several properties in Figure 3. We only used Bandera's slicing capabilities in these checks; Bandera can also abstract program data to extract compact models. Slicing is driven by the expressions used in assertions and predicates in the properties being checked and is fully automatic. We omit timing data noting only that the total time to perform these checks was less than a minute in all cases (including slicing, model extraction, and model checking). By default, Bandera will extract a model suitable for deadlock checking. We used SPIN's deadlock checking ability for the first two checks; slicing has a modest impact on the state space since most of this small program can influence the execution of Java locking operations and **wait** statements. The `BufferAssertions` checks were obtained by enabling assertion checking with SPIN; slicing has a dramatic effect here since the program dependences [15] from the assertion expressions allow the thread that polls for emptiness to be sliced away. The last four checks illustrate that the overhead of BSL's quantification is not prohibitive. We only show data for sliced models, the non-sliced models are significantly larger. It is interesting to note that the embedding of the temporal formula to be checked in the formula from step 4 in Section 5.3 causes a non-trivial increase in the size of the automaton (never-claim) used in checking the property. For `IndexRangeInvariant`, the basic invariant property requires a 2 state automaton and this increases to 14 states with quantification. For `FullToNonFull`, the response property requires a

4 state automaton and this increases to 25 states with quantification. It is difficult to assess the impact that this blowup has on the cost of checking properties
since we optimize the model for each property. We are studying this question
empirically to understand the cost of quantification over a broader collection of
programs and properties.

7   Related Work

There is a long history of work on temporal logics for specifying properties of
concurrent systems. LTL [23] is one of the most popular such logics. Efforts to
make such logics easier to use have taken several directions including developing
diagrammatic forms [2,9] and using stylized English [6,13].

   In recent years, increasing attention has been devoted to formally specifying
properties of design or object models, such as those supported in the unified modeling language (UML). UML's object constraint language (OCL) [24] provides
for specification of program invariants and pre/post conditions on operations.
Weaknesses of OCL-based approaches include the lack of ability to reason about
such specifications and the fact that current tool support does not provide a
mechanism to transfer to such specifications to the code. Both of these are being
addressed by different research efforts. Alloy [20] is an object-modeling language
that has an associated tool for checking specifications written about the model. Tools that support design-by-contract for Java programs such as iContract
[21], support a subset of OCL that has been tailored to Java syntax. Such tools
instrument the program to dynamically check invariants and method pre/post
conditions. Our work fits in this context by pushing OCL-like Java-based specifications in several directions to make them more checkable (ala Alloy) and
to incorporate temporal specifications. The added benefit is that by exploiting
model checking technology we can perform restricted checks for defects or exhaustive verification of properties; this makes our approach more suitable for the
subtle defects that are found in multi-threaded Java systems.

   The JML project [22] is attempting to provide a fully featured specification
system for Java code. It provides for invariant, pre and post-conditions as do
the approaches discussed above, but it aims to be enable users to completely describe the behavior of the code. In contrast, our work is aimed at supporting the
description of partial correctness properties that can be automatically checked
against code descriptions.

   Recently, Iosif and Sisto have independently developed a language for specifying LTL properties of Java source code that is similar in many respects to
ours [19]. Like ours, their language includes mechanisms for defining predicates on source code features such as variable values and common control points
(e.g., method activation, method exit, and labeled statements). A limited form
of support is given for using specification patterns, but no support is given for
defining and selectively enabling assertion specifications. Their language does
not include a mechanism for object quantification, but it does include quantification over integers. This integer quantification cannot be implemented directly

(due to the unbounded nature of the domain), but they suggest that abstraction techniques may be incorporated in the future to address this problem. They plan to implement their language as part of a larger collection of tools that they are building for model-checking software source code [7,8].

8   Conclusion

We have defined a language framework for expressing correctness properties of dynamic Java programs. A property expressed in this framework can be rendered in terms of commonly available features in the input languages of existing model checking tools. This framework is integrated into the Bandera system so that information about the property to be checked can be exploited to reduce the size of the program model. We have implemented the core functionality of BSL and are beginning to use it to check properties of Java code.

Work on the core of BSL has led us to pursue several extensions to allow for a wider range of properties to be expressed. One of the most interesting of these extensions is the application of our approach to class instance quantification, from Section 5.3, to quantify over the elements of an array. The basic idea is to use non-determinism to choose from a range of indices and then bind the array element at that index for use in subsequent temporal formulae. We believe that this can be applied to any container built using arrays, such as java.util.Vector. We are experimenting with these extensions to find the ones that add useful new capabilities to BSL and we plan to report on those in the future.

Acknowledgements. Thanks to Tom Ball, Sriram Rajamani, and Radu Iosif for interesting discussions during the preparation of this paper.

References

1. Thomas Bal and Sriram K. Rajamani. Boolean programs : A model and process for software analysis. Technical Report 2000-14, Microsoft Research, 2000.
2. I. A. Browne, Z. Manna, and H. B. Sipma. Generalized temporal verification diagrams. *Lecture Notes in Computer Science*, 1026, 1995.
3. A. Cimatti, E. Clarke, F. Giunchiglia, and M. Roveri. NuSMV : a new symbolic model checker. *International Journal on Software Tools for Technology Transfer*, 2000. to appear.
4. James C. Corbett, Matthew B. Dwyer, John Hatcliff, Shawn Laubach, Corina S. Păsăreanu, Robby, and Hongjun Zheng. Bandera : Extracting finite-state models from Java source code. In *Proceedings of the 22nd International Conference on Software Engineering*, June 2000.
5. James C. Corbett, Matthew B. Dwyer, John Hatcliff, and Robby. Bandera : A source-level interface for model checking Java programs. In *Proceedings of the 22nd International Conference on Software E ngineering*, June 2000.
6. R. Darimont and A. van Lamsweerde. Formal refinement patterns for goal-driven requirements elaboration. In *Proceedings of the Fourth ACM SIGSOFT Symposium on Foundations of Software Engineering*, pages 179–190, October 1996.

7. C. Demartini, R. Iosif, and R. Sisto. A deadlock detection tool for concurrent Java programs. *Software - Practice and Experience*, 29(7):577–603, July 1999.

8. C. Demartini, R. Iosif, and R. Sisto. dspin : A dynamic extension of SPIN. In *Theoretical and Applied Aspects of SPIN Model Checking (LNCS 1680)*, September 1999.

9. Laura K. Dillon, G. Kutty, Louise E. Moser, P. M. Melliar-Smith, and Y. S. Ramakrishna. A graphical interval logic for specifying concurrent systems. *ACM Transactions on Software Engineering and Methodology*, 3(2):131–165, April 1994.

10. Matthew B. Dwyer, George S. Avrunin, and James C. Corbett. Property specification patterns for finite-state verification. In Mark Ardis, editor, *Proceedings of the Second Workshop on Formal Methods in Software Practice*, pages 7–15, March 1998.

11. Matthew B. Dwyer, Corina S. Pasareanu, and James C. Corbett. Translating Ada programs for model checking : A tutorial. Technical Report 98-12, Kansas State University, Department of Computing and Information Sciences, 1998.

12. M.B. Dwyer, G.S. Avrunin, and J.C. Corbett. A System of Specification Patterns. |http://www.cis.ksu.edu/santos/spec-patterns—, 1998.

13. M.B. Dwyer, G.S. Avrunin, and J.C. Corbett. Patterns in property specifications for finite-state verification. In *Proceedings of the 21st International Conference on Software Engineering*, May 1999.

14. David Paul Grove. *Effective Interprocedural Optimization of Object-oriented Languages*. PhD thesis, University of Washington, 1998.

15. John Hatcliff, James C. Corbett, Matthew B. Dwyer, Stefan Sokolowski, and Hongjun Zheng. A formal study of slicing for multi-threaded programs with JVM concurrency primitives. In *Proceedings of the 6th International Static Analysis Symposium (SAS'99)*, September 1999.

16. K. Havelund and T. Pressburger. Model checking Java programs using Java PathFinder. *International Journal on Software Tools for Technology Transfer*, 1999.

17. Gerard J. Holzmann. The model checker SPIN. *IEEE Transactions on Software Engineering*, 23(5):279–294, May 1997.

18. Gerard J. Holzmann and Margaret H. Smith. Software model checking : Extracting verification models from source code. In *Proceedings of FORTE/PSTV'99*, November 1999.

19. Radu Iosif and Riccardo Sisto. On the specification and semantics of source level properties in java. In *Proceedings of the First International Workshop on Automated Program Analysis Testing and Verification*, June 2000. (Held in conjunction with the 2000 Internation Conference on Software Engineering).

20. Daniel Jackson. Alloy: A lightweight object modelling notation.

21. Reto Kramer. iContract—the Java Design by Contract tool. In *Proceedings of Technology of Object-Oriented Languages and Systems, TOOLS-USA*. IEEE Press, 1998.

22. Gary T. Leavens, Albert L. Baker, and Clyde Ruby. JML: a Java modeling language. In *Formal Underpinnings of Java Workshop (at OOPSLA'98)*, October 1998.

23. Z. Manna and A. Pnueli. *The Temporal Logic of Reactive and Concurrent Systems: Specification*. Springer-Verlag, 1991.

24. Jos Warmer and Anneke Kleppe. *The Object Constraint Language: Precise Modeling with UML*. Addison-Wesley, 1998.

Model-Checking Multi-threaded Distributed Java Programs*

Scott D. Stoller

Computer Science Dept., Indiana University,
Bloomington, IN 47405-7104 USA

Abstract. Systematic state-space exploration is a powerful technique
for verification of concurrent software systems. Most work in this area
deals with manually-constructed models of those systems. We propose a
framework for applying state-space exploration to multi-threaded distributed systems written in standard programming languages. It generalizes
Godefroid's work on VeriSoft, which does not handle multi-threaded systems, and Bruening's work on ExitBlockRW, which does not handle
distributed (multi-process) systems. Unlike ExitBlockRW, our search algorithms incorporate powerful partial-order methods, guarantee detection of deadlocks, and guarantee detection of violations of the locking
discipline used to avoid race conditions in accesses to shared variables.

1 Introduction

Systematic state-space exploration (model-checking) is a powerful technique for
verification of concurrent software systems. Most work in this area actually deals
with manually-constructed models (abstractions) of those systems. The models
are described using restricted languages, not general-purpose programming languages. Use of restricted modeling languages can greatly facilitate analysis and
verification, leading to strong guarantees about the properties of the model. However, use of such models has two potentially significant disadvantages: first,
the effort needed to construct the model (in addition to the actual implementation of the system), and second, possible discrepancies between the behavior
of the model and the behavior of the original system. One approach to avoiding
these disadvantages is automatic translation of general-purpose programming
languages into modeling languages, as in [STMD96,HS99,DIS99,CDH+00]. This
facilitates applying abstractions, but automatic translation that handles all language features (including dynamic memory allocation) and standard libraries
and yields tractable models is very difficult.

Another approach is to apply state-space exploration directly to software
written in general-purpose programming languages, such as C++ or Java. This
approach is used in VeriSoft [God97,GHJ98]. Capturing and storing the state

* The author gratefully acknowledges the support of ONR under Grant N00014-
99-1-0358 and the support of NSF under CAREER Award CCR-9876058. Email:
stoller@cs.indiana.edu   Web: http://www.cs.indiana.edu/~stoller/

K. Havelund, J. Penix, and W. Visser (Eds.): SPIN 2000, LNCS 1885, pp. 224–244, 2000.
© Springer-Verlag Berlin Heidelberg 2000

of a program written in a general-purpose programming language is difficult, so VeriSoft uses *state-less search*; this means that the search algorithm does not require storage of previously-visited states. State-less search might visit a state multiple times. VeriSoft uses partial-order methods—specifically, persistent sets and sleep sets (see Section 3) to reduce this redundancy. VeriSoft is targeted at "distributed" systems, specifically, systems containing multiple single-threaded processes that do not share memory. Processes interact via *communication objects*, such as semaphores or sockets.

ExitBlock [Bru99] is based on similar ideas as VeriSoft but targets a different class of systems. ExitBlock can test a single multi-threaded Java process that uses locks to avoid race conditions in accesses to variables shared by multiple threads. Specifically, ExitBlock assumes that the process satisfies the mutual-exclusion locking discipline (MLD) of Savage *et al.* [SBN+97]. ExitBlock exploits this assumption to reduce the number of explored interleavings of transitions of different threads. Bruening shows that if a system satisfies MLD, then for the purpose of determining reachability of control points and deadlocks, it suffices to consider schedules in which context switches between threads occur only when a lock is released, including the implicit release performed by Java's wait operation.

This paper combines the ideas in VeriSoft and ExitBlock and extends them in several ways. Our framework targets systems of multi-threaded processes that interact via communication objects and use locks to avoid race conditions in accesses to shared variables. Thus, it handles a strict superset of the systems handled by VeriSoft or ExitBlock. Related work is discussed further in Section 11.

Our results fall into two categories: results in Sections 4–8 for systems known to satisfy MLD, and results in Section 9 for systems expected to satisfy MLD. Static analyses like Extended Static Checking [DLNS98], types for safe locking [FA99], and protected variable analysis [Cor00] can conservatively check whether a system satisfies MLD. If it does, MLD constrains the set of objects that may be accessed by a transition (based on the set of locks held by the thread performing the transition), and this information can be used to constrain dependency between transitions and thereby to compute smaller persistent sets. In the absence of such guarantees, MLD can be checked dynamically during the selective search, using a variant of the lockset algorithm [SBN+97]. Since MLD is expected to hold, we propose to still exploit MLD when computing persistent sets. This introduces a potentially dangerous circularity. If a transition t that violates MLD is incorrectly assumed to be independent of other transitions, this error might cause the persistent-set algorithm to return a set that is too small (*e.g.*, does not include t) and is not actually persistent. Since the explored set of transitions is not persistent, there is *a priori* no guarantee that the selective search will actually find a violation of MLD. Bruening does not address this issue. We show that this can happen with MLD but not with a slightly stricter variant MLD'.

2   System Model

We adopt Godefroid's model of concurrent systems [God96], except that we call the concurrent entities threads rather than processes, disallow transitions that affect the control state of multiple threads, and divide objects into three categories. A *concurrent system* is a tuple $\langle \Theta, \mathcal{O}, \mathcal{T}, s_{init}, \mathcal{O}_{unsh}, \mathcal{O}_{syn}, \mathcal{O}_{mtx} \rangle$, where

Θ is a finite set of threads. A thread is a finite set of elements called *control points*. Threads are pairwise disjoint.

$\mathcal{O}$ is a finite set of objects. An *object* is characterized by a pair $\langle Dom, Op \rangle$, where *Dom* is the set of possible values of the object, and *Op* is the set of operations that can be performed on the object. An *operation* is a partial function that takes an input value and the current value of the object and returns a return value and an updated value for the object.

$\mathcal{T}$ is a finite set of transitions. A transition t is a tuple $\langle S, G, C, F \rangle$, where: S is a control point of some thread, which we denote by *thread*(t); F is a control point of the same thread; G is a guard, *i.e.*, a boolean-valued expression built from read-only operations on objects and mathematical functions; and C is a command, *i.e.*, a sequence of expressions built from operations on objects and mathematical functions. We call S and F the *starting* and *final* control points of t.

s_{init} is the initial state. State is defined below.

$\mathcal{O}_{unsh} \subseteq \mathcal{O}$ is the set of unshared objects, *i.e.*, objects accessed by at most one thread.

$\mathcal{O}_{syn} \subseteq \mathcal{O}$ is the set of synchronization objects, defined in Section 2.1.

$\mathcal{O}_{mtx} \subseteq \mathcal{O}$ is the set of objects for which MLD, defined in Section 2.2, is used.

A *state* is a pair $\langle L, V \rangle$, where L is a collection of control points, one from each thread, and V is a collection of values, one for each object. For a state s and object o, we abuse notation and write $s(o)$ to denote the value of o in s. Similarly, we write $s(\theta)$ to denote the control point of thread θ in state s.

A transition $\langle S, G, C, F \rangle$ of thread θ is *pending* in state s if $S = s(\theta)$, and it is *enabled* in state s if it is pending in s and G evaluates to true in s. For a concurrent system $\mathcal{A}$, let $pending_{\mathcal{A}}(s, \theta)$ and $enabled_{\mathcal{A}}(s, \theta)$ denote the sets of transitions of θ that are pending and enabled, respectively, in state s (in system $\mathcal{A}$). Let $enabled_{\mathcal{A}}(s)$ denote the set of transitions enabled in state s. When the system being discussed is clear from context, we elide the subscript. If a transition $\langle S, G, C, F \rangle$ is enabled in state $s = \langle L, V \rangle$, then it can be executed in s, leading to the state $\langle (L \setminus \{S\}) \cup \{F\}, C(V) \rangle$, where $C(V)$ represents the values obtained by using the operations in C to update the values in V. $s \overset{t}{\rightarrow} s'$ means that transition t is enabled in state s and that executing t in s leads to state s'.

A *sequence* is a function whose domain is the natural numbers or a finite prefix of the natural numbers. Let $|\sigma|$ denote the length of a sequence σ. Let $\sigma(i..j)$ denote the subsequence of σ from index i to index j. Let $last(\sigma)$ denote $\sigma(|\sigma| - 1)$. Let $\langle a_0, a_1, \ldots \rangle$ denote a sequence containing the indicated elements; $\langle \rangle$ denotes the empty sequence. Let $\sigma_1 \cdot \sigma_2$ denote the concatenation of sequences σ_1 and σ_2.

An *execution* of a concurrent system $\mathcal{A}$ is a finite or infinite sequence σ of transitions of $\mathcal{A}$ such that there exist states $s_0, s_1, s_2, \ldots$ such that $s_0 \overset{\sigma(0)}{\rightarrow} s_1 \overset{\sigma(1)}{\rightarrow}$ $s_2 \cdots$ and $s_0 = s_{init}$. Operations are deterministic, so the sequence of states $s_1, s_2, \ldots$ is completely determined by the sequence of transitions and s_{init}. When convenient, we regard that sequence of states as part of the execution. A state is *reachable* (in a system) if it appears in some execution (of that system). A control point is *reachable* if it appears in some reachable state.

Objects in $\mathcal{O} \setminus (\mathcal{O}_{unsh} \cup \mathcal{O}_{syn} \cup \mathcal{O}_{mtx})$ are called *communication objects*. For example, a system containing Java processes communicating over a socket involves some instances of java.net.Socket, which are in $\mathcal{O}_{mtx}$, and an underlying socket, which is a communication object.

2.1 Synchronization Objects

We plan to apply our framework to model-checking of Java programs, so we focus on the built-in synchronization operations in Java. In our framework, a synchronization object embodies the synchronization-related state that the JVM maintains for each Java object or class. (Java does not contain distinct synchronization objects; every Java object contains its own synchronization-related state. This difference is inconsequential.)

The fields of a synchronization object are: *owner* (name of a thread, or *free*), *depth* (number of unmatched acquire operations), and *wait* (list of waiting threads). We assume that the lock associated with each synchronization object is free in the initial state. The "operations" on synchronization objects are: acquire, release, wait, notify, and notifyAll. Each of these high-level "operations" is represented in a straightforward way as one or more transitions that use multiple (lower-level) operations on the synchronization object. For concreteness, we describe one such representation here. Other encodings are possible.

Thread θ acquiring o's lock corresponds to a transition with guard $o.owner \in \{free, \theta\}$ and command $o.owner := \theta; o.depth++$. Thread θ releasing o's lock corresponds to two transitions: one with guard contains $o.owner \neq \theta$ and a command that throws an IllegalMonitorStateException, and one with guard $o.owner = \theta$ and command $o.owner := (o.depth = 1)\,?\,free : \theta; o.depth--$.[1]

Let $tmpDepth$ denote an unshared natural-number-valued object used by θ. Thread θ waiting on o corresponds to three transitions: one with guard $o.owner \neq \theta$ and a command that throws an IllegalMonitorStateException, and one with guard $o.owner = \theta$ and command $o.wait.add(\theta); tmpDepth = o.depth; o.depth := 0; o.owner := free$ followed by one with guard $o.owner = free \wedge \theta \notin o.wait$ and command $o.owner := \theta; o.depth := tmpDepth$. Thread θ doing notify on o corresponds to two transitions: one with guard $o.owner \neq \theta$ and a command that throws an IllegalMonitorStateException, and one with guard

---

[1] The definition of command does not allow conditionals. The first assignment statement in this command is syntactic sugar for $o.ownerRelease(o.depth, \theta)$, which is an operation that has exactly the same effect as the assignment statement.

$o.owner = \theta$ and command $o.waitRemove()$, which removes an arbitrary element of the set. notifyAll is similar, except that $Remove$ is replaced with $RemoveAll$.

We informally refer to acquire, release, *etc.*, as operations on synchronization objects, when we actually mean the operations used by the corresponding transitions. An important observation is:

SyncWithoutLock: If a thread θ executes an operation op other than acquire on a synchronization object o in a state s in which θ does not hold o's lock, then (1) execution of op in s does not modify the state of o, and (2) execution of op in s has the same effect (*e.g.*, it throws IllegalMonitorStateException) regardless of other aspects of o's state (e.g., regardless of whether o's lock is held by another thread or free, and regardless of whether any threads are blocked waiting on o).

One might hope that synchronization objects could be included in $\mathcal{O}_{mtx}$ and not treated specially in the proofs below. Special consideration is needed for operations on synchronization objects, because they access $o.owner$ in a way that violates MLD. Classifying synchronization objects as communication objects would mean that all operations on them are visible, which would increase the cost of the selective search.

Our results are sensitive to the operations on synchronization objects. For example, consider introducing a non-blocking operation Free? that returns true iff the object's lock is free. This operation violates SyncWithoutLock and would require that release be classified as visible (see Section 2.3).

2.2   Mutex Locking Discipline (MLD)

The MLD of [SBN+97] allows objects to be initialized without locking. Initialization is assumed to be completed before the object becomes shared (*i.e.*, accessed by two different threads). The guard or command of a transition *accesses* object o if it contains an operation on o. Transition t *accesses* object o in state s if (1) t is pending in s and t's guard accesses o or (2) t is enabled in s and t's command accesses o. Thread θ *accesses* object o in state s, denoted $access(s, \theta, o)$, if there exists a transition in $pending(s, \theta)$ that accesses o in s. $startShared(\sigma, o)$ is the index of the first state in σ in which an access to o that is not part of initialization of o occurs; formally, letting σ be $s_0 \xrightarrow{\sigma(0)} s_1 \xrightarrow{\sigma(1)} s_2 \cdots$, $startShared(\sigma, o)$ is the least value of i such that $(\exists i_1, i_2 \leq i : \exists \theta_1, \theta_2 \in \Theta : \theta_1 \neq \theta_2 \wedge access(s_{i_1}, \theta_1, o) \wedge access(s_{i_2}, \theta_2, o))$, or $|\sigma|$ if no such values exist.

Mutex Locking Discipline (MLD): A system $\langle \Theta, \mathcal{O}, \mathcal{T}, s_{init}, \mathcal{O}_{mtx}, \mathcal{O}_{syn} \rangle$ satisfies MLD iff for all executions $\sigma = s_0 \xrightarrow{\sigma(0)} s_1 \xrightarrow{\sigma(1)} s_2 \cdots$ of the system, for all objects $o \in \mathcal{O}_{mtx}$,

MLD-R: o is read-only after it becomes shared, *i.e.*, there exists a constant c such that for all $i \geq startShared(\sigma, o)$, $s_i(o) = c$.

MLD-L: o is properly locked after it becomes shared, *i.e.*, there exists a synchronization object $o_1 \in \mathcal{O}_{syn}$ such that, for all $i \geq startShared(\sigma, o)$, for all $\theta \in \Theta$, if $access(s_i, \theta, o)$, then θ owns o_1's lock in s_i.

Godefroid [God96] defines: transition t uses object o iff t's guard or command contains an operation on o. A use of o by the command of a disabled transition cannot be detected by run-time monitoring, so we do not want the definition of MLD to depend on such uses. This motivates our definition of "accesses".

2.3 Visible and Invisible

Operations are classified into two categories: visible and invisible. Informally, visible operations are points in the computation at which the scheduler takes control and possibly causes a context switch between threads.

All operations on communication objects are visible, as in [God97]. The operations on synchronization objects that may block are visible; thus, acquire and wait (specifically, for wait, the operations in the transition that blocks, not the operations in the other two transitions) are visible. All other operations are invisible. A transition is *visible* if its command or guard contains a visible operation; otherwise, it is *invisible*. A control point S is *visible* if all transitions with starting control point S are visible; otherwise, it is *invisible*. A state s is *visible* if all control points in s are visible; otherwise, it is *invisible*. Visible states correspond to global states in [God97]. We define some conditions on systems:

Separation: Visible and invisible transitions are "separated", *i.e.*, for every thread θ, for every control point $S \in \theta$, all transitions with starting control point S are visible, or all of them are invisible.
Initial Control Locations are Visible (InitVis): For   every   thread θ, $s_{init}(\theta)$ is visible.
Bound on Invisible Transition Sequences (BoundedInvis): There exists a bound b on the length of contiguous sequences of invisible transitions by a single thread. Thus, in every execution, for every thread θ, every contiguous sequence of $b + 1$ transitions executed by θ (ignoring interspersed transitions of other threads) contains at least one visible transition.
Determinism of Invisible Control Points (DetermInvis): In every reachable state, for every thread θ, θ has at most one enabled invisible transition.
Non-Blocking Invisible Control Points (NonBlockInvis): For   every thread θ, for every invisible control point S of θ, for every reachable state s containing S, $enabled(s, \theta) \neq \emptyset$.

In a system satisfying DetermInvis, non-determinism may still come from two sources: concurrency (*i.e.*, different interleavings of transitions) and visible transitions (*e.g.*, VeriSoft's VS_Toss operation [God97]).

A straightforward generalization (not considered further in this paper) is to allow conditional invisibility (*i.e.*, let operations be invisible in some states and visible in others) and to classify an acquire operation by θ as invisible in states where $owner = \theta$.

3   State-Less Selective Search

The material in this section is paraphrased from [God97]. Two techniques used to make state-less search efficient are persistent sets and sleep sets. Both attempt to reduce the number of explored states and transitions. Persistent sets exploit the static structure of the system, while sleep sets exploit information about the history of the search. Informally, a set T of transitions enabled in a state s is persistent in s if, for every sequence of transitions starting from s and not containing any transitions in T, all transitions in that sequence are independent with all transitions in T.

Dependency Relation. Let T and *State* be the sets of transitions and states, respectively, of a concurrent system A. $D \subseteq T \times T$ is an *unconditional dependency relation* for A iff D is reflexive and symmetric and for all $t_1, t_2 \in T$, $\langle t_1, t_2 \rangle \notin D$ ("t_1 and t_2 are independent") implies that for all states $s \in State$, (1) if $t_1 \in enabled(s)$ and $s \xrightarrow{t_1} s'$, then $t_2 \in enabled(s)$ iff $t_2 \in enabled(s')$ (independent transitions neither disable nor enable each other), and (2) if $\{t_1, t_2\} \subseteq enabled(s)$, then there is a unique state s' such that $s \xrightarrow{t_1} s_1 \xrightarrow{t_2} s'$ and $s \xrightarrow{t_2} s_2 \xrightarrow{t_1} s'$. (enabled independent transitions commute). $D \subseteq T \times T \times State$ is a *conditional dependency relation* for A iff for all $t_1, t_2 \in T$ and all $s \in State$, $\langle t_1, t_2, s \rangle \notin D$ ("t_1 and t_2 are independent in s") implies that $\langle t_2, t_1, s \rangle \notin D$ and conditions 1 and 2 above hold. This definition of conditional dependency assumes that commands of transitions satisfy the *no-access-after-update* restriction [God96, p. 21]: an operation that modifies the value of an object o cannot be followed by any other operations on o.

Persistent Set. A set $T \subseteq enabled(s)$ is *persistent* in s iff, for all nonempty sequences of transitions σ such that $s_0 \xrightarrow{\sigma(0)} s_1 \xrightarrow{\sigma(1)} s_2 \cdots \xrightarrow{\sigma(n-1)} s_n \xrightarrow{\sigma(n)} s_{n+1}$, if $s_0 = s$ and $(\forall i \in [0..n] : \sigma(i) \notin T)$, then $\sigma(n)$ is independent in s_n with all transitions in T.

Godefroid's state-less selective search (SSS) using persistent sets and sleep sets appears in Figure 1, where *exec* and *undo* are specified by: if $s \xrightarrow{t} s'$, then $exec(s, t) = s'$ and $undo(s', t) = s$. PS(s) returns a set of transitions that is persistent in s. D is an unconditional dependency relation. SSS diverges if the state space contains cycles; in practice, divergence is avoided by limiting the search depth.

Following Godefroid [God96] but deviating from standard usage, a *deadlock* is a state s such that $enabled(s)$ is empty. We focus on determining reachability of deadlocks and control points. Reachability of control points can easily encode information about values of objects. For example, a Java program might assert that a condition e_1 holds using the statement if (!e_1) throw e_2; violation of this assertion corresponds to reachability of the control point at the beginning of throw e_2. If necessary (as in Section 5), assertion violations can easily be encoded

Global variables: *stack, curState;*

```
SSS() {
    stack := empty;
    curState := s_init;
    DFS(∅);
}
```

```
DFS(sleep) {
    T := PS(curState) \ sleep;
    while (T is not empty)
        remove a transition t from T;
        push t onto stack;
        curState := exec(curState, t);
        sleep' := {t' ∈ sleep | ⟨t, t'⟩ ∉ D};
        DFS(sleep')
        pop t from stack;
        curState := undo(curState, t);
        sleep := sleep ∪ {t};
}
```

Fig. 1. State-less Selective Search (SSS) using persistent sets and sleep sets.

as reachability of visible control points, by introducing a communication object with a single (visible) operation that is called when any assertion is violated.

Theorem 1. *Let A be a concurrent system with a finite and acyclic state space. A deadlock d is reachable in A iff SSS explores d. A control point S is reachable in A iff SSS explores a state containing S.*

Proof: This is a paraphrase of Theorem 2 of [God97].   □

4   Invisible-First Selective Search

Persistent sets can be used to justify not exploring all interleavings of invisible transitions.

Theorem 2. *Let A be a concurrent system satisfying MLD and Separation. For all threads θ and all reachable states s, if $enabled(s, \theta)$ contains an invisible transition, then $enabled(s, \theta)$ is persistent in s.*

Proof: Let σ be a sequence of transitions as in the definition of persistent set. Let $t \in enabled(s, \theta)$. Separation implies that t is invisible. It suffices to show that $\sigma(n)$ is independent in s_n with t. First, we show that σ does not contain transitions of $thread(t)$; second, we show the desired independence. Roughly, MLD implies that accesses to objects in $\mathcal{O}_{mtx}$ do not cause dependence; invisibility of t implies that accesses to communication objects do not cause dependence; and SyncWithoutLock implies that accesses to synchronization objects do not cause dependence. For details, see [Sto00].   □

Suppose the system satisfies MLD, Separation, BoundedInvis, and DetermInvis. If a thread θ has an enabled invisible transition in a state s, then Separation and DetermInvis imply that θ has exactly one enabled transition in s. Theorem 2 implies that it is sufficient to explore only that transition from s. This can be done repeatedly, until θ has an enabled visible transition. BoundedInvis implies that this iteration terminates. Let $execInvis_A(s, \theta)$ be the unique state obtained

Global variables: *stack, curState*;

IF-SSS() {
   stack := empty;
   curState := s_{init};
   $DFS_{if}(\emptyset)$;
}

$DFS_{if}(sleep)$ {
   $T := PS(curState) \setminus sleep$;
   while (T is not empty)
      remove a transition t from T;
      push t onto *stack*;
      curState := $exec(curState, t)$;
      curState := $execInvis_A(curState, thread(t))$;
      $sleep' := \{t' \in sleep \mid \langle t, t' \rangle \notin D\}$;
      $DFS_{if}(sleep')$;
      pop t from *stack*;
      curState := $undo(curState, t)$;
      $sleep := sleep \cup \{t\}$;
}

Fig. 2. Invisible-First State-less Selective Search (IF-SSS) using persistent sets and sleep sets.

by performing this procedure starting from state s; if θ has no enabled invisible transitions in state s, then we define $execInvis_A(s, \theta) = s$. Specializing SSS to work in this way yields Invisible-First State-less Selective Search (IF-SSS), given in Figure 2.

Theorem 3. *Let A be a concurrent system with a finite and acyclic state space and satisfying MLD, Separation, BoundedInvis, and DetermInvis. A deadlock d is reachable in A iff IF-SSS explores d. A control point S is reachable in A iff IF-SSS explores a state containing S.*

Proof: This follows from Theorems 1 and 2, and the fact that transitions in *sleep* are independent with invisible transitions executed by *execInvis* (this follows from Separation, DetermInvis, and Theorem 2), so it is safe not to explicitly check that independence when computing $sleep'$. For details, see [Sto00].   □

5   Composing Transitions

In some cases, a stronger partial-order reduction can be obtained by amalgamating a visible transition and the subsequent sequence of invisible transitions explored by IF-SSS into a single transition; an example appears in Section 6. Transitions are amalgamated (composed) as follows. Given a sequence σ of transitions, let $cmd_{seq}(\sigma)$ be the sequential composition of the commands of the transitions in σ, and let $guard_{seq}(\sigma)$ be the weakest predicate ensuring that when each transition t in σ is executed, t's guard holds. Let $final(t)$ denote the final control point of transition t.

   Given a concurrent system $A = \langle \Theta, \mathcal{O}, \mathcal{T}, s_{init}, \mathcal{O}_{unsh}, \mathcal{O}_{syn}, \mathcal{O}_{mtx} \rangle$ satisfying MLD, Separation, BoundedInvis, and DetermInvis, $\mathcal{C}(A)$ is $\langle \Theta, \mathcal{O}, \mathcal{T}', s_{init}, \mathcal{O}_{unsh}, \mathcal{O}_{syn}, \mathcal{O}_{mtx} \rangle$, where $\mathcal{T}'$ is as follows. Let b be the bound in BoundedInvis for A. For each visible transition $t = \langle S, G, C, F \rangle$ in $\mathcal{T}$, for each sequence σ of invisible transitions of length at most b such that $guard_{seq}(\langle t \rangle \cdot \sigma) \neq$ false and $final(last(\sigma))$ is visible, $\mathcal{T}'$ contains the transition $\langle S, guard_{seq}(\langle t \rangle \cdot \sigma), cmd_{seq}(\langle t \rangle \cdot \sigma), final(last(\sigma)) \rangle$. Elements of $\mathcal{T}'$ are analogous to process transitions [God97].

Theorem 4. *Let $\mathcal{A}$ be a concurrent system satisfying MLD, Separation, InitVis, BoundedInvis, and DetermInvis. s is a reachable visible state of $\mathcal{A}$ iff s is a reachable visible state of $\mathcal{C}(\mathcal{A})$.*

Proof: A proof sketch follows; for details, see [Sto00].

($\Leftarrow$): Let s be a reachable visible state of $\mathcal{C}(\mathcal{A})$. Let σ be an execution of $\mathcal{C}(\mathcal{A})$ containing s. Expanding each transition in σ into the sequence of transitions of $\mathcal{A}$ from which it is composed yields an execution of $\mathcal{A}$ that contains s.

($\Rightarrow$): Let s be a reachable visible state of $\mathcal{A}$. Let σ be an execution of $\mathcal{A}$ containing s. We re-arrange σ as follows: for each thread θ, move the invisible transitions of θ that appear between the i'th and $(i+1)$'th visible transitions of θ backwards so that those invisible transitions form a contiguous subsequence of the re-arranged execution starting immediately after the i'th visible transition of θ. We use MLD and Theorem 2 to show that this can be achieved by interchanging independent transitions. From the re-arranged execution of $\mathcal{A}$, we can easily form an execution of $\mathcal{C}(\mathcal{A})$ containing s. □

Theorem 5. *Let $\mathcal{A}$ be a concurrent system with a finite and acyclic state space and satisfying MLD, Separation, InitVis, BoundedInvis, and DetermInvis. A deadlock d is reachable in $\mathcal{A}$ iff SSS applied to $\mathcal{C}(\mathcal{A})$ explores d. A control point S is reachable in $\mathcal{A}$ iff SSS applied to $\mathcal{C}(\mathcal{A})$ explores a state containing S.*

Proof: This follows directly from Theorems 1 and 4 and the observation that $\mathcal{A}$ and $\mathcal{C}(\mathcal{A})$ have the same set of reachable deadlocks, which follows from NonBlockInvis (which implies that all deadlocks of $\mathcal{A}$ are visible) and Theorem 4. □

6   Comparison of Invisible-First and Composition

Sections 4 and 5 describe two approaches to achieving similar partial-order reductions. The invisible-first approach (Section 4) is worthwhile for three reasons. First, Theorem 2 shows that this reduction is a special case of persistent sets, thereby showing the relationship to existing partial-order methods. Second, Theorem 3 shows that, with IF-SSS, operations in invisible transitions do not need to be recorded (because they do not introduce dependencies that would cause transitions to be removed from sleep sets); we are investigating whether an analogous optimization is possible for SSS applied to $\mathcal{C}(\mathcal{A})$. Third, the guards of composed transitions sometimes introduce dependencies that cause SSS applied to $\mathcal{C}(\mathcal{A})$ to explore more interleavings than IF-SSS. For example, consider a thread θ that is ready to execute **if** (x_1) { **if** (x_2) c_1 **else** c_2 } **else** { **if** (x_3) c_3 **else** c_4 }, where $x_i \in \mathcal{O}_{mtx}$ and the c_i do not contain visible operations. Let S denote the starting control point of this statement. In the original system $\mathcal{A}$, θ accesses only x_1 at S. In the composed system, θ accesses x_1, x_2, and x_3 at S, because the composed transitions with starting control point S have guards like $x_1 \wedge x_2$ and

$x_1 \wedge \neg x_3$. In a state s with $s(\theta) = S$ and $s(x_1) = \text{false}$, the access by θ to x_3 in the composed system is an artifact of composition. Such accesses introduce dependencies that could cause persistent sets to be larger in $C(\mathcal{A})$ than $\mathcal{A}$, if the calculation of persistent sets—specifically, the calculation of *pendInvisOps*, defined in Section 8—exploits information from static analysis.

The composition approach (Section 5) is worthwhile because it sometimes achieves a stronger partial-order reduction. For example, suppose two threads are both ready to acquire the lock that protects a shared variable v, copy v's value into an unshared variable, and then release the lock. In $C(\mathcal{A})$, each thread can do this with a single transition, and those two transitions are independent, so SSS applied to $C(\mathcal{A})$ could explore a single interleaving. In $\mathcal{A}$, each thread does this with a sequence of three transitions, and the transitions that manipulate the lock are not independent, so IF-SSS applied to $\mathcal{A}$ explores multiple interleavings. A more detailed example appears in [Sto00].

7   Computing Sleep Sets

Consider refining DFS (in Figure 1) to use a conditional dependency relation when computing *sleep'*; this can produce larger sleep sets and hence more efficient search. Dependency of t and t' should be evaluated in the state prior to execution of t; thus, the line that computes *sleep'* should be moved immediately above the line containing *exec*, and $\langle t, t' \rangle \notin D$ should be replaced with $\langle t, t', curState \rangle \notin D$. Theorem 1 holds for the modified algorithm, provided the transitions satisfy no-access-after-update. In VeriSoft [God97], this refinement works fine, because only visible operations affect dependency (invisible operations are on unshared objects), and visible operations can only appear as the first operation in a transition's command, so determining that visible operation (by intercepting it) before the transition actually executes is straightforward.

Our framework does not impose those restrictions, so operations on shared objects used by a transition t are not known until after t has been executed, so the calculation of *sleep'* cannot easily be moved above the line containing *exec*. One solution is to execute and undo t in order to determine its guard and command, but this is expensive, because undo is expensive (especially if implemented using reset+replay or checkpointing). A more efficient approach is to observe that conditional dependency typically depends only on a relatively small and well-defined amount of information about the system's state; in such cases, we can record that information and use it to evaluate *sleep'* after t is executed. For example, for a transition that manipulates a FIFO queue, one might use the conditional dependency relation in [God96, Section 3.4] and therefore record two booleans indicating whether the queue is empty or full.

Dependency relations for transitions are typically derived in a modular way from dependency relations for (the operations of) each object [God96, Definitions 3.15, 3.21]. For some types of objects, it might be difficult or expensive to record the parts of the state that affect conditional dependency. Also, conditional dependency (as defined in [God96]) cannot be used for objects that are accessed in a way that violates the no-access-after-update restriction. We simply use unconditional dependency for such objects; this is easy, because unconditional dependency is a special case of conditional dependency. As an exception, we can use conditional dependency for some transitions whose accesses to synchronization objects violate the no-access-after-update restriction, e.g., transitions that acquire and then release a lock, as in the example at the end of Section 5.

8 Computing Persistent Sets

Computing persistent sets requires information about the future transitions of each thread. When model-checking standard languages, the exact set of transitions is not known, so statically determined upper bounds on the set of operations that each thread may perform (ignoring operations on unshared objects) are used to compute persistent sets. Let $allowedOps(\theta)$ denote such an upper bound for thread θ. Let $allowedInvisOps(\theta)$ be the set of invisible operations in $allowedOps(\theta)$. Let $usedVisOps(t)$ be the set of visible operations used by t. We assume that in each visible state s, for each thread θ, the following set is known:

$$pendVisOps(s,\theta) = \bigcup_{t \in pending(s,\theta)} usedVisOps(t) \qquad (1)$$

To compute small persistent sets, it is important to have information about the set of invisible operations used by pending transitions of θ in s. A non-trivial upper bound $pendInvisOps(s,\theta)$ on that set can be obtained by exploiting MLD. For concreteness, we describe how to obtain such a bound based on the data structures maintained by the lockset algorithm [SBN+97]. We assume in this section that the system satisfies MLD; the lockset algorithm is used here only to obtain information about which locks protect accesses to each object. If that information is available from whatever static analysis was used to ensure that MLD holds, then running the lockset algorithm during the search is unnecessary.

The lockset algorithm uses the following data structures. For each object o, the following values are maintained: $o.mode$, which is virgin (allocated but uninitialized), exclusive (accessed by only one thread), shared (accessed by multiple threads, but threads after the first did not modify the object), or shared-modified (none of the above conditions hold); $o.firstThread$, which is the first thread that accessed o (i.e., the thread that initializes o; $o.firstThread$ is undefined when o is in virgin mode); and $o.candLockSet$ ("candidate lock set"), which is the set of locks that were held during all accesses to o after initialization (i.e., starting with the access that changed $o.mode$ from exclusive to shared or shared-modified). We assume that $o.candLockSet$ contains all locks (i.e., equals $\mathcal{O}_{syn}$) while o is in exclusive mode. For each thread θ, $held(s,\theta)$, the set of synchronization objects whose locks are held by θ in state s, is maintained, in order to efficiently update candidate lock sets. $acquiring(s,\theta)$ is the set of synchronization objects o such that $pendVisOps(s,\theta)$ contains an acquire operation on o.

$$pendInvisOps(s, \theta) =$$

$$\bigcup_{o_1 \in held(s,\theta) \cup acquiring(s,\theta)} \{o.op \in allowedInvisOps(\theta) \mid MLDallows(s, \theta, o_1, o)\}$$

$$MLDallows(s, \theta, o_1, o.op) =$$

$\quad \lor\ o.mode = \text{virgin} \land mayInit(s, \theta, o)$

$\quad \lor\ o.mode = \text{exclusive} \land (\theta = o.firstThread \lor rdOnly(op) \lor o_1 \in o.candLockSet)$

$\quad \lor\ o.mode = \text{shared} \land (rdOnly(op) \lor o_1 \in o.candLockSet)$

$\quad \lor\ o.mode = \text{shared-modified} \land o_1 \in o.candLockSet$

where $rdOnly(op)$ holds if op is read-only, and $mayInit(s, \theta, o)$ holds if θ can be the first thread to access a virgin object o in state s. For example, in Java, for non-static variables, one might require that θ be the thread that allocated o (for static variables of a class C, θ is the thread that caused class C to be loaded).

For systems that satisfy the following stricter version of MLD-L, we can modify how $o.candLockSet$ is computed in a way that can lead to smaller persistent sets: in every execution in which o is shared, the same lock protects accesses to o; formally, this corresponds to switching the order of the quantifications "for all executions of $\mathcal{A}$" and "there exists $o_1 \in \mathcal{O}_{syn}$". With this stricter requirement, we can modify undo so that it does not undo changes to the candidate lock set. This has the desired effect of possibly making $o.candLockSet$ smaller (hence possibly producing smaller persistent sets) without affecting whether a violation of the requirement is reported.

Persistent sets can be computed using the following variant of Algorithm 2 of [God96], which is based on Overman's Algorithm. We call this Algorithm 2-MLD.

1. Select one transition $t \in enabled(s)$. Let $T = \{thread(t)\}$.
2. For each $\theta \in T$, for each operation $op \in pendVisOps(s, \theta) \cup pendInvisOps(s, \theta)$, for each thread $\theta' \in \Theta \setminus T$, if $(\exists op' \in allowedOps(\theta') : op \rhd_s op')$, then insert θ' in T.
3. Repeat step 2 until no more processes can be added. Return $\bigcup_{\theta \in T} enabled(s, \theta)$.

Theorem 6. *Let $\mathcal{A}$ be a concurrent system satisfying MLD. In every state s of $\mathcal{A}$, Algorithm 2-MLD returns a set that is persistent in s.*

Proof: This follows from correctness of Algorithm 2 of [God96]. $\square$

9 Checking MLD During Selective Search

If the system is expected to satisfy MLD but no static guarantee is available, MLD can be checked during the selective search using the lockset algorithm [SBN+97]. As explained in Section 1, the results in Sections 4–8 do not directly apply in this case, because they compute persistent sets assuming that the system satisfies MLD. Here we extend those results to ensure that, if the system violates a slightly stronger variant of MLD, then the selective search finds a violation.

Savage *et al.* observe that their liberal treatment of initialization makes Eraser's checking undesirably dependent on the scheduler [SBN+97, p. 398]. For the same reason, IF-SSS might indeed miss violations of MLD. Consider a system in which θ_1 can perform the sequence of three transitions (control points are omitted in this informal shorthand) $\langle v := 0, sem.up(), v := 1 \rangle$, and θ_2 can perform the sequence of four transitions $\langle sem.down(), o.acquire(), v := 2, o.release() \rangle$, where $v \in \mathcal{O}_{mtx}$ is an integer variable, $o \in \mathcal{O}_{syn}$, and semaphore sem (a communication object) is initially zero. This system violates MLD, because $v := 1$ can occur after $v := 2$, and θ_1 holds no locks when it executes $v := 1$. IF-SSS does not find a violation, because after $sem.Up()$, $execInvis$ immediately executes $v := 1$.

We strengthen the constraints on initialization by requiring that the thread (if any) that initializes each object be specified in advance and by allowing at most one initialization transition per object (a more flexible alternative is to allow multiple initialization transitions per object, but to require that the initializing thread not perform any visible operations between the first access to o and the last access to o that is part of initialization of o). Formally, we require that a partial function $initThread$ from objects to threads be included as part of the system, and we define $startShared'(\sigma, o)$ to be: if o is not in the domain of $initThread$, then zero, otherwise the second smallest i such that $(\exists \theta \in \Theta : access(s_i, \theta, o))$, where σ is $s_0 \overset{\sigma(0)}{\rightarrow} s_1 \overset{\sigma(1)}{\rightarrow} s_2 \cdots$. Let MLD′ denote MLD with $startShared$ replaced with $startShared'$, and extended with the requirement that for each object o in the domain of $initThread$, $initThread(o)$ is the first thread to access o.[2] The lockset algorithm can easily be modified to check MLD′. We assume that accesses to objects in $\mathcal{O}_{mtx}$ by the guard of a transition t are checked in each state in which t is pending (in other words, we assume that in each state, guards of all pending transitions are evaluated). It suffices to check accesses to objects in $\mathcal{O}_{mtx}$ by the command of a transition only when that transition is explored by the search algorithm; to see this, note that the following variant of MLD′-L is equivalent to MLD′-L, in the sense that it does not change the set of systems satisfying MLD′:

MLD′-L1: o is properly locked after it becomes shared, *i.e.*, there exists a synchronization object $o_1 \in \mathcal{O}_{syn}$ such that, for all $i \geq startShared'(\sigma, o)$, (1) if $access(s_i, \sigma(i), o)$, then $thread(\sigma(i))$ owns o_1's lock in s_i, and (2) for all $\theta \in \Theta$, if $pending(s_i, \theta)$ contains a transition whose guard accesses o, then θ owns o_1's lock in s_i.

For a state s, sequence σ of transitions, and transition t that is pending after execution of σ from s, let $s \overset{\sigma}{\Longrightarrow}$ denote execution of σ starting from s, and let $s \overset{\sigma;t}{\Longrightarrow}$ denote execution of σ starting from s followed by evaluation of t's guard and, if t is enabled, execution of t's command.

---

[2] It is easy to show that MLD′ is stricter than MLD (*i.e.*, a system that satisfies MLD′ also satisfies MLD). This does not enable one to easily prove the theorems in this section from the unprimed theorems in previous sections or *vice versa*.

Theorem 2′. *Let A be a concurrent system satisfying Separation. For all threads θ and all reachable states s, if enabled(s, θ) contains an invisible transition, then either enabled(s, θ) is persistent in s or enabled(s, θ) contains a transition t such that either $s \xrightarrow{\langle\rangle;t}$ violates MLD′ or $s \xrightarrow{t} s'$ and a violation of MLD′ is reachable from s'.*

Proof: MLD′ is relatively insensitive to the order in which accesses occur. Let σ be a sequence of transitions as in the definition of persistent set. One can show (roughly) that if a violation of MLD′ occurs when σ is executed before t, then a violation also occurs if t is executed before σ. For details, see [Sto00].   □

Theorem 3′. *Let A be a concurrent system with a finite and acyclic state space and satisfying Separation, BoundedInvis, and DetermInvis. A violates MLD′ iff IF-SSS finds a violation of MLD′.*

Proof: An invariant I is used to show that violations of MLD′ are eventually detected, even if they cause persistent sets or sleep sets to be computed incorrectly. The proof of invariance of I is based on Theorem 2′. For details, see [Sto00].
    □

Theorem 5′. *Let A be a concurrent system with a finite and acyclic state space and satisfying Separation, InitVis, BoundedInvis, and DetermInvis. A violates MLD′ iff $C(A)$ violates MLD′.*

Proof: ($\Leftarrow$): Let σ be an execution of $C(A)$ violating MLD′. Expanding each transition in σ into the sequence of transitions of A from which it is composed yields an execution of A that violates MLD′.

($\Rightarrow$): Theorem 3′ implies that IF-SSS explores an execution σ of A that violates MLD′. Composing sequences of transitions in A to form transitions of $C(A)$ yields an execution of $C(A)$ that violates MLD′.   □

The stricter constraints on initialization in MLD′ allow the definition of *pendInvisOps* to be tightened. Let *pendInvisOps′* denote that variant of *pendInvisOps*. Let Algorithm 2-MLD′ denote the variant of Algorithm 2-MLD that uses *pendInvisOps′*.

Theorem 6′. *Let A be a concurrent system. In every state s of A, Algorithm 2-MLD′ returns a set P such that either P is persistent in s or P contains a transition t such that t violates MLD′ in s.*

Proof: In Algorithm 2-MLD′, only the calculation of *pendInvisOps′* depends on MLD′, and *pendInvisOps′*(s, θ) is invoked only for threads θ that have already been added to T. Suppose for all threads θ in T, all transitions in enabled(s, θ) satisfy MLD′ in s. Then all invocations of *pendInvisOps′* in this invocation of Algorithm 2-MLD′ returned accurate results, so P is persistent in s. Suppose there exists a thread θ in T such that some transition t in enabled(s, θ) violates MLD′ in s. Then P contains t, and t violates MLD′ in s.   □

Let A be a concurrent system with a finite and acyclic state space and satisfying Separation, InitVis, BoundedInvis, and DetermInvis. Consider applying SSS with Algorithm 2-MLD′ to $C(A)$ augmented with the lockset algorithm, modified slightly to check MLD'. Theorem 6' implies that if no violation of MLD' is found, then $C(\mathcal{A})$ satisfies MLD' and hence MLD. Theorem 3 Theorem 5' then implies that $\mathcal{A}$ satisfies MLD. Theorem 5 can then be used to conclude that reachability of control points and deadlocks was correctly determined during the search.

Let $\mathcal{A}$ be a concurrent system with a finite and acyclic state space and satisfying Separation, InitVis, BoundedInvis, and DetermInvis. Consider applying IF-SSS with Algorithm 2-MLD' to $\mathcal{A}$ augmented with the lockset algorithm, modified slightly to check MLD'. Theorems 3' and 6' imply that if no violation of MLD' is found, then $\mathcal{A}$ satisfies MLD' and hence MLD. Theorem 3 implies that reachability of control points and deadlocks was correctly determined during the search. Similarly, consider applying SSS to $C(\mathcal{A})$ augmented to check MLD'. Theorem 6' implies that if no violation of MLD' is found, then $C(\mathcal{A})$ satisfies MLD', so Theorem 5' implies that $\mathcal{A}$ satisfies MLD' and hence MLD. Theorem 5 implies that reachability (in $\mathcal{A}$) of control points and deadlocks was correctly determined during the search.

10   Implementation

A prototype implementation for multi-threaded single-process systems is mostly complete, thanks to Gregory Alexander, Aseem Asthana, Sean Broadley, Sriram Krishnan, and Adam Wick. It transforms Java class files (application source code is not needed) by inserting calls to a scheduler at visible operations and inserting calls to a variant of the lockset algorithm at accesses to shared objects. The scheduler, written in Java, performs state-less selective search. The JavaClass toolkit [Dah99] greatly facilitated the implementation.

The scheduler runs in a separate thread. The scheduler gives a selected user thread permission to execute (by unblocking it) and then blocks itself. The selected user thread executes until it tries to perform a visible operation, at which point it unblocks the scheduler and then blocks itself (waiting for permission to continue). Thus, roughly speaking, only one thread is runnable at a time, so the JVM's built-in scheduler does not affect the execution.

The tool exploits annotations indicating which objects are (possibly) shared. Object creation commands can be annotated as creating unshared objects, accesses to which are not intercepted, or as creating tentatively unshared objects, accesses to which are intercepted only to verify that the objects are indeed unshared. Objects created by unannotated commands are potentially shared; accesses to them are intercepted to check MLD and, if necessary, are recorded to determine dependencies. Currently, annotations are provided by the user; escape analysis, such as [WR99], could provide them automatically.

By default, classes have *field granularity*, *i.e.*, the intercepted operations are field accesses (getfield and putfield instructions). For some classes, it is desirable for operations to correspond to method calls. We say that such classes have *method granularity*. For example, with semaphores, operations seen by the scheduler should be up (also called V or signal) and down (also called P or wait), not reads and writes of fields. Intercepting operations at method granularity reduces overhead and allows use of class-specific dependency relations. The annotation file indicates which classes have method granularity.

When methods are considered as operations, the boundaries of the operation must be defined carefully, because a method can invoke methods of and directly access fields of other objects. In our framework, by default, an intercepted method invocation i represents accesses to this performed by i but not accesses to this performed by methods invoked within i; it does not represent accesses to other objects. Accesses by i to instances of other classes are intercepted based on the granularities of those other classes; indicating that a class C has method granularity determines only how accesses to instances of C are intercepted. We require that methods of classes with method granularity perform no visible operations, except that the methods may be synchronized.

Ideally, for a class C with method granularity, *all* accesses to instances of C are intercepted at the level of method invocations. If C has non-private fields that are accessed directly by other classes, those field accesses would also need to be recorded. Therefore, we require that method granularity be used only for classes whose instance fields (including inherited ones) are all private or final (accesses to final fields are ignored). Similarly, an invocation of a method $C.m$ can access private fields of instances of C other than this. We disallow method granularity for classes that perform such accesses; a simple static analysis can conservatively check this requirement. If this turns out to be undesirably restrictive (e.g., for classes that use such accesses to implement comparisons, such as equals), we can deviate from the above ideal and explicitly record such field accesses; a simple static analysis can identify getfield and putfield instructions that possibly access instances other than this.

Classes may be annotated as having *atomic granularity*. An intercepted invocation i of a method (including, as always, inherited methods) of such a class represents all computations performed by i, including computations of other methods invoked from i except methods invoked on other instances of atomic classes. Requirements for atomic granularity include the three above requirements for method granularity. Furthermore, in order to ensure that invocations of atomic methods are dependent only with invocations of atomic methods on the same object, we require that an instance o_{na} of a non-atomic class accessed by a method of an instance o_a of an atomic class be "encapsulated" within o_a; specifically, if the computation represented by an intercepted invocation of a method of o_a accesses o_{na} in a way other than testing whether it is an instance of an atomic class (this accommodates "equals" methods), then all accesses to o_{na} occur in computations represented by intercepted invocations of methods of o_a. We also require that methods of an atomic class C do not access static variables of classes other than C, and that all static fields of C are private. A proof that these conditions are sufficient is left for future work.

Currently, the user is responsible for checking the requirements for using method or atomic granularity; static analysis could provide conservative automatic checks. The Sun JDK 1.2.2 reference implementation of the java.util.Collection

API mostly satisfies the requirements for atomic granularity, except for methods that return a collection backed by another collection, such as the keySet, values, and entrySet methods in java.util.AbstractMap. Atomic granularity can be used for Collection classes in programs that do not invoke such methods.

Synchronized methods and methods of classes with method or atomic granularity are intercepted using automatically generated wrapper classes. Unshared objects are instances of the original class C; shared objects are instances of C's wrapper class, which extends C. For each such method m, the wrapper class contains a wrapper method that overrides m. If m is synchronized, the wrapper indicates that it is trying to acquire a lock, yields control to the scheduler, waits for permission to proceed, invokes super.m, and then releases the lock. If the class has method or atomic granularity, the wrapper calls the lockset algorithm and possibly records the operation. An "invokevirtual $C.m$" instruction requires no explicit modification; the JVM's method lookup efficiently determines whether the instance is shared. For method invocations on unshared instances, the overhead is negligible. An obvious alternative approach, which we call Outside, is to insert near each invocation instruction a segment of bytecode that explicitly tests whether the instance is shared and, if so, performs the steps described above. With Outside, the overhead is non-negligible even for unshared instances. Another benefit of using wrappers to intercept invokevirtual is that, when generating a wrapper, it is easy to determine whether the method being wrapped is synchronized. With Outside, if the instance is shared, the inserted bytecode would need to explicitly check the class of the instance, because a synchronized method can override an unsynchronized method, and *vice versa*.

Field accesses, array accesses, invokespecial instructions, and synchronization instructions (monitorenter and monitorexit) are intercepted using Outside. The bytecode inserted near these instructions must efficiently determine whether an object is shared. Inserting in java.lang.Object a boolean field would be a nice solution if it didn't give the JVM (Sun JDK 1.2.1) a heart attack. We insert in java.lang.Object a boolean-valued method with body "return false". It is overridden in all wrapper classes by a method with body "return true".

Certain calls to java.util.Random are treated as non-deterministic, *i.e.*, all possible return values are explored; this is like VS_Toss in VeriSoft [God97].

$undo(s, t)$ can be implemented by reverse computation, reset+replay, or checkpointing. Reverse computation is attractive in theory but difficult to implement. Our prototype uses reset+replay (like VeriSoft), mainly because it is easy to implement. ExitBlock [Bru99] and Java PathFinder [BHPV00] use checkpointing, which requires a custom JVM. Checkpointing is more efficient than reset+replay for CPU-intensive programs. Experiments comparing the efficiency of checkpointing and reset+replay for typical applications of these testing tools are needed. Such tools are typically applied to small problem instances that consume relatively little CPU time.

Our prototype has been applied to some simple programs (e.g., dining philosophers) but is under construction and currently has some limitations: array accesses are not intercepted; support for notifyAll, communication objects, and

RMI are unimplemented; Algorithm 2-MLD' and dependency relations for sema-phores, queues, *etc.*, are unimplemented, so *enabled(s)* is used as the persistent set, and a simple read/write dependency relation is used to compute sleep sets.

11   Related Work

The framework in [God97] can be regarded as the special case of ours that handles systems with $\mathcal{O}_{syn} = \emptyset$ and $\mathcal{O}_{mtx} = \emptyset$.

Java PathFinder [BHPV00] incorporates a custom JVM, written in Java, that supports traditional selective search. It ensures that each state is explored at most once but probably has more overhead than our bytecode rewriting. It uses partial-order reductions but does not exploit MLD, so in principle, every access to a shared variable needs to be intercepted to check for dependencies.

Corbett's protected variable reduction [Cor00] exploits MLD to make state-space exploration more efficient. Corbett proposes a static analysis that conser-vatively checks whether objects are accessed in a way that satisfies MLD. In [Cor00], Corbett does not provide results on checking MLD during state-space exploration and does not consider making release, notify, and notifyAll invisible (except for releases that do not make the lock free).

In [Bru99], Bruening considers only threads interacting via shared variables; the partial-order methods used in our framework also accommodate arbitrary communication objects. ExitBlock corresponds roughly to IF-SSS with PS(s) = enabled(s) and, for the calculation of sleep sets, the trivial dependency relation $\mathcal{T} \times \mathcal{T}$. ExitBlockRW corresponds roughly to IF-SSS with PS(s) = enabled(s) and, for the calculation of sleep sets, the unconditional dependency relation that recognizes the independence of operations on different objects and of read operations on the same object.

IF-SSS (or SSS applied to $\mathcal{C}(\mathcal{A})$) allows the use of any persistent-set algo-rithm and any dependency relation. This flexibility allows properties of common synchronization constructs to be exploited. For example, for threads interacting via a shared FIFO queue, IF-SSS can exploit the fact that in states where the queue is non-empty, an insertion and a removal are independent. Similarly, for interaction involving a semaphore, IF-SSS can exploit the fact that in states where the semaphore's value is positive, an up operation is independent with a down operation. Accesses to fields of synchronization objects (*e.g.*, *owner* and *wait*) and to fields of other synchronization constructs (*e.g.*, the value field of a semaphore) are included in ExitBlockRW's read and write sets and therefore cause dependencies based on the simple read/write dependency relation.

ExitBlock treats release as visible and acquire as invisible. This complicates deadlock detection in ExitBlock, and ExitBlockRW might miss deadlocks. IF-SSS and SSS find all reachable deadlocks.

ExitBlockRW requires recording information about invisible operations—specifically, it records the sets of objects read and written by each block. With IF-SSS, invisible operations do not need to be recorded; they do need to be intercepted, mainly to check MLD', unless the system is known to satisfy MLD.

Bruening's proof that ExitBlock finds all assertion violations [Bru99, Theorem 3, pp. 47-48] is incomplete, because the proof implicitly assumes that all accesses satisfy MLD. Accesses to synchronization-related state (*e.g.*, *o.owner*) need not follow MLD and therefore require special consideration in the proof.

Bruening does not prove that ExitBlock (or ExitBlockRW) is guaranteed to find a violation of MLD for systems that violate MLD. Even if violations of MLD are manifested as assertion violations, the (incomplete) proof that ExitBlock finds all assertion violations [Bru99, Theorem 3, pp. 47-48] does not imply that ExitBlock finds all violations of MLD, because that proof presupposes that the system satisfies MLD.

In Bruening's proof that ExitBlockRW finds all assertion violations [Bru99, pp. 53-54], the requirements on s_i' and s_{i-1}' are symmetric, so two swapped segments can be swapped again, so the meaning of "Move each segment in this way as far as possible to the left" is unclear. Our Theorem 2 clearly shows how the idea of exploiting MLD is related to persistent sets. Bruening does not relate ExitBlock or ExitBlockRW to existing partial-order methods.

References

[BHPV00] Guillaume Brat, Klaus Havelund, Seung-Joon Park, and Willem Visser. Model checking programs. In *IEEE International Conference on Automated Software Engineering (ASE)*, September 2000.

[Bru99] Derek L. Bruening. Systematic testing of multithreaded Java programs. Master's thesis, Massachusetts Institute of Technology, 1999.

[CDH+00] James C. Corbett, Matthew Dwyer, John Hatcliff, Corina Pasareanu, Robby, Shawn Laubach, and Hongjun Zheng. Bandera: Extracting finite-state models from Java source code. In *Proc. 22nd International Conference on Software Engineering (ICSE)*, June 2000.

[Cor00] James C. Corbett. Using shape analysis to reduce finite-state models of concurrent Java programs. *ACM Transactions on Software Engingeering and Methodology*, 9(1):51–93, January 2000.

[Dah99] Markus Dahm. Byte code engineering with the JavaClass API. Technical Report B-17-98, Institut für Informatik, Freie Universität Berlin, 1999.

[DIS99] Claudio Demartini, Radu Iosif, and Riccardo Sisto. A deadlock detection tool for concurrent Java programs. *Software: Practice and Experience*, 29(7):577–603, July 1999.

[DLNS98] David L. Detlefs, K. Rustan M. Leino, Greg Nelson, and James B. Saxe. Extended static checking. Research Report 159, Compaq SRC, 1998.

[FA99] Cormac Flanagan and Martín Abadi. Types for safe locking. In *Proc. European Symposium on Programming (ESOP)*, volume 1576 of *LNCS*, pages 91–108. Springer-Verlag, March 1999.

[GHJ98] Patrice Godefroid, Robert S. Hanmer, and Lalita Jagadeesan. Model checking without a model: An analysis of the heart-beat monitor of a telephone switch using VeriSoft. In *Proc. ACM International Symposium on Software Testing and Analysis (ISSTA '98)*, pages 124–133, 1998.

[God96] Patrice Godefroid. *Partial-Order Methods for the Verification of Concurrent Systems*, volume 1032 of *Lecture Notes in Computer Science*. Springer-Verlag, 1996.

[God97]   Patrice Godefroid. Model checking for programming languages using Ver-
            iSoft. In *Proc. 24th ACM Symposium on Principles of Programming Lan-
            guages (POPL)*, pages 174–186. ACM Press, 1997.
[HS99]   Klaus Havelund and Jens U. Skakkebæk. Applying model checking in
            Java verification. In *Proc. 5th and 6th International SPIN Workshops*, vo-
            lume 1680 of *Lecture Notes in Computer Science*, pages 216–231. Springer-
            Verlag, September 1999.
[SBN+97]   Stefan Savage, Michael Burrows, Greg Nelson, Patrick Sobalvarro, and
            Thomas E. Anderson. Eraser: A dynamic data race detector for multi-
            threaded programs. *ACM Transactions on Computer Systems*, 15(4):391–
            411, November 1997.
[STMD96]   S. M. Shatz, S. Tu, T. Murata, and S. Duri. An application of Petri
            net reduction for Ada tasking deadlock analysis. *IEEE Transactions on
            Parallel and Distributed Systems*, 7(12):1307–1322, December 1996.
[Sto00]   Scott D. Stoller. Model-checking multi-threaded distributed Java pro-
            grams. Technical Report 536, Computer Science Dept., Indiana University,
            2000.
[WR99]   John Whaley and Martin Rinard. Compositional pointer and escape ana-
            lysis for Java programs. In *Proc. ACM Conference on Object-Oriented
            Systems, Languages and Applications (OOPSLA)*, pages 187–206, Octo-
            ber 1999.

Using Runtime Analysis to Guide Model Checking of Java Programs

Klaus Havelund

QSS/Recom
NASA Ames Research Center
Moffett Field, CA, USA
havelund@ptolemy.arc.nasa.gov
http://ase.arc.nasa.gov/havelund

Abstract. This paper describes how two runtime analysis algorithms, an existing data race detection algorithm and a new deadlock detection algorithm, have been implemented to analyze Java programs. Runtime analysis is based on the idea of executing the program once, and observing the generated run to extract various kinds of information. This information can then be used to predict whether other different runs may violate some properties of interest, in addition of course to demonstrate whether the generated run itself violates such properties. These runtime analyses can be performed stand-alone to generate a set of warnings. It is furthermore demonstrated how these warnings can be used to guide a model checker, thereby reducing the search space. The described techniques have been implemented in the home grown Java model checker called Java PathFinder.

Keywords: Concurrent programs, runtime analysis, race conditions, deadlocks, program verification, guided model checking, Java.

1 Introduction

Model checking of programs has received an increased attention from the formal methods community within the last couple of years. Several systems have emerged that can model check source code, such as Java, C and C++ directly (typically subsets of these languages) [17,9,4,20,30,25]. The majority of these systems can be classified as *translators*, which translate from the programming language source code to the modeling language of the model checker. The Java PathFinder 1 (JPF1) [17], developed at NASA Ames Research Center, was such an early attempt to bridge the gap between Java [12] and the PROMELA language of SPIN [21]. A second generation of Java PathFinder (JPF2) [30] has recently been developed at NASA Ames, which diverges from the translation approach, and model checks bytecode directly. This system contains a home grown Java Virtual Machine (JVM) specifically designed to support memory efficient storage of states for the purpose of model checking. This system resembles the Rivet machine described in [3] in the sense that Rivet also provides its own new JVM.

K. Havelund, J. Penix, and W. Visser (Eds.): SPIN 2000, LNCS 1885, pp. 245–264, 2000.
© Springer-Verlag Berlin Heidelberg 2000

The major obstacle for model checking to succeed is of course the management of large state spaces. For this purpose abstraction techniques have been studied heavily in the past 5 years [18,2,13,8,1]. More recently, special focus has been put on abstraction environments for Java and C [5,6,31,20,14,25]. Alternatives to state recording model checking have also been tried, such as VeriSoft [11], which performs stateless model checking of C++ programs, and ESC [10], which uses a combination of static analysis and theorem proving to analyze Modula3 programs. Of course static program analysis techniques [7] is an entire separate promising discipline, although it yet remains to be seen how well they can handle concurrency. An alternative to the above mentioned techniques is *runtime analysis*, which is based on the idea of concluding properties of a program from a single run of the program. Hence, executing the program once, and observing the run to extract information, which is then used to predict whether other different runs may violate some properties of interest (in addition of course to demonstrate whether the generated run violates such properties). The most known example of a runtime analysis algorithm is perhaps the data race detection algorithm Eraser [26], developed by S. Savage, M. Burrows, G. Nelson, and P. Sobalvarro, which has been implemented in the Visual Threads tool from Compaq [27]. A data race is the simultaneous access to an unprotected variable by several threads. An important characteristic of this algorithm is that a run itself does not have to contain a data race in order for data races in other runs to be detected. This kind of algorithm will not guarantee that errors are found since it works on an arbitrary run. It may also yield false positives. What is attractive, however, is that the algorithm scales very well since only one run needs to be examined. Also, in practice Eraser often seems to catch the problems it is designed to catch independently of the run chosen. That is, the randomness in the choice of run does not seem to imply a similar randomness in the analysis results.

The work presented in this paper describes an extension to JPF2 to perform runtime analysis on multi-threaded Java programs in simulation mode, either stand-alone, or as a pre-run to a subsequent model checking, which is guided by the warnings generated during the runtime analysis. We implement the generic Eraser algorithm to work for Java, and furthermore develop and implement a new runtime analysis algorithm, called GoodLock, that can detect deadlocks. We furthermore implement a third runtime dependency analysis used to do dynamic slicing of the program before the model checker is activated on the set of runtime analysis warnings. Section 2 describes the Eraser algorithm from [26], and how it is implemented in JPF2 to work on Java programs. Section 3 describes the deadlock detection algorithm and its implementation. Section 4 describes how these analyses, in addition to being run stand alone, can be performed in a pre-run to yield warnings, that are then used to guide a model checker. This section includes a presentation of the runtime dependency analysis algorithm used to reduce the state space to be explored by the model checker. Finally, Section 6 contains conclusions and a description of future work.

2   Data Race Detection

This section describes the Eraser algorithm as presented in [26], and how it has been implemented in JPF2 to work on Java programs. A *data race* occurs when two concurrent threads access a shared variable and when at least one access is a *write*, and the threads use no explicit mechanism to prevent the accesses from being simultaneous. The Eraser algorithm detects data races in a program by studying a single run of the program, and from this trying to conclude whether any runs with data races are possible. We have implemented the generic Eraser algorithm described in [26] to work for Java's synchronization constructs. Section 2.1 illustrates with an example how JPF2 is run in Eraser mode. Section 2.2 describes the generic Eraser algorithm, while Section 2.3 describes our implementation of it for Java.

2.1   Example

The Java program in Figure 1 illustrates a potential data race problem.

```
1. class Value{
2.    private int x = 1;
3.
4.    public synchronized void add(Value v){x = x + v.get();}
5.
6.    public int get(){return x;}
7. }
8.
9. class Task extends Thread{
10.    Value v1; Value v2;
11.
12.    public Task(Value v1,Value v2){
13.      this.v1 = v1; this.v2 = v2;
14.      this.start();
15.    }
16.
17.    public void run(){v1.add(v2);}
18. }
19.
20. class Main{
21.    public static void main(String[] args){
22.      Value v1 = new Value(); Value v2 = new Value();
23.      new Task(v1,v2); new Task(v2,v1);
24.    }
25. }
```

Fig. 1. Java program with a data race condition.

Three classes are defined: The `Value` class contains an integer variable that is accessed through two methods. The `add` method takes another `Value` object as parameter and adds the two, following a typical object oriented programming style. The method is synchronized, which means that when called by a thread, no other thread can call synchronized methods in the same object. The `Task` class inherits from the system defined `Thread` class, and contains a constructor (lines 12-15) that is called when objects are created, and a `run` method that is called when these objects are started with the **start** method. Finally, the **main** method in the Main class starts the program. When running JPF2 in simulation mode with the Eraser option switched on, a data race condition is found, and reported as illustrated in Figure 2.

```
********************************
Race condition!
--------------------------------
Variable x in class Value
is accessed unprotected.
********************************
From Task thread:
--------------------------
read access
Value.get line 6
Value.add line 4
Task.run line 17

From Task thread:
--------------------------
write access
Value.add line 4
Task.run line 17
==============================
```

Fig. 2. Output generated by JPF2 in Eraser simulation mode.

The report tells that the variable x in class Value is accessed unprotected, and that this happens from the two Task threads, from lines 4 and 6, respectively, also showing the call chains from the top-level run method. The problem detected is that one Task thread can call the add method on an object, say v1, which in turn calls the unsynchronized get method in the other object v2. The other thread can simultaneously make the dual operation, hence, call the add method on v2. Note that the fact that the add method is synchronized does not prevent its simultaneous application on two different Value objects by two different threads.

2.2 Algorithm

The basic algorithm works as follows. For each variable x, a set of locks $set(x)$ is maintained. At a given point in the execution, a lock l is in $set(x)$ if each thread that has accessed x held l at the time of access. As an example, if one thread has the lock l_1 when accessing a variable x, and another thread has lock l_2, then $set(x)$ will be empty after those two accesses, since there are no locks that both threads have when they access the variable. If the set in this way becomes empty, it means that there does not exist a lock that protects it, and a warning can be issued, signaling a potential for a data race.

The set of locks protecting a variable can be calculated as follows. For each thread t is maintained the set, $set(t)$, of locks that the thread holds at any time. When a thread for example calls a synchronized method on an object, then the thread will lock this object, and the set will be updated. Likewise, when the thread leaves the method, the object will be removed from the lock set, unless the thread has locked the object in some other way. When the thread t accesses a variable x (except for the first time), the following calculation is then performed:

$\text{set}(x) := \text{set}(x) \cap \text{set}(t);$
if $\text{set}(x) = \{\}$ **then** issue warning

The lock set associated to the variable is *refined* by taking the intersection with the set of locks held by the accessing thread. The initial set, $\text{set}(x)$, of locks of the variable x is in [26] described to be the set of all locks in the program. In a Java program objects (and thereby locks) are generated dynamically, hence the set of all locks cannot be pre-calculated. Instead, upon the first access of the variable, $\text{set}(x)$ is assigned the set of locks held by the accessing thread, hence $\text{set}(t)$.

The simple algorithm described above yields too many warnings as explained in [26]. First of all, shared variables are often *initialized* without the initializing thread holding any locks. In Java for example, a thread can create an object by the statement **new** $C()$, whereby the $C()$ constructor will initialize the variables of the object, probably without any locks. The above algorithm will yield a warning in this case, although this situation is safe. Another situation where the above algorithm yields unnecessary warnings is if a thread creates an object, where after several other threads read the object's variables (but no-one is writing after the initialization).

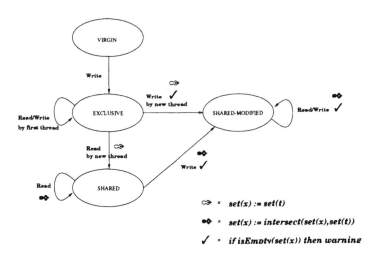

Fig. 3. The Eraser algorithm associates a state machine with each variable x. The state machine describes the Eraser analysis performed upon access by any thread t. The pen heads signify that lock set refinement is turned on. The "ok" sign signifies that warnings are issued if the lock set becomes empty.

To avoid warnings in these two cases, [26] suggests to extend the algorithm by associating a state machine to each variable in addition to the lock set. Figure 3 illustrates this state machine. The variable starts in the VIRGIN state. Upon the first write access to the variable, the EXCLUSIVE state is entered. The lock set of the variable is not refined at this point. This allows for initialization without locks. Upon a read access by another thread, the SHARED state is entered, now with the lock refinement switched on, but without yielding warnings in case the lock set goes empty. This allows for multiple readers (and not writers) after the initialization phase. Finally, if a new thread writes to the variable, the SHARED-MODIFIED state is entered, and now lock refinements are followed by warnings if the lock set becomes empty.

2.3   Implementation

The Eraser algorithm has been implemented by modifying the home grown Java Virtual machine to perform this analysis when the `eraser` option is switched on. Two new Java classes are defined: `LockSet`, implementing the notion of a set of locks, and `LockMachine`, implementing the state machine and lock set, that is associated with each variable.

Lock Sets Associated with Threads. Each thread is associated with a `LockSet` object, which is updated whenever a lock on an object is taken or released. The interface of this class is:

```
interface iLockSet{
  void    addLock(int objref);
  void    deleteLock(int objref);
  void    intersect(iLockSet locks);
  boolean contains(int objref);
  boolean isEmpty();
}
```

This happens for example when a `synchronized` statement such as:

```
synchronized(lock){
  ...
}
```

is executed. Here `lock` will refer to an object, the object reference of which will then be added to the lock set of the thread that executes this statement. Upon exit from the statement, the lock is removed from the thread's lock set, if the lock has not been taken by an enclosing synchronized statement. This can occur for example in a statement like[1]:

```
synchronized(lock){
  synchronized(lock){
    ...
  };
  (*)
}
```

---

[1] This statement illustrates a principle and does not represent a programming practice.

In this case, leaving the inner `synchronized` statement should not cause the lock to be removed from the thread's lock set since the outer statement still causes the lock to be held at point (∗). The JPF2 JVM already maintains a counter that tracks the nesting, and this counter is then used to update the lock sets correctly. Note that conceptually a synchronized method such as:

```
public synchronized void doSomething(){
   ...
}
```

can be regarded as short for:

```
public void doSomething(){
  synchronized(this){
     ...
  }
}
```

State Machines Associated with Variables. The `LockMachine` class has the following interface:

```
interface iLockMachine{
  void checkRead(ThreadInfo thread);
  void checkWrite(ThreadInfo thread);
}
```

An object of the corresponding class is associated to each variable, and its methods are called whenever a variable field is read from or written to. Variables include instance variables as well as static variables of a class, but not variables local to methods since these cannot be shared between threads.

Instrumenting the Bytecodes. A Java program is translated into bytecodes by the compiler. The bytecodes manipulate a stack of method frames, each with an operand stack. Objects are stored in a heap. The add method of the `Value` class in Figure 1, for example, is by the Java compiler translated into the following bytecodes:

```
Method synchronized void add(Value)
    0 aload_0
    1 aload_0
    2 getfield #7 <Field int x>
    5 aload_1
    6 invokevirtual #6 <Method int get()>
    9 iadd
   10 putfield #7 <Field int x>
   13 return
```

The reference (*this*) of the object on which the add method is called, is loaded twice on the stack (0 and 1), where after the x field of *this* object is extracted by the `getfield` bytecode, and put on the stack, replacing the topmost *this* reference. The object reference of the argument v is then loaded on the stack (5), and the `get` method is called by the `invokevirtual` bytecode, the result being stored on the stack. Finally the results are added and restored in the x field of *this* object.

The JPF2 JVM accesses the bytecodes via the JavaClass package [23], which for each bytecode delivers a Java object of a class specific for that bytecode (recall that JPF2 itself is written in Java). The JPF2 JVM extends this class with an execute method, which is called by the verification engine, and which represents the semantics of the bytecode. The runtime analysis is obtained by further annotating the execute method. For example, a getfield bytecode is delivered to the JPF2 JVM as an object of the following class, containing an execute method, which makes a conditional call (if the Eraser option is set) of the checkRead method of the lock machine of the variable being read.

```
public class GETFIELD extends AbstractInstruction {
  public InstructionHandle execute(SystemState s) {
    ...

    if (Eraser.on){
      da.getLockMachine(objref,fieldName).checkRead(th);
    }

    ...
  }
}
```

A similar annotation is made for the PUTFIELD bytecode. Similar annotations are also made for static variable accesses such as the bytecodes GETSTATIC and PUTSTATIC, and all array accessing bytecodes such as for example IALOAD and IASTORE. The bytecodes MONITORENTER and MONITOREXIT, generated from explicit synchronized statements, are annotated with updates of the lock sets of the accessing threads to record which locks are owned by the threads at any time; just as are the bytecodes INVOKEVIRTUAL and INVOKESTATIC for calling synchronized methods. The INVOKEVIRTUAL bytecode is also annotated to deal with the built-in wait method, which causes the calling thread to release the lock on the object the method is called on. Annotations are furthermore made to bytecodes like RETURN for returning from synchronized methods, and ATRHOW that may cause exceptions to be thrown within synchronized contexts.

3   Deadlock Detection

In this section we present a new runtime analysis algorithm, called GoodLock, for detecting deadlocks. A classical deadlock situation can occur where two threads share two locks, and they take the locks in different order. This is illustrated in Figure 4, where thread 1 takes the lock Ll first, while thread 2 takes the lock L2 first, where after each of the two threads is now prevented from getting the remaining lock because the other thread has it.

3.1   Example

To demonstrate this situation in Java, suppose we want to correct the program in Figure 1, eliminating the data race condition problem by making the get method synchronized, as shown in Figure 5, line 6 (we just add the synchronized keyword to the method signature).

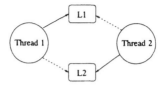

Fig. 4. Classical deadlock where task 1 takes lock Ll first and task 2 takes lock L2 first.

```
1. class Value{
2.    private int x = 1;
3.
4.    public synchronized void add(Value v){x = x + v.get();}
5.
6.    public synchronized int get(){return x;}
7. }
```

Fig. 5. Avoiding the data race condition by making the **get** method synchronized.

Now the x variable can no longer be accessed simultaneously from two threads, and the Eraser module will no longer give a warning. When running JPF2 in simulation mode with the GoodLock option switched on, however, a lock order problem not present before is now found, and reported as illustrated in Figure 6.

Fig. 6. Output generated by JPF2 in GoodLock simulation mode.

The report explains that the two object instances of the Value class, identified by the internal object numbers #0 and #1, are taken in a different order by the two Task threads, and it indicates the line numbers where the threads may deadlock, hence where the access to the second lock may fail. That is, line 4 contains the call of the get method from the add method. The problem arises due to the fact that the get method has become synchronized. One task may now call the add operation on a Value object, say v1, which in turn calls the get method on the other object v2; hence locking v1 and then v2 in that order.

Since the other task will do the reverse, we have a situation as illustrated in Figure 4.

An algorithm that detects such lock cycles must in addition take into account that a third lock may protect against a deadlock like the one above, if this lock is taken as the first thing by both threads, before any of the other two locks are taken. In this situation no warnings should be emitted. Such a protecting third lock is called a *gate lock*. The algorithm below does *not* warn about a lock order problem in case a gate lock prevents the deadlock from ever happening.

3.2   Algorithm

The algorithm for detecting this situation is based on the idea of recording the locking pattern for each thread during runtime as a lock tree, and then when the program terminates to compare the trees for each pair of threads as explained below. If the program does not terminate by itself, the user can terminate the execution by a single stroke on the keyboard, when he or she believes enough information has been recorded, which can be inferred by information being printed out. The lock tree that is recorded for a thread represents the nested pattern in which locks are taken by the thread. As an artificial example, consider the code fragments of two threads in Figure 7. Each thread executes an infinite loop, where in each iteration four locks, L1, L2, L3 and L4, are taken and released in a certain pattern. For example, the first thread takes L1; then L3; then L2; then it releases L2; then takes L4; then releases L4; then releases L3; then releases L1; then takes L4; etc.

```
Thread 1: while(true){                Thread 2: while(true){
            synchronized(L1){                     synchronized(L1){
              synchronized(L3){                     synchronizd(L2){
                synchronized(L2){};                   synchronized(L3){}
                synchronized(L4){}                  }
              }                                   };
            };
            synchronized(L4){                     synchronized(L4){
              synchronized(L2){                     synchronized(L3){
                synchronized(L3){}                    synchronized(L2){}
              }                                     }
            }                                     }
          }                                   }
```

Fig. 7. Synchronization behavior of two threads.

This pattern can be observed, and recorded in a finite tree of locks for each thread, as shown in Figure 8, by just running the program for a large enough period to allow both loops to be iterated at least once. As can be seen from the tree, a deadlock is potential because thread 1 in its left branch locks L3 (node identified with 2) and then L4 (4), while thread 2 in its right branch takes these locks in the opposite order (11, 12). There are furthermore two additional ordering problems between L2 and L3, one in the two left branches (2, 3 and 9, 10), and one in the two right branches (6, 7 and 12, 13). However, neither of these pose a deadlock problem since they are protected by the *gate locks* L1 (1, 8) respectively L4 (5, 11). Hence, one warning should be issued, corresponding to the fact that this program would deadlock if thread 1 takes lock L3 (left branch of thread 1 in Figure 8) and thread 2 takes lock L4.

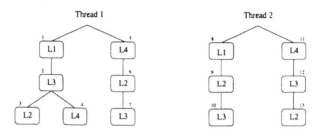

Fig. 8. Lock trees corresponding to threads in Figure 7.

The tree for a thread is built as follows. Each time an object *o* is locked, either by calling a synchronized method *m* on it, as in *o.m*(...), or by executing a statement of the form: `synchronized(o){...}`, the 'lock' operation in Figure 9 is called. Likewise, when a lock is released by the return from a synchronized method, or control leaves a `synchronized` statement, the 'unlock' operation is called. The tree has at any time a *current node*, where the path from the root (identifying the thread) to that node represents the *lock nesting* at this point in the execution: the locks taken, and the order in which they were taken. The lock operation creates a new child of the current node if the new lock has not previously been taken with that lock nesting. The unlock operation just backs up the tree if the lock really is released, and not owned by the thread in some other way. For the program in Figure 7, the trees will stabilize after one iteration of each loop, and will not get updated further. A print statement can inform the user whenever a new lock pattern is recognized and thereby a tree is updated, thereby making it easier for the user to decide when to terminate the program in case it is infinitely looping (if nothing is printed out after a while it is unlikely that new updates to the tree will occur).

```
lock(Thread thread,Lock lock){
    if thread does not already own lock{
        if lock is a son of current{
            current = that son
        }else{
            add lock as a new son of current;
            current = new son;
            print("new pattern identified");}}}

unlock(Thread thread,Lock lock){
    if thread does not own lock in another way{
        current = parent of current node;}}
```

Fig. 9. Operations 'lock' and 'unlock' used for creating a lock tree.

When the program terminates, the analysis of the lock trees is initiated by a call of the 'analyze' operation in Figure 10. This operation compares the trees for each pair of threads[2]. For each pair (t_1, t_2) of trees, such as those in Figure 8, the operation 'analyzeThis' is called recursively on all the nodes n_1 in t_1; and for every node n_2 in t_2 with the same lock as n_1, it is checked that no lock below n_1 in t_1 is above n_2 in t_2. In order to avoid issuing warnings when a *gate lock* prevents a deadlock, nodes in t_2 are marked after being examined, and nodes below marked nodes are not considered until the marks are removed when the analyzeThis operation backtracks from the corresponding node in t_1. This will prevent warnings from being issued about locks L2 and L3 in Figure 8, since the nodes 8 and 11 of thread 2 will get marked, when the trees below nodes 1 respectively 5 of thread 1 get examined. This reflects that nodes L1 and L4 are such gate locks preventing deadlocks due to lock order conflicts lower down the trees.

```
analyze(){
    for each pair (t₁,t₂) of thread trees{
        for each immediate child node n₁ of t₁'s topnode{
            analyzeThis(n₁,t₂);}}}

analyzeThis(LockNode n,LockTree t){
    Set N = {nₜ ∈ t | nₜ.lock == n.lock ∧ nₜ is not below a mark};
    for each nₜ in N{
        check(n,nₜ);
    };
    mark nodes in N;
    for each child nᶜʰⁱˡᵈ of n{
        analyzeThis(nᶜʰⁱˡᵈ,t);
    };
    unmark nodes in N;}

check(n₁,n₂){
    for each child node n₁ᶜʰⁱˡᵈ of n₁{
        if n₁ᶜʰⁱˡᵈ.lock is above n₂{
            conflict()
        }else{
            check(n₁ᶜʰⁱˡᵈ,n₂)}}}
```

Fig. 10. Operations 'analyze', 'analyzeThis', and 'check' used for analyzing lock trees.

The program in Figure 1 with the change indicated in Figure 5 has a potential for deadlock, which is detected by the GoodLock algorithm since each of the lock trees describes two locks on Value objects taken one after the other, but in different order in the two trees. Note, however, that the detection of a deadlock potential is not a proof of the existence of a deadlock. The program may prevent the deadlock in some other way. It is just a warning, which may focus our attention towards a potential problem. Note also, that the algorithm as described only detects deadlock potentials between pairs of threads. That is, although the analyzed program can have a very large number of threads, which is the

---

[2] The operation is symmetric such that only one ordering of a pair needs to be examined.

major strength of the algorithm, deadlocks will only be found if they involve two threads. A generalization is needed to identify deadlocks between more than two threads. The generalization must identify a subset of threads (trees) which together create a conflict. Consider for example three threads, each taking 2 out of 3 locks L1, L2 and L3 as follows: <L1,L2>, <L2,L3> and <L3,L1>. One can easily detect this deadlock by observing that as their first steps they together take all the locks, which prevent them from taking their second step each.

3.3 Implementation

The major new Java class defined is LockTree, which describes the lock tree objects that are associated with threads, and that are updated during the runtime analysis, and finally analyzed after program termination. Its interface is:

```
interface iLockTree{
  void lock(Lock lock);
  void unlock();
  void analyze(iLockTree otherTree);
}
```

The following bytecodes will activate calls of the lock and unlock operations in these tree objects for the relevant threads: MONITORENTER and MONITOREXIT for entering and exiting monitors, INVOKEVIRTUAL and INVOKESTATIC for calling synchronized methods or the built-in wait method of the Java threading library, bytecodes like RETURN for returning from synchronized methods, and ATRHOW that may cause exceptions to be thrown within synchronized contexts. Methods are in addition provided for printing out the lock trees, a quite useful feature for understanding the lock pattern of the threads in a program.

4 Integrating Runtime Analysis with Model Checking

The runtime analyses as described in the previous two sections can provide useful information to a programmer as stand alone tools. In this section we will describe how runtime analysis furthermore can be used to guide a model checker. The basic idea is to first run the program in simulation mode, with all the runtime analysis options turned on, thereby obtaining a set of warnings about data races and lock order conflicts. The threads causing the warnings, called the *race window*, is then fed into the model checker, which will then focus it attention on the threads that were involved in the warnings. For this to work, the race window often must be extended to include threads that create or otherwise influence the threads in the original window. A runtime dependency analysis is used as a basis for this extension of the race window.

4.1 Example

Consider the program in Figure 1, troubled by a deadlock potential caused by the change indicated in Figure 5. If, instead of applying the runtime analysis, we apply the JPF2 model checker to this program, the deadlock is immediately found and reported via an error trail leading from the initial state to the deadlocked state. Suppose, however, that this program is a subprogram of a larger program that spawns other threads not influencing the behavior of the two tasks involved in the deadlock. In this case the model checker will likely fail to find the deadlock since the state space becomes to big. Furthermore, if the other threads don't deadlock, then the global system never deadlocks, although the two tasks may. Hence, since the JPF2 model checker currently only looks for global deadlocks, it will never be able to find this local one.

As an experiment, the program was composed with an environment consisting of 40 threads, grouped in pairs, each pair sharing access to an object by updating it (each thread assigns $10,000$ different values to the object). This environment has more than 10^{160} states. When running JPF2 in runtime analysis mode, it prints out 44 messages, one for each time a new locking pattern is recognized (40 of the patterns come from the environment). When these messages no longer get printed, after 25 seconds, one can assume[3] that all patterns have been detected, and by hitting a key on the keyboard, the lock analysis is started. This identifies the original two Task threads as being the sinners. The model checker is now launched where only the Main thread, and the two Task threads are allowed to execute, and the deadlock is found by the model checker in 1.6 seconds. The Main thread is included because it starts the Task threads, as concluded based on a dependency analysis.

4.2   Algorithm

Most of the work has already been done during runtime analysis. An additional data structure must be introduced, the *race window*, which contains the threads that caused warnings to be issued. Before the model checker is activated, an *extended race window* is calculated, which includes additional threads that may influence the behavior of threads in the original window. The extension is calculated on the basis of a *dependency graph*, created by a dependency analysis also performed during the execution (a third kind of runtime analysis). This extended window is then used in the subsequent model checking by freezing all threads not in the window. That is, the scheduler simply does not schedule threads outside the window.

Figure 11 illustrates the state variables and operations needed to create the window and dependency graph, and the operation for extending the window. The window is just a set of threads. The dependency graph (dgraph) is a mapping from threads t to triples (A, R, W), where A is the ancestor thread that spawned t, R is the set of objects that t reads from, and W is the set of objects that t writes to. Whenever a runtime warning is issued, the 'addWarning' operation is called for each thread involved, adding it to the window. The operations 'start-Thread', 'readObject', and 'writeObject' update the dependency graph, which after program termination is used by the 'extendWindow' operation to extend

---

[3] This is a judgment call of course.

the window. The dependency graph is updated when a thread starts another thread with the start() method, and when a thread reads from, or writes to a variable in an object. The 'extendWindow' operation performs a fix-point calculation by creating the set of all threads *"reachable"* from the original window by repeatedly including threads that have spawned threads in the window, and by including threads that write to objects that are read by threads in the window. The extended window is used to evaluate whether a thread should be scheduled or not.

```
type Window = setof Thread;
type Dgraph = map from Thread to (Thread × setof Object × setof Object);

Window window;      (* updated when a runtime warning is issued *)
Dgraph dgraph;      (* updated when a thread starts a thread or accesses an object *)

addWarning(Thread thread){
    window = window ∪ {thread}}

startThread(Thread father,Thread son){
    dgraph = dgrap + [son ↦ (father, {}, {})]}

readObject(Thread thread,Object object){
    let (A, R, W) = dgraph(thread){
        dgraph = dgraph + [thread ↦ (A, R ∪ {object}, W)]}}

writeObject(Thread thread,Object object){
    let (A, R, W) = dgraph(thread){
        dgraph = dgraph + [thread ↦ (A, R, W ∪ {object})]}}

Window extendWindow(Window window,Dgraph dgraph){
    Window passed = {};
    Window waiting = window;
    while (waiting ≠ {}){
        get thread from waiting;
        if (thread ∉ passed){
            passed = passed ∪ {thread};
            let (A, R, W) = dgraph(thread){
                if (A ≠ "topmost thread") waiting = waiting ∪ {A};
                waiting = waiting ∪
                    {thread' | let(_, _, W') = dgraph(thread') in W' ∩ R ≠ {}};
        }
    }
};
return passed;}
```

Fig. 11. Operations for creating dependency graph and window.

4.3   Implementation

Two classes, whose interfaces are given below, represent respectively the dependency graph and the race window. The dependency graph can be updated when threads start threads, or access objects. Finally, a method allows to calculate the set of threads reachable from an initial window, based on the dependencies recorded. The race window is used to record threads involved in warnings. Before the model checker is launched the extendWindow method will include threads that influence the original window by calling the reachable method. The model checker scheduler will finally call the `contains` method whenever it needs to determine whether a particular thread is in the window, in which case it will be allowed to execute.

```
interface iDepend{
  static void     startThread(ThreadInfo father,ThreadInfo son);
  static void     readObject(ThreadInfo th,int objref);
  static void     writeObject(ThreadInfo th,int objref);
  static HashSet  reachable(HashSet threads);
}

interface iRaceWindow{
  static void     addWarning(ThreadInfo th);
  static void     extendWindow();
  static boolean  contains(String threadName);
}
```

The following bytecodes are instrumented to operate on the dependency graph: INVOKEVIRTUAL for invoking the `start` method on a thread; and PUTFIELD, GETFIELD, PUTSTATIC, GETSTATIC for accessing variables.

5   The RAX Example

In this section we present an example drawn from a real NASA application. The Remote Agent (RA) [24] is an AI-based spacecraft controller programmed in LISP, that has been developed by NASA Ames Research Center and NASA's Jet Propulsion Laboratory. It consists of three components: a Planner that generates plans from mission goals; an Executive that executes the plans; and finally a Recovery system that monitors the RA's status, and suggests recovery actions in case of failures. The Executive contains features of a multi-threaded operating system, and the Planner and Executive exchange messages in an interactive manner. Hence, this system is highly vulnerable to multi-threading errors. In fact, during real flight in space on board the Deep-Space 1 spacecraft in May 1999, the RA deadlocked, causing the ground crew to put the spacecraft on standby. The ground crew located the error using data from the spacecraft, but asked as a challenge our group if we could locate the error using model checking. This resulted in an effort described in [15], which in turn refers to earlier work on the RA described in [16]. Here we shall give a short account of the error and show how it could have been located with runtime analysis, and furthermore potentially be confirmed using model checking. For this purpose we have modeled the error situation in Java. Note that this Java program represents a small model of part of the RA, as described in [15]. However, although this is not an automated application to a real full-size program, it is a sufficiently convincing illustration of the approach in a real context.

The major two components to be modeled are events and tasks, as illustrated in Figure 12. The figure shows a Java class `Event` from which event objects can be instantiated. The class has a local counter variable and two synchronized methods, one for waiting on the event and one for signaling the event, releasing all threads having called `wait_for_event`. In order to catch events that occur while tasks are executing, each event has an associated event counter that is increased whenever the event is signaled. A task then only calls wait_for_event in case this counter has not changed, hence, there have been no new events since it was last restarted from a call of wait_for_event. The figure shows the definition of one of the tasks, the planner. The body of the run method contains an infinite loop, where in each iteration a conditional call of wait_for_event is executed. The condition is that no new events have arrived, hence the event counter is unchanged.

```
class Event {
  int count = 0;

  public synchronized void wait_for_event() {
    try{wait();}catch(InterruptedException e){};
  }

  public synchronized void signal_event(){
    count = (count + 1) % 3;
    notifyAll();
  }
}

class Planner extends Thread{
  Event event1,event2;
  int count = 0;

  public void run(){
    while(true){
      if (count == event1.count)
        event1.wait_for_event();
      count = event1.count;
      /* Generate plan */
      event2.signal_event();
    }
  }
}
```

Fig. 12. The RAX Error in Java.

To illustrate JPF2's integration of runtime analysis and model checking, the example is made slightly more realistic by adding extra threads as before. The program has 40 threads, each with $10,000$ states, in addition to the Planner and Executive threads, yielding more than 10^{160} states in total. Then we apply JPF2 in its special runtime analysis/model checking mode. It immediately identifies the data race condition using the Eraser algorithm: the variable count in class Event is accessed unsynchronized by the Planner's run method in the line: "if (count == event1.count)", specifically the expression: event1.count. This may be enough for a programmer to realize an error, but only if he or she can see the consequences. The JPF2 model checker, on the other hand, can be used to analyze the consequences. Hence, the model checker is launched on a thread window consisting of those threads involved in the data race condition: the Planner and the Executive, locating the deadlock - all within 25 seconds. The error trace shows that the Planner first evaluates the test "(count == event1.count)", which evaluates to true; then, before the call of event1.wait_for_event() the Executive signals the event, thereby increasing the event counter and notifying all waiting threads, of which there however are none yet. The Planner now unconditionally waits and misses the signal. The solution to this problem is to enclose the conditional wait in a critical section such that no events can occur in between the test and the wait. This error caused the deadlock on board the spacecraft.

6   Conclusions and Future Work

We have presented the GoodLock algorithm for detecting deadlock possibilities in programs caused by locks being taken in different orders by parallel running threads. The algorithm is based on an analysis of a single run of the program, and is therefore an example of a runtime analysis algorithm in the same family as the Eraser algorithm which detects data races. The Visual Threads tool [27] also provides a deadlock analysis. It still remains to explore how this relates to the one presented here. The Assure tool [28] is another tool that performs program runtime analysis, but the exact algorithms used have not been obtainable. The GoodLock algorithm seems to be unique in preventing false positives in the presence of *gate locks* that "protect" lock order problems "further down". We have furthermore suggested how to use the results of a runtime analysis to guide a model checker for their mutual benefit: the warnings yielded by the runtime analysis can help focus the search of the model checker, which in turn can help eliminate false positives generated by the runtime analysis, or generate an error trace showing how the warnings can manifest themselves in an error. In order to create the smallest possible self-contained sub-program to be model checked based on warnings from the runtime analysis, a runtime dependency analysis is introduced, which very simply records dependencies between threads and objects. In addition to implementing all of the above mentioned techniques, we have implemented the existing generic Eraser algorithm to work for Java by instrumenting bytecodes.

Future work will consist of improving the Eraser algorithm to give less false positives, in particular in the context of initializations of objects. The GoodLock algorithm will also be generalized to deal with deadlocks between multiple threads. One can furthermore consider alternative kinds of runtime analysis, for example analyzing issues concerned with the use of the built-in wait and notify thread methods in Java. A runtime analysis typically cannot guarantee that a program property is satisfied since only a single run is examined. The results, however, are often pretty accurate because the chosen run does not itself have to violate the property, in order for the property's potential violation in other runs to be detected. In order to achieve even higher assurance, one can of course consider activating runtime analysis *during* model checking (rather than before as described in this paper), and we intend to make that experiment. Note that it will not be necessary to explore the entire state space in order for this simultaneous combination of runtime analysis and model checking to be useful. Even though runtime analysis scales relatively well, it also suffers from memory problems when analyzing large programs. Various optimizations of data structures used to record runtime analysis information can be considered, for example the memory optimizations suggested in [26]. One can furthermore consider only doing runtime analysis on objects that are really shared by first determining the sharing structure of the program. This in turn can be done using runtime analysis, or some form of static analysis. Of course, at the extreme the runtime analysis can be performed on a separate computer. We intend to investigate how the runtime analysis information can be used to feed a program slicer [14], as an alternative to the runtime dependency analysis described in this paper.

References

1. S. Bensalem, V. Ganesh, Y. Lakhnech, C. Muñoz, S. Owre, H. Rueß, J. Rushby, V. Rusu, H. Saïdi, N. Shankar, E. Singerman, and A. Tiwari. An Overview of SAL. In *Proceedings of the 5th NASA Langley Formal Methods Workshop*, June 2000.
2. S. Bensalem, Y. Lakhnech, and S. Owre. Computing Abstractions of Infinite State Systems Compositionally and Automatically. In *CAV'98: Computer-Aided Verification*, number 1427 in LNCS, pages 319–331. Springer-Verlag, 1998.
3. D. L. Bruening. Systematic Testing of Multithreaded Java Programs. Master's thesis, MIT, 1999.
4. T. Cattel. Modeling and Verification of sC++ Applications. In *Proceedings of TACAS98: Tools and Algorithms for the Construction and Analysis of Systems*, volume 1384 of *LNCS*, LISBON, April 1998.
5. J. Corbett. Constructing Compact Models of Concurrent Java Programs. In *Proceedings of the ACM Sigsoft Symposium on Software Testing and Analysis*, March 1998. Clearwater Beach, Florida.
6. J. Corbett, M. Dwyer, J. Hatcliff, C. Pasareanu, Robby, S. Laubach, and H. Zheng. Bandera : Extracting Finite-state Models from Java Source Code. In *Proceedings of the 22nd International Conference on Software Engineering*, Limerich, Ireland, June 2000. ACM Press.
7. P. Cousot and R. Cousot. Abstract Interpretation Frameworks. *Journal of Logic and Computation*, 4(2):511–547, August 1992.
8. S. Das, D. Dill, and S. Park. Experience with Predicate Abstraction. In *CAV '99: 11th International Conference on Computer Aided Verification*, volume 1633 of *LNCS*, 1999.
9. C. Demartini, R. Iosif, and R. Sist. A Deadlock Detection Tool for Concurrent Java Programs. *Software Practice and Experience*, 29(7):577–603, July 1999.
10. D. L. Detlefs, K. R. M. Leino, G. Nelson, and J. B. Saxe. Extended Static Checking. Technical Report 159, Compaq Systems Research Center, Palo Alto, California, USA, 1998.
11. P. Godefroid. Model Checking for Programming Languages using VeriSoft. In *Proceedings of the 24th ACM Symposium on Principles of Programming Languages*, pages 174–186, Paris, January 1997.
12. J. Gosling, B. Joy, and G. Steele. *The Java Language Specification*. Addison Wesley, 1996.
13. S. Graf and H. Saidi. Construction of Abstract State Graphs with PVS. In *CAV '97: 6th International Conference on Computer Aided Verification*, volume 1254 of *LNCS*, 1997.
14. J. Hatcliff, J.C. Corbett, M.B. Dwyer, S. Sokolowski, and H. Zheng. A Formal Study of Slicing for Multi-threaded Programs with JVM Concurrency Primitives. In *Proc. of the 1999 Int. Symposium on Static Analysis*, 1999.

15. K. Havelund, M. Lowry, S. Park, C. Pecheur, J. Penix, W. Visser, and J. White. Formal Analysis of the Remote Agent Before and After Flight. In *Proceedings of the 5th NASA Langley Formal Methods Workshop*, June 2000.

16. K. Havelund, M. Lowry, and J. Penix. Formal Analysis of a Space Craft Controller using SPIN. In *Proceedings of the 4th SPIN workshop, Paris, France*, November 1998. To appear in IEEE Transactions of Software Engineering.

17. K. Havelund and T. Pressburger. Model Checking Java Programs using Java Path-Finder. *International Journal on Software Tools for Technology Transfer (STTT)*, 2(4):366–381, April 2000. Special issue of STTT containing selected submissions to the 4th SPIN workshop, Paris, France, 1998.

18. K. Havelund and N. Shankar. Experiments in Theorem Proving and Model Checking for Protocol Verification. In M-C. Gaudel and J. Woodcock, editors, *FME'96: Industrial Benefit and Advances in Formal Methods*, volume 1051 of *LNCS*, pages 662–681. Springer-Verlag, 1996. An experiment in program abstraction.

19. K. Havelund and J. Skakkebæk. Applying Model Checking in Java Verification. In *Proceedings of the 7th Workshop on the SPIN Verification System*, volume 1680 of *LNCS*, Toulouse, France., September 1999.

20. G. Holzmann and M. Smith. A Practical Method for Verifying Event-Driven Software. In *Proc. ICSE99, International Conference on Software Engineering, Los Angeles*. IEEE/ACM, May 1999.

21. G.J. Holzmann. The Model Checker Spin. *IEEE Trans. on Software Engineering*, 23(5):279–295, May 1997. Special issue on Formal Methods in Software Practice.

22. R. Iosif, C. Demartini, and R. Sisto. Modeling and Validation of JAVA Multithreaded Applications using SPIN. In *Proceedings of the Fourth Workshop on the SPIN Verification System*, Paris, November 1998.

23. JavaClass. http://www.inf.fu-berlin.de/~dahm/JavaClass.

24. N. Muscettola, P. Nayak, B. Pell, and B. Williams. Remote Agent: To Boldly Go Where No AI System Has Gone Before. *Artificial Intelligence*, 103(1-2):5–48, August 1998.

25. D. Park, U. Stern, and D. Dill. Java Model Checking. In *Proc. of the First International Workshop on Automated Program Analysis, Testing and Verification, Limerick, Ireland*, June 2000.

26. S. Savage, M. Burrows, G. Nelson, and P. Sobalvarro. Eraser: A Dynamic Data Race Detector for Multithreaded Programs. *ACM Transactions on Computer Systems*, 15(4):391–411, November 1997.

27. Visual Threads. http://www.unix.digital.com/visualthreads/index.html.

28. Assure. http://www.kai.com/assurej.

29. W. Visser, K. Havelund, G. Brat, and S. Park. Java PathFinder - Second Generation of a Java Model Checker. In *Proc. of Post-CAV Workshop on Advances in Verification, Chicago*, July 2000.

30. W. Visser, K. Havelund, G. Brat, and S. Park. Model Checking Programs. In *Proc. of ASE'2000: The 15th IEEE International Conference on Automated Software Engineering*. IEEE CS Press, September 2000.

31. W. Visser, S. Park, and J. Penix. Using Predicate Abstraction to Reduce Object-Oriented Programs for Model Checking. In *Proceedings of the 3rd ACM SIGSOFT Workshop on Formal Methods in Software Practice*, August 2000.

Communication Topology Analysis for Concurrent Programs

Matthieu Martel and Marc Gengler

Laboratoire d'Informatique de Marseille (LIM)
Parc Scientifique et Technologique de Luminy
163, avenue de Luminy - Case 901 F
13288 Marseille Cedex 9, France
{Matthieu.Martel, Marc.Gengler}@esil.univ-mrs.fr

Abstract. In this article, we address the problem of statically determining an approximation of the communication topology of concurrent programs. These programs may contain dynamic process and channel creations and may communicate channel names as well as functions, possibly containing other communications.
We introduce a control flow analysis which builds finite state automata to improve its precision. The method is twofold. First, we build an automaton for each process in the concurrent system yielding an approximation of how the synchronizations realized by the sequential components are ordered. Second, we extract the communication topology from a reduced product automaton, which size is polynomial in the size of the original program. This analysis was implemented and we apply it to the verification of a circuit allocation mechanism.

1 Introduction

Static analysis is a widely used technique to establish properties satisfied by programs, independently of a given execution context. Most common applications include compile-time optimizations and program verification. However, this scope is extended by concurrency which introduces new problems as well as new applications. Recently, much research has been done in this area, including Amtoft et al. [2], Bodei et al. [4,5], Jagannathan [10], Kobayashi et al. [11], Marinescu and Goldberg [12], Nielson and Nielson [14,15,16,18].

In this article, we present a static analysis which computes a fine approximation of the communication topology of Concurrent ML programs [22] and, more generally, which analyzes the whole synchronizations of concurrent programs. By determining, for each reception, the set of possibly matching emissions, we find an approximation of the possibly received values.

Our analysis is a control flow analysis (CFA). Concerning sequential functional languages, the aim of a CFA is to detect which functions an expression can evaluate to [17,19,23,24]. For higher order concurrent functional languages, such as Concurrent ML [22], this task is more complicated. Channel names may be

K. Havelund, J. Penix, and W. Visser (Eds.): SPIN 2000, LNCS 1885, pp. 265–286, 2000.
© Springer-Verlag Berlin Heidelberg 2000

dynamically created and communicated anywhere in the program, new processes can be dynamically created and functions are first-class values which may be communicated. Hence, a piece of code in the source program (possibly containing communications) may be executed by any process. Such analyses have been proposed by Bodei et al. [4], Colby [6], Solberg et al. [25] and Mercouroff [13]. However, the precision of the CFA is closely related to the approximations made on the topology of the communications. Hence, we address the problem of minimizing for each emission, the set of possible receptors. Eliminating some impossible communications improves the annotations at reception points and, consequently, on the sequential parts of the program using the received values.

From a technical point of view, we proceed as follows. First, we order the synchronization primitives of the sequential processes in the system. This is done by building a finite automaton $\widehat{\mathcal{A}}_p$ for each process p. A labeled path denotes one possible sequence of synchronizations in p. Second, we approximate how the different processes may interact altogether by building the product of the $\widehat{\mathcal{A}}_p$'s. This product automaton possibly has size exponential in the size of the program. Hence, we introduce a reduced product automaton size is polynomial and which conservatively approximates the product automaton.

Applications of CFA for concurrent languages are twofold. First, mixing a CFA with another static analysis usually improves the precision of this latter. For instance, partial evaluation [7] of concurrent languages has been discussed by Marinescu and Goldberg [12] and by Gengler and Martel [8,9]. Marinescu and Goldberg [12] also introduce a binding time analysis (BTA) which collects informations used by the partial evaluator. However, this BTA makes rough approximations due to the lack of informations about the topology of communications. Using a CFA would improve the performances of the partial evaluator. Second, as outlined by Bodei et al. [4], another application of CFA for concurrent languages are security and program verification. For a concurrent program, a CFA allows one to statically determine whether two given processes P_1 and P_2 may communicate together at one stage of their execution, or to statically approximate the set of channels which are shared by P_1 and P_2 during their execution. For instance, these results enable one to check access rights properties.

Section 2 gives an informal overview of the techniques developed in this article. Section 3 briefly introduces the subset of Concurrent ML we use. We introduce the analysis in Sections 4 and 5 First, in Section 4 we define an analysis for the individual processes and second, in Section 5, we introduce two ways to analyze a pool of processes, respectively based on product and reduced product automata. This analysis was implemented and results are discussed in Section 6 for a virtual circuit allocation mechanism, similar to the one used in ATM.

2   General Description

To compute precise annotations, a CFA has to use a fine approximation of the topology of the communications realized by a program. In this Section, we illustrate how our analysis works using the concurrent program of Figure 1 a).

In this system, Processes p_1 and p_3 respectively realize two and one emissions, and p_2 realizes three receptions. We assume that all the communications are made on the same channel. Communications are synchronous, i.e. an emission or a reception blocks the process until the communication occurs. In the remainder of this article, we use the following vocabulary. A *communication* is the synchronous interaction between an *emission point* and a *reception point*. A *synchronization* is either a communication or a new process creation (a fork). A *synchronization point* is either a communication point or a fork point.

A first way to conservatively annotate p_2 is to consider that any reception may receive its value from any emission on the same channel [25]. Let us call s_1 and s_2 the emissions of p_1, s_3 the emission of p_3, and r_1, r_2 and r_3 the receptions of p_2. Let $\widehat{C}(s_i)$ (resp. $\widehat{C}(r_j)$) be the abstract value sent (resp. received) at s_i (resp. r_j), $1 \leq i, j \leq 3$. Such an analysis assigns to $\widehat{C}(r_1)$, $\widehat{C}(r_2)$ and $\widehat{C}(r_3)$ the values

$$\widehat{C}(r_j) = \bigcup_{i \in \{1,2,3\}} \widehat{C}(s_i) \quad j \in \{1,2,3\} \tag{1}$$

As sketched in Figure 1 b), Equation (1) describes a correct approximation of the communication scheme of Figure 1 a). However, it is a trivial matter of fact that s_1 cannot communicate with r_3 nor s_2 with r_1.

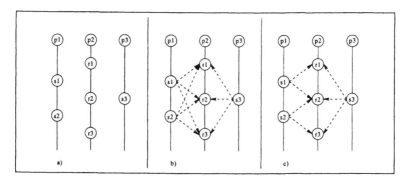

Fig. 1. a) A system made of communicating processes. b) Approximation of the communication topology computed by classical methods. c) Approximation of the topology computed by our CFA.

In order to assign a fine abstract value to receptions, a CFA has to approximate closely the communication topology of programs. This problem is twofold and we address it as follows.

– Obviously, the communication graph of a concurrent program depends on how the communications are ordered on each process. In this article, this point is addressed as follows. We build a finite state automaton $\widehat{A}$ which indicates how the synchronization points possibly follow each other. For each labeled sub-expression e^l in the program, we use an automaton whose initial and final states are identified by the nodes B_l and E_l. The transitions between these nodes depends on the expression. The transitions between sub-expressions indicate their respective evaluation order. A transition related to a sequential reduction step is labeled ε and we introduce a l-transition to denote the occurrence of a synchronization point labeled l. The result is an approximation of the communication scheme of each process.

– Knowing how the synchronizations are ordered on each process, we have to determine their interactions. A first way to address this problem is to consider the product of the automata related to the different processes in the program. Based on the collection $\widehat{S} = (\widehat{A}_p)_{p \in \text{Dom}(P)}$ of automata describing the synchronization points of the different processes, we show that the product automaton $A_{\otimes}^{\natural}(\widehat{S})$ describes a correct approximation of the synchronizations the program may realize. However, on one hand the size of $A_{\otimes}^{\natural}(\widehat{S})$ is possibly exponential in the size of the program, while on the other hand it contains more informations than really needed for the analysis. Intuitively, the only relevant informations in $A_{\otimes}^{\natural}(\widehat{S})$ for the analysis are the points which may synchronize together. Hence, we introduce a reduced product automaton $A_{\otimes}^{\sharp}(\widehat{S})$ which is polynomial in the size of the source program and we prove that $A_{\otimes}^{\sharp}(\widehat{S})$ correctly approximates $A_{\otimes}^{\natural}(\widehat{S})$. The result is an approximation of the possible interactions between processes.

In Figure 1 c), we show the approximation of the topology obtained using the method described above for the communication scheme of Figure 1 a). In the remainder of this Section we discuss the approximations made by our CFA.

First, the abstract value attached to a sub-expression is the union of all the abstract values carried by the different reduction paths of a non-deterministic program. For communications, this means that the value attached to a reception is the union of all the values carried by the potential emitters. This corresponds to the approximation done in Figure 1 c). Such approximations make the control flow annotations grow. However, any abstract value collected this way is related to one of the concrete values in one of the possible communication schemes.

Other approximations are obviously done during the analysis of the body of loops. First, different channel names created by the same channel() instruction inside a loop are identified. Hence, communications over such channels are assumed to be possible, even though the emitter and the receptor use different instances of the same instruction.

Second, a process p may communicate with the communication points occurring inside the body b of a loop, as long as p assumes that the loop has not terminated. However, thanks to the sequential automata, the analysis keeps track of the communication ordering inside b. The only sequences allowed are those corresponding to an unfolding of b.

For instance, let us consider the program of Figure 2 which describes a multiplexer-demultiplexer of channels. This program is made of two processes p_1 and p_2 written in Concurrent ML. Each sub-expression is labeled by an integer. p_1 alternatively receives data on channels ι_1 and ι_2. These data are transmitted on a channel γ. p_2 receives on γ the multiplexed data and transmits them on o_1 and o_2. We assume that γ is only shared by p_1 and p_2. So, the data sent on o_1

(resp. o_2) are the ones the multiplexer received on ι_1 (resp. ι_2). Finally, a process p_3 sends new channel names to the multiplexer on ι_1 and ι_2.

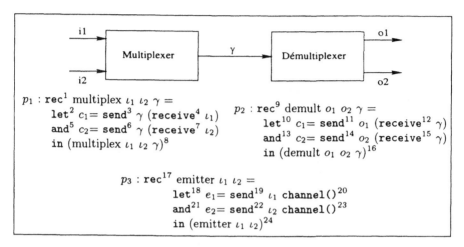

$p_1 : \mathbf{rec}^1$ multiplex $\iota_1\ \iota_2\ \gamma =$
$\quad \mathbf{let}^2\ c_1 = \mathbf{send}^3\ \gamma\ (\mathbf{receive}^4\ \iota_1)$
$\quad \mathbf{and}^5\ c_2 = \mathbf{send}^6\ \gamma\ (\mathbf{receive}^7\ \iota_2)$
$\quad \mathbf{in}\ (\text{multiplex}\ \iota_1\ \iota_2\ \gamma)^8$

$p_2 : \mathbf{rec}^9$ demult $o_1\ o_2\ \gamma =$
$\quad \mathbf{let}^{10}\ c_1 = \mathbf{send}^{11}\ o_1\ (\mathbf{receive}^{12}\ \gamma)$
$\quad \mathbf{and}^{13}\ c_2 = \mathbf{send}^{14}\ o_2\ (\mathbf{receive}^{15}\ \gamma)$
$\quad \mathbf{in}\ (\text{demult}\ o_1\ o_2\ \gamma)^{16}$

$p_3 : \mathbf{rec}^{17}$ emitter $\iota_1\ \iota_2 =$
$\quad \mathbf{let}^{18}\ e_1 = \mathbf{send}^{19}\ \iota_1\ \mathbf{channel}()^{20}$
$\quad \mathbf{and}^{21}\ e_2 = \mathbf{send}^{22}\ \iota_2\ \mathbf{channel}()^{23}$
$\quad \mathbf{in}\ (\text{emitter}\ \iota_1\ \iota_2)^{24}$

Fig. 2. Multiplexer - demultiplexer written in Concurrent ML.

Our implementation of the analysis determines that the abstract value emitted at point 11 (resp. 14) is the singleton {20} (resp. {23}). As stated before, different channel names created at the same point are not distinguished. However, the CFA detects that the instance of the first reception on γ (point 12) only may receive a value sent by an instance of the first emission (point 3). Similar observations can be done for the second emission and reception on γ.

3   Concurrent ML

In this Section, we introduce the subset of Concurrent ML [3,20,21] used in this article to illustrate how our analysis works. The syntax is defined in Figure 3.

Labels are attached to terms. They are used during the analysis which assumes that each sub-expression in the initial program has a unique label. This property is not maintained by reduction. The language contains conditionals, a **let** construct, and the operator **rec** for recursive functions. $\mathbf{channel}()^l$ denotes a function call which creates and returns a new channel name k different from all the existing ones. $(\mathbf{fork}\ e_0^{l_0})^l$ creates a new process which computes $e_0^{l_0}$ and evaluates to $()$ (the value of type unit). $(\mathbf{send}\ e_0^{l_0}\ e_1^{l_1})^l$ is the blocking emission of the value of $e_1^{l_1}$ on the channel resulting from the evaluation of $e_0^{l_0}$. $e_0^{l_0}$ and $e_1^{l_1}$ respectively are the *subject* and the *object* of the communication. Once the communication is done, a send evaluates to the value of its object. $(\mathbf{receive}\ e_0^{l_0})^l$ is the blocking reception of a value on the channel name described by $e_0^{l_0}$ (the subject of the reception). Values are in the domains of basic types or channel names or functions.

$$e ::= v^l \mid x^l$$
$$\mid (e_0^{l_0} \ e_1^{l_1})^l \mid (\text{if } e_0^{l_0} \ e_1^{l_1} \ e_2^{l_2})^l$$
$$\mid (\text{let } x^{l_2} = e_0^{l_0} \text{ in } e_1^{l_1})^l \mid \text{channel}()^l$$
$$\mid (\text{fork } e_0^{l_0})^l \mid (\text{send } e_0^{l_0} \ e_1^{l_1})^l$$
$$\mid (\text{receive } e_0^{l_0})^l$$

$$E ::= [] \mid (E \ e_1^{l_1})^l \mid (v^{l_0} \ E)^l \mid (\text{if } E \ e_1^{l_1} \ e_2^{l_2})^l$$
$$\mid (\text{let } x^{l_2} = E \text{ in } e_1^{l_1})^l$$
$$\mid (\text{send } E \ e_1^{l_1})^l \mid (\text{send } v^{l_0} \ E)^l$$
$$\mid (\text{receive } E)^l$$

$$v ::= B \mid \text{fun } x^{l_1} \Rightarrow e_0^{l_0}$$
$$\mid \text{rec } f^{l_1} \ x^{l_2} \Rightarrow e_0^{l_0}$$

$$B ::= () \mid i \mid b \mid k$$

$$i ::= \ldots - 1 \mid 0 \mid 1 \ldots$$
$$b ::= \text{true} \mid \text{false}$$
$$k ::= k_0 \mid k_1 \ldots$$

$$P ::= \langle p : e \rangle \mid P :: P'$$
$$p ::= p \mid q \ldots$$

Fig. 3. Language definition.

$$\frac{e_0^{l_0} \hookrightarrow e_2^{l_2}}{(e_0^{l_0} \ e_1^{l_1})^l \hookrightarrow (e_2^{l_2} \ e_1^{l_1})^l} \qquad\qquad \frac{e_1^{l_1} \hookrightarrow e_2^{l_2}}{(v^{l_0} \ e_1^{l_1})^l \hookrightarrow (v^{l_0} \ e_2^{l_2})^l}$$

$$((\text{fun } x^{l_0} \Rightarrow e_1^{l_1})^{l_2} \ v^{l_3})^l \hookrightarrow e_1^{l_1}\{x \leftarrow v^{l_3}\}$$

$$(\text{rec } f^{l_0} \ x^{l_1} \Rightarrow e_2^{l_2})^l \hookrightarrow (\text{fun } x^{l_1} \Rightarrow e_2^{l_2}\{f \leftarrow (\text{rec } f^{l_0} \ x^{l_1} \Rightarrow e_2^{l_2})^l\})^l$$

$$\frac{e_0^{l_0} \hookrightarrow e_1^{l_1}}{K, P :: \langle p : E[e_0^{l_0}]\rangle \xrightarrow{[\varepsilon]} K, P :: \langle p : E[e_1^{l_1}]\rangle}$$

$$\frac{k \notin \text{dom}(K)}{K, P :: \langle p : E[(\text{channel}())^l]\rangle \xrightarrow{[\varepsilon]} K[k \mapsto l], P :: \langle p : E[k^l]\rangle}$$

$$\frac{q \notin \text{dom}(P)}{K, P :: \langle p : E[(\text{fork } e_0^{l_0})^l]\rangle \xrightarrow{[l,l]} K, P :: \langle p : E[()^l]\rangle :: \langle q : e_0^{l_0}\rangle}$$

$$K, P :: \langle p_s : E_s[(\text{send } k^{l_0} \ v^{l_1})^{l_s}]\rangle :: \langle p_r : E_r[(\text{receive } k^{l_2})^{l_r}]\rangle$$
$$\xrightarrow{[l_s, l_r]} K, P :: \langle p_s : E_s[v^{l_1}]\rangle :: \langle p_r : E_r[v^{l_1}]\rangle$$

Fig. 4. Language semantics.

The operational semantics, given in Figure 4, are based on the language λ_{cv} defined by Reppy [20]. $\hookrightarrow$ is used for sequential reduction steps. $e_0^{l_0}\{x \leftarrow e_1^{l_1}\}$ denotes the term obtained by discarding the labels of the occurrences of x in $e_0^{l_0}$ and substituting $e_1^{l_1}$ to x.

$\xrightarrow{[\ell]}$ is used for concurrent reduction steps. These steps are annotated with labels $\ell \in \text{Lab}^2 \cup \{\varepsilon\}$ which only are used in order to prove the correctness of the analysis. An ε-labeled step corresponds to a sequential reduction step made by one of the processes in the pool. The transition related to a communication between two instructions labeled l_s and l_r is annotated l_s, l_r and the reduction step related to a process creation is annotated l_f, l_f where l_f is the label of the fork. Following Reppy [20], we use evaluation contexts E defined in Figure 3.

In addition, we use the classical notion of *configuration* K, P to denote a concurrent system in Concurrent ML. K is the environment for channels and P, the *process pool*, is defined in Figure 3.

A process is defined by $\langle p : e^l \rangle$, p being the name associated to the process which computes e^l. In Figure 3, $\xrightarrow{[c]}$ is defined over process pools. Inside a process, a sequential reduction step is done using $\hookrightarrow$.

For the instruction $(\mathtt{channel}())^l$, a new channel name k is assigned to the expression and the set K of used channel names is enriched with k. When an expression is forked, the father evaluates to $()$ and the new process is named q, where q is a fresh process name. Finally, a communication may occur between an emitting process p_s and a receiving process p_r which use the same channel. In this case, both p_s and p_r evaluate to the value exchanged.

4   Analysis of the Sequential Expressions

In this Section, we introduce the basic analysis within a sequential process. Section 5 presents the analysis between processes. Note that there are not separable analyses, because the interactions between processes affect the control-flow analysis of the individual processes. If e^l contains $\mathtt{fork}$'s, the bodies of the child processes are analyzed at the same time as e^l, but not their interactions whose analysis is deferred to Section 5.

The analysis of an expression e^l is a triple $(\widehat{\mathcal{C}}, \widehat{\mathcal{E}}, \widehat{\mathcal{A}})$. Let Lab and Id respectively denote the sets of labels and variables occurring in e^l. $\widehat{\mathcal{C}}$, $\widehat{\mathcal{E}}$ and $\widehat{\mathcal{A}}$ are defined as follows.

- $\widehat{\mathcal{C}}$: Lab $\to \wp(\text{Lab})$ is the abstract cache which approximates, for any subexpression e^l in the program, the set $\widehat{\mathcal{C}}(l)$ of values e^l may evaluate to. The abstract values either are functions denoted by their labels or channel names denoted by the label of the instruction $\mathtt{channel}()$ which created them. Type discipline ensures that no confusion is made between both kinds of values and avoids the introduction of two different caches.
- $\widehat{\mathcal{E}}$: Id $\to \wp(\text{Lab})$ is the abstract environment which binds free variables during the analysis.
- $\widehat{\mathcal{A}} = (\Sigma, \mathtt{B}, Q, Q_f, \delta)$ is a finite automaton which indicates how the synchronizations are ordered inside the expression we analyze. $\Sigma = \text{Lab} \cup \{\varepsilon, \mu\}$ is the alphabet, Q is the set of state, $\mathtt{B} \in Q$ is the initial state, $Q_f = \{\mathtt{E}\} \subseteq Q$ contains a unique final state. $\delta \in (Q \times \Sigma) \to \wp(Q)$ is the transition function.

In Figure 5, we define inductively on the structure of the terms the constraints a triple $(\widehat{\mathcal{C}}, \widehat{\mathcal{E}}, \widehat{\mathcal{A}})$ has to satisfy in order to define a correct analysis for an expression e^l. If so, we write $\widehat{\mathcal{C}}, \widehat{\mathcal{E}}, \widehat{\mathcal{A}} \vdash e^l$.

We use the following notations. $[\![\mathtt{s} \xrightarrow{\ell} \mathtt{s}']\!]$ denotes an automaton whose initial and final state respectively are $\mathtt{s}$ and $\mathtt{s}'$ and such that $Q = \{\mathtt{s}, \mathtt{s}'\}$ and $\mathtt{s}' \in \delta(\mathtt{s}, \ell)$.

$$\widehat{C}, \widehat{\mathcal{E}}, \widehat{A} \vdash c^l \Leftrightarrow [\![\mathrm{B}_l \xrightarrow{\varepsilon} \mathrm{E}_l]\!] \sqsubseteq \widehat{A} \qquad \widehat{C}, \widehat{\mathcal{E}}, \widehat{A} \vdash x^l \Leftrightarrow \widehat{\mathcal{E}}(x) \subseteq \widehat{C}(l),\ [\![\mathrm{B}_l \xrightarrow{\varepsilon} \mathrm{E}_l]\!] \sqsubseteq \widehat{A}$$

$$\widehat{C}, \widehat{\mathcal{E}}, \widehat{A} \vdash (\texttt{fun } x^{l_1} \texttt{ => } e_0^{l_0})^l \Leftrightarrow \begin{cases} l \in \widehat{C}(l),\ \widehat{C}, \widehat{\mathcal{E}}[x \mapsto \widehat{C}(l_1)], \widehat{A}_0 \vdash e_0^{l_0},\ \widehat{A}_0 \sqsubseteq \widehat{A} \\ [\![\mathrm{B}_l \xrightarrow{\varepsilon} \mathrm{E}_l]\!] \sqsubseteq \widehat{A},\ [\![\mathrm{B}_l \xrightarrow{\mu} \mathrm{B}_{l_0}]\!] \sqsubseteq \widehat{A},\ [\![\mathrm{E}_{l_0} \xrightarrow{\mu} \mathrm{E}_l]\!] \sqsubseteq \widehat{A} \end{cases}$$

$$\widehat{C}, \widehat{\mathcal{E}}, \widehat{A} \vdash (\texttt{rec } f^{l_1}\ x^{l_2} \texttt{ => } e_0^{l_0})^l \Leftrightarrow \begin{cases} l \in \widehat{C}(l),\ \widehat{C}(l) \subseteq \widehat{C}(l_1),\ \widehat{A}_0 \sqsubseteq \widehat{A} \\ \widehat{C}, \widehat{\mathcal{E}}[f \mapsto \widehat{C}(l_1)][x \mapsto \widehat{C}(l_2)], \widehat{A}_0 \vdash e_0^{l_0} \\ [\![\mathrm{B}_l \xrightarrow{\varepsilon} \mathrm{E}_l]\!] \sqsubseteq \widehat{A},\ [\![\mathrm{B}_l \xrightarrow{\mu} \mathrm{B}_{l_0}]\!] \sqsubseteq \widehat{A},\ [\![\mathrm{E}_{l_0} \xrightarrow{\mu} \mathrm{E}_l]\!] \sqsubseteq \widehat{A} \end{cases}$$

$$\widehat{C}, \widehat{\mathcal{E}}, \widehat{A} \vdash (e_0^{l_0}\ e_1^{l_1})^l \Leftrightarrow \begin{cases} \widehat{C}, \widehat{\mathcal{E}}, \widehat{A}_0 \vdash e_0^{l_0},\ \widehat{C}, \widehat{\mathcal{E}}, \widehat{A}_1 \vdash e_1^{l_1} \\ \widehat{A}_0 \sqsubseteq \widehat{A},\ \widehat{A}_1 \sqsubseteq \widehat{A},\ [\![\mathrm{B}_l \xrightarrow{\varepsilon} \mathrm{B}_{l_0}]\!] \sqsubseteq \widehat{A},\ [\![\mathrm{E}_{l_0} \xrightarrow{\varepsilon} \mathrm{B}_{l_1}]\!] \sqsubseteq \widehat{A} \\ \forall l_2 \in \widehat{C}(l_0)\ :\ (\texttt{fun } x^{l_4} \texttt{ => } e_3^{l_3})^{l_2} \in \mathrm{prg}, \\ \widehat{C}(l_1) \subseteq \widehat{C}(l_4),\ \widehat{C}(l_3) \subseteq \widehat{C}(l),\ [\![\mathrm{E}_{l_1} \xrightarrow{\varepsilon} \mathrm{B}_{l_3}]\!] \sqsubseteq \widehat{A}, [\![\mathrm{E}_{l_3} \xrightarrow{\varepsilon} \mathrm{E}_l]\!] \sqsubseteq \widehat{A} \\ \forall l_2 \in \widehat{C}(l_0)\ :\ (\texttt{rec } f^{l_4}\ x^{l_5} \texttt{ => } e_3^{l_3})^{l_2} \in \mathrm{prg}, \\ \widehat{C}(l_1) \subseteq \widehat{C}(l_5),\ \widehat{C}(l_3) \subseteq \widehat{C}(l) \\ [\![\mathrm{E}_{l_1} \xrightarrow{\varepsilon} \mathrm{B}_{l_3}]\!] \sqsubseteq \widehat{A},\ [\![\mathrm{E}_{l_3} \xrightarrow{\varepsilon} \mathrm{E}_l]\!] \sqsubseteq \widehat{A} \\ [\![\mathrm{E}_{l_1} \xrightarrow{\varepsilon} \mathrm{E}_l]\!] \sqsubseteq \widehat{A},\ [\![\mathrm{E}_{l_3} \xrightarrow{\varepsilon} \mathrm{B}_{l_3}]\!] \sqsubseteq \widehat{A} \end{cases}$$

$$\widehat{C}, \widehat{\mathcal{E}}, \widehat{A} \vdash \texttt{channel}()^l \Leftrightarrow l \in \widehat{C}(l),\ [\![\mathrm{B}_l \xrightarrow{\varepsilon} \mathrm{E}_l]\!] \sqsubseteq \widehat{A}$$

$$\widehat{C}, \widehat{\mathcal{E}}, \widehat{A} \vdash k^l \Leftrightarrow l \in \widehat{C}(l),\ [\![\mathrm{B}_l \xrightarrow{\varepsilon} \mathrm{E}_l]\!] \sqsubseteq \widehat{A}$$

$$\widehat{C}, \widehat{\mathcal{E}}, \widehat{A} \vdash (\texttt{fork } e_0^{l_0})^l \Leftrightarrow \widehat{C}, \widehat{\mathcal{E}}, \widehat{A}_0 \vdash e_0^{l_0},\ [\![\mathrm{B}_l \xrightarrow{l} \mathrm{E}_l]\!] \sqsubseteq \widehat{A},\ \widehat{A}_0 \sqsubseteq \widehat{A},\ [\![\mathrm{B}_l \xrightarrow{l} \mathrm{B}_{l_0}]\!] \sqsubseteq \widehat{A}$$

$$\widehat{C}, \widehat{\mathcal{E}}, \widehat{A} \vdash (\texttt{send } e_0^{l_0}\ e_1^{l_1})^l \Leftrightarrow \begin{cases} \widehat{C}, \widehat{\mathcal{E}}, \widehat{A}_0 \vdash e_0^{l_0},\ \widehat{C}, \widehat{\mathcal{E}}, \widehat{A}_1 \vdash e_1^{l_1},\ \widehat{C}(l_1) \subseteq \widehat{C}(l) \\ \widehat{A}_0 \sqsubseteq \widehat{A},\ \widehat{A}_1 \sqsubseteq \widehat{A},\ [\![\mathrm{B}_l \xrightarrow{\varepsilon} \mathrm{B}_{l_0}]\!] \sqsubseteq \widehat{A} \\ [\![\mathrm{E}_{l_0} \xrightarrow{\varepsilon} \mathrm{B}_{l_1}]\!] \sqsubseteq \widehat{A},\ [\![\mathrm{E}_{l_1} \xrightarrow{l} \mathrm{E}_l]\!] \sqsubseteq \widehat{A} \end{cases}$$

$$\widehat{C}, \widehat{\mathcal{E}}, \widehat{A} \vdash (\texttt{receive } e_0^{l_0})^l \Leftrightarrow \begin{cases} \widehat{C}, \widehat{\mathcal{E}}, \widehat{A}_0 \vdash e_0^{l_0} \\ \widehat{A}_0 \sqsubseteq \widehat{A},\ [\![\mathrm{B}_l \xrightarrow{\varepsilon} \mathrm{B}_{l_0}]\!] \sqsubseteq \widehat{A},\ [\![\mathrm{E}_{l_0} \xrightarrow{l} \mathrm{E}_l]\!] \sqsubseteq \widehat{A} \end{cases}$$

Fig. 5. Specification of the analysis.

$\widehat{A} \sqsubseteq \widehat{A}'$ states that $\widehat{A}$ is a sub-automaton of $\widehat{A}'$, i.e. $Q \subseteq Q'$ and $\delta \subseteq \delta'$. Hence, $[\![\mathrm{s} \xrightarrow{\ell} \mathrm{s}']\!] \sqsubseteq \widehat{A}$ indicates that there is a ℓ-transition from s to s' in $\widehat{A}$. The analysis builds for each expression e^l an automaton $\widehat{A}$ which initial and final states respectively are $\mathrm{Start}(\widehat{A}) = \mathrm{B}_l$ and $\mathrm{End}(\widehat{A}) = \{\mathrm{E}_l\}$. These automata are defined inductively on the structure of the terms. Their graphical representation is given in Figure 6. ε-transitions denote sequential reduction steps.

Because the evaluation of a first order constant c^l does not involve any synchronization, the automaton associated to this expression is made of an ε-transition from the initial state B_l to the final state E_l, as shown in Figure 6. This is ensured by the constraint $[\![\mathrm{B}_l \xrightarrow{\varepsilon} \mathrm{E}_l]\!] \sqsubseteq \widehat{A}$ in the specification of Figure 5.

For a variable x^l, $\widehat{\mathcal{E}}(x)$ is added to $\widehat{C}(l)$ indicating that the abstract value of point l depends on the abstract value of x in the environment. In addition,

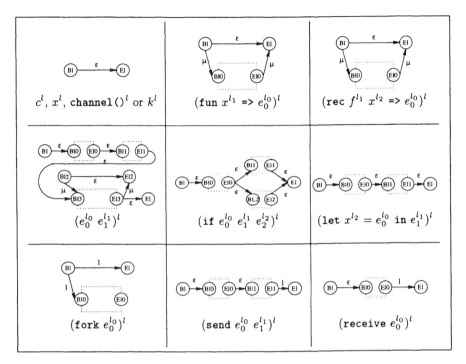

Fig. 6. Automata attached to the expressions during the analysis.

because no reduction may come from the evaluation of a variable, the automaton related to x^l is made of an ε-transition between the states B_l and E_l. Again, this is ensured by the constraint $[\![B_l \xrightarrow{\varepsilon} E_l]\!] \sqsubseteq \widehat{\mathcal{A}}$.

(fun x^{l_1} => $e_0^{l_0}$)^l and (rec f x^{l_1} => $e_0^{l_0}$)^l are values. Their evaluation does not require any computation. Hence, just like for first order constants, the initial state B_l of the automaton is linked to the final state E_l by an ε-transition. In addition, the body $e_0^{l_0}$ is analyzed, yielding an automaton $\widehat{\mathcal{A}}_0$ with B_{l_0} and E_{l_0} as initial and final states. As depicted in Figure 6, we connect $\widehat{\mathcal{A}}_0$ to $\widehat{\mathcal{A}}$ by a μ-transitions *via* the constraints $[\![B_l \xrightarrow{\mu} B_{l_0}]\!] \sqsubseteq \widehat{\mathcal{A}}$ and $[\![E_{l_0} \xrightarrow{\mu} E_l]\!] \sqsubseteq \widehat{\mathcal{A}}$. μ-transitions only are used to link both parts of the automaton and never describe a valid path between nodes. Concerning the abstract cache, l is added to $\widehat{\mathcal{C}}(l)$, indicating that the current function is among the ones which may occur at this point.

The analysis of an application $(e_0^{l_0} \ e_1^{l_1})^l$ first relies on these of $e_0^{l_0}$ and $e_1^{l_1}$ which yield two automata $\widehat{\mathcal{A}}_0$ and $\widehat{\mathcal{A}}_1$. Because of the evaluation order, the synchronizations made by $e_0^{l_0}$ precede the ones made by $e_1^{l_1}$. Also, assuming that $e_0^{l_0}$ evaluates to (fun x^{l_4} => $e_3^{l_3}$)^{l_2}, the synchronizations made by $e_1^{l_1}$ precede the ones resulting from the evaluation of $e_3^{l_3}$ with the right value for x. Hence we build the following automaton. B_l is linked to the initial state of $\widehat{\mathcal{A}}_0$ and $\widehat{\mathcal{A}}_0$'s final state is linked to $\widehat{\mathcal{A}}_1$ initial state by ε-transitions. This corresponds to the constraints $\widehat{\mathcal{A}}_0 \sqsubseteq \widehat{\mathcal{A}}$, $\widehat{\mathcal{A}}_1 \sqsubseteq \widehat{\mathcal{A}}$, $[\![B_l \xrightarrow{\varepsilon} B_{l_0}]\!] \sqsubseteq \widehat{\mathcal{A}}$ and $[\![E_{l_0} \xrightarrow{\varepsilon} B_{l_1}]\!] \sqsubseteq \widehat{\mathcal{A}}$.

Next, $\widehat{\mathcal{C}}(l_0)$ denotes the labels of the functions $e_0^{l_0}$ may evaluate to. For each function $(\mathtt{fun}\ x^{l_4}\ \Rightarrow\ e_3^{l_3})^{l_2}$ such that $l_2 \in \widehat{\mathcal{C}}(l_0)$, we indicate that the synchronizations in the body $e_3^{l_3}$ follow these in $e_1^{l_1}$ by asking $[\![\mathrm{E}_{l_1} \xrightarrow{\varepsilon} \mathrm{B}_{l_3}]\!] \sqsubseteq \widehat{\mathcal{A}}$. Finally, the final states of e^l and $e_3^{l_3}$ are linked by $[\![\mathrm{E}_{l_3} \xrightarrow{\varepsilon} \mathrm{E}_l]\!] \sqsubseteq \widehat{\mathcal{A}}$. prg denotes the program for which we compute an analysis. In Figure 6 we show the automaton resulting from the analysis of an expression $(e_0^{l_0}\ e_1^{l_1})^l$, assuming that $\widehat{\mathcal{C}}(l_0) = \{l_2\}$ and that $(\mathtt{fun}\ x^{l_4}\ \Rightarrow\ e_3^{l_3})^{l_2} \in \mathrm{prg}$.

The application of a recursive function is analyzed similarly. Because the body may be executed zero or many times, we add $[\![\mathrm{B}_l \xrightarrow{\varepsilon} \mathrm{E}_l]\!] \sqsubseteq \widehat{\mathcal{A}}$ and $[\![\mathrm{E}_{l_4} \xrightarrow{\varepsilon} \mathrm{B}_{l_4}]\!] \sqsubseteq \widehat{\mathcal{A}}$, where l_4 is the label of the body of the recursive function.

Channels are identified by their creation points. $\mathtt{channel()}$ being a function call, for an occurrence of $\mathtt{channel()}^l$ in the program, we collect l in $\widehat{\mathcal{C}}(l)$. So, no distinction is made between different channels created in a recursive function.

For an expression $(\mathtt{fork}\ e_0^{l_0})^l$, we only analyze the body $e_0^{l_0}$ of the child process at this stage of the analysis, obtaining an automaton $\widehat{\mathcal{A}}_0$. In Section 5, during the analysis of the interactions between processes, we consider $\mathtt{fork}$'s just like another communications. For now, $[\![\mathrm{B}_l \xrightarrow{l} \mathrm{E}_l]\!] \sqsubseteq \widehat{\mathcal{A}}$ indicates that the execution of the $\mathtt{fork}$ consists of doing a synchronization denoted l. On the other hand, the automaton $\widehat{\mathcal{A}}_0$ which describes the synchronizations realized by $e_0^{l_0}$ is included in $\widehat{\mathcal{A}}$ and linked to the initial state B_l of the expression we analyze by $[\![\mathrm{B}_l \xrightarrow{l} \mathrm{B}_{l_0}]\!] \sqsubseteq \widehat{\mathcal{A}}$. In Section 5.2, when considering the product automaton, $e_0^{l_0}$ stays frozen until it can synchronize on l with the $\mathtt{fork}$.

The specification of the analysis for an emission $(\mathtt{send}\ e_0^{l_0}\ e_1^{l_1})^l$ states that the sub-expressions are analyzed. $[\![\mathrm{E}_{l_0} \xrightarrow{\varepsilon} \mathrm{E}_{l_1}]\!] \sqsubseteq \widehat{\mathcal{A}}$ indicates that the execution of $e_0^{l_0}$ precedes the one of $e_1^{l_1}$ and $[\![\mathrm{E}_{l_1} \xrightarrow{l} \mathrm{E}_l]\!] \sqsubseteq \widehat{\mathcal{A}}$ states that l denotes the last synchronization point in $(\mathtt{send}\ e_0^{l_0}\ e_1^{l_1})^l$.

Receptions are treated similarly. $[\![\mathrm{E}_{l_0} \xrightarrow{l} \mathrm{E}_l]\!] \sqsubseteq \widehat{\mathcal{A}}$ states that the synchronizations in the sub-expression precede the synchronization related to the reception. Note that no constraint is introduced on the received abstract value at this stage of the analysis. This is due to the fact that $\widehat{\mathcal{C}}, \widehat{\mathcal{E}}, \widehat{\mathcal{A}} \vdash e^l$ only specifies the analysis of the different processes without considering their synchronizations. However, in a concurrent execution, a reception $(\mathtt{receive}\ e_0^{l_0})^l$ may receive either a basic value or a function or a name, depending on its type. Hence, in Sections 5.1 and 5.2, when considering process interactions, we introduce constraints indicating how $\widehat{\mathcal{C}}(l)$ is bound to. These constraints are specified in definitions 4 and 8.

As an intermediary result, we introduce some properties satisfied by the analysis defined in Figure 5. First we examine the existence of a best analysis for an expression e^l and, second, we focus on correctness. These results are used further in this article, when proving the main property concerning the correctness of the specification over concurrent reduction.

Let $(\widehat{\mathcal{C}}_1, \widehat{\mathcal{E}}_1, \widehat{\mathcal{A}}_1)$ and $(\widehat{\mathcal{C}}_2, \widehat{\mathcal{E}}_2, \widehat{\mathcal{A}}_2)$ be two analyses for the same expression e^l. $(\widehat{\mathcal{C}}_1, \widehat{\mathcal{E}}_1, \widehat{\mathcal{A}}_1) \prec (\widehat{\mathcal{C}}_2, \widehat{\mathcal{E}}_2, \widehat{\mathcal{A}}_2)$ denotes that $(\widehat{\mathcal{C}}_1, \widehat{\mathcal{E}}_1, \widehat{\mathcal{A}}_1)$ is more precise than

$(\widehat{C}_2, \widehat{\mathcal{E}}_2, \widehat{A}_2)$. $\prec$ is defined by

$$(\widehat{C}_1, \widehat{\mathcal{E}}_1, \widehat{A}_1) \prec (\widehat{C}_2, \widehat{\mathcal{E}}_2, \widehat{A}_2) \Leftrightarrow \begin{cases} \forall l \in \text{Lab}, \ \widehat{C}_1(l) \subseteq \widehat{C}_2(l) \\ \forall x \in \text{Id}, \ \widehat{\mathcal{E}}_1(x) \subseteq \widehat{\mathcal{E}}_2(x) \\ \widehat{A}_1 \sqsubseteq \widehat{A}_2 \end{cases} \tag{2}$$

The existence of a least analysis in the sense of $\prec$ stems from the fact that, for an expression e^l, the set $\{(\widehat{C}, \widehat{\mathcal{E}}, \widehat{A}) \ : \ \widehat{C}, \widehat{\mathcal{E}}, \widehat{A} \vdash e^l\}$ is a Moore family[1].

The main property introduced in this Section concerns sequential subject reduction and indicates that if a triple $(\widehat{C}, \widehat{\mathcal{E}}, \widehat{A})$ is a correct analysis for an expression e^l then it is still correct after a sequential reduction step $\hookrightarrow$ (Section 3). First, we introduce the order relation $<$ over automata.

Definition 1 *Let $\widehat{A}$ and $\widehat{A}'$ be two automata. $\widehat{A} < \widehat{A}'$ iff any path labeled $\ell_1 \dots \ell_n$ in $\widehat{A}$ is a path in $\widehat{A}'$.*

Intuitively, the labels of the transitions in an automaton $\widehat{A}$ built during the analysis of an expression e^l correspond to the synchronizations realized during the execution of e^l. Hence, a path in $\widehat{A}$ denotes one possible sequence of synchronizations the execution of e^l may lead to. Sequential reduction steps do not realize synchronizations but may discard some possible sequences of synchronizations. For instance, consider the execution of a conditional. Hence, if $e^l \hookrightarrow e'^{l'}$ then any possible sequence of communication in $e'^{l'}$ is a sequence of communication in e^l. Considering the automata $\widehat{A}$ and $\widehat{A}'$ built during the analysis for e^l and $e'^{l'}$, we have $\widehat{A}' < \widehat{A}$. This is summed up by the proposition below.

Proposition 2 (Sequential subject reduction) *If $\widehat{C}, \widehat{\mathcal{E}}, \widehat{A} \vdash e^l$ and $e^l \hookrightarrow e'^{l'}$ then $\widehat{C}, \widehat{\mathcal{E}}, \widehat{A}' \vdash e'^{l'}$ for some $\widehat{A}'$ such that $\widehat{A}' < \widehat{A}$.*

Analyzing separately the processes of an application allows us to order the synchronization points on each process. However this is not enough to obtain a fine approximation of the topology of communications. In the following Section, we consider the product automaton of the automata described above in order to compute the synchronization realized by the program.

5 Process Pool Analysis

In this Section, we focus on analyzing a process pool. Section 5.1 defines an analysis $\models^\natural$ based on the product automaton $A_\otimes^\natural(\widehat{S})$ of a collection $\widehat{S}$ of automata built as in Section 4. We prove the correctness of $\models^\natural$ by a subject reduction property. In Section 5.2, we introduce a second analysis $\models^\sharp$ based on a reduced product automaton $A_\otimes^\sharp(\widehat{S})$ which size is polynomial in the size of the original program. We prove that $\models^\sharp$ is a correct approximation of $\models^\natural$.

---

[1] A subset X of a complete lattice $(L, \le)$ is a Moore family iff for all set $Y \subseteq X$, $(\sqcap Y) \in X$. Notice that a Moore family X never is empty and admits a least element since $(\sqcap X) \in X$ (see [19]).

5.1   Product Automaton Based Analysis

Let $\widehat{S} = (\widehat{A}_p)_{p\in\text{Dom}(P)}$ be a collection of automata. The states in the product automaton $A_\otimes^\natural(\widehat{S})$ are products of the states of the automata in $\widehat{S}$. An ε-transition inside an automaton $\widehat{A}_p$ denotes a sequential reduction step and is transcribed in $A_\otimes^\natural(\widehat{S})$. An l-transition in $\widehat{A}_p$ denotes a synchronization point. We add (l, l')-transitions in $A_\otimes^\natural(\widehat{S})$ if l and l' are transitions in two automata of $\widehat{S}$ such that the instruction labeled l may synchronize with the instruction labeled l'.

Definition 3 (Product automaton) *Let $\widehat{S}$ be a collection of n automata. The product automaton $A_\otimes^\natural(\widehat{S})$ of the automata in $\widehat{S}$ is a tuple $(\Sigma^\natural, q_0^\natural, Q^\natural, \delta^\natural)$. The alphabet is $\Sigma^\natural \subseteq Lab^2 \cup \{\varepsilon, \mu\}$. $Q^\natural$ is made of k-tuples $(s_1, \ldots, s_k)$ in which s_i, $1 \leq i \leq k$, denotes the advancement of the ith automaton. $q_0^\natural$ is the initial state and $\delta^\natural \in (Q^\natural \times \Sigma^\natural) \to \wp(Q^\natural)$ is the transition function. $A_\otimes^\natural(\widehat{S})$ is built as follows.*

(i) *The initial state $q_0^\natural \in Q^\natural$ is the product of the initial states $Start(\widehat{A}_p)$ of the automata $\widehat{A}_p \in \widehat{S}$, i.e.*

$$q_0^\natural \overset{def}{=} \bigotimes_{\widehat{A}_p \in \widehat{S}} Start(\widehat{A}_p) \tag{3}$$

(ii) *For all $q^\natural \in Q^\natural$ such that $q^\natural = (s_0, \ldots, s_n)$,*

a) $\forall i, 1 \leq i \leq n, \forall \ell \in \{\varepsilon, \mu\},$
$$\left| \begin{array}{l} (\exists \widehat{A}_p \in \widehat{S} : [\![s_i \overset{\ell}{\to} s_i']\!] \sqsubseteq \widehat{A}_p) \Rightarrow \\ [\![q^\natural \overset{\ell}{\to} (s_1, \ldots, s_i', \ldots, s_n)]\!] \sqsubseteq A_\otimes^\natural(\widehat{S}) \end{array} \right.$$

b) $\forall i, j, 1 \leq i \neq j \leq n,$

$$\left(\exists \widehat{A}_p, \widehat{A}_{p'} \in \widehat{S} : \left| \begin{array}{l} [\![s_i \overset{l_s}{\to} s_{l_s}]\!] \sqsubseteq \widehat{A}_p \\ [\![s_j \overset{l_r}{\to} s_{l_r}]\!] \sqsubseteq \widehat{A}_{p'} \\ (\textbf{send } e_0^{l_0}\, e_1^{l_1})^{l_s} \in prg \\ (\textbf{receive } e_2^{l_2})^{l_r} \in prg \end{array} \right. \right)$$
$$\Rightarrow [\![q^\natural \overset{l_s, l_r}{\to} (s_1, \ldots, s_{l_s}, \ldots, s_{l_r}, \ldots, s_n)]\!] \sqsubseteq A_\otimes^\natural(\widehat{S}) \tag{4}$$

c)

$$\forall i, 1 \leq i \leq n, \left| \begin{array}{l} \left(\exists \widehat{A}_p \in \widehat{S} : \left| \begin{array}{l} [\![s_i \overset{l_f}{\to} s_{l_f}]\!] \sqsubseteq \widehat{A}_p \\ [\![s_i \overset{l_f}{\to} s_{l_0}]\!] \sqsubseteq \widehat{A}_p \\ (\textbf{fork } e_0^{l_0})^{l_f} \in prg \end{array} \right. \right) \\ \Rightarrow [\![q^\natural \overset{l_f, l_f}{\to} (s_1, \ldots, s_{l_f}, \ldots, s_n, s_{l_0})]\!] \sqsubseteq A_\otimes^\natural(\widehat{S}) \end{array} \right. \tag{5}$$

The product automaton is built incrementally. We start with the only state $q_0^\natural$ and any state $q^\natural = (s_1, \ldots, s_k)$ in $A_\otimes^\natural(\widehat{S})$ describes one of the possible advancements of the process pool. We add an ε-transition going out of $q^\natural$ every-time there is an ε-transition in one of the automata $\widehat{A}_p$ going out of s_i, $1 \leq i \leq k$. Doing so, we obtain a new state which also denotes one of the possible advancements.

Next, an l-transition denotes a synchronization point. Two processes may communicate together if they own matching synchronization points l_s and l_r related to an emission and a reception and which possibly are active at the same time. In this case there is a state $q^\natural = (s_1, \ldots, s_k)$ and two automata $\widehat{\mathcal{A}}_p$ and $\widehat{\mathcal{A}}_{p'}$ in $\widehat{\mathcal{S}}$ such that $[\![s_s \xrightarrow{l_s} s'_s]\!] \sqsubseteq \widehat{\mathcal{A}}_p$ and $[\![s_r \xrightarrow{l_r} s'_r]\!] \sqsubseteq \widehat{\mathcal{A}}_{p'}$, $1 \leq s, r \leq k$, $s \neq r$. Then the transition $q^\natural \xrightarrow{l_s, l_r} q^{\natural'}$ is added to the product automaton where $q^{\natural'}$ is a new state obtained by substituting s'_s and s'_r to s_s and s_r in $q^\natural$.

Notice that the product automaton allows a communication between any emitter s and any receptor r which possibly are active at the same time, independently of the channel they use. In Definition 4, the abstract value sent by s is added to the abstract value attached to r iff s and r possibly communicate on the same channel. Greater precision would be obtained by directly discarding these impossible communications in $\mathbb{A}_\otimes^\natural(\widehat{\mathcal{S}})$. However, the product automaton would not be defined independently of the analysis, overloading the notations.

Finally, a **fork** creates a new process. Hence, for any transition $[\![s_i \xrightarrow{l_f} s_{l_f}]\!] \sqsubseteq \widehat{\mathcal{A}}_p$ such that there exists a state $q^\natural = (s_1, \ldots, s_i, \ldots, s_k)$ in $Q^\natural$, the $(k+1)$ product state $(s_1, \ldots, s_{l_f}, \ldots, s_k, s_{l_0})$ is added to $Q^\natural$. This tuple denotes the state resulting from the execution of the **fork**. It contains one more component s_{l_0} which describes the advancement of the new process. Concerning the father process, the state denoting its advancement is updated to indicate that the process creation is done.

In the remainder of this Section, we specify the conditions a triple $(\widehat{\mathcal{C}}, \widehat{\mathcal{E}}, \widehat{\mathcal{A}}_\otimes^\natural)$ has to satisfy to be an analysis for a process pool P and we prove the correctness of this analysis. $\widehat{\mathcal{C}}$ and $\widehat{\mathcal{E}}$ are defined in the same way as in Section 4 and $\widehat{\mathcal{A}}_\otimes^\natural$ is the product of the automata $\widehat{\mathcal{A}}_p$ built for the sequential expressions of P. Also, we introduce a new order relation extending $\prec$ to deal with the way the product automata are related under concurrent reduction.

$\widehat{\mathcal{C}}, \widehat{\mathcal{E}}, \widehat{\mathcal{A}}_\otimes^\natural \models^\natural P$ denotes that the triple $(\widehat{\mathcal{C}}, \widehat{\mathcal{E}}, \widehat{\mathcal{A}}_\otimes^\natural)$ is an analysis for the process pool P, where $\models^\natural$ is specified in Definition 4. Intuitively, we require that all the expressions in the process pool are correctly abstracted using the automaton $\widehat{\mathcal{A}}_\otimes^\natural$ and that for any communication described in $\widehat{\mathcal{A}}_\otimes^\natural$, the abstract value sent by the emitter is contained in the abstract value attached to the receptor.

Definition 4 *A triple $(\widehat{\mathcal{C}}, \widehat{\mathcal{E}}, \widehat{\mathcal{A}}_\otimes^\natural)$ defines good annotations for a process pool P, denoted $\widehat{\mathcal{C}}, \widehat{\mathcal{E}}, \widehat{\mathcal{A}}_\otimes^\natural \models^\natural P$ iff*

(i) $\widehat{\mathcal{A}}_\otimes^\natural = \mathbb{A}_\otimes^\natural(\widehat{\mathcal{S}})$ for some collection $\widehat{\mathcal{S}}$ of automata such that $\widehat{\mathcal{S}} = (\widehat{\mathcal{A}}_p)_{p \in Dom(P)}$ and $\widehat{\mathcal{C}}, \widehat{\mathcal{E}}, \widehat{\mathcal{A}}_p \vdash e^l$ for all $\langle p : e^l \rangle \in P$.

(ii) For all $[\![q \xrightarrow{l_s, l_r} q']\!] \sqsubseteq \widehat{\mathcal{A}}_\otimes^\natural$ s.t. $\begin{cases} (\textbf{send } e_0^{l_0} \ e_1^{l_1})^{l'_i} \in prg \\ (\textbf{receive } e_2^{l_2})^{l'_j} \in prg \end{cases}$, $\widehat{\mathcal{C}}(l_0) \cap \widehat{\mathcal{C}}(l_2) \neq \varnothing$

implies $\widehat{\mathcal{C}}(l_1) \subseteq \widehat{\mathcal{C}}(l_r)$.

As stated in Section 4, the abstract cache $\widehat{\mathcal{C}}$ indifferently is used to collect abstract values denoting either channels or functions. In Definition 4, $e_0^{l_0}$ and $e_2^{l_2}$

have type Channel and consequently the condition $\widehat{\mathcal{C}}(l_0) \cap \widehat{\mathcal{C}}(l_2) \neq \varnothing$ considers abstract values related to channels in order to determine whether the emitter and the receptor may communicate. If so, the constraint $\widehat{\mathcal{C}}(l_1) \subseteq \widehat{\mathcal{C}}(l_r)$ involves abstract values denoting channels or functions, depending on the type of $e_1^{l_1}$.

Similarly to Section 4, the existence of a least analysis for a process pool P stems from the fact that the set $\{(\widehat{\mathcal{C}}, \widehat{\mathcal{E}}, \widehat{\mathcal{A}}_\otimes^\natural) \;:\; \widehat{\mathcal{C}}, \widehat{\mathcal{E}}, \widehat{\mathcal{A}}_\otimes^\natural \models^\natural P\}$ of correct analysis for a process pool P is a Moore family w.r.t. the relation $\prec$ of Equation (2).

In order to prove that an analysis is preserved under reduction, we introduce a new order relation $\overset{\ell}{<}$ which extends $<$ as follows. A path in $\widehat{\mathcal{A}}_\otimes^\natural$ describes the sequence of synchronizations realized by one possible execution of the program. This relation allows us to state that if $K, P \xrightarrow{[\ell]} K', P'$ then the product automaton $\widehat{\mathcal{A}}_\otimes^\natural{}'$ which abstracts P' contains all the paths in $\widehat{\mathcal{A}}_\otimes^\natural$ starting from $q^{\natural'}$ where $q^{\natural'}$ is a state we access from $q_0^\natural$ by an ℓ-transition. So, any sequence of synchronizations in $\widehat{\mathcal{A}}_\otimes^\natural{}'$ is a sequence of synchronization in $\widehat{\mathcal{A}}_\otimes^\natural$ following the synchronization described by ℓ.

Definition 5 *Let $\widehat{\mathcal{A}}_\otimes^\natural$ and $\widehat{\mathcal{A}}_\otimes^\natural{}'$ be two product automata and $\ell \in \Sigma$ a letter in the alphabet. $\widehat{\mathcal{A}}_\otimes^\natural \overset{\ell}{<} \widehat{\mathcal{A}}_\otimes^\natural{}'$ iff for each path labeled $\ell_1 \ldots \ell_n$ in $\widehat{\mathcal{A}}_\otimes^\natural$ there exists a path labeled $\ell.\ell_1 \ldots \ell_n$ in $\widehat{\mathcal{A}}_\otimes^\natural{}'$.*

Notice that $\widehat{\mathcal{A}}_\otimes^\natural \overset{\varepsilon}{<} \widehat{\mathcal{A}}_\otimes^\natural{}'$ iff $\widehat{\mathcal{A}}_\otimes^\natural < \widehat{\mathcal{A}}_\otimes^\natural{}'$. Finally, we introduce the following property which describes how the annotations behave under reduction.

Proposition 6 (Concurrent subject reduction) *Let P be a process pool such that $\widehat{\mathcal{C}}, \widehat{\mathcal{E}}, \widehat{\mathcal{A}}_\otimes^\natural \models^\natural P$. Then if $K, P \xrightarrow{[\ell]} K, P'$ then $\widehat{\mathcal{C}}, \widehat{\mathcal{E}}, \widehat{\mathcal{A}}_\otimes^\natural{}' \models^\natural P'$ for some product automaton $\widehat{\mathcal{A}}_\otimes^\natural{}'$ such that $\widehat{\mathcal{A}}_\otimes^\natural{}' \overset{\ell}{<} \widehat{\mathcal{A}}_\otimes^\natural$.*

5.2 Polynomial Size Analysis

In this Section, we introduce an automaton $A_\otimes^\sharp(\widehat{S})$ which is a reduced version of $A_\otimes^\natural(\widehat{S})$. While the size of the product automaton is possibly exponential in the size n of the program, $A_\otimes^\sharp(\widehat{S})$ has size $O(n^3)$. We show that $A_\otimes^\sharp(\widehat{S})$ can be used instead of $A_\otimes^\natural(\widehat{S})$ for the analysis.

Intuitively, the only relevant informations needed by the analysis are the pairs of synchronizations points which may interact together. For instance, we are interested in the set of potential emission points which may communicate with a given reception point, independently of any notion of ordering, i.e. of the place of this communication in a trace of the execution.

The product automaton $A_\otimes^\natural(\widehat{S})$ contains all the sequences of synchronizations of the whole possible executions, which is more precise than needed for our purpose. Hence, we reduce its size by discarding such irrelevant informations and still keeping enough precision to eliminate non possible synchronizations.

This compromise is obtained in $A_\otimes^\sharp(\widehat{S})$ by building an automaton able to answer to the question: "which are the possible synchronization points possibly following a given synchronization?". Let l_0 and l_1 be the labels of matching synchronization points. The state q_{l_0,l_1} denotes this synchronization in $A_\otimes^\sharp(\widehat{S})$ and the set of synchronization points following the interaction is given by $L(q_{l_0,l_1})$.

A new synchronization between points l_2 and l_3 is allowed if both l_2 and l_3 belong to $L(q_{l,l'})$ for some previous synchronization denoted by $q_{l,l'}$. In this case, we add an (l_2,l_3)-transition from $q_{l,l'}$ to q_{l_2,l_3} and $L(q_{l_2,l_3})$ is updated.

Let S denote the set of states terminating an (l_s,l_r)-transition in $A_\otimes^\sharp(\widehat{S})$. S is approximated in $A_\otimes^\sharp(\widehat{S})$ by a single state q_{l_s,l_r}. Hence, any (l_s,l_r)-transition in $A_\otimes^\sharp(\widehat{S})$ terminates in q_{l_s,l_r}. In addition, $A_\otimes^\sharp(\widehat{S})$ keeps track of the advancement of the sequential automata after the synchronization denoted by (l_s,l_r) via $L(q_{l_s,l_r})$ which contains all the nodes s such that s occurs in q for some $q \in S$.

Definition 7 (Reduced product automaton) *Let $\widehat{S}$ be a collection of n automata. The reduced product automaton $A_\otimes^\sharp(\widehat{S})$ of the automata in $\widehat{S}$ is a tuple $(\Sigma^\sharp, q_0^\sharp, Q^\sharp, \delta^\sharp, L)$. The alphabet is $\Sigma^\sharp = Lab^2$. The states belong to $Q^\sharp = \{q_{l,l'} : l,l' \in Lab\} \cup \{q_0^\sharp\}$ where $q_0^\sharp$ is a fresh initial state. $\delta^\sharp \in (Q^\sharp \times \Sigma^\sharp) \to \wp(Q^\sharp)$ is the transition function. $L : Q^\sharp \to \wp(Q_P)$, where $Q_P = \cup_{\widehat{A}_p \in \widehat{S}} State(\widehat{A}_p)$, assigns to any state $q_{l,l'}$ the possibly active states of the $\widehat{A}_p \in \widehat{S}$ once the points l and l' have synchronized together. $A_\otimes^\sharp(\widehat{S})$ is built as follows.*

(i) $q_0^\sharp \in Q^\sharp$ and $L(q_0^\sharp) = \cup_{\widehat{A}_p \in \widehat{S}} Start(\widehat{A}_p)$.

(ii) For all $q \in Q^\sharp$,

   a) $\forall s \in L(q),\ (\exists \widehat{A}_p \in \widehat{S} : [\![s \xrightarrow{\varepsilon} s']\!] \sqsubseteq \widehat{A}_p) \Rightarrow \{s'\} \subseteq L(q)$

   b) For all $s_s \in L(q),\ s_r \in L(q)$,

$$
\left(\exists \widehat{A}_p, \widehat{A}_{p'} \in \widehat{S} : \begin{cases} [\![E_{l_1} \xrightarrow{l_s} s_{l_s}]\!] \sqsubseteq \widehat{A}_p \\ [\![E_{l_2} \xrightarrow{l_r} s_{l_r}]\!] \sqsubseteq \widehat{A}_{p'} \\ (\textbf{send}\ e_0^{l_0}\ e_1^{l_1})^{l_s} \in prg \\ (\textbf{receive}\ e_2^{l_2})^{l_r} \in prg \end{cases} \right) \Rightarrow \begin{cases} [\![q \xrightarrow{l_s,l_r} q_{l_s,l_r}]\!] \sqsubseteq A_\otimes^\sharp(\widehat{S}) \\ \Lambda(q) \setminus \{E_{l_1}, E_{l_2}\} \subseteq L(q_{l_s,l_r}) \\ \{s_{l_s}, s_{l_r}\} \subseteq L(q_{l_s,l_r}) \end{cases}
$$

$$(6)$$

   c) $\forall s_f \in L(q)$,

$$
\left(\exists \widehat{A}_p \in \widehat{S} : \begin{cases} [\![B_{l_f} \xrightarrow{l_f} s_{l_f}]\!] \sqsubseteq \widehat{A}_p \\ [\![B_{l_f} \xrightarrow{l_f} s_{l_0}]\!] \sqsubseteq \widehat{A}_p \\ (\textbf{fork}\ e_0^{l_0})^{l_f} \in prg \end{cases} \right) \Rightarrow \begin{cases} [\![q \xrightarrow{l_f,l_f} q_{l_f,l_f}]\!] \sqsubseteq A_\otimes^\sharp(\widehat{S}) \\ L(q) \setminus \{B_{l_f}\} \subseteq L(s_{l_f,l_f}) \\ \{s_{l_f}, s_{l_0}\} \subseteq L(s_{l_f,l_f}) \end{cases}
$$

$$(7)$$

$A_\otimes^\sharp(\widehat{S})$ is built incrementally. We start with a fresh initial state $q_0^\sharp$. $L(q_0^\sharp)$ contains the initial states of the automata in $\widehat{S}$ indicating that the related points belong to the set of possible active points at the beginning of the execution. An ε-transition in some $\widehat{A}_p \in \widehat{S}$ denotes an internal reduction step of the process p. Hence, every time that s $\in L(q)$ and $[\![s \xrightarrow{\varepsilon} s']\!] \sqsubseteq \widehat{A}_p$ for some s $\in Q_P$ and $q \in Q^\sharp$, s' is added to $L(q)$ indicating that s' also is a possibly active point after execution of the synchronization denoted by q and before any other synchronization. This is done in (2a).

Next, consider the transitions $[\![E_{l_1} \overset{l_s}{\to} S_{l_s}]\!]$ and $[\![E_{l_2} \overset{l_r}{\to} S_{l_r}]\!]$ of two automata $\widehat{\mathcal{A}}_p$ and $\widehat{\mathcal{A}}_{p'}$. The communication is possible if E_{l_1} and E_{l_2} possibly are active at the same time, i.e. if E_{l_1} and E_{l_2} both belong to $L(q)$ for some state $q \in Q^\sharp$. If so, the transition $[\![q \overset{l_s,l_r}{\to} q_{l_s,l_r}]\!]$ is added to $A^\sharp_\otimes(\widehat{S})$ and $L(q_{l_s,l_r})$ has to contain the active points once the synchronization has been done. Hence $L(q)$ contains the points active before the synchronization except E_{l_1} and E_{l_2}, as well as the points following the communication, namely S_{l_s} and S_{l_r}. This is done in (6). forks are treated similarly in (7). A new state q_{l_f,l_f} is added to $Q^\sharp$ and $L(q_{l_f,l_f})$ is updated in the same way as for communications.

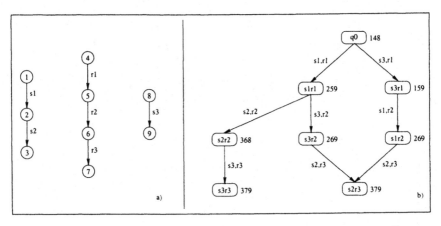

Fig. 7. a) Collection of automata for the program of Fig. 1. b) Reduced product automaton for the previous collection. Values in front of the states correspond to $L(q)$.

Figure 7 shows the reduced product automaton corresponding to the example of Figure 1. In this example, one can see that there is an exact correspondence between the states of the product automaton and the values of the function L. In this case, the reduced automaton is as precise as the product automaton and strictly described the same possible communications.

Based on $A^\sharp_\otimes(\widehat{S})$, we introduce a new analysis $\models^\sharp$ for a process pool P. Again, we used the sets $\widehat{\mathcal{C}}, \widehat{\mathcal{E}}$ defined in Section 4 as well as a reduced product automaton denoted $\widehat{\mathcal{A}}^\sharp_\otimes$. $\models^\sharp$ is obtained by substituting the reduced product automaton to the product automaton in the definition of $\models^\natural$.

Definition 8 *A triple* $(\widehat{\mathcal{C}}, \widehat{\mathcal{E}}, \widehat{\mathcal{A}}^\sharp_\otimes)$ *defines good reduced annotations for a process pool* P, *denoted* $\widehat{\mathcal{C}}, \widehat{\mathcal{E}}, \widehat{\mathcal{A}}^\sharp_\otimes \models^\sharp P$ *iff*

(i) $\widehat{\mathcal{A}}^\sharp_\otimes = A^\sharp_\otimes(\widehat{S})$ *for some collection* $\widehat{S}$ *of automata such that* $\widehat{S} = (\widehat{\mathcal{A}}_p)_{p \in Dom(P)}$ *and* $\widehat{\mathcal{C}}, \widehat{\mathcal{E}}, \widehat{\mathcal{A}}_p \vdash e^l$ *for all* $\langle p : e^l \rangle \in P$.

(ii) For all $[\![q \xrightarrow{l_s, l_r} q']\!] \sqsubseteq A^\natural_\otimes(\widehat{S})$ *s.t.* $\begin{cases} (\textbf{send } e_0^{l_0} \ e_1^{l_1})^{l_s} \in prg \\ (\textbf{receive } e_2^{l_2})^{l_r} \in prg \end{cases}$, $\widehat{C}(l_0) \cap \widehat{C}(l_2) \neq \varnothing$

implies $\widehat{C}(l_1) \subseteq \widehat{C}(l_r)$.

Again, the existence of a least analysis in the sense of $\prec$ stems from the fact that $\{(\widehat{C}, \widehat{\mathcal{E}}, \widehat{\mathcal{A}}^\natural_\otimes) \ : \ \widehat{C}, \widehat{\mathcal{E}}, \widehat{\mathcal{A}}^\natural_\otimes \models^\natural P\}$ is a Moore family.

The reduced automaton $A^\natural_\otimes(\widehat{S})$ collapses the states of the product automaton $A^\natural_\otimes(\widehat{S})$ following a given synchronization. As a consequence, any transition going out of a state $q^\natural$ in $A^\natural_\otimes(\widehat{S})$ corresponds to an outgoing transition going out of $q^\sharp$ in $A^\natural_\otimes(\widehat{S})$ where $q^\sharp$ is the state approximating $q^\natural$. Hence any path in $A^\natural_\otimes(\widehat{S})$ also is a path in $A^\natural_\otimes(\widehat{S})$. We use this observation to prove $A^\natural_\otimes(\widehat{S})$ may be substituted to $A^\natural_\otimes(\widehat{S})$. Doing so, we state that the reduced automaton contains all the sequences of synchronizations of the product automaton.

Proposition 9 (Equivalence of automata) *Let P be a process pool and $\widehat{S} = (\widehat{\mathcal{A}}_p)_{p \in Dom(P)}$ a collection of automata such that for all $\langle p : e^l \rangle \in P, \widehat{C}, \widehat{\mathcal{E}}, \widehat{\mathcal{A}}_p \vdash e^l$. We have $A^\natural_\otimes(\widehat{S}) \prec A^\sharp_\otimes(\widehat{S})$*

Hence, $\models^\sharp$ can be used instead of $\models^\natural$ without discarding the properties established in Section 5.1. So, if $\widehat{C}, \widehat{\mathcal{E}}, \widehat{\mathcal{A}}^\sharp_\otimes \models^\sharp P$ then $\widehat{C}, \widehat{\mathcal{E}}, \widehat{\mathcal{A}}^\natural_\otimes \models^\natural P$ for some $\widehat{\mathcal{A}}^\natural_\otimes$ such that $\widehat{\mathcal{A}}^\natural_\otimes \prec \widehat{\mathcal{A}}^\sharp_\otimes$. We end this Section by introducing the following property about the the size of the reduced product automaton.

Proposition 10 (Size of the reduced automaton) *Let $\widehat{S}$ be a collection of k automata of size $O(m)$ and let $n = km$. The reduced product automaton $A^\sharp_\otimes(\widehat{S})$ has size $O(n^4)$.*

Proposition 10 stems from the following observations. There is at most $O(n)$ synchronization points in the program. So, the number of state in $A^\sharp_\otimes(\widehat{S})$ is $O(n^2)$ and the transition function has size $O(n^4)$. For a given $q \in Q^\sharp$, $L(q)$ contains all the labels of the program in the worst case, i.e. $L(q)$ has size $O(n)$. Hence L has size $O(n^3)$ and the whole size of the automaton consequently is $O(n^4)$, due to the transition function.

Because of the size limitations, we do not show how to automatically compute an analysis for a process pool P. However, one can generate a set $c[P]$ of constraints such that a solution $(\widehat{C}, \widehat{\mathcal{E}}, \widehat{\mathcal{A}}_\otimes)$ to $c[P]$ satisfies $\widehat{C}, \widehat{\mathcal{E}}, \widehat{\mathcal{A}}_\otimes \models^\sharp P$. The least solution can be computed in polynomial time. One method consists of using a graph formulation of the constraints [19,25]. Each set constrained by $c[P]$ corresponds to a node in a graph G and edges are related to constraints. In this case, the complexity of the resolution of $c[P]$ for a process pool P described by a program of size $O(n)$ stems from the following observations. G contains at most $O(n^4)$ vertices and $O(n^4)$ edges. A node is examined as many times as its related value is modified. Since values have size $O(n^2)$, the whole complexity of this resolution method is $O(n^6)$.

6   Application

In this Section, we comment the results given by an implementation of the CFA. We consider a virtual circuit allocation mechanism similar this of ATM [1,26].

6.1   Virtual Circuit Allocation

Virtual circuit creation follows the scheme of Figure 8. The different nodes of the network are linked to their neighbors by control channels. These channels are used to forward a circuit creation message from the source node to the destination node. The latter creates a link with its neighbor which proceeds similarly until the source node is reached (still using control channels). Next, each intermediary node propagates the data received on its input link to its output link.

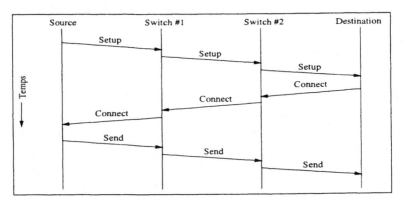

Fig. 8. Principle of virtual circuit allocation.

A full implementation of this mechanism was realized in the core language treated in this article. For simplicity, we give a simplified version written in an imperative pseudo-language (Figure 9). We only use one intermediary node.

We assume that processes p_1, p_2 and p_3 are concurrently running on three different nodes of the network. #ctrl_12 (resp. #ctrl_23) is a bidirectional control channel linking the nodes of p_1 and p_2 (resp. p_2 and p_3). In addition, since p_1 creates two different circuits a and b, the pieces of code given for process p_2 are executed twice. In our implementation, we use a 0-CFA [19] for the sequential parts of the language. This enforces us to duplicate these pieces of code in order to keep enough precision. It could be avoided by using a more sophisticated analysis (1-CFA). So, in Figure 9, the two labels annotating some instructions correspond to the unique labels of two copies of the same piece of code.

p_1, p_2 and p_3 work as follows. p_1 successively asks for two new circuit creations. Function **connect** sends an initialization message on the control channel #ctrl_12 and binds variable virt_ch_a to the channel name to be used for a.

Processus p_1 (source)	Processus p_2 (switch)	Processus p_3 (destination)
| ```
function connect(dest) =
{ send #ctrl_12 init(dest);
  ch ← receive 7,19 #ctrl_12;
  return ch;
}
function main()
{ virt_ch_a ← connect(3)13;
  virt_ch_b ← connect(3)25;
  send  virt_ch_a data_a30;
  send  virt_ch_b data_b35;
}
``` | ```
...
ctrl_msg ← receive 51,84 #ctrl_12;
send  #ctrl_23 ctrl_msg;
ch_out ← receive 56,89 #ctrl_23;
ch_in ← channel()58,91;
send  #ctrl_12 ch_in;
fork (while do
      send  ch_out
         (receive 62,95 ch_in)
);
...
``` | ```
...
ctrl_msg ← receive #ctrl_23;
ch_dest ← channel()124,129;
send  #ctrl_23 ch_in;
receive 132,134 ch_in;
...
``` |

Fig. 9. Implementation of the virtual circuit allocation mecanism. Procedure connect as well as the pieces of code of processes p_2 and p_3 are executed twice.

This scheme is repeated for b. Finally, data are transmitted on virt_ch_a and virt_ch_b.

p_2 corresponds to the node between the source and the destination. When a virtual circuit creation request is received on #ctrl_12, it is transmitted to the destination on the control channel #ctrl_23. p_2 next receives the output channel name to use and binds variable ch_out. Next, it creates a new channel ch_in which is sent to the source process. The last operation consists of creating a new process which forwards on ch_out the values received on ch_in. The whole process is repeated for the virtual circuit b.

Finally, p_3 corresponds to the destination node. When the control message is received, p_3 creates a new channel and binds variable ch_in. This channel name is transmitted to p_2 via control channel #ctrl_23. Once the circuits are created, p_3 receives data on a and b.

6.2   Analysis

We used our analysis to check the correctness of a full implementation of the program described in Figure 9. Here we present the results we obtained, translated to the program of Figure 9. Figure 10 gives the abstract values obtained for the points of interest and for relevant variables. As indicated above, some pieces of code are executed twice. In Figure 10, we indicate for variables which execution is referenced by (a) and (b).

The main observation concerns the abstract values received by p_3 at points 132 and 134. These values, $\{30\}$ and $\{35\}$, are the ones emitted by p_1 on circuits a and b. This validates the mechanism. The values received on a (resp. b) are the ones emitted on this channel and only these ones. This guarantees that p_2 does not invert the data received on its input links and forwarded on its output links.

Concerning the virtual circuit a, one can check that the variables virt_ch_a and ch_dest (a) corresponding to the extremities of the circuit are bound to $\{58\}$ and $\{124\}$ which correspond to the channel names created at these points. The new process created by p_2 forwards on a name created at point 124 the data
```

Label	7	13	19	25	30	35	51	56	58
Value	{58}	{13}	{91}	{25}	{30}	{35}	{13}	{124}	{58}

Label	62	84	89	91	95	124	129	132	134
Value	{30}	{25}	{129}	{91}	{35}	{124}	{129}	{30}	{35}

Variable	#ctrl_12	#ctrl_23	virt_ch_a	virt_ch_b	ctrl_msg (a)	ctrl_msg (b)
Value	{1}	{2}	{58}	{91}	{13}	{25}

Variable	ch_in (a)	ch_in (b)	ch_out (a)	ch_out (b)	ch_dest (a)	ch_dest (b)
Value	{58}	{91}	{124}	{129}	{124}	{129}

Fig. 10. Abstract values attached to the labels of the program of Figure 9.

received on a name created at point 58 (variables ch_in (a) and ch_out (a)). Thus, the transmission of data from the source to the destination is ensured. In addition, it is possible to check that the channel names of abstract value {58} and {124} are not used elsewhere in the program. So, the data emitted on the virtual circuit a only are transmitted to the destination node. Similar observations can be done for the virtual circuit b.

Finally, let us take note that in order to obtain these results, the analysis has to use an approximation of the communication topology of the program. The same control channels #ctrl_12 et #ctrl_23 are used for both circuit creation. An analysis based on Equation (1) could not obtain these results. The result would be virt_ch_a = virt_ch_a = {58, 91} which does not enable us to check that no confusion is done between the data transmitted on both circuits.

We also used this analysis in order to verify security properties for an auction distributed application. This system is made of a server and several clients who send to the server public data (e.g. their price) as well as confidential data (e.g. their credit card number). Each client is linked to the server by one communication channel. The server broadcasts the public data and conserves the private ones. We show that, in our implementation, the only public data are actually broadcasted.

7   Conclusion

In this article, we introduced a static analysis able to depict a conservative image of the communication topology of a concurrent system written in Concurrent ML. The dynamic aspects of concurrency are managed, including forks, the transmission of functions and channel creations. This analysis is a CFA which builds a finite automaton in order to increase its precision. It was implemented and results are discussed in Sections 2 and 6.

Using product automata allows us to derive a fine approximation of the topology, as shown in Section 2. This represents the main contribution of this article. It enables to minimize the abstract value attached to reception points. Gains are twofold. First, this increase the precision of the analysis for the sequential part of the program following the reception. Second, since channel names are potentially communicated, we also define more concisely the pairs of possible emitters and receptors for further communications.

We believe that the gains due to the introduction of topological information in the CFA improve the analysis of many kinds of applications. For quite common deterministic communication schemes, such as a sequence of communications on the same channel between two processes, this makes possible to distinguish between the values sent at each stage. For more complicated communication schemes, precision may decrease at some points in the program, for instance because of alternatives, loops or non-determinism. However, precision will increase again once the ambiguities disappear, for instance after a global synchronization.

Now, we are interested in mixing it with other analyses, in order to increase the conciseness of the annotations. We focus on a binding time analysis [8,12] which uses topological informations during its analysis of programs. In this context, our CFA would enable to distinguish between the static and dynamic values sent on the same channel, while usual analyses consider a channel dynamic as soon as a dynamic value is sent on it.

References

1. Antony Alles. ATM Internetworking. Technical report, 1995. CISCO Systems Inc.
2. T Amtoft, Flemming Nielson, and Hanne Riis Nielson. Behaviour analysis and safety conditions: a case study in CML. In *FASE'98*, number 1382 in Lecture Notes in Computer Science, pages 255–269. Springer-Verlag, 1998.
3. Dave Berry, Robin Milner, and David N. Turner. A semantics for ML concurrency primitives. In *Proceedings of the ACM-SIGPLAN Symposium on Principles of Programming Languages POPL'92*. ACM, 1992.
4. Chiara Bodei, Pierpaolo Degano, Flemming Nielson, and Hanne Riis Nielson. Control flow analysis for the pi-calculus. In *Concur'98*, number 1466 in Lecture Notes in Computer Science, pages 84–98. Springer-Verlag, 1998.
5. Chiara Bodei, Pierpaolo Degano, Flemming Nielson, and Hanne Riis Nielson. Static analysis of processes for no read-up and no write-down. In *FOSSAC'99*, number 1578 in Lecture Notes in Computer Science, pages 120–134. Springer-Verlag, 1999.
6. Christopher Colby. Analyzing the communication topology of concurrent programs. In *Proceedings of the ACM-SIGPLAN Symposium on Partial Evaluation and semantic based program manipulations PEPM'95*, pages 202–213. ACM, 1995.
7. Charles Consel and Olivier Danvy. Partial evaluation: Principles and perspectives. In *Proceedings of the ACM-SIGPLAN Symposium on Principles of Programming Languages POPL'93*. ACM, 1993.
8. Marc Gengler and Matthieu Martel. Self-applicable partial evaluation for the pi-calculus. In *Partial Evaluation and Semantics-Based Program Manipulation, PEPM'97*, pages 36–46, 1997.
9. Marc Gengler and Matthieu Martel. Des étages en Concurrent ML. In *Rencontres Francophones du Parallélisme, Renpar10*, 1998.
10. Suresh Jagannathan. Locality abstractions for parallel and distributed computing. In *International Conference on Theory and Practice of Parallel Programming*, number 907 in Lecture Notes in Computer Science. Springer-Verlag, 1994.

11. Naoki Kobayashi, Motoki Nakade, and Akinori Yonezawa. Static analysis of communications for asynchronous concurrent programming languages. In *SAS'95*, volume 983 of *LNCS*, pages 225–242. Springer-Verlag, 1995.

12. Mihnea Marinescu and Benjamin Goldberg. Partial evaluation techniques for concurrent programs. In *ACM-SIGPLAN Symposium on Partial Evaluation and Semantic Based Program Manipulations PEPM'97*, pages 47–62. ACM, 1997.

13. Nicolas Mercouroff. An algorithm for analyzing communicating processes. *Lecture Notes in Computer Science*, 598:312–325, 1992.

14. Flemming Nielson and Hanne Riis Nielson. Constraints for polymorphics behaviours of Concurrent ML. In *Constraints in Computational Logics*, number 845 in Lecture Notes in computer Science, pages 73–88. Springer-Verlag, 1994.

15. Flemming Nielson and Hanne Riis Nielson. Higher-order concurrent programs with finite communication topology. In *Proceedings of the ACM-SIGPLAN Symposium on Principles of Programming Languages POPL'94*, pages 84–97. ACM, 1994.

16. Flemming Nielson and Hanne Riis Nielson. Static and dynamic processor allocation for higher-order concurrent languages. In *TAPSOFT'95*, number 915 in Lecture Notes in Computer Science, pages 590–604. Springer-Verlag, 1995.

17. Flemming Nielson and Hanne Riis Nielson. Infinitary control flow analysis: a collecting semantics for closure analysis. In *ACM-SIGPLAN Symposium on Principles of Programming Languages POPL'97*, pages 332–345. ACM, 1997.

18. Flemming Nielson and Hanne Riis Nielson. Communication analysis for Concurrent ML. In *ML with Concurrency*, Monograph in Computer Science, pages 185–251. Springer, 1999.

19. Flemming Nielson, Hanne Riis Nielson, and Chris Hankin. *Principles of Program Analysis*. Springer, 1999.

20. John H. Reppy. An operational semantics of first-class synchronous operations. Technical Report TR-91-1232, Department of Computer Science, Cornell University, Ithaca, NY 14853, 1991.

21. John H. Reppy. *Higher-order Concurrency*. PhD thesis, Department of Computer Science, Cornell University, Ithaca, NY 14853, 1992.

22. John H. Reppy. *Concurrent Programming in ML*. Cambridge University Press, 1999.

23. Olin Shivers. Control flow analysis in scheme. In *Proceedings of the ACM-SIGPLAN Conference on Programming Language Design and Implementation, PLDI'88*, pages 164–174. ACM, 1988.

24. Olin Shivers. *Control Flow Analysis of Higher Order Languages*. PhD thesis, Carnegie Mellon University, 1991. Technical Report CMU-CS-91-145.

25. Kirsten L Solberg, Flemming Nielson, and Hanne Riis Nielson. Systematic realisation of control flow analyses for CML. In *ACM-SIGPLAN International Conference on Functional Programming, ICFP'97*, pages 38–51. ACM, 1997.

26. Andrew S. Tanenbaum. *Computer Networks, Third Edition*. Prentice Hall, 1996.

Low-Fat Recipes for Spin

Theo C. Ruys

Faculty of Computer Science, University of Twente.
P.O. Box 217, 7500 AE Enschede, The Netherlands.
ruys@cs.utwente.nl

Abstract. Since the introduction of the first version of the model checker SPIN in 1991, many papers have been written on improvements to the tool and on industrial applications of the tool. Less attention has been given to the pragmatic use of SPIN. This paper presents several techniques to optimise both the modelling and verification activities when using SPIN.

Introduction

Since the introduction of the first version of the model checker SPIN [5] in 1991 (accompanying Gerard Holzmann's book [6] on SPIN), many papers have been published on technical improvements to SPIN. The extensive list of industrial applications [8] shows that SPIN has already been proven quite useful. The proceedings of the SPIN Workshops [18] give a good overview of the (applied) research on SPIN. It is surprising that less attention has been given to the pragmatic use of SPIN; there is not even a Frequently Asked Questions (FAQ) list for SPIN.

With respect to verification tools that need extensive user guidance – like theorem provers and proof checkers – model checkers are often put forward as 'press-on-the-button' tools: given a model and a property, pressing the 'verify' button of the model checker is enough for the tool to prove or disprove the property. If both the model and the property are readily available, this claim might be true. However, the formalization of both the model and the properties is usually not a trivial task. Furthermore, due to the infamous state space explosion problem, both the model and the property to be verified should be coded as efficient as possible for the model checker that is being used.

Now that model checking tools in general and SPIN in particular are becoming more widespread in use [7], these tools are starting to be adopted by people that only want to press the button and that do not know precisely what is 'under the hood' of such verification tools. During technology transfer projects and during the education of our students we experienced that – without proper guidance – PROMELA and SPIN are not being used in the most optimal way. On the one hand, PROMELA, because it resembles C [9], is regarded as a high level programming language. On the other hand, SPIN is seen as a magic tool that can verify even the largest systems. PROMELA models are being constructed as some sort of C programs that may be good specifications and functional models, but may not be as efficient to verify. Several solutions to this potential misuse of model checkers come to mind:

K. Havelund, J. Penix, and W. Visser (Eds.): SPIN 2000, LNCS 1885, pp. 287–321, 2000.
© Springer-Verlag Berlin Heidelberg 2000

- *More agressive tools.* If model checking tools would mimic optimizing compilers more closely, all non-efficiency could be optimised away. The limited price to pay would be a drop in compilation and runtime speed.
- *Restrict the language.* If the user of the model checker cannot use 'expensive' constructs, the model will be efficient by construction. The catch here is that in general it will be more difficult to model systems.
- *Educate the users.* If the users know what constructs should be avoided and what data and control structures are most efficient, the user can improve his modelling skills himself.

This paper aims to be helpful with respect to the last solution. We present some (shortened) selected techniques from "Effective SPIN" [15], a collection of proven best practices when using SPIN.

Effective Modelling and Verification. Press-on-the-button verification is only feasible for small to medium sized applications. Industrial size applications need aggressive use of the modelling language, the properties to be checked and the verification tool itself. As discussed above, there is generally a big difference in efficiency in the models developed by a 'casual' user and the models developed by an 'expert' user. Moreover, the 'expert' user knows how to exploit the directives and options of the model checker to optimise the verification runs. Efficient use of model checking tools seems to require an 'assembler programming' approach to model building: use all tricks of the model checker to minimise the state space of the model and make the verification process as efficient as possible. The 'expert' verification engineer resembles the seasoned programmer, who not only has a deep knowledge and understanding of data structures and algorithms but also knows the options and directives to tune the programming tools that he is using.

With model checking tools there is – just as with programming – a trade-off between time and space requirements. For the model checking process, however, the space requirements are much more important than the time requirements. Because of the state space explosion, it is crucial to reduce the number of states as much as possible. So reduction of the number of states is the first consideration. The minimization of the size of the state vector (i.e. the amount of memory which is needed to encode a single state) is the next concern. Only in the last case, reduction of the verification time should be taken into account. SPIN has several options and directives to tune the verification process. Not surprisingly, many of these options are related to the trade-off between space and time requirements. An efficient verification model is usually optimised and tuned towards the property that has to be verified. It is not unusual to have a different model for each different property. This differs from programming, where one usually has only a single program (and older superseded versions of that program).

This paper presents a couple of 'expert' techniques to optimise both the modelling and verification process when using SPIN.[1] These techniqes are mostly

---

[1] To determine whether one is already on the 'expert' level of PROMELA one could do the following: start XSPIN, press "Help" and read the last section "Reducing

concerned with the minimization of the number of states or the reduction of the state vector. The techniques discussed here are not answers to FAQs, but are more like 'recipes from a cookbook' in the style of [2] and [12]. The recipes are presented in a tutorial oriented manner. When appropriate, there will be pointers to more formal and technical discussions, though. This paper is intended to be useful for intermediate to advanced users of SPIN; [15] has more sections for novice users of SPIN.

All proposed techniques can be used with standard PROMELA and standard SPIN. No modifications to SPIN are needed. Some hints and tips will be trivial to experienced C/C++ programmers, but might be 'eye-openers' for SPIN users that originate from the 'formal methods community'. Several of the tips and techniques presented in this report, may even look like terrible 'hacks': horrible and unreadable deviations from the original specification or model.[2]

We hope that the recipes will not only be adopted as efficient ways to achieve specific goals in PROMELA or SPIN, but also induce a new way of thinking about the verification process with SPIN.

Experiments. The techniques discussed in this paper and the advice given are verified by numerous experiments with SPIN itself. Summaries of the results of (most of) these experiments are included in the report. All verification experiments are run on a Dell Inspiron 7000 Notebook computer running Red Hat Linux 6.1 (Linux kernel version 2.2.12). The Dell computer is driven by a Pentium II/300Mhz with 128Mb of main memory. For the **pan** verification runs we limited the memory to 64Mb though. For our experiments we used SPIN version 3.3.10.

Some verification runs have been repeated with certain optimization settings enabled or disabled. The different types of verification runs are identified as follows:

`default`	default XSPIN settings
`-o3`	disables SPIN's smart merging of safe sequences
`-DNOREDUCE`	disables partial order reduction
`-DCOLLAPSE`	a state vector compression mode
`-DMA=n`	uses a minimised DFA encoding for the state space

See [19] for details on these verification options.

Literate Programming. The recipes in the paper are illustrated by PROMELA code fragments. These PROMELA fragments are presented as *literate programs* [10,14]. Literate programming is the act of writing computer programs primarily as documents to be read by human beings, and only secondarily as instructions

---

Complexity". The SPIN user who already lives by all these rules of thumb, is on the right track.

[2] Some of the techniques discussed in this paper should probably be done by SPIN instead of the user. Future versions of SPIN might incorporate optimizations (e.g. assignment of arrays, *efficient* arrays of bits, checking for pure atomicity, etc.) which would make the discussions in this paper obsolete. Until then, one has to adopt these techniques manually.

to be executed by computers [14]. A literate program combines source code and documentation in a single file. Literate programming *tools* then parse such a file to produce either readable documentation or compilable source code.

We use **noweb**, developed by Norman Ramsey as our literate programming tool. **noweb** [14,13] is similar to Knuth's **WEB**, only simpler. Unlike **WEB**, **noweb** is independent of the programming language to be literated.

We briefly introduce the reader to the **noweb** style of literate programming. A literate document consists of *code chunks* and *document chunks*. What follows is a code chunk.

```
1     ⟨sample code chunk 1⟩≡
      proctype Silly()
      {
         ⟨Silly's body 2⟩
      }
```

In this code fragment, the chunk ⟨*sample code chunk* 1⟩ is defined. In the left margin, **noweb** shows the unique number of the *code chunk*.[3] When the name of a code chunk appears in the definition of another code chunk, it stands for the corresponding replacement text. In our simple example, ⟨*sample code chunk* 1⟩ uses the code chunk ⟨*Silly's body* 2⟩, which is defined as follows.

```
2     ⟨Silly's body 2⟩≡                                    (1) 3▷
      do
      :: skip
      od ;
```

In the right margin of the definition of a chunk, between parenthesis, the tags of the code chunks that *use* this particular code chunk are listed. In this case, this list only contains the tag of ⟨*sample code chunk* 1⟩. It's possible and common practice to give the same name to several different code chunks. Continuing our example, we can expand our **Silly** process as follows.

```
3     ⟨Silly's body 2⟩+≡                                   (1) ◁2
      assert(0) ;
```

The +≡ here indicates that the code chunk ⟨*Silly's body*⟩ has appeared before. The PROMELA code following +≡ will be appended to the previous replacement text for the same name. When such continuations of code chunk definitions are used, **noweb** provides more information in the right margin; it indicates the previous definition (◁) and the next definition (▷) of the same code chunk.

Recipe 1 – Macros, `inline` Definitions, and `m4`

Unlike most programming languages, PROMELA does not support the concept of procedures or functions to structure a PROMELA model. Instead, PROMELA offers the macro mechanism of the `cpp` preprocessor [9] and – since SPIN version 3.2.0

---

[3] In this paper the **WEB** style of chunk numbering is used. Another popular way of chunk identification is a tag *page.n*, where *n* indicates the *n*-th chunk on page *page*.

– the semantically equivalent `inline` construct. As the name of the construct already suggests, an invocation of an `inline` definition amounts to the automatic inlining of the text of the `inline` definition into the body of the process that invokes it.

Although limited with respect to native procedures or functions, `inline` definitions can still be quite helpful to structure a PROMELA model. The cpp macro mechanism is convenient for defining constants and symbolic propositions (e.g. XSPIN's dialog window for LTL verification runs). Furthermore, the cpp preprocessor can be used to parameterise a PROMELA model.

Note that SPIN's on-line documentation [19] suggests a third method to simulate **procedures**. A seperate server process needs to be declared with the body of the procedure. This server process responds to the user processes via a special globally defined channel, and responding to these requests via an user provided local channel. In the light of our 'assembler modelling' approach it will be clear that this method is rejected for its inefficiency.

In this section, we discuss some common cpp macros and `inline` tricks that have proven useful within the context of PROMELA models. We will also show some of the limitations of `inline` definitions with respect to parameterising PROMELA models and introduce the reader to m4, a more powerful macro processor than cpp.

1.1 Some cpp Macros

To get a feeling of cpp macros, we first introduce some useful cpp one-liners. These macros will be used in other parts of this report as well.

IF/FI. PROMELA does not support a pure deterministic conditional statement, To model a deterministic conditional one has to reside to the following construct:

```
if
:: ⟨boolean expression⟩ -> ⟨then part⟩
:: else -> ⟨else part⟩
fi ;
```

If the ⟨else part⟩ is missing (i.e. equal to `skip`), the construct becomes a rather clumsy way to model the equivalent of the following piece of C code:

```
if ( ⟨boolean expression⟩ ) {
⟨then part⟩
}
```

The following two macros IF and FI can be used as a convenient shorthand for a deterministic conditional:

4   ⟨cpp macros 4⟩≡   5▷
```
#define IF if ::
#define FI :: else fi
```

Now we can write:

```
IF ⟨boolean expression⟩ -> ⟨then part⟩
FI;
```

IMPLIES. When checking properties in an `assert` statement, it often happens that one needs to check a logical implication: $p \Rightarrow q$. The $\Rightarrow$ operator does not have a direct counterpart in PROMELA. Instead we encode the equivalent $\neg p \vee q$ as a cpp macro:

5   ⟨cpp macros 4⟩+≡   ◁4
```
    #define IMPLIES(p,q) ((!p) || (q))
```

1.2   A Poor Man's Assignment

Although PROMELA supports `arrays` and `typedef` variables, these structured types are not (yet) 'first class citizens' of the language. For example, it is not possible to use PROMELA's assignment statement (i.e. '=') to copy one `array` or `typedef` variable to another.[4] Here, the cpp macro or `inline` construct can be helpful to implement a "poor man's assignment" or copy procedure. As an example, suppose a PROMELA model contains the following `typedef` definition:

6   ⟨typedef Foo 6⟩≡
```
    typedef Foo {
      byte b1 ;
      byte b2 ;
    } ;
```

The `inline` definition to copy one Foo variable to another is now trivial:

7   ⟨inline CopyFoo 7⟩≡
```
    inline CopyFoo(src,dest)
    {
      d_step {
        dest.b1 = src.b1 ;
        dest.b2 = src.b2 ;
      }
    }
```

---

[4] If one tries to assign a complete `typedef` variable, SPIN will issue an 'incomplete structure ref' error. But beware: if one tries to assign a complete `array` variable, SPIN will *not* complain. SPIN even allows assignment of incompatible arrays (i.e. different base type or different number of elements). But instead of copying the complete `array`, SPIN will only copy the first element of the `array`. The reason for this is that the name of an `array` variable is treated as an alias to the first element of the particular `array`.
Please note that PROMELA does allow initialisation of a complete array in the declaration of the array, though. The declaration
    ⟨type⟩ a[N]=val ;
initialises all N elements of a to val.

Similarly, one can use the following `inline` definition to assign the value `val` to the elements of an array `a` of length `n`.

8   ⟨*inline AssignArray* 8⟩≡

```
inline AssignArray(a,n,val)
{
  byte i ;
  d_step {
    i=0 ;
    do
    ::  i <  n -> a[i] = val ; i++
    ::  i >= n -> break
    od ;
    i=0 ;
  }
}
```

Note that the variable `i` is *not* local to the `inline` definition, but instead will be a local variable in all processes that invoke the `AssignArray` definition. To make sure that the overhead of the local variable is kept to a minimum, the variable `i` is reset to 0 at the end of the `d_step`. In this way, system states will not differ on the basis of the temporary variable `i`. See Recipe 5 for details on this idiom.

It would even have been more efficient if we would be able to 'hide' the variable `i` from the state vector using the PROMELA keyword `hidden`. Unfortunately, the current version of SPIN only allows global variables to be declared as `hidden` variables. So in order to hide `i`, we should declare `i` as a global variable and remove the declaration of `i` from the `inline` macro.

Note that one has to supply `inline` definitions for all `typedef` objects or `array` variables that have to copied or initialised.

1.3   Parameterised Protocols

Communication protocols are often parameterised by some symbolic constants. Typical parameters are the number of processes, the length of the communication buffers, the window size of the protocol, etc. When modelling such a parameterised protocol in PROMELA one usually uses the macro mechanism of the preprocessor `cpp` to define the parameters at the start of the PROMELA model. For example, we could use the following PROMELA fragment

```
#define N       3
#define WSIZE   4
#define CL      2
```

to specify `N` protocol instances, a windowsize of `WSIZE` and a channel length of `CL` elements.

Each time the PROMELA model has to be validated with different values of the parameters, the constants need to be changed explicitly in the PROMELA model. To really make the constants parameters to the PROMELA model, SPIN provides the preprocessor related options -D and -E to move the definition of such parameters outside the PROMELA model:

-Dyyy   pass -Dyyy to the preprocessor

-Eyyy   pass yyy to the preprocessor

Instead of defining the parameters in the PROMELA model itself, one can run SPIN as follows:

spin -DN=3 -DWSIZE=4 -DCL=2 ⟨promela file⟩

Consequently, the ⟨promela file⟩ does not have to be changed for different values of the protocol parameters. When parameters are set in this way using the command-line, it is recommended to specify default values for the parameters in the PROMELA model itself. For example:

```
#ifndef N
#define N 3
#endif
```

In practice, changing one of the parameters of a PROMELA model often means that some other statements have to be altered as well. For example, consider the following PROMELA fragment, where a message MSG is non-deterministicly sent to one of the available N processes. We assume that the sending over the channels to[i] cannot be blocked.

9   ⟨non-deterministic send - if 9⟩≡
```
      if
      ::   to[0] ! MSG
      ::   to[1] ! MSG
      ::   to[2] ! MSG
      ::   to[3] ! MSG
      fi ;
```

In this case N is equal to 4. The number of processes parameter is hardcoded into the model; if N is changed from 4 to 7, we have to add three more lines. We could make the sending of the MSG depend on N using PROMELA's do statement:[5]

10   ⟨non-deterministic send - do 10⟩≡
```
      byte i ;
      atomic {
        i=0 ;
        do
        ::   i<N-1   -> i++
        ::   i<N-1   -> to[i]    ! MSG ; break
        ::   i>=N-1 -> to[N-1] ! MSG ; break
        od ;
        i=0 ;
      }
```

This do-solution is less efficient than the straightforward if clause: not only do we need an extra variable to loop through the possible processes 0..N, the do-

---

[5] Note that the do-solution is only semantically equivalent to the if-solution if the sending over the channels to[i] cannot be blocked.

Table 1. Some cpp macros and their m4 counterparts

cpp macro	m4 macro
#define MAX 5	define('MAX','5')
#define P (a>5 && b<10)	define('P','a>5 && b<10')
#define IMPLIES(x,y) ((!x) || (y))	define('IMPLIES','((!$1) || ($2))')
#include "filename"	include('filename')

construct also performs worse with respect to the execution time and the search depth.[6] Moreover, the do-solution is clearly less readable than the original if construct. The only advantage of the do-solution is that it is parameterised in N.

Unfortunately enough, the cpp preprocessor is not expressive enough to let a macro expand to the if solution: cpp does not have a looping construct that depends on some numeric constant. A more powerful preprocessor is needed.

1.4   The m4 Macro Processor

Like cpp, m4 [16] is a macro processor in the sense that it copies its input to the output, expanding macros as it goes. m4 is being used either as a front-end to compilers, or as a macro processor in its own right. m4 is much more powerful and flexible than cpp. m4 is widely available on all UNIXes.[7] In the context of PROMELA and SPIN, m4 has turned out to be valuable tool for making PROMELA models more generic without losing efficiency.

The use of a different preprocessor than SPIN's is anticipated in SPIN with the -Pxxx option. To make SPIN use m4 instead of cpp, one simply issues the command

    spin -Pm4 -E-s[8]

This report is not the place to describe m4 in great detail. The interested reader should refer to [16] instead. We will only briefly discuss some differences between cpp and m4 to make a migration to m4 easier. And of course we will present the parameterised m4 macro that expands to the ⟨non-deterministic send - if 9⟩ chunk of the previous section.

Table 1 shows some cpp macros and their m4 equivalent counterparts. The m4 macro processor uses *quoted strings* (i.e. a string between the characters ' and ') to specify the arguments of the **define** macros. Naturally, m4 also provides constructs to conditionally include or exclude some program fragments. For example, the cpp construct

---

[6] In Recipe 3 "Randomness" we discuss the differences between the if and do solutions in greater detail.

[7] A warning on m4 from [16]: "Some people found m4 to be fairly addictive. ... Beware that m4 can be dangerous for the health of compulsive programmers."

[8] The option -s which is passed to m4 using SPIN's -E option, is needed to ensure the correct synchronisation of line numbers and file names within the PROMELA source file(s). See [16] for details.

<table>
<tr><td>

```
#ifdef name
⟨then ...⟩
#else
⟨else ...⟩
#endif
```

</td><td>

has the following
m4 counterpart:

</td><td>

```
ifdef('name','
⟨then ...⟩ ','
⟨else ...⟩ ')
```

</td></tr>
</table>

And the if, the ifndef and undef constructs of cpp have equivalent commands within m4 as well.

Comments in m4 input files are normally delimited by the characters '#' and a newline character. These comment delimiters can be changed to any string, using m4's built-in macro changecom. To retain PROMELA style comments – i.e. the cpp style comments – we change the comment delimiters to /* and */.

11   ⟨m4 macros 11⟩≡   12▷
```
changecom('/*','*/')
```

Besides counterparts for all cpp commands, m4 supports several additional pre-processing features. To implement a general looping construct, only the stack-like redefinition macros, the recursion construct and the integer arithmetic operations of m4 are needed, though. The following forloop macro is from [16]:

12   ⟨m4 macros 11⟩+≡   ◁11
```
define('forloop',
  'pushdef('$1', '$2')_forloop('$1', '$2', '$3', '$4')popdef('$1')')
define('_forloop',
  '$4''ifelse($1, '$3', ,
  'define('$1', incr($1))_forloop('$1', '$2', '$3', '$4')')')
```

Understanding the implementation of the forloop macro is not really needed, only the result of an invocation of forloop is important here. The forloop macro expects 4 parameters. The first parameter is the looping variable. The second and third parameter are the start and end value of the looping variable, respectively. The last argument of forall is the string that should be written for each value of the looping variable.

For example, the macro invocation
```
forloop('i', 1, 8, 'i ')
```
expands to
```
1 2 3 4 5 6 7 8
```
For each value of i, the string 'i ' is written, with the actual value substituted for i. Using forloop, we now are able to write a parameterised version of ⟨non-deterministic send - if 9⟩:

13   ⟨non-deterministic send - if using m4 13⟩≡
```
if
forloop('i', 0, eval(N-1), ':: to[i] ! MSG
')fi ;
```

If N has been defined to be 4, this chunk 13 will expand exactly to chunk 9. Although we managed to parameterise the guards of the if clause, the m4 construct using forloop is clearly less readable than both the original static if clause and the do solution. In Recipe 3, though, we will show that the m4 construct proves to be an efficient and parameterised solution.

The forloop macro can also be quite useful in a (boolean) expression. Suppose that a process waits for all N processes to become ready, i.e. the boolean ready[i] is true for all $i \in 0..N-1$:

```
ready[0] && ready[1] && ... && ready[N-1]
```

Again, we cannot use cpp to build this expression which depends on the parameter N. The forloop macro is straightforward, however:

```
forloop('i', 0, eval(N-1), 'ready[i] &&') true
```

Conclusions. To structure a PROMELA model or to parameterise the model, the use of cpp and inline constructs usually suffices. The power user, however, might consider to add m4 to his (verification) toolbox: this macro processor is more powerful than cpp and the parameterising of the PROMELA model is usually more elegantly. Moreover – as we will see in Recipe 3 – the resulting PROMELA model can be more efficient in terms of the number of states or the needed search depth. It is possible to mix m4 and cpp constructs in a single PROMELA model. This is not considered good practice, though.

As a last remark, remember that PROMELA is a protocol *meta language*, not a programming language. Shorthands like IF and forloop should be used with caution.

Recipe 2 – Atomicity

This section discusses issues related to the atomic and d_step constructs of PROMELA, which both introduce a sequence of statements that is to be executed indivisibly. The atomic sequence is allowed to contain non-deterministic choices, whereas the d_step (i.e. the deterministic step) may only contain deterministic statements.[9]

Both constructs can be used to reduce the complexity of the validation model and to improve the efficiency of verification runs [19]. As we will see in Recipe 5, the d_step construct can also be seen as a mechanism to define an indivisible statement in the language at the user-level, and thus to extend the semantics of PROMELA itself [20].

The semantics of the atomic clause of PROMELA has changed over the years. In version 1.x of SPIN, it would causes a run-time error if any statement, other than the first statement, blocks in an atomic sequence [17]. However, since version 2 of SPIN, it is legal for an atomic sequence to block. If any statement within the atomic sequence blocks, the atomicity is lost, and other processes are allowed to execute arbitrarily many statements [20]. The d_step is not allowed to block, though. The pan verifier will abort the verification if it detects a blocking d_step.

---

[9] Although the d_step clause should only contain 'deterministic' statements, the pan verifier will not check this. If the verifier encounters a non-deterministic choice, it will just choose the first alternative.

2.1   Atomicity of Single Statements

Before turning to the `atomic` and `d_step` constructs themselves, we briefly discuss the granularity of PROMELA statements. In the realm of (competing) parallel processes that share global memory, the implementation of computations and assignment statements is liable to result in incorrect behaviour due to race conditions between the processes. The abstraction level of PROMELA is higher: a single statement is assumed to be indivisible. For example, an assignment like

```
a = b+c*d-e*f ;
```

is considered to be atomic within PROMELA. If one wants to check the correctness of a possible low-level implementation of such an assignment, one should manually split up the assignment using temporary variables. For example:

```
x1 = c*d ;
x2 = e*f ;
x1 = b+x1 ;
a  = x1-x2 ;
```

To exclude the temporary variables `x1` and `x2` from the state vector, they should be defined as `hidden` global variables.

2.2   Atomic is Not Always Atomic

New users often expect the version 1.x semantics of SPIN: placing an `atomic` clause around a sequence of statements should *ensure* the atomicity of the statements. This erroneous perspective can lead to unexpected errors that are hard to find. For example, suppose a PROMELA model contains an `atomic` clause which is assumed to be indivisible. During a verification run, however, the `atomic` clause blocks and control is passed to one of the other processes. Later during the search, the property that is being checked is violated, due to the premature ending of the `atomic` clause. Still assuming the atomicity of the clause, the user does not understand why the property has been violated.

The statement that causes an `atomic` clause to block is often an `if` or `do` statement. If the set of guards of the `if` or `do` statement is not complete and the `else` statement is missing, the particular statement might block. This error can easily slip into the model, when behaviour is added to the PROMELA model (i.e. new possible values for variables, new `mtype` messages that are sent over a channel), that is not anticipated by the particular `if` or `do` statement.

Although the semantics of the `atomic` clause have changed, it is still relatively easy to check whether `atomic` clauses are 'pure' in the sense that they are not exited prematuraly due to a blocking statement. The following steps are sufficient:

- declare a *global* bit variable `aflag`;
- set `aflag` to 1 on entrance of each `atomic` block that has to be checked for 'pure atomicity': immediately after the first statement or guard of the `atomic` block;

- set aflag to 0 on leaving those atomic blocks: immediately before the closing '}' of the block;
- use SPIN to verify that aflag is always equal to zero, i.e. verify that the invariant property []P holds, where P is equal to !aflag.

For example, to verify the following atomic clause

14   ⟨*atomic block* 14⟩≡
```
        atomic {
          guard ;
            . . .
        }
```

for 'pure atomicity', it would have to be changed to

15   ⟨*atomic block with* aflag 15⟩≡
```
        atomic {
          guard ;
          aflag=1 ;
            . . .
          aflag=0 ;
        }
```

A drawback of this method is that all atomic clauses have to be altered in the PROMELA model to check for 'pure atomicity'. Instead, we could also use cpp macros such that the checking can be done conditionally. The ⟨*aflag declarations* 16⟩ chunk below defines the necessary macros:

16   ⟨*aflag declarations* 16⟩≡
```
        #ifdef CHECK_ATOMICITY
        bit aflag ;
        #define SET_AFLAG        aflag=1
        #define RESET_AFLAG      aflag=0
        #else
        #define SET_AFLAG        skip
        #define RESET_AFLAG      skip
        #endif
```

The SET_AFLAG and RESET_AFLAG macros are only 'active' when CHECK_ATOMICITY is defined. The ⟨*atomic block with* aflag 15⟩ fragment can now be changed to:

17   ⟨*atomic block with* AFLAG *macros* 17⟩≡
```
        atomic {
          guard ;
          SET_AFLAG ;
            . . .
          RESET_AFLAG ;
        }
```

2.3 Infinity and Atomicity

Most reactive systems – like communication protocols – execute forever. Spin does not have problems verifying such systems with infinite behaviour.[10] Infinity and the **atomic** and **d_step** constructs do not mix, though. Consider the following trivial infinite loop in PROMELA:

18   ⟨*infinite loop* 18⟩≡   (19–21)

```
bit b ;
do
::   b=1-b
od ;
```

which is encapsulated in the following **proctype**:

19   ⟨*infinite-normal.pr* 19⟩≡

```
active proctype Infinite()
{
   ⟨infinite loop 18⟩
}
```

When this PROMELA model is checked (e.g. for invalid endstates), **pan** will terminate normally and report that 2 states are stored with a maximum search depth of 1.

Things change, however, if we enclose the ⟨*infinite loop* 18⟩ into an **atomic** clause:

20   ⟨*infinite-atomic.pr* 20⟩≡

```
active proctype Infinite()
{
   atomic { ⟨infinite loop 18⟩ }
}
```

There will still be only one state, but **pan** cannot 'get out' of the **atomic** loop; the **pan** verifier will continue to execute the assignment statement. Luckily, **pan** will (eventually) complain that the search depth was too small: every execution of the assignment will have been put onto the stack. When we enclose the ⟨*infinite loop* 18⟩ in a **d_step**, we get into trouble, though.

21   ⟨*infinite-d_step.pr* 21⟩≡

```
active proctype Infinite()
{
   d_step { ⟨infinite loop 18⟩ }
}
```

The **pan** verifier will never be able to complete its **d_step** transition and will keep executing the assignment statement; all in a single search step. The verifier will get into an endless (livelock) loop and will never allow one of the other processes to proceed. This error is not easy to spot as it seems as if **pan** is very busy traversing the state space.

---

[10] Note that PROMELA models always define finite state systems. Thus infinite behaviour in PROMELA involves looping: visiting a state that has already been visited before.

Although this example is trivial, an endless loop in a d_step clause is not unlikely to occur in practice. For example, consider the inline definition of ⟨inline AssignArray 8⟩, which initialises an array a of length n. The increment statement i++ in the do-loop can easily be forgotten.

So before putting a computation into a d_step one should make sure that the computation does not contain an infinite loop. A simple way to check this is to first enclose the computation sequence into an atomic clause. If the maximum search depth turns out to be too small due to the atomic clause, the clause probably contains an infinite loop.

Conclusions. In this recipe we discussed the 'atomicity' constructs of PRO-MELA. We have shown how to check for 'pure atomicity' when using the atomic clause. Furthermore, we discussed the pitfalls regarding infinite behaviour in combination with atomic and d_step.

Recipe 3 – Randomness

The file rand.html from [19] mentions the following: "There is no random number generation function in PROMELA. ... In almost all cases, PROMELA's notion of non-determinism can replace the need for a random number generator." In general this is true. Randomness is a concept used in program *implementation* (e.g. in simulutation and testing), whereas non-determinism is a concept used in the *specification* of systems and hence, in model checking and verification. An attempt to construct a random generator in PROMELA often reflects a misunderstanding of the user with respect to the model. For verification, in general, only specific possibilities (e.g. boundary values, valid and invalid choices) need modelling.

Still, there sometimes seems to be a need for an explicit randomise construct. Especially users new to SPIN and less familiar with non-deterministic choices, expect a random number generation function in PROMELA. Furthermore, in the initial phase of the modelling of a system, an explicit random construct can be quite useful.

In this section we investigate and compare several possibilities to add a **random** definition to the PROMELA language. The randomness example proves to be a nice example to get a feeling of the "assembler programming" approach to model building.

do solution. A natural first attempt to an explicit randomise construct – which is commonly seen – is the following piece PROMELA definition:

22   ⟨inline: random - plain do 1st try 22⟩≡

```
inline random(i,N)
{
    ⟨random - do 1st try⟩
}
```

where the body of ⟨random - do 1st try 23⟩ could be defined as:

23   ⟨random - do *(1st attempt)* 23⟩≡

```
    i=0 ;
    do
    :: i<N  -> i++
    :: i<N  -> break
    :: i>=N -> break
    od ;
```

The do-loop is used to non-deterministically increment the variable i or to break out of the loop. After the loop the variable i will have a value from the range 0..N. We see that for both guards i<N and i>=N we can always break out of the loop. So, an elegant and slightly more efficient randomise construct is the following:

24   ⟨*inline: random - plain* do 24⟩≡

```
    inline random(i,N)
    {
       ⟨random - do 25⟩
    }
```

where ⟨random - do 25⟩ is defined as:

25   ⟨random - do 25⟩≡   (24 26)

```
    i=0 ;
    do
    :: i<N -> i++
    :: break
    od ;
```

The construction can improved even further by placing the complete ⟨*random do*⟩ chunk in an atomic clause.[11]

26   ⟨*inline: random - atomic* do 26⟩≡

```
    inline random(i,N)
    {
       atomic { ⟨random - do 25⟩ }
    }
```

if solution. Similar to ⟨*non-deterministic send - if* 9⟩, we can also use an if-clause to set the random value in a single transition. For example, if N is 4, we could also set i to a random value between 0 and N using the following code:

```
  if
  :: i=0
  :: i=1
  :: i=2
  :: i=3
  :: i=4
  fi ;
```

---

[11] Note that we cannot use a d_step clause here, because the random choice is based on the non-deterministic guards in the do-loop.

SPIN will non-deterministicly choose one of guards to set i to a value in the range 0..4. The drawback of the if solution is that the code chunk has to be altered when the constant N is changed. As explained in Recipe 1, we cannot use the cpp preprocessor to let a macro expand dynamically to a variable number of guards, based on the parameter N. Instead we use the m4 macro forloop defined in ⟨m4 macros 12⟩ to dynamically build the if clause:[12]

```
27    ⟨inline: random - if 27⟩≡
          inline random(i)
          {
            if
          forloop('j', 0, eval(N), '   :: i=j
          ') fi ;
          }
```

Pseudo-random Generator. Apart from the non-deterministic techniques that we discussed above, one can also model a deterministic, pseudo-random generator in PROMELA. For example, after defining the macro

```
#define RANDOM (seed*3 + 14) % 100
```
every subsequent assignment
```
seed = RANDOM ;
```
will set seed to a "pseudo-random" value between 0 and 99. It will be clear that this is a different kind of randomness than the non-deterministic do and if techniques. In the remainder of this recipe, we will not discuss pseudo-random generators any further.

3.1   Comparison

To compare the different implementations of the random definition, we have run two types of test series with SPIN:

- We have verified a PROMELA model where random(i,N) was called only once with N==50.
- To check the verification time of the random construct, we also verified a PROMELA model where the random(i,N) definition was invoked 10000 times with N==10.

We distinguish between setting a local or global variable. The reason for making this distinction is that declaring variables to be local to a process *or* global to the complete model can have consequences on the effectiveness of the verification runs. Although semantically equal (unless the global variable is used in some other process), SPIN can optimise the use of local variables more aggressively because, by definition, a *local* variable will never be used by other processes. Thus, SPIN can savely apply live-variable analysis [1] on local variables within a process, whereas SPIN cannot do this for global variables.

---

[12] The only drawback of this m4 approach is that we cannot make N a parameter of the inline definition; the value of N has to be known at macro expansion time.

Table 2. local - 50. Comparing different implementations to set a *local* variable to a random value between 0 and 50.

implementation	options	depth reached	states stored	states matched	transitions
plain do	default	53	104	50	154
atomic do	default	55	104	50	154
if	default	2	53	50	103
plain do	-o3	104	205	50	255
atomic do	-o3	105	104	50	154
if	-o3	3	104	50	154

Table 3. local - 10000x10. Comparing different implementations to set a *local* variable 10000 times to a random value between 0 and 10.

implementation	options	depth reached	states stored	transitions	total memory (Mb)	time (sec)
plain do	default	130002	330003	430003	10.669	2.23
atomic do	default	150002	330003	1429900	11.149	11.05
if	default	20002	220003	1319900	6.390	6.21
plain do	-o3	250002	650003	750003	18.669	4.13
atomic do	-o3	260002	440003	1539900	15.770	14.07
if	-o3	40002	440003	1539900	10.250	6.69

For the 'local variable' verification runs, for example, we used the following `Test` process:

```
28      ⟨random-local-var.pr 28⟩≡
        active proctype Test()
        {
          byte i ;
          random(i) ;
          assert((0<=i) && (i<=N)) ;
        }
```

Furthermore, we repeated the verification runs with different optimization settings enabled and disabled. Enabling or disabling partial order reduction did not make any significant difference. On the other hand, disabling the "sequence merge mode" of SPIN (using the -o3 option) gave different results. Tables 2-5 summarise the results of the various verification runs.

Local Table 2 and Table 3 list the results of randomly setting a local variable. The tables show that the plain do and atomic do solutions behave more or less the same for the default setting of SPIN. If the "sequence merge mode" is disabled with -o3, though, the plain do solution generates many more states than the atomic do construct. We also can conclude that using an atomic construct

Table 4. global - 50. Comparing different implementations to set a *global* variable to a random value between 0 and 50.

implementation	options	depth reached	states stored	states matched	transitions
plain do	default	104	255	0	255
atomic do	default	55	154	0	154
if	default	3	154	0	154
plain do	-o3	104	255	0	255
atomic do	-o3	105	154	0	154
if	-o3	3	154	0	154

Table 5. global - 10000x10. Comparing different implementations to set a *global* variable 10000 times to a random value between 0 and 10.

implementation	options	depth reached	states stored	transitions	total memory (Mb)	time (sec)
plain do	default	250002	650013	750003	18.669	7.56
atomic do	default	160002	440013	1539900	13.130	18.35
if	default	40002	440013	1539900	10.250	10.52
plain do	-o3	250002	650013	750003	18.669	7.46
atomic do	-o3	260002	440013	1539900	15.770	20.64
if	-o3	40002	440013	1539900	10.250	10.71

has negative influence on the running time of the verification: the atomic do solution is much slower than the plain do construct.

In the default setting, the if random solution behaves superior to both do solutions: the number of states is less and the depth of the if construct is constant, whereas the depth of both do solutions is linear in N. For -o3, the if solution results in as many states as the atomic do solution, but the search depth is still constant. The if solution is slightly slower than the plain do construct but a factor two faster than the atomic do.

Global. Table 4 and Table 5 show the results of randomly setting a global variable. Now the number of states for the if and atomic do solutions are the same for both the default and -o3 verification runs. Still, the depth of the if solution is superior. The plain do solution generates more states in both settings and only excels in its execution speed. Note that only the search depth of the atomic do construct is affected by changing the verification run from default to -o3.

Conclusions. The if solution is favorable with respect to the number of states and the depth reached. For the same reason, even despite its fast running times, the *plain* do solution should be avoided. The atomic do solution suffers from the linear depth and the somewhat slower execution time. The advantage of the atomic do solution is that it can be used for general N without changing the PROMELA source code. In the rare event, that you need an explicit randomise function, the atomic do will therefore suffice. For a general and efficient implementation, one should try the m4 implementation of the if solution.

Recipe 4 − Array of Bits - Bitvector

PROMELA has borrowed the array mechanism of C to group related values into a single array variable. All PROMELA datatypes can be stored in an array. When modelling a system in PROMELA, an array of bits is quite useful to encode the (local) state of the system. For example, an array of bits can be used to model

- a collection of on/off switches of the system (e.g. a factory plant); or
- a set of processes in the system (e.g. in a multicast protocol)

Unfortunately, when using arrays of bits, SPIN will issue the following unnerving warning:

```
spin: warning: bit-array ⟨array-name⟩ mapped to byte-array
```

In other words, SPIN will allocate 8 times as much memory for the bit array in the state vector as was expected! In this section we will discuss a different way to encode arrays of bits in PROMELA, which is superior to SPIN's mapping to byte-arrays.

4.1   Bitvector

To implement an equivalent to PROMELA's array-mechanism, we define a library of bitvectors. A bitvector is an (unsigned) piece of memory, where each bit can be individually set, reset and tested. We use PROMELA's built-in integer types to represent the bitvectors: byte (max. 8 bits), short (max. 16 bits) and int (max. 32 bits). PROMELA also supports a variable length unsigned type (max. 8 bits). The following aspects of the various integer types have to be taken into account:

- The byte type is an *unsigned* type. The short and int types are *signed* integer types, which means that we have to be careful with the sign bit (leftmost bit). Special care is needed in combination with logical shift operations to the right, because such operations also shift the signbit to the right.
- In numerical expressions, SPIN converts the operands to (32-bit) *signed* int values. Consequently, a bitvector int consisting of 32 ones (i.e. ~0) is considered to be a negative int value. SPIN will generate a truncation warning when converting an int value back to an *unsigned* byte.
- Consequently, it is also not wise to use −1 (i.e. 16 ones) for a short. In numerical expressions this value is converted to the int value ffff, which results in similar truncation warnings.

To be on the safe side, one should not use *signed* values (i.e. non-negative integers) to encode `bitvectors`, so:

- use bytes or `unsigned` variables for `bitvectors` with 2–8 bits;
- use `shorts` for `bitvectors` with 9–15 bits;
- use `ints` for `bitvectors` with 16–31 bits;

We define the following shorthands for `bitvector` declarations.

29   ⟨bitvector *macros* 29⟩≡   (34) 30▷
```
#define BITV_U(x,n)      unsigned x : n
#define BITV_8           byte
#define BITV_16          short
#define BITV_32          int
```

The suffixes _8, _16 and _32 indicate the number of bits the corresponding `bitvector` occupies.

30   ⟨bitvector *macros* 29⟩+≡   (34) ◁29 31▷
```
#define ALL_1S           2147483647
```

The constant `ALL_1S` is equal to 2^{31} and is represented by a zero followed by 31 ones. The constant `ALL_1S` is used to set all bits in a bitvector to 1.

The bits of a `bitvector` are manipulated using the logical *bitwise* operators of PROMELA: ~, &, |, ^, << and >>. More details on these operators can be found in traditional textbooks on the programming language C (e.g. [9]). We define some basic operations to manipulate `bitvectors`. The following macros set the i-th bit of the `bitvector` bv to 0 and 1, respectively:

31   ⟨bitvector *macros* 29⟩+≡   (34) ◁30 32▷
```
#define SET_0(bv,i)      bv=bv&(~(1<<i))
#define SET_1(bv,i)      bv=bv|(1<<i)
```

We can also set all bits of a bitvector to 0 or 1 in a single instruction:

32   ⟨bitvector *macros* 29⟩+≡   (34) ◁31 33▷
```
#define SET_ALL_0(bv)    bv=0
#define SET_ALL_1(bv,n)  bv=ALL_1S>>(31-n) ;
```

The parameter n to `SET_ALL_1` denotes the number bits to set to 1. It seems natural to let `SET_ALL_1` just assign `ALL_1S` to bv. However, SPIN will issue a truncation error when bv is a `byte` or a `short`. The following two macros can be used to test whether the i-th bit is 0 or 1, respectively:

33   ⟨bitvector *macros* 29⟩+≡   (34) ◁32
```
#define IS_0(bv,i)       (!(bv&(1<<i)))
#define IS_1(bv,i)       (bv&(1<<i))
```

The ⟨bitvector *macros*⟩ now provide the same functionality as the original array manipulation operations. Instead of writing a[i]=1 one has to invoke the macro SET_1(a,i) and the boolean test a[i] now boils down to IS_1(a,i).
All `bitvector` macros are stored in the 'header' file `bitvector.lpr`:

34   ⟨*bitvector.lpr* 34⟩≡
```
    ⟨bitvector macros 29⟩
```

Bigger bitvectors: revival of byte-arrays. If one needs a bitvector with more than 31 individual bits, one can use an array of bytes to encode such a 'big' bitvector. The following macros again hide the implementation details from the user.

```
35      ⟨bitvector macros using byte-arrays 35⟩≡
            #define BITV(bv,n)      byte bv[n]
            #define SET_0(bv,i)     bv[i/8] = bv[i/8] & (~(1<<(i%8)))
            #define SET_1(bv,i)     bv[i/8] = bv[i/8] | (1 << (i%8))
            #define IS_0(bv,i)      (!(bv[i/8]&(1<<(i%8))))
            #define IS_1(bv,i)      (bv[i/8]&(1<<(i%8)))
```

The array of bytes approach also becomes attractive if the number of bits that have to be stored is between 17 and 24; this would save one byte compared to the int implementation. A drawback of using an array of bytes to encode bitvectors is that manipulation of a complete bitvector is more problematic. For instance, testing whether all bits are equal to zero (or one) cannot be done using a cpp macro definition. In the remainder of this recipe we will only use bitvectors that are implemented by the simple data types: byte, short and int.

Note that encoding bitvectors using an array of bytes is as efficient as the implementation using the simple data types: byte, short and int. The results of the verification runs of bitvectors implemented by arrays of bytes can be found in [15].

4.2   Comparison

To compare SPIN's byte-array implementation to the newly developed bitvector macros, we have written a simple PROMELA specification that models a *bridge* between two places A and B. At the start of the system, N persons are at A and they all have to cross the bridge to get to B.

The places A and B are modelled by PROMELA processes and the bridge itself is a (handshake) channel between A and B. The choice for the next person to cross the bridge is made non-deterministically.[13] We use the variable person to encode the presence of a person at either A or B. The variable person is either defined as a bit-array (and converted to a byte-array by SPIN) or as as bitvector. If person[i] is 1 (or IS_1(person,i) is true) in process A it means that the i-th person is still at A.

To illustrate the usage of the bitvector operations, we include the definition of process B for the N=8 case:

```
36      ⟨proctype B - one bridge 36⟩≡
            active proctype B()
            {
              BITV_8   person ;
              byte     i ;
```

---

[13] Analogous to ⟨inline: random - if 27⟩, the 'random' choice for the next person to cross the bridge has been implemented by an if guard using m4.

Table 6. One bridge, 8 persons: byte-array vs. bitvector.

implementation	options	state vector	depth reached	states stored	total memory (Mb)	time (sec)
byte-array	default	36	54	7702	2.507	0.07
bitvector	default	24	54	7702	2.404	0.09
byte-array	-DCOLLAPSE	36	54	7702	2.507	0.13
bitvector	-DCOLLAPSE	24	54	7702	2.507	0.11
byte-array	-DMA=60	36	54	7702	0.819	1.60
bitvector	-DMA=60	24	54	7702	0.512	1.98

```
SET_ALL_0(person) ;
do
:: (!ALL_HERE(8)) -> bridge ? i ; SET_1(person,i) ;
:: else -> break
od
\}
```

where ALL_HERE is defined as:

37   ⟨bridge: macros 37⟩≡
          #define ALL_HERE(N)   ((person^((~0)<<N))==(~0))

We have verified three cases:

- One bridge, N=8. There is only one bridge between A and B. The number of persons at A is 8. The information stored in the person array can be coded in a single byte (i.e. BITV_8).
- One bridge, N=14. There is only one bridge between A and B. The number of persons at A is 14. Earlier experiments have shown that N=14 is the largest parameter for which the model can be verified exhaustively within 64Mb of memory.
- Two bridges, N=7. There are three processes A, B and C and there are two bridges: one between A and B and one between B and C. At the start there are 7 persons at A that have to go to C via B.

SPIN's approach to map bit-arrays to byte-arrays may not be extremely problematic. If the state vector compression techniques of SPIN would be able to compress the 7 extra zeros that are allocated for each bit in the byte-arrays, not much harm will be done. For that reason we have also verified the bridge models with two of SPIN's advanced compressions methods enabled: -DCOLLAPSE and -DMA=60.

The results of the experiments are summarised in the Tables 6-8. The results show that the bitvector implementation indeed results in a much smaller state vector. Consequently, the verification of the bitvector models needs (much) less memory than SPIN's byte-array implementation. Surprisingly enough, the

Table 7. One bridge, 14 persons: byte-array vs. bitvector.

implementation	options	state vector	state vector - stored	state vector - overhead	depth reached	states stored	total memory (Mb)	time (sec)
byte-array	default	52	40	8	90	1204260	60.058	18.94
bitvector	default	28	16	8	90	1204260	31.180	15.78
byte-array	-DCOLLAPSE	52	24	12	90	1204260	45.209	32.63
bitvector	-DCOLLAPSE	28	18	12	90	1204260	38.143	28.43
byte-array	-DMA=60	52	-	-	90	1204260	66.358	456.63
bitvector	-DMA=60	28	-	-	90	1204260	36.865	454.29

Table 8. Two bridges, 7 persons: byte-array vs. bitvector.

implementation	options	state vector	state vector - stored	state vector - overhead	depth reached	states stored	total memory (Mb)	time (sec)
byte-array	default	52	36	8	86	316379	16.127	5.07
bitvector	default	36	20	8	86	316379	11.109	4.62
byte-array	-DCOLLAPSE	52	10	12	86	316379	9.265	7.46
bitvector	-DCOLLAPSE	36	10	12	86	316379	9.163	7.01
byte-array	-DMA=60	52	-	-	86	316379	2.560	64.88
bitvector	-DMA=60	36	-	-	86	316379	1.638	72.92

bitvector implementation is also faster than the byte-array implementation
(except for the -DMA=60 compression verification runs). The -DCOLLAPSE compression mode behaves spectacular on the byte-array verification runs, but only
brings it closer to the bitvector implementation.

The bitvector implementation seems to be extremely efficient and difficult
to compress any further. In the one bridge/N=14 case (Table 7), the default case
of the bitvector run performs better than the two compressed verification runs.

Conclusions. From the results we conclude that there is no reason to stick to
SPIN's byte-array implementation. With respect to state space considerations,
the bitvector implementation is superior in all cases, including the compressed
verification runs. Furthermore, the bitvector macros seem slightly faster than
the array indexing implementation of SPIN.

Recipe 5 – Extending Promela - Deque

PROMELA is a protocol *modelling* language; it is not a specification language. One
of the complaints about PROMELA that is often heard is that PROMELA resembles
the programming language C [9] too much. The lack of more abstract datatypes
than the built-in types bit, byte, array, etc., is seen as serious disadvantage.
This view on PROMELA is not correct, though. The PROMELA language is rich

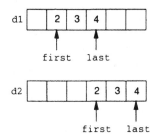

Fig. 1. Erroneous implementation of a circular **deque** in PROMELA, using dynamic **first** and **last** pointers.

enough to add user-defined datatypes. The **typedef** construct can be used to define new datatypes and the **inline** or **cpp** macros (see Recipe 1) can be used to define operations on such new datatypes. If the bodies of the operations are enclosed in **d_step** clauses, the implementation will be highly efficient, as SPIN treats a complete **d_step** clause as a single transition.

The most important rule that should be followed when adding a new datatype T to PROMELA is that a value t of T is always represented by the same sequence of bits. The reason for this is that two states are considered equal by SPIN if the memory representation of both states is exactly the same. If the same value t can have several different memory footprints, SPIN will not be able to conclude that the same value t is used.

For example, suppose we would try to implement a double-ended **deque**-like datatype on top of the built-in **array** type of PROMELA. We treat the **array** as a circular buffer, using **first** and **last** pointers which point to the first element and last element of the **deque**, respectively. Such implementation allows the addition and removal of elements at both sides of the **deque**, which can be done quite efficiently. Figure 1 shows the **array** representations of **deque** d1 and d2 that are semantically equal. Both **deques** contain the values 2, 3 and 4. However, apart from the fact that the **first** and **last** pointers of d1 and d2 are different, the array representation of d1 and d2 are clearly not equal. So, SPIN will treat the two **deques** as being different.

5.1 Deque

To illustrate the power and elegance of PROMELA, we present a *correct* implementation of a double-ended **Deque** datatype in PROMELA. Elements can be added and removed from the front and the back of a **Deque** object. First we define the **Deque** datatype itself.

```
38    ⟨typedef Deque 38⟩≡
         typedef Deque {
            byte  a[N] ;
            byte  length ;
            byte  i ;
         } ;
```

The array a is used to hold the elements of the Deque. The array a can hold at most N elements of type byte. The field length holds the number of elements in the deque. The first element (i.e. the 'front') of a Deque variable will always be stored in a[0], whereas the last element (i.e. the 'back') will reside in a[length-1]. Entries in a that are not used (i.e. a[length..N-1]) will always have value 0.

The field i is only used as a temporary index variable within the array a. Outside of the Deque operations, it will always have the value 0. Instead of having a *local* temporary field i for each Deque, one could also choose to use a single global variable for all Deque variables.[14] Having a single global temporary variable is more efficient with respect to the state vector, especially when the PROMELA model uses several Deque variables. The advantage of having the local i field in the typedef definition of Deque, though, is that the typedef definition is self-sufficient; the user can use the typedef definitions together with the Deque operations without having to declare additional variables. There is no danger for having nameclashes.

A clear disadvantage of the ⟨*typedef* Deque 38⟩ definition is that the type of the elements (i.e. byte) and the number of elements (i.e. N) are hardcoded into the Deque definition. If one needs another Deque in which the type of the elements or the maximum number of elements differs, one has to define a new typedef definition. To be more generic, we make both the type and the number of elements a parameter to the Deque datatype:

39   ⟨Deque *definition* 39⟩≡   (48) 42▷
```
#define DECLARE_DEQUE(T,MAX) \
typedef Deque_##T##MAX { \
   T      a[MAX] ; \
   byte   length ; \
   byte   i ; \
}
```

The ## operation in the typedef is cpp's string concatenation operator. Thus, the macro application DECLARE_DEQUE(type,N) will expand to a typedef definition with the name Deque_typeN.[15] For example,

40   ⟨Deque *example:* Deque *declarations* 40⟩≡
```
DECLARE_DEQUE(byte,3) ;
DECLARE_DEQUE(short,5) ;
```

will define the following typedef definitions:

41   ⟨Deque *example:* Deque *declarations expansions* 41⟩≡
```
typedef Deque_byte3 { ... } ;
typedef Deque_short5 { ... } ;
```

---

[14] In the programming language C++ we would have made i a static variable to the class Deque.

[15] The reader familiar with C++ [21] will recognise the similarity between the DECLARE_DEQUE construct and C++'s template mechanism. In fact, early C++ compilers used macro expansion to implement templates.

Table 9. Deque operations.

PUSH_FRONT(deq,x)	adds a new element x at the front of deq
PUSH_BACK(deq,x)	adds a new element x at the back of deq
FRONT(deq)	returns the first element of deq
BACK(deq)	returns the last element of deq
POP_FRONT(deq)	removes the first element of deq
POP_BACK(deq)	removes the last element of deq
CLEAR(deq)	removes all elements from deq
COPY(src,dest)	copies the elements of Deque src to Deque dest
PRINT(deq)	writes the contents of deq to the standard output
SIZE(deq)	returns the number of elements in deq
IS_EMPTY(deq)	returns true if deq does not contain any elements

To ease the declaration of Deque variables, we also define a short hand for the Deque_... names:

42   ⟨Deque *definition* 39⟩+≡   (48)   ◁39
```
      #define DEQUE(T,MAX) Deque_##T##MAX
```

Now we can introduce Deque variables as follows:

43   ⟨Deque *example:* Deque *variables* 43⟩≡
```
      DEQUE(byte,3)    d1 ;
      DEQUE(short,5)   d2 ;
```

Deque operations. For the implementation of the Deque operations we use PROMELA's inline construct and cpp macros. We use PROMELA's d_step construct to encode the operations as efficient as possible. Table 9 shows the operations that we defined for Deque in [15].[16]

In this paper, we only present the definitions of PUSH_FRONT, PUSH_BACK, COPY, FRONT, BACK, SIZE and IS_EMPTY. The other Deque operations are left as an exercise.

44   ⟨Deque *operations* 44⟩≡   (48)   45▷
```
      inline PUSH_FRONT(deq,x)
      {
        d_step {
          deq.i=deq.length ;
          do
          :: deq.i > 0  -> deq.a[deq.i]=deq.a[deq.i-1] ; deq.i--
          :: deq.i == 0 -> break
          od ;
          deq.a[0]=x ;
          deq.length++ ;
          deq.i=0 ;
        }
      }
```

---

[16] We borrowed the names for the Deque operations from C++'s Standard Template Library (STL) [21].

The operation PUSH_FRONT(deq,x) adds the element x to deq by shifting all elements of deq to the right in array deq.a. The 'local' field deq.i is used to iterate through the array deq.a. At the end of the operation this temporary variable is resetted to 0.

The danger of PUSH_FRONT is that if the array deq.a is full, the operation will still try to add a new element. Fortunately, the **pan** verifier will trigger this "index out of bounds" error on run-time.[17] It would have nicer been though, if we had added an assertion like assert(deq.length<N) to the operation. Unfortunately, this is not possible as N is not fixed: there may be several Deques defined, all with different MAX arguments. We could have solved this by storing the size of the array into the **typedef** definition of Deque, but this would have enlarged the Deque objects.

PUSH_FRONT is an expensive operation: all elements in the **deque** have to be shifted one place to the right in order to insert a single element. Still, due to the **d_step** construct the complete operation only uses a single transition within SPIN.

The Deque type is a double-ended List, so we can also add elements to the back of the Deque object:

45   ⟨Deque *operations* 44⟩+≡   (48) ◁44 46▷
```
    inline PUSH_BACK(deq,x)
    {
      d_step {
        deq.a[deq.length]=x ;
        deq.length++ ;
      }
    }
```

Like with PUSH_FRONT, there is no explicit check for an "index out of bounds" error. The operation PUSH_BACK is more efficient than PUSH_FRONT. In fact, when using an **array** to implement a Deque type, adding to the back of the **array** is always more efficient than to the front of the **array**.[18]

Because **typedef** and **array** objects in PROMELA are not assignable, we also need a operation to copy the contents of one Deque variable to another Deque variable.

46   ⟨Deque *operations* 44⟩+≡   (48) ◁45 47▷
```
    inline COPY(src,dst)
    {
      d_step {
        CLEAR(dst) ;
        dst.length=src.length ;
        dst.i=0 ;
        do
```

---

[17] Unless the **pan** verifier has been compiled using the directive -DNOBOUNDCHECK.

[18] It will be clear that the implementation of a Stack-like datatype on top of an **array** is most efficient: addition and removal of elements is always done at the back of the array.

```
      ::   dst.i <  dst.length -> dst.a[dst.i] = src.a[dst.i] ; dst.i++
      ::   dst.i >= dst.length -> break
      od ;
      dst.i=0 ;
   \}
\}
```

Note that we first call CLEAR on dst to set all elements of dst.a to 0.
Below we define the operations on Deque objects that return a value:

47   ⟨Deque *operations* 44⟩+≡   (48) ◁46
```
            #define FRONT(deq)      (deq.a[0])
            #define BACK(deq)       (deq.a[deq.length-1])
            #define SIZE(deq)       (deq.length)
            #define IS_EMPTY(deq)   (deq.length==0)
```

Note that the macros FRONT and BACK do not check whether deq is non-empty.

Here our Deque implementation is ended. In [15] all Deque definitions and operations are defined and stored (using noweb) in a single 'header' file deque.hpr:

48   ⟨*deque.hpr* 48⟩≡
            ⟨Deque *definition* 39⟩
            ⟨Deque *operations* 44⟩

PROMELA models that need Deque objects can simply #include this file.

Conclusions. In this recipe we have shown that PROMELA allows the definition of efficient user-defined types. A double-ended Deque type has been defined. In the same way, other abstract data types like single-ended Queues, Lists and Stacks can be defined and offered to the user via the usual #include mechanism.

Recipe 6 – Invariance

Manna and Pnueli [11] consider three main classes of temporal properties of reactive programs: *invariance*, *response* and *precedence* properties. This section is devoted to checking *invariance* properties with SPIN. An invariance property refers to a boolean expression P, and it requires that P is an invariant (i.e. is equal to true) over all reachable states of all computations [11]. In temporal logic notation, invariance properties are expressed by $\Box P$ for a state formula P.

Dwyer et. al. [4] have conducted a valuable survey on the practical use of temporal properties with respect to finite-state verification. They collected more than 500 temporal specifications to classify temporal properties into property patterns. One of the results of [4] is that 25% of the temporal properties that are being checked are invariance properties (i.e. universality or absence patterns in the terminoloy of [4]).[19]

For novice users of SPIN, the invariance property is easy to grasp and probably one of the first properties that they will verify with SPIN. There are several

---

[19] *Response* properties are even more common: they constitute nearly 50% of the temporal properties.

ways to verify an invariance property $\Box P$ with SPIN. In this recipe we discuss five of them. We have tested the different invariance schemes on several PROMELA specifications to find out which is most efficient. Our approach only allows references to *global* variables to appear in the expression P. This does not restrict the approach as local variables can always be declared globally. Using global variables may be less efficient than using local variables, though.

1. monitor process. The first method that we investigate is the method that is proposed in `assert.html` of [19]. This method is also the method of choice for people (relatively) new to SPIN. To express system invariance it suffices to place the invariant in an independently executed process.

49   ⟨*invariance - monitor process* 49⟩≡

```
active proctype monitor()
{
  assert(P) ;
}
```

Since the `monitor` process is executed independently from the rest of the system, the `assert(P)` statement may be evaluated at any time. Alternatively, one could add the `assert` statement to the `init` process after all processes have been started. Note that in this case the property P is not checked in the initial state of the system.

Even before running experiments with SPIN, however, we can predict that the 'independence' execution of the `monitor` process will be expensive. As the `assert` statement will be enabled in all states of the system, the number of states could – in the worst case – be doubled.

2. never claim - do assert. The SPIN documentation [19] also suggests another method to check for invariance.

50   ⟨*invariance - **never do assert** 50*⟩≡

```
never {
  do
  :: assert(P)
  od
}
```

The **never** claim ensures that after every step of the system the assertion is checked. In this way the number of states is not doubled, only the search depth of the verification run.

A minor drawback of this method is the fact that SPIN always gives the following warning after verifying a **never** claim:

```
warning: for p.o. reduction to be valid the never claim must be stutter-closed
(never claims generated from LTL formulae are stutter-closed)
```

As this **never** claim is not generated from a LTL formula, the novice SPIN user is not likely to trust the verification results after this warning about 'stutter-closed'-ness. In [15], stuttering is discussed in more detail. Here we only assure the reader that the **never do assert** method is always safe with respect to partial order reduction. And the warning can thus be ignored.

3. LTL property. The most *logical* way to check for invariance is to use SPIN's support for Linear Temporal Logic (LTL) formulae. SPIN's command line option -f translates a LTL formula to a **never** claim, encoding the corresponding Büchi acceptance condition.

The LTL formula $\Box P$ is translated to the following (stutter-closed) **never** claim:

```
51      ⟨invariance - LTL never claim 51⟩≡
        never {
        TO_init:
          if
          ::  (!P) -> goto accept_all
          ::  (1)  -> goto TO_init
          fi ;
        accept_all:
          skip
        }
```

4. guarded monitor process. A drawback of the ⟨*invariance - monitor process* 49⟩ method is that the **assert** statement is enabled in *every* state. To verify $\Box P$, though, it suffices to check that $\Diamond \neg P$ does not hold.

```
52      ⟨invariance - guarded monitor process 52⟩≡
        proctype monitor()
        {
        end:
          atomic { !P -> assert(P) ; }
        }
```

The **atomic** statement only becomes executable when P itself is not **true**. The end label is needed because if the **atomic** clause never becomes executable, the **monitor** process would have a 'non-valid end-state'.

5. unless. Our last method to check for invariance uses PROMELA's **unless** statement. The idea is to enclose the ⟨*body*⟩ of one of the processes of the system into the following **unless** clause:

```
53      ⟨invariance: unless 53⟩≡
        proctype Foo()
        {
          { ⟨body⟩
          } unless { atomic { !P -> assert(P) ; } }
        }
```

Whenever P becomes **false**, the ⟨*body*⟩ will be interrupted and SPIN will conclude that the invariant property P does not hold. The **unless** method has some advantages, but these are outweigthed by the disadvantages:

+   No extra `proctype` is needed, which saves 4 bytes in the state vector.
+   The local variables of the process can also be used in the property P.
−   The definition of a `proctype` has to be changed. This involves even more work when the process contains labels and `goto`'s.
−   The `unless` construct can reach inside `atomic` clauses, which means that if the property P is `false` inside an `atomic` clause, the `unless` method will erroneously report an error.
−   The partial order reduction may be invalid if rendez-vous communication is used within the body.
−   The ⟨*body*⟩ of the process is not allowed to end, because otherwise the `unless` statement also terminates, preventing subsequent tests on !P.

6.1 Comparison

To compare the different invariance methods we used these methods to verify the following four (standard) PROMELA specifications:

> brp   a bounded retransmission protocol (from [3]).
>
> leader   a leader election protocol (part of SPIN's 3.3.10 distribution).
>
> philo   a model for the well-known dining philosophers problem; we used N=7 for the `default` runs and N=6 for the `-DNOREDUCE` runs.
>
> pftp   a flow control protocol (from [6] and part of SPIN's 3.3.10 distribution).

We conducted two types of verification runs. In the `default` case, we used SPIN's default settings and only adjusted the depth of the depth first search (DFS) stack (via option `-m`) when needed. Because the `unless` method is not reliable in combination with rendez-vous communication and partial order reduction (i.e. for the brp and philo runs), we repeated the verification runs with partial order reduction disabled (i.e. `-DNOREDUCE`).

Tables 10-13 list the results of verifying some trivial invariance properties using the methods discussed. The columns correspond with the 5 invariance methods. We verified two versions of the 'monitor process' method: in 1a the `monitor` process is started first, whereas in 1b the `monitor` process is started last. The 'best' results in a row are typeset using **boldface**.

Tables 10 and 12 report the total memory used by the verification runs in the `default` and `-DNOREDUCE` case, respectively. Tables 11 and 13 report the verification time (i.e. user+system time) of the runs. Due to space considerations, we have not included other significant parameters of the verification runs, like 'depth reached' or 'number of states stored'.

Conclusions. First we consider the results in the columns 1a and 1b. The only difference between the PROMELA models of 1a and 1b is the activation order of the `monitor` process. Still the results for 1a and 1b show significant differences. If the `monitor` process is started last (1b) the verification statistics are worse. The reason for this is that SPIN's DFS will select the processes in reverse order; i.e. the last process started will be considered first. And because the `monitor` process is always enabled, this step will always be executed before any other

Table 10. Invariance `default`: total memory used (Mb).

	1a	1b	2	3	4	5
brp	27.157	38.115	**14.971**	15.688	26.338	22.135
leader	**2.542**	**2.542**	**2.542**	**2.542**	**2.542**	9.648
philo	16.318	21.336	**11.710**	11.915	**11.710**	12.510
pftp	**9.441**	11.285	**9.441**	9.953	**9.441**	9.744

Table 11. Invariance `default`: verification time (sec).

	1a	1b	2	3	4	5
brp	11.11	16.42	**4.90**	5.77	9.39	10.24
leader	0.03	**0.02**	**0.02**	0.03	**0.02**	3.36
philo	23.26	35.11	11.41	13.84	**11.31**	12.01
pftp	**1.53**	2.01	1.67	2.06	1.56	1.62

Table 12. Invariance `-DNOREDUCE`: total memory used (Mb).

	1a	1b	2	3	4	5
brp	40.777	59.415	22.140	24.735	40.572	**21.048**
leader	7.725	10.387	**5.062**	5.307	**5.062**	14.011
philo	11.504	16.317	**7.203**	7.835	**7.203**	17.973
pftp	30.644	40.679	**20.608**	22.037	**20.608**	22.307

Table 13. Invariance `-DNOREDUCE`: verification time (sec).

	1a	1b	2	3	4	5
brp	24.13	37.16	10.86	12.54	21.09	**9.60**
leader	2.66	4.18	1.30	1.37	**1.19**	5.76
philo	19.67	30.67	9.61	12.07	**9.57**	35.27
pftp	13.70	19.34	8.19	9.22	**7.84**	8.34

process can advance a step. But although **1a** performs better than **1b**, its results are still worse than the other invariance methods. So we conclude that to check for invariance one should not use the 'monitor process' solution. But if you do, be sure to activate the `monitor` process as the first process.

Although the `unless` method sometimes shows the best statistics (i.e. when partial order reduction is disabled) it has too many restrictions to be general applicable. ¿From the other three methods, method '4. guarded monitor process' seems to perform quite well. However, the results of method '2. `never do assert`' are always close or better. For the verification of the `brp`, method 2 performs even much better than method 4. It is also interesting to see that, although it never performs bad, there is no verification run where method '3. LTL property' shows the best results. Using this method to check for invariance is not a bad choice, but method 2 and 4 perform better.

To conclude we recommend to use method '2. `never do assert`' when checking invariance with SPIN.

Conclusions

In this paper we presented six 'recipes' to cook more efficient PROMELA models and to use the model checker SPIN more effectively. In Recipe 1 we showed how macros and `inline`s can help to structure and parameterise PROMELA models. Recipe 2 discussed some issues regarding the `atomic` and `d_step` constructs. In Recipe 3 we investigated the most efficient way to model randomness in PROMELA. In Recipe 4 we developed a `bitvector` library that is more efficient than SPIN's own `byte`-array implementation. In Recipe 5 we combined the ingredients of Recipe 1 and 2 to show how to add efficient data types to PROMELA. And in Recipe 6 we investigated the effectiveness of five different methods to check for invariance with SPIN.

This paper and the forthcoming [15] are not claimed to constitute a complete and finished collection of best practices for SPIN. On the contrary, the author hopes that this collection of techniques will stimulate other SPIN users to contribute their own best practices and experiences to this list. In this way not only the common knowledge on modelling and verification with SPIN will grow, it will also yield opportunities to optimise and improve the SPIN system itself.

Acknowledgements. First of all, the author wants to thank Gerard Holzmann, the SPIN master, who is always available for patiently answering naive questions and personal wishes regarding SPIN. I would like to thank Pim Kars for showing me – already in 1996 – several efficient PROMELA tricks, that changed my attitude towards the application of verification tools. Ed Brinksma is thanked for sharing his experiences as a 'novice' SPIN user (i.e. Recipe 2 and 4). Yaroslav Usenko is thanked for his suggestion for a more elegant and slightly more efficient `do` solution for the `random` construct (i.e. Recipe 3). I want to thank Rom Langerak and especially the anonymous referees for their very useful suggestions to improve both the contents and readability of this paper.

References

1. Alfred V. Aho, Ravi Sethi, and Jeffrey D. Ullman. *Compilers: Principles, Techniques, and Tools*. Addison-Wesley, Reading, Massachusetts, 1986.
2. Dov Bulka and David Mayhew. *Efficient C++ (Performance Programming Techniques)*. Addison-Wesley, Reading, Massachusetts, 2000.
3. Pedro R. D'Argenio, Joost-Pieter Katoen, Theo C. Ruys, and G. Jan Tretmans. The Bounded Retransmission Protocol must be on time! (Full Version). CTIT Technical Report Series 97-03, Centre for Telematics and Information Technology, University of Twente, Enschede, The Netherlands, 1997. Also available from URL: http://wwwtios.cs.utwente.nl/~dargenio/brp/.
4. Matthew B. Dwyer, George S. Avrunin, and James C. Corbett. Patterns in Property Specifications for Finite-State Verification. In *Proceedings of the 1999 International Conference on Software Engineering (ICSE'99)*, pages 411–420, Los Angeles, CA, U.S.A., May 1999. ACM Press.
5. Gerard J. Holzmann. SPIN homepage: http://netlib.bell-labs.com/netlib/spin/whatispin.html.

6. Gerard J. Holzmann. *Design and Validation of Computer Protocols*. Prentice Hall, Englewood Cliffs, New Jersey, 1991.
7. Gerard J. Holzmann. SPIN Model Checking - Reliable Design of Concurrent Software. *Dr. Dobb's Journal*, pages 92–97, October 1997.
8. Gerard J. Holzmann. The Model Checker SPIN. *IEEE Transactions on Software Engineering*, 23(5):279–295, May 1997.
9. Brian Kernighan and Dennis Ritchie. *The C Programming Language*. Prentice Hall, second edition, 1988.
10. Donald E. Knuth. *Literate Programming*. Number 27 in CSLI Lecture Notes. Center for the Study of Language and Information (CSLI), Stanford University, California, 1992.
11. Zohar Manna and Amir Pnueli. Tools and Rules for the Practicing Verifier. In R.F. Rashid, editor, *Carnegie Mellon Computer Science: A 25th Anniversary Commemorative*, pages 125–159. ACM Press, New York, 1991.
12. Scott Meyers. *Effective C++ (50 Specific Ways to Improve Your Programs and Designs)*. Addison-Wesley, Reading, Massachusetts, second edition, 1998.
13. Norman Ramsey. noweb – homepage. Available from URL: http://www.cs.virginia.edu/~nr/noweb/.
14. Norman Ramsey. Literate Programming Simplified. *IEEE Software*, 11(5):97–105, September 1994.
15. Theo C. Ruys. Effective SPIN. CTIT Technical Report Series, Centre for Telematics and Information Technology, University of Twente, Faculty of Computer Science, Enschede, The Netherlands, August 2000. To appear.
16. René Seindal. *GNU m4, version 1.4*. Free Software Foundation, Inc., 59 Temple Place - Suite 330, Boston, MA 02111, USA, 1.4 edition, November 1994. Available from URL: http://www.gnu.org.
17. SPIN Documentation. Basic SPIN Manual. Part of SPIN's online HTML documentation.
18. SPIN Documentation. Proceedings of the SPIN Workshops. Part of SPIN's online HTML documentation.
19. SPIN Documentation. SPIN Version 3.3: Language Reference - Man-Pages and Semantics Definition. Part of SPIN's online HTML documentation.
20. SPIN Documentation. What's New in SPIN Versions 2.0 and 3.0 - Summary of changes since Version 1.0. Part of SPIN's online HTML documentation.
21. Bjarne Stroustrup. *The C++ Programming Language*. Addison-Wesley, Reading, Massachusetts, third edition, 1997.

Tutorial on FDR and Its Applications

Philippa Broadfoot and Bill Roscoe

Oxford University Computing Laboratory
Wolfson Building, Parks Road
Oxford OX1 3QD, UK
{pb,awr}@comlab.ox.ac.uk

FDR [1] is a refinement checker for the process algebra CSP [2,4], based on that language's well-established semantic models. FDR stands for Failures-Divergences Refinement, after the premier model. In common with many other model checkers, it works by "determinising" (or normalising) a specification and enumerating states in the cartesian product of this and the implementation. Unlike most, the specification and implementation are written in the same language. Under development by its creators, Formal Systems (a spin-off of the Computing Laboratory) since 1991, it now offers a range of state compression methods. On current workstations it can work at up to 20M states/hour with only a small degradation on moving to disc-based storage.

Adaptations of FDR have been, or are being made, to accommodate other input notations such as UML, but in this tutorial we will concentrate on CSP. We will give a brief introduction to the CSP input language, and demonstrate FDR's use in modelling

- Timed systems
- Fault tolerance
- Cryptographic protocols: FDR was, we believe, the first general-purpose model checker to be used for these, and we will demonstrate the Casper protocol-to-CSP compiler [3].
- Information flow analysis

as well as discussing the techniques it uses for addressing the state explosion problem.

FDR has been much used in industrial work in areas such as computer security, safety-critical systems, communications networks and telecommunications.

References

1. Formal Systems. FDR web site:
   http://www.formal.demon.co.uk/FDR2.html
2. C. A. R. Hoare. "Communicating Sequential Processes", Prentice Hall (1985).
3. Gavin Lowe. Casper web site:
   http://www.mcs.le.ac.uk/~gl7/Security/Casper/
4. A. W. Roscoe. "The Theory and Practice of Concurrency", Prentice Hall (1998).

K. Havelund, J. Penix, and W. Visser (Eds.): SPIN 2000, LNCS 1885, p. 322, 2000.
© Springer-Verlag Berlin Heidelberg 2000

The Temporal Rover and the ATG Rover

Doron Drusinsky

Time-Rover, Inc.
11425 Charsan Ln., Cupertino, CA 95014, USA
doron@time-rover.com, www.time-rover.com

Abstract. The Temporal Rover is a specification based verification tool for applications written in C, C++, Java, Verilog and VHDL. The tool combines formal specification, using Linear-Time Temporal Logic (LTL) and Metric Temporal Logic (MTL), with conventional simulation/execution based testing. The Temporal Rover is tailored for the verification of complex protocols and reactive systems where behavior is time dependent. The Temporal Rover generates executable code from LTL and MTL assertions written as comments in the source code. This executable source code is compiled and linked as part of the application under test. During application execution the generated code validates the executing program against the formal temporal specification requirements. Using MTL, real time and relative time constraints can be validated. A special code generator supports validation of such constraints in the field, on an embedded target.

1 Temporal Logic Overview

Temporal Logic [5] is a special branch of modal logic that investigates the notion of time and order. In [6], Pnueli suggested using Linear-Time Propositional Temporal Logic (LTL) for reasoning about concurrent programs. Since then, several researchers have used LTL to state and prove correctness of concurrent programs, protocols, and hardware (e.g., [2], [3], [4]).

Metric Temporal Logic (MTL) extends Temporal Logic with real time constraints and was suggested by Chang, Pnueli, and Manna as a vehicle for the verification of real time systems [1].

Throughout this article we will refer to TL assertions being LTL assertions with or without MTL extensions.

2 Linear-Time Temporal Logic

Linear-Time Temporal Logic (LTL) is an extension of propositional logic where, in addition to the propositional logic operators (and (&&), or (||), xor (^), not (!), etc.) there are four future-time operators and four dual past time operators. The following syntax is used by the Temporal Rover for these four operators:

- Always in the future, and Always in the past. You can use the English keywords *Always* and *AlwaysInThePast*, or a box ([], [-]) to represent the always operators.

K. Havelund, J. Penix, and W. Visser (Eds.): SPIN 2000, LNCS 1885, pp.323–330, 2000.
© Springer-Verlag Berlin Heidelberg

- Sometime in the future, and Sometime in the past. You can use the English keywords *Sometime* and *SometimeInThePast*, or a diamond (<>, <->) to represent a sometime operators.
- Until (for the future), and Since (for the past). You can use the English keywords *Until* and *Since*, or U and S to represent the until and since operators.
- Next cycle (for the future), and Previous cycle (for the past). You can use the English keywords *Next* and *Previous*, or a circle ((), (-)) to represent these operators.

3 Metric Temporal Logic

Metric Temporal Logic (MTL) extends LTL by supporting the specification of relative time and real time constraints. All four LTL future time operators (*Sometime, Always, Until, Next*) can be characterized by relative time and real time constraints specifying the duration of the temporal operator.

The following are some examples of MTL constraints (text inside curly brackets implies a prepositional-logic formula):

1. $Always_{<10}(\{readySignal == 1\}$ Implies $()\{ackSignal == 0\})$
   which reads: always, within the next ten cycles, readySignal == 1 implies that one cycle later ackSignal == 0.
2. $Always_{timer1[5,10]}(\{readySignal == 1\}$ Implies
   $Eventually_{timer2 >= 20}\{ackSignal == 0\})$
   which reads: always, between 5 and 10 timer1 real time units in the future, readySignal == 1 implies that eventually, at least 20 timer2 real time units further in the future, ackSignal == 0.

MTL constraints can specify lower bounds, upper bounds, and ranges for relative time and real time constraints. In the first example a relative time upper bound is specified for the always operator. It is relative in that the bound is counted in clock cycles (see *The Temporal Rover's Notion of Time* below). In the second example two real time constraints are specified, using virtual clocks named *timer1* and *timer2*. A separate *TRClock* statement maps these virtual clocks to system calls, system clocks or any other counting device.

4 Proprietary Operators

The following two operators are Temporal Rover specific and are not part of LTL or MTL as described in the literature. Both operators can be used only in the MTL form namely, with a constraint.

- ρ RepeatedUntil$_{constraint}$ φ. This operator counts the number of occurrences of ρ until the occurrence of φ. It is used with MTL syntax, such as ρ RepeatedUntil$_{<=5}$ φ which succeeds if and only if ρ occurred five times or less until the occurrence of φ. Note that the constraint (written as <=5) does not represent real-time or relative clock ticks but rather is the number of times ρ succeeds in a *final* way (finality issues are discussed in the sequel).

- Repeated$_{constraint}$ ρ. This operator counts the number of occurrences of ρ in the future. It is used with MTL syntax, such as Repeated$_{[4,7]}$ ρ which succeeds if and only if ρ occurred between four and seven times in the future.

5 Using the Temporal Rover

The Temporal Rover is a code generator whose input is a Java, C, C++, Verilog, or VHDL source code program, where TL assertions are written as source code comments. The Temporal Rover parser converts this program file into a new file, which is identical to the original file except for the TL assertions that are now implemented in source code.

5.1 Writing Temporal Logic Assertions within a Program

The following example illustrates the way assertions are written inside source code. A Traffic-Light Controller (TLC) function is repeatedly invoked by a scheduler. Being a typical state machine, in each invocation cycle it computes its next state based on it's current state and the values of variables at the time. The TL assertions describes temporal requirements for this TLC.

```
void myScheduler() {
        while (1) {
                … /* schedule various system modules */
                trafficLightController()
        }
…
void trafficLightController() {
… /* Traffic Light Controller functionality */

/* TRBegin
// Asserting that always, if light is Green, camera
// is not on  (not shooting), namely CameraOn == 0.
TRAssert{ Always({Color_Main == GREEN} Implies
                {CameraOn == 0})
        }
=>
// These actions are customizable and provided by
// the user
  {
      printf("Assertion 1: so far: SUCCESS\n");
      printf("Assertion 1: so far: FAIL\n");
                                      TRProcessLastRe
                                      sult("Assertion
                                      1\n");
      printf("Assertion 1: DONE! your last result is FINAL!\n");
  }
TREnd */

} // end of trafficLightController function
```

The assertion has the following general syntax:

TRAssert {<TL-formula>} => {<*Four optional actions*>}

The list of four optional actions are, in order:

1. Action to perform every cycle in which the TL formula succeeds.
2. Action to perform every cycle in which the TL formula fails.
3. Action to perform every cycle (see *The Temporal Rover's Notion of Time* below).
4. Action to perform every cycle in which the TL formula succeeds or fails in a final way (see *Finite Executions vs. Infinite TL Sequences* below).

5.2 The Temporal Rover's Notion of Time

In the Traffic Light Controller example above, the assertion is written inside the *trafficLightController* function. This location of the assertion within the program defines the clock tick for the TL assertion. A new cycle for this assertion is considered to occur when the assertions location in the code is reached in run-time. For example, an assertion

Always({Color_Main == GREEN} Implies Next {CameraOn == 0})

Within the *trafficLightController* function will consider the *Next* cycle to be the next time *trafficLightController* is reached.

5.3 Finite Executions vs. Infinite TL Sequences

TL is semantically defined for infinite sequences or at least for sequences whose end point is known. For example, the TL formula *Eventually {x>0}* semantically evaluates to true if there is a point within the input sequence where $x>0$. However, when executing an on-going reactive program it is not known a priori whether the program has ended yet or not. Hence, if x is 0 until cycle 1000 there are two possibilities:

- The program will not continue executing.
- The program will continue executing and possibly $x>0$ sometime thereafter.

In the first case *Eventually {x>0}* should semantically fail, whereas in the second it might succeed. The Temporal Rover cannot know in run time whether the program will continue executing or not. Therefore, the best it can conclude is that *so far, the assertion failed.* In contrast, when $x>0$ this assertion succeeds and the Temporal Rover knows that no future value of x will be able to change this fact. This is the reason for the fourth optional Temporal Rover action. This action executes when the success/fail result is *final* and cannot change in the future.

Another example is *Always{x>0}*. It will succeed in a non final way as long as $x>0$. It will fail in a final way once x is not greater than 0.

5.4 The Embedded Systems Code Generator

Embedded systems applications face the following special constraints:

- Limited memory. The target application in many automotive, consumer, and communication applications is limited in RAM.
- The target application has real-time constraints.
- Due to the memory size limitations many embedded applications have no on-board operating system. Such systems have no file system for logging verification and test reports. In addition, they cannot perform dynamic memory allocation, which is essential for all TL implementations.

The Temporal-Rover has a special code generator targeted at embedded applications. The generated verification code has almost no memory overhead on the target, and performs overhead computation on a host PC. The generated verification code requires no OS on the target side

Using this code generator, a host computer performs almost all verification code. The target is required to perform only basic computations of propositional sub-formulae and to communicate the results to the host.

The host and target code segment communicate via serial port, RPC, or any other communication protocol, using a customizable protocol. Since all verification code is executing on host side, there is full access to a file system for logging and comparing test results.

5.5 Concurrency

The Temporal Rover supports assertions for concurrent systems using the following approach. Let A and B be two concurrent entities, such as processes, tasks, threads, modules, etc. Entity A may mark a block of code as a section, such as CriticalSectionA. Having done that, entity B can refer to this block of code in it's assertions. For example:

```
Eventually(
        {y==0} And
        ({x!=0) Until {TRWithin("CriticalSectionA")})
)
```

Where TRWithin is a special TemporalRover construct that examines, during execution whether entity A is indeed inside the marked block of code or not.

6 Complexity and Scalability

The Tableau method is commonly used by model-checkers for formal verification of TL properties. It was conceived as a method for solving the validity problem for LTL ([7]). As such, it is considered as a possible method for run-time evaluation of LTL. The Tableau method creates a non-deterministic state machine (called the Tableau) whose size is exponential in the size of the TL formula. For example, the size of the formula/assertion *Always (x==1 Implies Next y==1)* is 5, counting 3 operators and 2 propositions. The corresponding Tableau will therefore have 32 states. Being non-deterministic, a Tableau requires an implementation where most states are in memory every clock cycle. Obviously, such an exponential method is not scaleable, and cannot be used for the verification of large applications and protocols. Consider a temporal logic specification of a real-life protocol such as the PCI-bus protocol, with over 100 assertions, of length 15 each. Consider also an efficient Tableau implementation of 50 bytes per state. The run-time memory requirement will be 160MBytes, leaving almost no memory for the actual PCI-bus simulation.

Some PCI-bus assertions are listed on our Web site at http://www.time-rover.com, where it is evident that assertions are often of length 20 or more, requiring 1,000,000 states or more per assertion, implying memory consumption in the order of Gigabytes.

Note that the size of the Tableau is directly related to speed in that it represents the number of states that need to be evaluated and processed every clock cycle.

The Temporal Rover does not use the Tableau method. The complexity of it's algorithm is n^2 thereby yielding much better scalability than the Tableau. This complexity is not in contrast with known exponential lower bounds for the TL validity problem, as the Temporal Rover does not attempt to solve the validity problem.

7 The ATG Rover

The ATG-Rover is a program that automatically generates test sequences that cover high-level specifications written in TL, using the same specification syntax used by the Temporal Rover.

The sequences generated by the ATG-Rover are well suited for testing a requirement driven application in that:

- Only sequences relevant to the specification requirements are generated thereby reducing the size of the test bench considerably.
- The generated sequences have the same flexibility as the high-level requirements. Hence for example, a requirement that *Every two consecutive Requests must be separated by an Acknowledgement* has the flexibility of allowing the *Acknowledgement* to appear any time between two consecutive *Requests*. Therefore, ATG should generate test sequences that pass for any combination of *<Request, Acknowledgement, Request>* triplet, no matter how far apart the events are from one another. Formally speaking, the ATG Rover needs to accommodate TL's inherent non-determinism.
- Redundant test sequences are not generated.

Rather than generating the test bench itself, the output of the ATG-Rover is a program that generates tests, given in source code. This eliminates the need to store a very large amount of tests, and enables the test engineer to modify the generated program so that only a particular subset of tests will be generated. The generated program becomes the driver of the system under test, for the purpose of testing particular units within the system. The ATG-Rover accommodates TL's inherent non-determinism by incorporating a TemporalRover verification cycle within each ATG-Rover test cycle.

The generated program generates all possible input sequences for a given maximal sequence length. For every time stamp within the sequence it generates all possible input combinations. For each such combination, the generated program does the following:

1. Feeds the unit under test with it's current inputs.
2. Fires the unit.
3. Fires the Temporal Rover to validate the unit's response against the specified response.

References

1. E. Chang, A. Pnueli, Z. Manna - Compositional Verification of Real-Time Systems, Proc. 9'th *IEEE Symp. On Logic In Computer Science*, 1994, pp. 458-465.
2. B. T. Hailpern, S. Owicki - *Modular Verification of Communication Protocols.* IEEE Trans of comm. **COM-31**(1), No. 1, 1983, pp. 56-68.
3. Z. Manna, A. Pnueli - *Verification of Concurrent Programs: Temporal Proof Principles,* Proc. of the Workshop on Logics of Programs, Springer Verlag, LNCS, 1981 pp. 200-252.
4. S. Owicki, L. Lamport - *Proving Liveness Properties of Concurrent Programs,* TOPLAS 4(3) (1982), 455-495.
5. A. Prior - *Past, Present and Future,* Oxford University Press, 1967.
6. A. Pnueli - *The Temporal Logic of Programs,* Proc. 181977 *IEEE Symp.. on Foundations of Computer Science*, pp. 46-57.
7. A. P. Sistla, E. M. Clarke - *The Complexity of Linear Propositional Temporal Logic*, Journal of the ACM **32** (1985), pp. 733-749.

Appendix: Assertion Examples

- ev1 and ev2 happen or do not happen simultaneously:
  Always ({ ev1 } Iff { ev2 })

- if ev1 then ev2 two cycles later:
  Always ({ ev1 } Implies (2){ ev2 })

- ev2 not before ev1:
  Always (Not{ev2} Until {ev1})

- ev2 within n cycles after ev1:
  Always ({ev1} Implies Eventually $_{<=n}${ev2})

- ev2 within n1 and n2 cycles after ev1:
  Always ({ev1} Implies Eventually $_{[n1,n2]}${ev2})

- ev2 any number of cycles after ev1:
  Always ({ev1} Implies Eventually {ev2})

- ev2 after n cycles of no ev1:
  Always $_{<=n}$Not{ev1} Implies Eventually $_{>n}${ev2}

- ev2 any number of cycles after ev1, with no ev3 in between:
  Always ({ev1} Implies ((Not{ev3} Until {ev2}) And Eventually {ev2}))

- ev1 after the last ev2 and before ev3:
  Always (Last{ev2} Implies Eventually ({ev1} And AlwaysInThePast Not{ev3}))

- if ev1, then ev2 must not occur for n cycles:
  Always ({ev1} Implies Always $_{<=n}$Not{ev2})

- if ev2, then ev1 must have occurred 3 cycles earlier:
  Always ({ev2} Implies Previous Previous Previous {ev1})

- if ev2, then ev1 must have occurred sometime earlier (not including present time):
  Always ({ev2} Implies Previous SometimeInThePast {ev1})

- evMid occured at least once between evStart and evStop:
  Always ({ evStart } Implies {evMid}Before{evStop})

- val==VAL between evStart and evStop:
  Always ({ evStart } Implies ({val==VAL} Until {evStop}))

Runtime Checking of Multithreaded Applications with Visual Threads

Jerry J. Harrow, Jr.

Compaq Computer Corporation, Business Critical Servers Group,
110 Spit Brook Rd, Nashua, NH, USA
Jerry.Harrow@Compaq.com

Abstract. Multithreaded applications are notoriously difficult to design and build while avoiding defects. Many of Compaq's customers need to employ threads to implement high-performance, scalable applications that address their needs in business and science. In order to ensure their success using threads, Compaq provides a runtime debugging and analysis tool for multithreaded applications called Visual Threads. This paper describes the automatic runtime checking for multithreaded applications incorporated in Visual Threads.

1   Introduction

While the performance of computer systems continues to improve at a rapid rate, many problems in science and business continue to outstrip the ability of a single processor. This has given rise to computer systems built using Symmetric Multiprocessing (SMP), and programming interfaces to enable an application to enlist those processors. One such programming interface standard is IEEE POSIX 1003.1-1996, which is commonly referred to as *pthreads* [1]. The POSIX threads library enables an application to create and control additional threads of execution, and provides synchronization primitives to allow the threads to coordinate their work. Java ™ provides similar capabilities through its language syntax. All the threads in an application run inside the same process and therefore share the same address space, terminal, and open files. Depending upon the operating system[1], the threads may be scheduled across the available processors, thereby enabling true concurrent execution of the threads.

The challenges of threads are many. Primary of these challenges is the increased program complexity caused by the need to synchronize access to shared data structures, the potential for timing-dependent failures, errors using the programming interface, and the difficulty of debugging and optimizing the application.

---

[1] Compaq's *OpenVMS* and *Tru64*™ UNIX® operating systems both provide a POSIX threads library implementation that enables true concurrent execution of threads on systems with multiple processors.

K. Havelund, J. Penix, and W. Visser (Eds.): SPIN 2000, LNCS 1885, pp.331–342, 2000.
© Springer-Verlag Berlin Heidelberg

2   Development of Visual Threads

The genesis of Visual Threads was the observation that many of the problems reported by our customers in their multithreaded applications were in fact programming errors on their part. The vision of the development manager for the threads group was that if we could help customers find these problems, it would greatly improve customer satisfaction, and reduce support costs. The goal of Visual Threads therefore became: *To help Compaq's customers succeed with threads.*

With almost no other competitive tools available in the industry, the development team brainstormed to build a list of all common thread-related programming errors that an application may experience. This list was then prioritized to reflect the relative usefulness of detecting each error to the programmer. After weighing the benefits of the various types of tools that could be built, the team decided to focus on automatic runtime-based checking. The primary factors influencing this choice are listed below.

– Can be applied to code already written
– Provides the most capability without user input
– Does not require buy-in to a particular design model
– Programming-language independence
– Addresses the widest range of errors
– Works when not all code is available as source code

With the tool paradigm selected, the team started the detailed design of what specific errors this runtime-based checking tool would address. The set of analysis rules were chosen very pragmatically. The team commenced to design and implement the largest set of runtime checking that we could reasonably expect to complete within the time and resource constraints of 5-6 engineers and 6-12 months design and implementation. Additional analysis rules have been added in on-going releases.

3   Visual Threads Architecture

Visual Threads integrates many distinct technologies into a single development tool to hide the underlying complexity, and make it easy to use. The primary components that make up Visual Threads are listed below.

– Graphical User Interface implemented in Java
– An optional connection from the user interface to the analysis engine running on a remote server via the Java Remote Method Invocation facility
– Analysis engine implemented in C++ and accessed via Java native method calls
– Shared-memory transport between analysis engine and application to be analyzed
– A binary instrumentation tool to add analysis code into an existing application
– A POSIX threads implementation that provides data gathering hooks

These technologies and components are used together to enable a programmer to apply the computation power of today's sophisticated computer systems toward solving their problem of producing robust, scalable, efficient code.

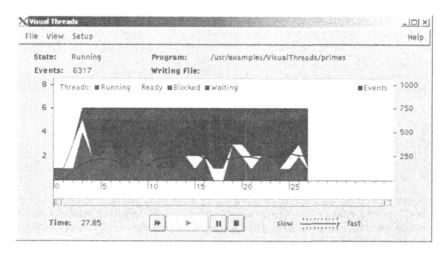

Fig. 1. The main window of the Visual Threads user interface provides execution controls, and a summary of thread activity over time. This graph is dynamically drawn in conjunction with the analysis of the application as it executes.

The primary unit of data processed by Visual Threads is the *event*. This data is provided directly from the library that implements the threads programming interface. A significant state change in the threads library results in an event being generated. This event is encoded as a small binary record and transmitted from the application process to Visual Threads via a shared memory ring buffer. Visual Threads uses these events to model the execution of the application via a state machine. The runtime checking is then applied to this state machine and any errors detected are reported via the user interface. In some cases, additional events are generated by other analysis code that Visual Threads injects into the application executable. In particular, the support for detecting race conditions on data shared between multiple threads without synchronization is performed by such injected code. If violations of this rule are detected, events are generated describing the violation.

4   Automatic Runtime Checking

The heart of Visual Threads' runtime checking is a set of rules that are applied to the threads-related activity in the application. The automatic error-detection rules can be classified into the categories of deadlock, data protection, and other programming errors. In addition to the error-detection rules, there are rule templates that allow a programmer to create customized rules to analyze the behavior of their particular application.

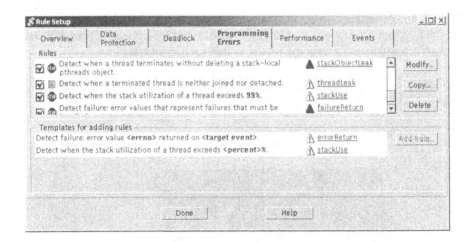

Fig. 2. Rules are enabled, disabled, and created via the Rule Setup dialog. The top section lists the currently defined rules in the *Programming Errors* category, if they are enabled, and what action to take when the rule is violated. The bottom section provides templates that can be used to create additional rules.

When a given rule is enabled, Visual Threads evaluates the rule condition relative to the thread events generated by the application. When a rule is violated, Visual Threads responds with a rule action (such as stopping the application or ignoring the violation) and provides the necessary data to help diagnose the error in the application. Consider the following naïve implementation of Dykstra's classic dining philosophers problem [2].

```
#include <pthread.h>

pthread_t philosopher[5];
pthread_mutex_t chopstick[5];

void *dine(void *arg) {
    long left = (long) arg;
    long right = (left + 1) % 5;
    while (1) {
        pthread_mutex_lock(&chopstick[left]);
        pthread_mutex_lock(&chopstick[right]);
        // Eating...
        pthread_mutex_unlock(&chopstick[left]);
        pthread_mutex_unlock(&chopstick[right]);
        sleep(1);
    }
}

void main() {
    // Create chopsticks
    for (int c = 0; c < 5; c++)
        pthread_mutex_init(&chopstick[c], NULL);
```

```
        // Create philosophers
        for (int p = 0; p < 5; p++)
            pthread_create(&philosopher[p], NULL,
                           &dine, (void *)p);
        sleep(100);
}
```

When executed under Visual Threads, the following alarm is generated.

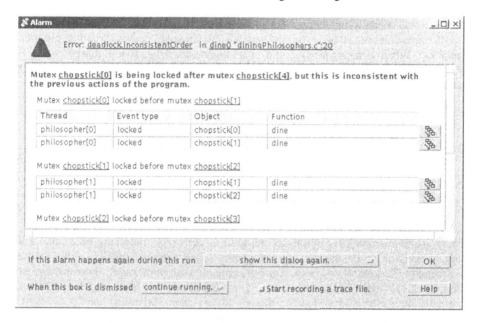

Fig. 3. This alarm reports the detection of an inconsistent lock hierarchy during the execution of the program. The white center area of the dialog is dedicated to describing the actions of the program that violate the *inconsistentOrder* rule. Each line in the tables displayed depicts an action in the program, and provides access to more information about each philosopher (thread), chopstick (mutex), the callstack, and the location in the source where the action occurred.

The entire Visual Threads system is targeted for efficient analysis of running programs. Under the default configuration all rules except those dealing with data protection are enabled. Each class of rules are described in the following sections.

4.1   Deadlock-Related Rules

The problem of deadlock is common in parallel programming. Deadlock can occur whenever multiple shared resources are required to accomplish a task. If not done correctly, two threads may end up each holding one resource but waiting for a second held by the other thread. If neither releases a resource until they complete their respective tasks, both will wait indefinitely. Visual Threads detects just this situation in the use of the POSIX threads programming interface. The set of resources analyzed by Visual Threads are mutexes, read-write locks (write portion), and threads (join operations). When a deadlock situation is detected, the error message provides all the relevant information necessary to diagnose the underlying cause of the error. For each thread involved in the deadlock, the location where the resource was acquired, and the location where the thread is waiting for the other resource is displayed.

Explicit Deadlock. Deadlock is a circularity in the dependency graph for the threads. It is detected via a simple recursive mark-search algorithm directly applied to the model representation of the program that Visual Threads constructs as the program executes. When a thread blocks on a synchronization point, a new marker value is allocated. A recursive routine is then invoked specifying the thread object and the marker value. The algorithm for this routine is described in pseudo code below.

```
CheckDeadlock (object, mark) {
    // If we find current mark, then cycle detected
    if object.mark == mark then report deadlock;

    object.mark = mark;

    for each o on which object depends
        CheckDeadlock (o, mark);
}
```

There are two noteworthy optimizations used to keep this processing efficient. The first of these is to invoke the algorithm only when a thread blocks. This avoids overhead in the case when a lock is not contended (a common case). Fortunately, the data collection hooks utilized by Visual Threads provide this level of detail, which is normally only available within the threads library implementation itself. A second optimization was to eliminate the need to clear previous marks. This was accomplished by always using a unique mark value on every search. Mark values are simply a 32-bit integer quantity incremented for every search. While it is theoretically possible for an application to be executed long enough to perform 2^{32} searches for deadlock, thereby causing mark values to be re-used, the probability of this is negligible.

Potential Deadlock. While detecting actual deadlock is useful, it is relatively obvious when it occurs because the application never completes. Visual Threads goes beyond this, however, to detect various conditions that may lead to deadlock. These are much more important to ensuring program correctness because they detect situations that may not typically have any visible symptoms, but at some point in the future may cause the application to fail. One such rule detects when locks (mutexes and/or read-write locks) are acquired in an inconsistent order sometime during the application run. Visual Threads does this by monitoring the lock acquisition order, and verifying that all future acquisitions are performed in the same order. If the locks are acquired inconsistently, there is the potential for the application to deadlock.

The algorithm for detecting inconsistent lock order maintains a set of must-not-be-locked-before relationship pairs. When a new lock is acquired a search is performed to find any existing lock order pairs involving the new lock and each of the other locks already held by the thread. Note that the must-not-be-locked-before relationship is transitive and therefore the search function recursively follows chains of relationships. If a match is found, an error is reported. The error message (see Figure 3 as an example) includes each of the locations in the source code that contributed to the observed lock order. If the search fails to find any inconsistencies with previous execution behavior, then new must-not-be-locked-before relationship pairs are created using the new lock and each lock currently held.

If the application was designed based upon a lock acquisition hierarchy (i.e. a consistent order in which to acquire locks is part of the application definition), then application-specific rules can be configured that enable Visual Threads to validate that the lock acquisition order specified by the design is in fact honored.

Priority Inversion. Another deadlock-related rule is the detection of priority inversion. Visual Threads detects high-priority threads that are waiting for a lock held by a low-priority thread when another medium-priority thread is currently executing. This rule, along with a warning about sharing locks between threads of differing priorities, helps to pinpoint other programming errors that can lead to poor performance or more drastic failures.

4.2   Data Protection Rules

The most powerful Visual Threads analysis rule finds data shared between multiple threads without the protection afforded by a mutex, read-write lock, or atomic hardware instruction sequence. In the rest of this section the generic term *lock* will be used to refer to all of those synchronization primitives. Unsynchronized access to data that is shared between multiple threads and is also modified can result in timing-related errors such as incorrect results, or memory corruption. The algorithm starts with the premise that the sharing of a read-write data item *d* should be governed by some lock *l*, or by the implicit synchronization of thread creation or join (a join allows a thread to wait for the termination of another thread). Violations of this premise are reported as potential errors in the application being analyzed. There are three significant facets of the algorithm used to detect and report these potential errors.

- Memory-usage markings to handle initialization, and shared read data.
- Lockset refinement to detect that a lock does not protect the data.
- Thread segment identification to handle create/terminate synchronization

Basic Algorithm. Visual Threads data protection rules are based upon the algorithms and implementation of the Eraser tool. The complete details of the underlying Eraser algorithm are available in a separate paper [3], but it can be summarized as follows. At the start of the algorithm all data is marked as NEW (see Table 1), and is protected by a candidate *lockset* containing all the locks in the application.

To account for initialization and read-only sharing of data, error reports are deferred until a data address reaches the SHARED-MODIFIED state, as depicted in Figure 4. Once a thread modifies the data, it is associated with that thread and marked EXCLUSIVE. If read or written by any other thread, the memory is then marked SHARED or SHARED-MODIFIED respectively.

Table 1. Memory-usage Markings

State	Description
NEW	Newly allocated memory, not yet accessed, no lock sets.
EXCLUSIVE	Memory is identified as being exclusively accessed by a particular thread, no lock sets.
SHARED	Identifies shared, read-only data. The set of locks in effect during all accesses is updated. No errors are reported.
SHARED-MODIFIED	Identifies shared, writable data. The set of locks in effect during all accesses is updated. If empty, an error is generated.

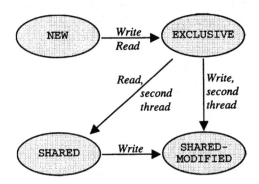

Fig. 4. Checking for consistent synchronization is deferred until the memory is actually shared between two or more threads and is being modified. Earlier state transitions accommodate memory allocated and initialized by a single thread, then shared with other threads either in a read-only fashion, or with synchronization.

When the data becomes shared, the candidate lockset presumed to protect the data is updated. The lockset is reduced to the intersection of the previous lockset and the set of locks held by the thread on the current access. This progressively removes locks from the lockset that are only incidentally locked during some access to the data. If the lockset ever becomes empty an error is reported because no single lock protects all access to the data. A pseudo-code representation of the Eraser algorithm is depicted below.

```
Let locks_held(t) be the set of locks held by thread t.
Let update_use(d,a,t) update the marking of data d
    by thread t using access a as shown in Figure 4.
For each data item d:
    mark[d] := NEW
    lockset[d] := { all locks }

On each access a (read or write) to d, by a thread t:
    update_use(d,a,t)
    if mark[d] in { SHARED, SHARED-MODIFIED }
        lockset[d] := lockset[d] ∩ locks_held(t)
    if mark[d] = SHARED-MODIFIED and,
        lockset[d] = { }, then report error
```

Thread Segment Extension to Eraser Algorithm.   Not all data shared between threads without the use of a lock is an application error. There are types of indirect synchronization that may eliminate the need for explicit locks. In particular, a very common paradigm is for the initial thread to allocate and initialize some data, create worker threads to perform some transformations on this data, and then after the threads have all completed, display the result. The original Eraser algorithm was extended to reduce the number of false reports due to this type of implicit synchronization, by introducing the concept of thread segment. A thread segment delineates time in addition to just thread identity. By utilizing the thread segment identifiers in the algorithm instead of simply using the thread identity, we can distinguish accesses that cannot happen concurrently. No thread segment spans beyond the creation of a new thread, or a join. When a parent thread creates a new child thread, the parent's thread segment id is updated, and the child's thread segment id is assigned. Similarly, after a join operation, the parent's thread segment id is updated (the child no longer exists). Each running thread is represented as a leaf in the graph. Figure 5 shows how thread segments are assigned over time.

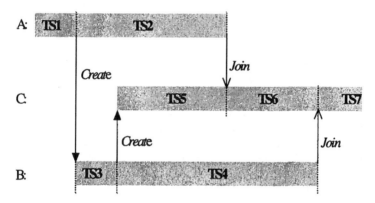

Fig. 5. A single thread may have many thread segments over time. Thread A creates Thread B, and Thread B creates Thread C. Thread C synchronizes with Thread A by waiting for it to terminate. Similarly, Thread C then waits for Thread B to terminate. This results in the seven thread segments **T1** through **T7**.

These thread segments are kept in a directed graph that indicates which thread segments cannot occur concurrent with each other. As you can see from Figure 5, **S1** happens before **TS2-TS7**, **TS3** happens before **TS5-TS7**, **TS2** happens before **TS6** and **TS7**, and so forth. The modification of the Eraser algorithm to incorporate thread segments is relatively straightforward.

1. When data *d* is marked as EXCLUSIVE, associate it with the thread segment id of the current thread instead of the thread id.
2. If data *d* is marked as EXCLUSIVE to thread segment **TS***i*, and is being touched by *TSj* (where $i \neq j$), and **TS***i* happens before **TS***j* in the graph, then instead of moving the data to one of the shared states, associate *d* with **TS***j*.   The marking remains EXCLUSIVE.

This extension allows exclusive-use data to be "passed" from parent thread to child thread (and back) as long as the thread segments involved in the access cannot be concurrent due to the known points of thread creation and termination (as determined by the thread segment graph). If the two thread segments are potentially concurrent, then the data is marked as either SHARED or SHARED-MODIFIED as appropriate and the standard checking is applied.

Implementation Details.   The basic technique used to detect this type of error involves monitoring every load and store of all global and heap data in the application.   The code for monitoring memory access is injected into an existing application executable using a binary code modification tool called Atom [4]. Information is maintained for each data address in a corresponding *shadow* address. Since access to the state information is very frequent, the shadow data is efficiently determined by a table lookup and offset calculation.   The table lookup is kept small by using large shadow segments (16MB) to minimize search time on the table.   This table lookup was added for improved robustness necessary in a product, even at the cost of some additional execution overhead.   The data maintained in the shadow area is listed below.

– Type of sharing (as listed in Table 1)
– Set of locks protecting this data, if marked SHARED or SHARED-MODIFIED.
– Owner thread segment, if marked EXCLUSIVE

Protecting Unsafe Libraries and Functions.   In addition to detecting unsynchronized access to shared data, Visual Threads also allows the definition of application-specific rules that identify particular libraries or functions that are known not to be thread safe.   There are many extensively used libraries (such as user-interface toolkits) that are not thread safe.   Typically, the programmer must surround any call to such a library with a lock to prevent other threads from calling into the library concurrently.   Programmers can then identify this requirement, and have Visual Threads verify that the application has been coded properly.

4.3   Other Programming Error Rules

The remaining error-detection rules validate various facets of using the POSIX threads programming interface correctly. For the most part, the rules listed below are simply checks that are performed during state changes in the model maintained by Visual Threads.

– Detect attempts to relock a non-recursive mutex.
– Detect attempts to unlock a lock the thread did not previously lock.
– Detect when a condition variable is associated with more than one mutex.
– Detect when mixed scheduling policy is used.
– Detect attempts to wait on a condition variable when the mutex is not locked.
– Detect when a thread terminates while holding a mutex or read-write lock.
– Detect when a thread terminates without deleting a stack-local threads object.
– Detect when a terminated thread is neither joined nor detached.

- Detect when stack utilization of a thread exceeds 99%.
- Detect when the threads programming interface returns an error value that represents a failure that must be handled.

While many of these errors may seem minor, often they have indeterminate effects upon the application state. This can lead to unexpected behavior at some later time, which can be extremely difficult to debug due to the distance from the original problem.

4.4   Detecting Errors by Observation and Heuristics

While this paper has focused primarily on the program validation aspects, Visual Threads also provides visualization of the state of thread and synchronization objects in the application, as well as statistical analysis of overall execution behavior. Unlike the relatively absolute errors detected by rule checking, some errors are recognized only by the degree of their severity. For this class of errors, Visual Threads provides a heuristic-based summary of the program execution as shown in Figure 6. The types of analysis reported in this manner are listed below.

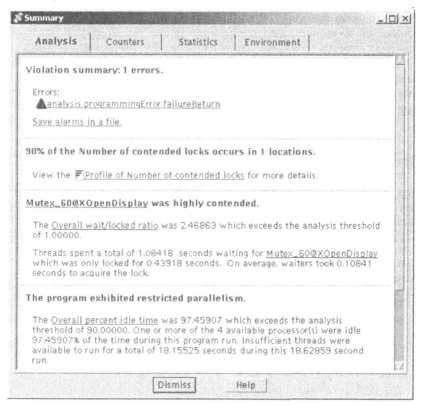

Fig. 6. The Analysis Summary is automatically displayed when the program completes. In addition to summarizing errors, it generates observations about the program execution.

 – Locks with high levels of contention
 – Locks with granularity that is too coarse
 – Level of processor utilization
 – Mutex with the highest percentage of contended locks
 – Mutex with the highest total wait time
 – Mutex with the highest number of concurrent waiters
 – Inefficient use of mutex attributes

Often such analysis is helpful in performance tuning, but it can also highlight coding or design errors that result in high lock contention, poor lock granularity, or poor processor utilization.

5   Summary

Visual Threads provides extensive automatic runtime validation of a running multithreaded application. Through pragmatic selection of targeted analysis and efficient algorithms, even the most complex application domain can benefit from automated program checking. While far from exhaustively validating the overall correctness of a multithreaded application, it can be invaluable in detecting programming errors that may lead to program instability and unexpected failures.

Visual Threads is available on Compaq's *OpenVMS* and *Tru64*™ UNIX® operating systems which run on the 64-bit Alpha microprocessor. It is able to analyze multithreaded programs whether written in C, C++, Fortran, or the Java programming language.

References

1. 9945-1:1996 (ISO/IEC) [IEEE/ANSI Std 1003.1 196 Edition] Information Technology – Portable Operating System Interface (POSIX)—Part 1: System Application: Program Interface (API) [C Language] (ANSI), IEEE Standards Press, ISBN 1-55937-573-6, 1996.
2. Dijkstra, E.W. Co-operating Sequential Processes. *Programming Languages*, Genuys, F. (ed.), Academic Press, 1965.
3. Savage, S., Burrows, M., Nelson, G., Sobalvarro, P., Anderson, E.: Eraser: A dynamic data race detector for multi-threaded programs. ACM Transactions on Computer Systems (TOCS), 15(4): 391-411, November 1997. Also appeared in Proceedings of the Sixteenth ACM Symposium on Operating System Principles, October 5-8, 1997, St. Malo, France, Operating System Review 31(5), ACM Press, 1997, ISBN 0-89791-916-5, pp 27-37.
4. Compaq Computer Corporation: Compaq Tru64 UNIX Programmers Guide V5.0, July 1999.

Author Index

Lecture Notes in Computer Science

For information about Vols. 1–1825
please contact your bookseller or Springer-Verlag

Vol. 1865: K.R. Apt, A.C. Kakas, E. Monfroy, F. Rossi (Eds.), New Trends Constraints. Proceedings, 1999. X, 339 pages. 2000. (Subseries LNAI).

Vol. 1866: J. Cussens, A. Frisch (Eds.), Inductive Logic Programming. Proceedings, 2000. X, 265 pages. 2000. (Subseries LNAI).

Vol. 1867: B. Ganter, G.W. Mineau (Eds.), Conceptual Structures: Logical, Linguistic, and Computational Issues. Proceedings, 2000. XI, 569 pages. 2000. (Subseries LNAI).

Vol. 1868: P. Koopman, C. Clack (Eds.), Implementation of Functional Languages. Proceedings, 1999. IX, 199 pages. 2000.

Vol. 1869: M. Aagaard, J. Harrison (Eds.), Theorem Proving in Higher Order Logics. Proceedings, 2000. IX, 535 pages. 2000.

Vol. 1872: J. van Leeuwen, O. Watanabe, M. Hagiya, P.D. Mosses, T. Ito (Eds.), Theoretical Computer Science. Proceedings, 2000. XV, 630 pages. 2000.

Vol. 1873: M. Ibrahim, J. Küng, N. Revell (Eds.), Database and Expert Systems Applications. Proceedings, 2000. XIX, 1005 pages. 2000.

Vol. 1874: Y. Kambayashi, M. Mohania, A M. Tjoa (Eds.), Data Warehousing and Knowledge Discovery. Proceedings, 2000. XII, 438 pages. 2000.

Vol. 1875: K. Bauknecht, S.K. Madria, G. Pernul (Eds.), Electronic Commerce and Web Technologies. Proceedings, 2000. XII, 488 pages. 2000.

Vol. 1876: F. J. Ferri, J.M. Iñesta, A. Amin, P. Pudil (Eds.), Advances in Pattern Recognition. Proceedings. 2000. XVIII, 901 pages. 2000.

Vol. 1877: C. Palamidessi (Ed.), CONCUR 2000 – Concurrency Theory. Proceedings, 2000. XI, 612 pages. 2000.

Vol. 1878: J.P. Bowen, S. Dunne, A. Galloway, S. King (Eds.), ZB 2000: Formal Specification and Development in Z and B. Proceedings, 2000. XIV, 511 pages. 2000.

Vol. 1879: M. Paterson (Ed.), Algorithms – ESA 2000. Proceedings, 2000. IX, 450 pages. 2000.

Vol. 1880: M. Bellare (Ed.), Advances in Cryptology – CRYPTO 2000. Proceedings, 2000. XI, 545 pages. 2000.

Vol. 1881: C. Zhang, V.-W. Soo (Eds.), Design and Applications of Intelligent Agents. Proceedings, 2000. X, 183 pages. 2000. (Subseries LNAI).

Vol. 1882: D. Kotz, F. Mattern (Eds.), Agent Systems, Mobile Agents, and Applications. Proceedings, 2000. XII, 275 pages. 2000.

Vol. 1883: B. Triggs, A. Zisserman, R. Szeliski (Eds.), Vision Algorithms: Theory and Practice. Proceedings, 1999. X, 383 pages. 2000.

Vol. 1884: J. Štuller, J. Pokorný, B. Thalheim, Y. Masunaga (Eds.), Current Issues in Databases and Information Systems. Proceedings, 2000. XIII, 396 pages. 2000.

Vol. 1885: K. Havelund, J. Penix, W. Visser (Eds.), SPIN Model Checking and Software Verification. Proceedings, 2000. X, 343 pages. 2000.

Vol. 1886: R. Mizoguchi, J. Slaney /Eds.), PRICAI 2000: Topics in Artificial Intelligence. Proceedings, 2000. XX, 835 pages. 2000. (Subseries LNAI).

Vol. 1888: G. Sommer, Y.Y. Zeevi (Eds.), Algebraic Frames for the Perception-Action Cycle. Proceedings, 2000. X, 349 pages. 2000.

Vol. 1889: M. Anderson, P. Cheng, V. Haarslev (Eds.), Theory and Application of Diagrams. Proceedings, 2000. XII, 504 pages. 2000. (Subseries LNAI).

Vol. 1890: C Linnhoff-Popien, H.-G. Hegering (Eds.), Trends in Distributed Systems: Towards a Universal Service Market. Proceedings, 2000. XI, 341 pages. 2000.

Vol. 1891: A.L. Oliveira (Ed.), Grammatical Inference: Algorithms and Applications. Proceedings, 2000. VIII, 313 pages. 2000. (Subseries LNAI).

Vol. 1892: P. Brusilovsky, O. Stock, C. Strapparava (Eds.), Adaptive Hypermedia and Adaptive Web-Based Systems. Proceedings, 2000. XIII, 422 pages. 2000.

Vol. 1893: M. Nielsen, B. Rovan (Eds.), Mathematical Foundations of Computer Science 2000. Proceedings, 2000. XIII, 710 pages. 2000.

Vol. 1895: F. Cuppens, Y. Deswarte, D. Gollmann, M. Waidner (Eds.), Computer Security – ESORICS 2000. Proceedings, 2000. X, 325 pages. 2000.

Vol. 1896: R. W. Hartenstein, H. Grünbacher (Eds.), Field-Programmable Logic and Applications. Proceedings, 2000. XVII, 856 pages. 2000.

Vol. 1897: J. Gutknecht, W. Weck (Eds.), Modular Programming Languages. Proceedings, 2000. XII, 299 pages. 2000.

Vol. 1898: E. Blanzieri, L. Portinale (Eds.), Advances in Case-Based Reasoning. Proceedings, 2000. XII, 530 pages. 2000. (Subseries LNAI).

Vol. 1899: H.-H. Nagel, F.J. Perales López (Eds.), Articulated Motion and Deformable Objects. Proceedings, 2000. X, 183 pages. 2000.

Vol. 1900: A. Bode, T. Ludwig, W. Karl, R. Wismüller (Eds.), Euro-Par 2000 Parallel Processing. Proceedings, 2000. XXXV, 1368 pages. 2000.

Vol. 1901: O. Etzion, P. Scheuermann (Eds.), Cooperative Information Systems. Proceedings, 2000. XI, 336 pages. 2000.

Vol. 1902: P. Sojka, I. Kopeček, K. Pala (Eds.), Text, Speech and Dialogue. Proceedings, 2000. XIII, 463 pages. 2000. (Subseries LNAI).

Vol. 1906: A. Porto, G.-C. Roman (Eds.), Coordination Languages and Models. Proceedings, 2000. IX, 353 pages. 2000.

Vol. 1912: Y. Gurevich, P.W. Kutter, M. Odersky, L. Thiele (Eds.), Abstract State Machines. Proceedings, 2000. X, 381 pages. 2000.

Vol. 1913: K. Jansen, S. Khuller (Eds.), Approximation Algorithms for Combinatorial Optimization. Proceedings, 2000. IX, 275 pages. 2000.

Vol. 1923: J. Borbinha, T. Baker (Eds.), Research and Advanced Technology for Digital Libraries. Proceedings, 2000. XVII, 513 pages. 2000.

Vol. 1924: W. Taha (Ed.), Semantics, Applications, and Implementation of Program Generation. Proceedings, 2000. VIII, 231 pages. 2000.

Vol. 1926: M. Joseph (Ed.), Formal Techniques in Real-Time and Fault-Tolerant Systems. Proceedings, 2000. X, 305 pages. 2000.